THE FIRST FREEMASONS

THE
FIRST
FREEMASONS

Scotland's Early Lodges and their Members

David Stevenson

Second Edition

Grand Lodge of Scotland

First published 1988 (Hardback)
Reprint edition 1989 (Paperback)

© David Stevenson 1988

Second Edition
First Published 2001

© David Stevenson 2001

British Library Cataloguing in Publication Data

Stevenson, David, *1942*–
  The first freemasons: Scotland's early
  lodges and their members.
  1. Scotland. Freemasons. Lodges
  I. Title
  366'.1'09411

ISBN 902324 65 9

Printed in Scotland
Geo. Stewart & Co. Ltd.
Edinburgh

For Robert, Elisha, Anne-Marie and Kathryn

CONTENTS

List of illustrations — ix
Abbreviations and Conventions — xi
Preface to the second edition — xv
Preface to the first edition — xvii

1 Masons and freemasons — 1
2 Edinburgh
The Lodge of Edinburgh (Mary's Chapel) — 12
The Lodge of Canongate Kilwinning — 35
The Lodge of Canongate and Leith, Leith and Canongate — 39
The Lodge of Journeymen Masons, Edinburgh — 42

3 The Lothians
The Lodge of Aitchison's Haven — 52
The Lodge of Haddington — 60
The Lodge of Linlithgow — 62

4 The West
The Lodge of Kilwinning — 63
The Lodge of Glasgow — 74
The Lodge of Dumfries — 78
The Lodge of Kirkcudbright — 82
The Lodge of Hamilton — 83

5 Fife and Tayside
The Lodge of St Andrews — 90
The Lodge of Dunfermline — 91
The Lodge of Dundee — 94

6 Central
The Lodge of Stirling — 98
The Lodge of Scone (Perth) — 101
The Lodge of Dunblane — 107

7 The Borders
The Lodge of Melrose — 113
The Lodge of Kelso — 117
The Lodge of Haughfoot — 119

8 The North
The Lodge of Aberdeen — 124
The Lodge of Inverness — 150
The Lodge of Banff — 151
The Lodge of Kilmolymock (Elgin) — 152

9 Early Scottish freemasonry — 156

Notes — 162

Appendix 1
  List and map of early (pre-1710) masonic lodges in Scotland — 182

Appendix 2
  Inventory of early (pre-1710) Scottish masonic records — 184

Appendix 3
  William Geddes's Encomiastick Epigram, 1690 — 206

Appendix 4
  Alan Ramsay, To Dr John Theophilus Desaguliers — 209

Index — 211

ILLUSTRATIONS

1	Alexander Hamilton, general of the artillery and member of the Lodge of Edinburgh	29
2	Sir John Clerk of Penicuik, member of the Lodge of Edinburgh	34
3	Geometria	51
4	William Aytoun, Master Mason, and his wife	54
5	Charter Chest of the Incorporation of Masons of Glasgow, 1684	77
6	The stonemason supreme among the building crafts	89
7	Minute of the Lodge of Kilwinning, 1677	112
8	Patrick Whyte, hookmaker, member of the Lodge of Aberdeen	129
9	The Pillars of Solomon's Temple - perhaps	132
10	The Aberdeen Mark Book: list of entered apprentices	137
11	The Aberdeen Mark Book: list of masters of the lodge	141
12	The Aberdeen Mark Book: masons' tools	144
13	The Aberdeen Mark Book	144
14	Lodge of Aberdeen: the house bought as a meeting place in 1700	148
15	The Mason Box of the Lodge of Aberdeen	155
16	Lodge of Aberdeen: accounts, 1699	161

ABBREVIATIONS AND CONVENTIONS

AQC	*Ars Quatuor Coronatorum. Transactions of the Quatuor Coronati Lodge No.2076,* London.
BL	British Library, London.
Carr, *Edinburgh*	*The minutes of the Lodge of Edinburgh, Mary's Chapel, No.1, 1598-1738,* ed. H. Carr (Quatuor Coronatorum Antigrapha. Masonic Reprints, xiii, London, 1962).
Carr, *Kilwinning*	H. Carr, *Lodge Mother Kilwinning, No.0. A study of the earliest minute books, 1642 to 1842* (London, 1961).
Carr, *Mason and burgh*	H. Carr, *The mason and the burgh. An examination of the Edinburgh register of apprentices and the burgess rolls* (London, 1954).
Colvin, *Architects*	H.M. Colvin, *A biographical dictionary of British architects* (London, 1978).
Complete baronetage	*Complete baronetage,* ed. G.E. C[okayne].(6 vols., Exeter, 1900-9).
Complete peerage	*Complete peerage of England, Scotland, Ireland, Great Britain and the United Kingdom,* ed. G.E. C[okayne] (revised edn., 14 vols., London, 1910-59).
DNB	*Dictionary of National Biography* (63 vols., 1885-1900).
EUL	Edinburgh University Library.
GLS	Grand Lodge of Scotland, Edinburgh.
GLSYB	*Grand Lodge of Scotland Year Book* (Edinburgh, 1952-).
HMC	Historical Manuscripts Commission.
Inventory	Inventory of early Scottish masonic records (Appendix 2 of this book).
Knoop, *Catechisms*	*Early masonic catechisms,* ed. D. Knoop, G.P. Jones & D. Hamer (2nd edn, London, 1973).
Knoop, *Genesis*	D. Knoop & G.P. Jones, *The Genesis of freemasonry* (Manchester, 1947).
Knoop, *Scottish mason*	D. Knoop & G.P. Jones, *The Scottish mason and The Mason Word* (Manchester, 1939)

Lyon, *Edinburgh*	D.M. Lyon, *History of the Lodge of Edinburgh (Mary's Chapel), No.1, embracing an account of the rise and progress of freemasonry in Scotland* (2nd or tercentenary edn, London, 1900).
Mr of works accs.	*Accounts of the masters of works,* ed. H.M. Paton (vol. i) and J. Imrie and J.G. Dunbar (2 vols., Edinburgh, 1957-82).
MacGibbon, *Architecture*	D. MacGibbon and R. Ross, *The castellated and domestic architecture of Scotland* (5 vols., Edinburgh, 1887-92).
Miller, *Aberdeen*	A.L. Miller, *Notes on the early history and records of the Lodge, Aberdeen, No.1ter on the roll of the Grand Lodge of Ancient, Free and Accepted Masons of Scotland* (Aberdeen, 1919).
Mylne, *Master Masons*	R.S. Mylne, *The master masons to the crown of Scotland* (Edinburgh, 1893).
NLS	National Library of Scotland, Edinburgh
Poole, *Gould's History*	*Gould's History of freemasonry,* ed. H. Poole (4 vols., London, 1951).
PSAS	*Proceedings of the Society of Antiquaries of Scotland.*
RCAHMS	Royal Commission on the Ancient and Historical Monuments of Scotland, Inventories.
RPCS	*Register of the privy council of Scotland* (38 vols., Edinburgh, 1887-1970).
SBRS	Scottish Burgh Record Society.
Scots peerage	*The Scots peerage,* ed. Sir J.B. Paul (9 vols., Edinburgh, 1904-14).
SHS	Scottish History Society.
Smith, *Dumfries*	James Smith, *History of the Old Lodge of Dumfries* (Dumfries, 1892).
SRO	Scottish Record Office, Edinburgh. The SRO has now changed its name to The National Archives of Scotland (NAS).
SRS	Scottish Record Society.
Stevenson, *Origins*	D. Stevenson, *The origins of freemasonry. Scotland's century, 1590-1710* (Cambridge, 1988).
Vernon, *History*	W.F. Vernon, *History of freemasonry in the province of Roxburgh, Peebles and Selkirkshires, from 1674 to the present time* (London, 1893).

Money. All references are to Scots money unless otherwise stated. From the seventeenth century £1 Scots = 1*s*.8*d*. Sterling (or £12 Scots = £1 Sterling). A Merk = 13*s*. 4*d*. Scots.

Dating. Days and months are cited Old Style, as this was retained in Britain until 1752. In accordance with the convention of the 'historical year', years are taken to begin on 1 January and not (as in Scotland until 1600 and in England until 1752) on 25 March, dates being silently adjusted where necessary.

Quotations. Original spelling is retained for quotations unless otherwise stated, though abbreviations have been silently extended. In case of difficulty in understanding quotations it often helps to concentrate not on the spelling but on how words look as if they should sound, taking into account the frequent interchangeability of 'u', 'v' and 'w', and the Scots tendency to replace 'w' with 'qu'.

PREFACE TO THE SECOND EDITION

I am most grateful to the Grand Lodge of Scotland for the opportunity to publish a second edition of *The First Freemasons*, especially as the bankruptcy of the original publisher meant that distribution of the first edition was less effective than it might have been. I must also express my appreciation of the help and encouragement of Bob Cooper, the Grand Lodge Librarian

The purpose of the book remains unchanged: to shed light on the emergence of freemasonry, both for freemasons and for a wider audience, by studying the earliest known lodges, those which emerge in seventeenth-century Scotland. In Britain (unlike continental Europe), freemasonry has generally been ignored (or consciously avoided) by academic historians. Partly this is due to the fact that freemasonry in Britain never aspired to the political, social and cultural roles that many branches of the craft undertook on the Continent, partly to present day paranoia about the movement. While a historian can research Hitler without being suspected of Nazism, I have found that many suspect that anyone researching freemasonry must be a member of the craft. On occasion, such silliness carried to extremes has led to my assertion that I am not a freemason being disbelieved, and to me being told that I must be a secret initiate, commissioned as part of a conspiracy to issue masonic propaganda disguised as academic research. This, it seems to me, underlines how quite overdue a move is towards treating the history of freemasonry like that of any other social and cultural institution.

The main differences between this second edition of the book and the first consist of the addition of two new appendices, both poetic. One reproduces a previously unknown verse on the mason craft by William Geddes, dated 1690, while in the other Alan Ramsay addresses John Theophilus Desaguliers in Scots, commemorating the latter's visit to Edinburgh in 1721. The addition of two new masonic catechisms to Appendix 2 demonstrates that new evidence relating to early masonic history is still being discovered. Otherwise changes to the first edition text is confined to minor alterations in wording and a few corrections – the most significant being the putting right of a nasty blunder concerning the early members of the Lodge of Canongate and Leith.

David Stevenson

PREFACE TO THE FIRST EDITION

The early Scottish lodges of freemasons, most of which still exist and still possess records dating from the seventeenth century, are by far the oldest such lodges in the world. It is therefore remarkable that no attempt has ever been made to study them systematically, though very useful histories of a few lodges exist. This book represents an attempt to fill this gap by surveying the history of the individual lodges and examining their membership, their activities, and their relationships with each other and with craft gilds or incorporations which included masons. Much remains obscure, for the lodges were secret institutions and practised secret rituals, and though a remarkable amount of record material relating to them survives it is nonetheless fragmentary. Moreover, most lodge members were men of relatively humble social status, which makes identifying and tracing them difficult (especially when their names are common ones). Much work remains to be done in using lodge records in conjunction with other local records, but a start has been made.

There is much confusion and uncertainty as to the origins of freemasonry. In my book *The origins of freemasonry. Scotland's century* (Cambridge, 1988) I have sought to demonstrate that, in spite of much obscurity, the evidence indicates that something that is recognisably modern freemasonry first emerges in seventeenth-century Scotland, and then spreads to England, though the anglocentric assumptions of most masonic historians has led them to claim the movement to be essentially English, the embarrassing Scottish evidence being explained away by ingenious but unconvincing arguments. The evidence and my arguments relating to the essentially Scottish origins of the movement are summarised in chapter one below to provide a context for the studies of the individual lodges which follow.

I am not myself a freemason, but obviously this book could not have been written unless lodges had given me access to their early records, and I here record my gratitude to these lodges and their officials. Sadly a few lodges either declined to answer my letters or refused to let me consult their records. The willingness of the Grand Lodge of Scotland to give me access to its library to consult both printed works and early manuscript ones has greatly facilitated my work and is much appreciated.

I also gratefully acknowledge grants from the University of Aberdeen and the Carnegie Trust for the Universities of Scotland towards travel and other costs relating to my research, and from the Leverhulme Trust to finance leave of absence from teaching commitments.

I am grateful to the following for permission to reproduce copyright photographs as follows:

The duke of Hamilton (1)
The Scottish National Portrait Gallery (2)
Heriot's Hospital, Edinburgh (4)
The People's Palace Museum, Glasgow (5)
Dr Guild's Managers, Aberdeen (8, 9)

David Stevenson

1
MASONS AND FREEMASONS

Like other craftsmen, Medieval stonemasons had their own organisations, a mythical history of their craft stressing its antiquity and importance, and oaths of secrecy and initiation rites for new members of their craft.[1] Thus essentially the stonemasons were similar to other crafts. Nonetheless, they had some distinctive characteristics. Their mythical history was unusually elaborate and sweeping in its claims for the craft. Masonry was held to comprehend not merely manual labour but the theoretical work of the architect. Further, architecture was equated with geometry, being seen as constituting the practical application of mathematics. Thus the traditional histories of masonry claimed the great Greek mathematician Euclid as a mason, and indeed as one of the founders of the mason craft. The central episodes in the development of masonry were set in ancient Egypt (where Euclid makes his appearance—as an Egyptian) and at the building of Solomon's Temple in Jerusalem. Thus Medieval masons proudly equated their craft with the science of mathematics, and traced its origins to the oldest (and assumed to be the greatest) civilisation known to them in any detail, and to a central event in sacred scripture. In the late Middle Ages these claims emerge in the written accounts which appear in England known as the Old Charges, 'charges' being orders for the conduct of the trade included in these histories.

That the masons should produce a more elaborate mythology than other crafts is hardly surprising, for they were responsible for some of the greatest and most visible achievements of Medieval civilisation, the great castles and cathedrals and other churches which dominated the landscape. Standing before these awesome creations must have impressed all with the powers of the men that had built them, and encouraged the pretensions of the masons themselves to antiquity and to an importance above that of other crafts.

The masons also differed from other crafts in their relative geographical mobility. Most craftsmen worked in a single location, or within a town or small area. This was true of some masons as well, but the nature of their work forced many to travel. Great building projects might require many masons for many years, and masons would gather from wide areas to work on them, perhaps returning to their families in winter when building stopped. This mobility meant that the usual type of organisation for craftsmen in the Middle Ages, the craft guild, was inadequate for masons. Guilds were normally subordinate to the town or burgh authorities, supervising entry to crafts, regulating the careers and working lives of the craftsmen, and protecting the monopoly rights of members against interlopers—residents of the burgh who did not belong to the guild, or outsiders seeking work in the burgh.

Guilds of masons were common, and can be found emerging in Scotland (where guilds were generally known as incorporations) in the late Middle Ages. But guilds, being confined in membership to inhabitants of a town, could not fully meet the needs of mobile masons, and they therefore developed their own organisations. On building sites masons were provided with shelters known as lodges, for working in when the weather was bad and storing materials and tools. On larger sites, where masons were employed who did not live in the locality, masons often ate and slept in the lodge as well. Such site lodges often existed continuously for many years, for great churches often required constant attention from a few masons working on repairs and maintenance between phases of major building activity. Not surprisingly, in time these long-term site lodges developed their own customs and regulations, partly evolved by the masons themselves, partly imposed by town or church authorities. In Scotland such lodges, under burgh control, can be traced in Aberdeen and Dundee in the late fifteenth and early sixteenth centuries. But they appear to have declined or disappeared entirely shortly before or after the Reformation of 1560 brought a new protestant church to Scotland. In no case is there any evidence whatever of continuity between these semi-permanent Medieval site lodges and the lodges of freemasons which emerged in seventeenth-century Scotland. Temporary site lodges continued to come into existence in the seventeenth century, but again there is no overlap between them and the new type of freemasons' lodges.

The mobility of many masons led to the creation of site lodges in the Middle Ages in addition to guilds containing masons. But these lodges did not solve the problem, created by such mobility, of identifying properly qualified fellow masons. All craftsmen sought to regulate and restrict entry to their craft, and to keep their skills and techniques secret from outsiders. The guilds performed this function in towns: each guild had a fixed membership, and craftsmen knew one another. But when masons from different places gathered at a building site, how were they to tell regularly trained craftsmen from interlopers claiming to be master masons to boost their wages? Practical tests of skill would be cumbersome, and in any case a man might be fairly skilled without having been regularly trained and accepted as a master in the way craft exclusiveness required. On the Continent there is evidence of secret modes of recognition being used, signs or words revealed to men on their formal admission as master masons, signs which men unknown to each other could exchange to confirm that they were indeed both masters, and it seems likely that these signs existed among masons in Britain as well.

All crafts had their secrets relating to practical skills, and references to secrets in the Old Charges appear to refer solely to such matters. As with virtually any organisation in the Middle Ages, entry to a craft guild would involve initiation of some sort. This would stress the importance of the event as a turning-point in men's lives, and often involve ritual humiliation. Such initiations would also contain oaths binding initiates to keep the crafts' secrets:

but in the case of masons secret modes of recognition would doubtless also be taught during such ritual initiations.

The legacy of the Medieval masons obviously contains much that is later found in freemasonry: the mythical history of the craft; the identification of masonry with mathematics; organisation in 'lodges'; secret signs and words; and rituals of initiation. Yet (as most masonic historians now readily accept) it would be misleading to claim that this was already freemasonry. The mason craft in the Middle Ages certainly has some distinctive features setting it apart to some extent from other crafts, but in essence it is simply one craft among many, more like others than dissimilar to them. Moreover, there are major problems in linking this Medieval legacy directly to the emergence of freemasonry. The situation has, however, been unnecessarily complicated by two prevailing misconceptions. The first is the assumption that the emergence of freemasonry took place in England, a belief maintained in the face of the overwhelming preponderance of Scottish documentary evidence relating to the process, evidence which is often simultaneously explained away (as due to chances of survival, to a Scots passion for writing things down, or as not really concerned with freemasonry), and then used in an English context to make up for the lack of English evidence! The second misconception lies in assuming that freemasonry evolved gradually and steadily from the Medieval legacy in a supposedly continuous process, though this cannot be traced in the surviving evidence.

Looking at the Scottish evidence as a whole in the context of Scottish history indicates that the emergence of freemasonry involved an act of creation, not just evolution. In the years around 1600 the legacy of the Middle Ages was remodelled and combined with Renaissance themes and obsessions to create a new movement. Evolutionary developments subsequently brought about many alterations and elaborations of this movement, yet what appeared in Scotland around 1600 contains the essentials of modern freemasonry.

The man who more than anyone else deserves the title of creator of modern freemasonry was William Schaw. The younger son of a laird (landowner) with close connections with the court, Schaw developed a strong interest in architecture and in 1583 was appointed master of works by King James VI of Scotland. As master of works he supervised building work undertaken for the king, and controlled the employment of all workmen on such official building projects. By 1598 Schaw was calling himself not just master of works but general warden of the masons of Scotland. While he may have simply assumed this title, seeking to extend his authority from masons working on royal works to all masons, it is perhaps more likely that he had persuaded leading masons to agree to recognise his power over them. As general warden and master of works Schaw issued two codes of statutes, in 1598 and 1599. In these he laid down regulations for the organisation and practice of the mason craft through a system of 'lodges'. But these lodges were very different from the old type of building site lodges: they were clearly intended to contain *all* the masons in a burgh or district (not just those who happened to be working on a particular site), and to be permanent institutions with elected officials running them under the supervision of the general warden.

What was William Schaw trying to do—and why? At first sight it might seem that his statutes are solely concerned with the organisation and regulation of the working lives of stonemasons. Certainly this was central to his work, but there are enough hints in the statutes themselves, and in evidence which soon follows and relates to developments arising from the statutes, to make a very strong case for arguing that he was doing much more, reviving and developing Medieval masonic mythology and rituals in a Renaissance atmosphere. But naturally this secret and esoteric side of his work was not committed to writing in his statutes.

The Schaw Statutes define two grades or ranks of mason within the lodges, entered apprentice and fellow craft (alternatively known as master). These two degrees, here first defined, became standard in freemasonry until, in the late seventeenth and early eighteenth centuries, fellow craft and master were gradually divided into two separate grades (rather than alternate names for the same grade), giving the three degrees of modern craft freemasonry. The statutes moreover imply initiations to these grades, and though no Scottish copies of the Old Charges are known before the mid seventeenth century (and those that then appear clearly derive from English originals) the statutes suggest that these Medieval myths were as well known to Scots masons as to their English colleagues.

Within months of the issue of the First Schaw Statutes the first references to specific masonic lodges of the new type appear, and the minutes of two of them, Aitchison's Haven and Edinburgh, commence. The fact that there are no references whatever to the new-type lodges before the statutes surely indicates that they are essentially Schaw's creation—though doubtless individual lodges were sometimes based on earlier types of organisation and on masonic traditions in the localities. Lodge minutes, like the statutes, naturally avoid recording secrets, but in them the initiation of members to the grades of entered apprentice and fellow craft are usually recorded. By about 1630 evidence appears of public awareness that Scottish stonemasons had secrets. This takes the form of references in a variety of sources to 'the Mason Word'— though rather oddly few outsiders seem to have known of the existence of lodges until the end of the century. The early references to the Mason Word concentrate on secret modes of identification—words, postures, signs and gestures—but in fact the term had a wider application, denoting the rituals and secrets of the masons. This becomes clear in the 1690s when the early Scottish 'masonic catechisms', manuscript accounts of the rituals, appear. In addition to detailing recognition codes (question and answer sessions in which one mason could make sure that another was an initiate), the catechisms describe initiation ceremonies culminating in the communication of a secret word to the initiate.

This detailed evidence of ritual initiations does not come until the end of the seventeenth century, but as the rituals are known collectively as the Mason Word and that term was current early in the century, it seems safe to assume that these practices date back at least to that time: and indeed it seems likely that they date back further to William Schaw's creation of the lodges, though this cannot be proved.

As general warden William Schaw claimed authority over Scotland's masons. But he also gave his support to another claim to influence over them. In 1600 or 1601 he signed the so-called First St Clair Charter[2] whereby the masons recognised William Sinclair of Roslin as their patron and protector. It was said that the Sinclairs had long held this position, but how much truth there is in this is impossible to say. Cases can be found of landowners acting as protectors in the localities for men in wandering trades, and James VI had (perhaps at the request of William Schaw) confirmed the position of an Aberdeenshire laird as warden of the masons in North East Scotland in 1590, so there is nothing inherently implausible in the Sinclair claim. The masons renewed their recognition of Sinclair patronage in the Second St Clair Charter addressed to William Sinclair's son, Sir William, in 1627 or 1628, but by this time the king's masters of works, still claiming to be general wardens, bitterly opposed the Sinclairs instead of supporting their pretensions. After the 1630s both the Sinclairs and the masters of works gave up actively trying to assert control over the mason craft, so the lodge system created by William Schaw was left to evolve on its own. But the abortive St Clair Charters are valuable in that they were signed by representatives of a number of lodges: Edinburgh, Aitchison's Haven, St Andrews, Dunfermline and Haddington in the case of the first charter, Edinburgh, St Andrews, Stirling, Dunfermline, Glasgow and Dundee in the case of the second. These cannot be taken as complete lists of existing lodges: for example, Kilwinning Lodge, to which the Second Schaw Statutes had been addressed, evidently refused to have anything to do with other lodges as Schaw would only give it precedence as the second lodge of Scotland and not the first. But the St Clair Charters do provide the earliest evidence for the existence of a number of lodges, and as the century passes other lodges emerge from previous obscurity or are newly created. By 1710, the approximate end-date for this study, William Schaw's legacy totalled at least twenty-five lodges scattered throughout the Lowlands.

If the argument be accepted that the new-style lodges, with their grades of initiate and their rituals, were essentially Schaw's creation (however much he may have drawn on older traditions), what were his motives? Frustratingly little is known of Schaw personally, though he is known to have been a recusant, a Catholic in protestant Scotland, and he is known to have travelled in France and Denmark and may have visited other countries. Unfortunately he died in 1602, soon after his own two codes of statutes and the First St Clair Charter: had he lived longer his intentions might have been much clearer. However, in another book, *The origins of freemasonry. Scotland's century* it has been argued that he was instrumental in injecting into the traditional lore and institutions of the craft a complex mix of late Renaissance influences, a number of which seemed to single out the mason craft as being of exceptional significance. These influences can only be mentioned briefly here, but the fact that they were not simply Schaw's personal eccentricities but reflected major obsessions of the age is indicated by the way in which, in spite of his early death, the movement he inspired continued to flourish and increasingly to attract the fascinated interest of outsiders.

In the decades around 1600 secret societies thrived in Europe, many of them obsessed with the idea of finding some solution to the wars and religious disputes which seemed to be tearing European civilisation apart. These desperate attempts to solve the world's problem ranged from the relatively orthodox Christian (of one denomination or another) to pantheistic attempts to create a new religious synthesis. One feature common to many of these societies was the belief in the lost wisdom of past civilisations which, if recovered, would provide new understanding of the divine, of the universe and of man. This aspect of the Renaissance emphasis on the superiority of ancient civilisations to the Middle Ages was carried to extremes in the Hermetic movement.

Closely bound up with the search for wisdom through astrology and alchemy, Hermeticism assumed that as ancient Egypt predated the civilisations of Greece and Rome, its lost knowledge must be more valuable and pure. The movement got its name from the mythical figure of Hermes Trismegistes. The writings attributed to this supposed Egyptian sage in fact dated from the early Christian era, but they were believed to be many centuries older. Through study of these works and of ancient Egypt (especially of the hieroglyphics in which the Egyptians were supposed to have concealed their wisdom from the eyes of the profane) men hoped to unlock the mysteries of the distant past. But the search was not simply historical and scientific: in its essence it was a spiritual quest, and so purification and spiritual enlightenment were essential to success—as, many believed, was secrecy, for great mysteries were the preserve of the dedicated initiate. In the light of Hermetic ideas the Medieval myths of the masons take on a new importance. The myths claimed that the craft had its roots in ancient Egypt: and the Old Charges specifically assigned Hermes Trismegistus an important role in this process. In the generations in which the great Hermetic quest swept across Europe masons must have taken a particular pride in the role of the god-like Hermes in their craft histories, and considering the extent of the obsession it is not implausible to think of William Schaw as seeing one aspect of the secret lodges he created as being a grafting of the ambitions that led to the founding of secret Hermetic societies onto a craft which already claimed that it had a connection with Hermes and that some of its wisdom derived from ancient Egypt. In this light, the core of ritual which lay at the heart of the new lodges can been seen as involving them in some sense in the Hermetic quest. The idea of Schaw believing Scottish stonemasons had a part to play in recovering lost ancient wisdom essential to the future of mankind may seem absurd in cold blood: in the highly charged atmosphere of 1600 in which many felt all stability and certainty was collapsing it becomes plausible.

One branch of the Hermetic quest centred attention on the art of memory. This had originated in the Classical world as a purely practical mnemonic system, designed to aid in the memorising of long speeches. By the late sixteenth century many Hermetic writers had transformed the art of memory into something occult and mysterious, a technique which could harness mystical or magical powers in the pursuit of the lost wisdom of the ancients and of revelation of the divine. In his second code of statutes William Schaw had ordered that all masons be trained in the art of memory and be regularly tested in it. Which variety of the art Schaw espoused is unknown, but he must have made the same logical connection between the art on the one hand and masons on the other which led the modern historian of the art, Frances Yates, to argue that the art must have some part in the origins of freemasonry, even though she lacked any direct evidence.[3] In its most common forms, the art of memory had an architectural framework. To memorise a speech the practitioner created in his mind a complex building with many rooms, furnished with images or symbols in set locations. He then moved mentally through this building on a fixed route, assigning each idea in his speech in turn to one of the images. Then, in giving his speech, he again walked in his mind through this building, and as he came to them the images would remind him in the correct order of the ideas he wished to express. That the whole process may sound far more trouble than it is worth is, in the present context, besides the point. What matters is that the art of memory was widely respected and practised in Renaissance Europe, and that many believed it to possess occult properties closely linked to the search for spiritual enlightenment. And surely it was the architectural setting of the art which made Schaw believe it was peculiarly appropriate and important for masons. The great quest was to be pursued through a mystical building, and buildings were the creation of masons/architects. When, late in the seventeenth century, details of the rituals of the early Scottish freemasons become known, the descriptions of the lodge within which rituals were performed, and the symbolic significances assigned to different parts of the lodge and objects in it, this can be interpreted in terms of the lodge being envisaged as a temple of memory, still largely mental but given some concrete reality through the performance of rituals, in a room with, perhaps, marks on the floor indicating its supposed features. But if the lodge, in the sense of the framework within which freemasons performed their rituals, was indeed in conception a temple of memory (as well as a re-creation of the Temple of Solomon), this was (ironically) soon forgotten, as the art itself fell out of fashion.

The appearance of Hermes Trismegistus and ancient Egypt in the Medieval mythology of the masons assumed a new significance in the light of the intense interest in these topics during the Renaissance. The same is true of other aspects of these myths. The sixteenth century saw a most remarkable enhancement of the status of the architect in Renaissance thought. Mathemetics was hailed as the queen of the sciences, to which all others were subservient, and the architect was hailed as the supreme practitioner of the mathematical sciences. Renaissance thought, drawing on the writings of the Roman architect Vitruvius, conceived the architect as virtually the universal man, skilled in all the sciences. The coincidence of this exalted concept of the architect with the equation in the Old Charges of masonry with architecture (and therefore with geometry and mathematics) must have had a dual effect. On the one hand it must have greatly increased the pride of masons in their craft: the supreme importance of their work was now widely recognised. On the other hand, outsiders who heard the lore of the Old Charges were increasingly likely to take the pretensions of the masons seriously, and perhaps to seek contact with them to discover if the craft had among it secrets lost knowledge of the architectural sciences. A closely related development would have served to reinforce such attitudes. The Classical world had separated the philosophical and the practical. The philosopher's realm was abstract thought, and he should not debase himself or his ideas by seeking to demonstrate them in practice or to find practical applications for them. That would be debasing, encroaching on the despised world of manual labour. Even the architect was regarded as dirtying his hands by involvement in practical applications, though the fact that making of machines of war was regarded as part of architecture gave him some respectability: the manual labour of fighting and killing was seen as respectable. In the later Renaissance, however, such prejudices were increasingly challenged, and the belief emerged that the philosopher should come down from his ivory tower and consult with craftsmen, for they often had knowledge derived from seeking to solve practical problems, or inherited from past ages, which would serve to advance the sciences.

If, inspired by such a belief that craftsmen had valuable knowledge, one was to seek contact with craftsmen, were not masons the obvious men to approach, practitioners of a craft which had long claimed to practise the queen of the sciences and to derive knowledge from Hermes Trismegistus and ancient Egypt? Intellectual developments of the age seemed to conspire to point to a unique role for the masons. It cannot be proved that William Schaw was partly inspired in his remoulding of the mason craft in Scotland by the heady exaltation of the architect/mathematician, but as a practising architect it would be astonishing if he was not influenced by this fashionable concept. And certainly in the course of the seventeenth century plenty of evidence emerges that the concept was well known and accepted among Scottish masons—and to some degree at least among outsiders, as is indicated by the fact that a significant number of men with mathematical interests joined lodges.

Schaw organised Scottish masons into new-style permanent lodges, reinforcing older masonic lore with a heady mix of Renaissance ideas. Doubtless he intended the great majority of members of his lodges to be working stonemasons, with the lodges acting to some extent as trade guilds (paralleling the incorporations in the burghs) by regulating the trade. But he may well have contemplated some outsiders with relevant interests being initiated into the secrets of the masons. The fact that he died within three years of the appearance of the new lodges makes it impossible to be sure, but there is evidence of a laird being an initiate in 1600. Then, from the 1630s, outsiders begin to appear in the lodges, first in Edinburgh. The coming of these 'non-operatives' is a slow process with many setbacks, as will become clear in the following chapters, but by the end of the seventeenth century some lodges were dominated by gentleman, non-operative members of high social status.

There are, however, problems with the terminology adopted by most masonic historians when discussing the widening of membership of lodges. Members have usually been divided into 'operatives' on the one hand, working stone masons, and 'non-operatives' on the other. 'Non-operatives' are then equated with 'gentlemen' or 'speculative' masons. The first problem is that one type of member fits into neither category and is therefore seldom given its due place in discussing the membership of lodges. Many lodges had members who were neither stonemasons nor gentlemen, men of relatively humble status (often drawn from other crafts). From the point of view of the widening membership of the movement these are as interesting as the men of gentry status, and in this book are included in the term non-operatives. The term thus does not apply only to men of high social status, but to all lodge members who were not stonemasons.

Reserving the term 'speculative mason' for 'gentlemen' non-operatives has had a much more significant role in distorting understanding of the development of freemasonry. 'Speculative' in masonic history has come to denote respectability, acceptance as practitioners of something recognisable as freemasonry. That is reasonable, but then to equate 'speculative masons' with 'gentleman masons' is not. One of the central points of freemasonry is supposed to be that it over-rides differences of social status, yet this definition is based on a snobbish assumption that it is only when the gentry take over the movement that it becomes freemasonry. Rituals performed and ideals held by gentlemen are dignified, respectable freemasonry: their stonemason predecessors acting out the same rituals and holding the same beliefs are somehow not worthy of the name. In reality the Scottish operative stonemasons of the seventeenth century had as rich a life of ritual and belief as their gentry successors. Indeed, it might be argued that they were in some respects more 'speculative' than their modern descendants in that they lived in an age when symbolism was central to life and was held to have almost mystical power in seeking to understand reality, by contrast to its impoverished and degraded state in the modern world!

The masonic catechisms and other evidence make it clear that masonic ritual was, as today, based on the Medieval lore of the craft and on symbolical and allegorical interpretations of supposed events and of the tools, materials and practices of stonemasons. As in any guild or fraternity, the ideal of brotherhood among members was central. The equality of all as masons was also clearly stated: architecture/masonry was unique in binding together the highest and lowest in society. Another central feature of modern freemasonry is the claim to represent a morality without being a religion and without commitment to any specific religious denomination. This is usually seen as deriving from late seventeenth-century and eighteenth-century Enlightenment ideals: growing religious toleration on the one hand, moves towards broad deistic religious views on the other. But though these tendencies fitted in very well with emergent freemasonry, and indeed go far to account for its great popularity in the eighteenth century, the emphasis on a morality separated from religious worship probably had a very different origin, in religious intolerance rather than tolerance.

One of the most startling aspects of the sudden appearance of the masonic lodges and their rituals in seventeenth-century Scotland is that no attempt was made to suppress them. The Church of Scotland was not known for its tolerance, and its first reaction to news of secret societies practising rituals might have been expected to be that this was some heterodox religious phenomenen, probably Roman Catholic as elaborate rituals were involved (and of course

William Schaw himself was a known Catholic), and therefore to be ruthlessly suppressed. Yet apart from some doubts about the compatibility of the Mason Word with true religion being expressed in the years around 1650, the church seems to have felt no unease at the development of freemasonry. In the bitterly intolerant atmosphere of the age this is very hard to understand, but it must surely indicate that some tacit bargain had been struck between the new movement and the church, in which the freemasons made it absolutely clear that they had no intention of encroaching on the monopoly of the church by any involvement of the lodges in religious practices, while at the same time emphasising that they were nonetheless an organisation strongly committed to Christian morality. In these circumstances the church evidently accepted masonic rituals as tolerable: they were moral, but not religious. Even if some such agreement is assumed to have existed, however, the way in which the church turned a blind eye to elaborate masonic rituals at a time when it was zealously seeking to suppress ritual and traditional practices in all walks of life as superstitious and popish is hard to understand. The attraction of masonic rituals to both stonemasons and outsiders must surely, indeed, owe something to a sense of loss at the destruction of religious ritual at the Reformation: the incorporations had been religious fraternities as much as craft guilds. Yet the new protestant church evidently felt no alarm at this. Perhaps it even saw freemasonry as channelling a yearning for ritual which might otherwise have led to popery into a harmless activity.

Scotland's early freemasons, it would appear, probably kept specific religious practices out of their lodges as to do otherwise would have been to confront the church with an attack on its monopoly of religion: but at a later date the morality without religious worship of the lodges made freemasonry attractive to those developing tolerant or deistic attitudes. Other features of freemasonry also made it attractive to the new age of Enlightenment. From the mid seventeenth century onwards there is a very notable growth in Britain of informal sociability and of voluntary social institutions providing settings for this sociability outside the dominant groupings of family and occupation. Coffee and chocolate houses thrived, their clients (or groups among them) often forming clubs. The same sorts of development also often took place in inns and ale houses. Some of these new institutions were very nebulous, others came to have definite memberships and rules—and even developed their own rituals. Some were general in membership, others confined to people with particular interests, literary, scientific or political. In the Scottish masonic lodges many evidently sought, and found, existing institutions which provided a framework for this craving for sociability and ritual. The traditional history of masonry and the conflation of masons, architects and mathematicians also had relevance to a new age. The great days of the Hermetic quest might be over, though the belief in lost wisdom from the distant past lingered on, but the concept of the mason as mathematician remained influential and a source of attraction, for more than ever before mathematics was seen as the way to describe and understand the universe.

Thus the freemasonry born in seventeenth-century Scotland proved capable of adapting from the era of the late Renaissance in which it was born to that of the Enlightenment. It also proved capable of being exported successfully. The development of freemasonry in England in the seventeenth century is highly obscure, but the fragmentary evidence suggests that in the closing years of the seventeenth century and the opening years of the eighteenth it was transformed by an influx of Scottish influences, introducing for the first time permanent lodges, the degrees of entered apprentice and fellow craft/master, and the rituals of the Mason Word (though that term was little used in England). Thus many of the essentials of the freemasonry which developed so fast in early eighteenth-century England derived from earlier Scottish freemasonry. English leadership of the movement was to develop and elaborate it in new ways (and indeed to give it the very name freemasonry), but to this day craft freemasonry bears clear evidence of its Scottish origins.

Like it or loath it, it is undeniable that freemasonry, spreading round the world with astonishing speed in the eighteenth century, was a remarkable social and cultural phenomonen—and in some of its guises, important in politics and religion as well. To understand it and its appeal a study of the early Scottish lodges in which it originated, and of the members of these lodges, is essential.

2
EDINBURGH

The Lodge of Edinburgh (Mary's Chapel)

Edinburgh is the obvious starting point for an examination of Scotland's early masonic lodges not merely because it is the country's capital but because it is the only burgh for which minutes of both the lodge and the guild or incorporation which contained masons survive in the seventeenth century, though the two sets exist side by side only for the last third of it. Moreover, in 1599 William Schaw described Edinburgh as the first lodge of Scotland, and its minutes, commencing in July 1599, are the oldest of any lodge which still exists today (though the oldest minutes of all are those of the extinct Aitchison's Haven Lodge, beginning in January 1599).[1] The records of the incorporation have not fared so well. Judging from the statement made in the mid nineteenth century that the signature of William Schaw 'is of frequent occurrence in the early records of the Incorporation of Mary's Chapel'[2] extensive records, probably including minutes signed by Schaw, then existed. But for many years historians were refused access to these records,[3] and though many are now available for consultation the earliest known minutes date from 1669, only a few miscellaneous papers surviving from earlier years.[4] It is highly ironic that the 'secret' masonic lodge should have published its minutes in full for the seventeenth century, while the incorporation was so obsessively secretive and careless that many of its early records have evidently been lost without historians being able to study them. However, the recovery of the late seventeenth century minutes means that an attempt can now be made to tackle, for the last decades of the century, some of the questions concerning the relationship of incorporation and lodge which Harry Carr was frustrated at being unable to answer (in his extensive studies of Edinburgh masons) through lack of access to any of the incorporation records.[5]

The Incorporation of Masons and Wrights (the latter being carpenters) of Edinburgh was granted a 'seal of cause' by the burgh council formally constituting it in 1475, but it is a mistake to think of this as 'the beginning of mason trade organisation' in Edinburgh.[6] As in other trades, organisation of some sort had doubtless long existed, and the seal of cause was granted because it became customary in the late fifteenth century to regularise the position of guilds by such grants—nine Edinburgh incorporations received their seals between 1473 and 1505.[7] In 1601 the Incorporation acquired Mary's Chapel in Niddry's Wynd, and it subsequently became generally known as the

Incorporation of Mary's Chapel. Similarly the lodge (first known to have met in the chapel in 1613) became known as that of Mary's Chapel.[8]

Lodge and incorporation existed in Edinburgh as parallel organisations from 1599, meeting in the same building. But each (so far as their written records are concerned) remained silent as to the existence of the other, though they were closely linked in some ways. The incorporation was headed by two officials, the mason deacon and the wright deacon, elected annually by the incorporation and the burgh council, and each year the lodge silently accepted the mason deacon of the incorporation as the presiding official in the lodge—an arrangement which does much to explain why the incorporation was prepared tacitly to accept the emergence of the new-fangled lodge instead of treating it as a rival seeking to entice masons from their allegiance to the incorporation.

The career of the mason up to his full acceptance as a free craftsman normally involved membership of both bodies. An entrant to the trade would begin by serving an apprenticeship. If he came from outside the burgh a formal indenture setting down the terms of his apprenticeship would be drawn up and signed, and this would be 'booked' or registered with the consent of the incorporation in the burgh register of apprentices. If, however, a trainee's father was a burgess of the burgh he would probably not be booked as an apprentice. The sons of burgesses did not need to serve as indentured apprentices to qualify for burgess-ship, being entitled to it by right of kinship. Sometimes (especially if recruited to a trade different from their fathers') they did serve as apprentices, but more often they were trained informally.[9] A father training his son in his trade would not be expected to limit his parental control over the child by a written agreement like an indenture. This is the main explanation of the fact that only 149 mason apprentices were booked in Edinburgh in 1601-1700, while the records of the lodge, imperfect as they are, record the admission of 271 operative entered apprentices in the same period.[10]

Though the burgh kept the apprentice register, the relevant incorporation's consent, and payment of a fee to it were necessary before a craft apprentice could be booked,[11] and he like his master came under the incorporation's supervision. Indentured mason apprentices were generally bound to serve their masters for seven years (longer than in most trades), often with the additional stipulation that the apprentice should then serve another year or so for 'meat and fee'—that is, receiving a wage as well as his keep. Shorter apprenticeships for masons were quite common in rural areas, but the seven year's minimum was generally enforced in Edinburgh, the following being the terms of the eighty-two indentures booked in Edinburgh in 1584-1647:[12]

5 years	5	9 years	1
6 years	1	10 years	2
7 years	59	11 years	1
8 years	13		

Two or three years after beginning his service the apprentice joined the lodge, going through the first stage of his initiation and becoming an 'entered apprentice' to his master. Relatively few indentures of apprenticeship survive, but of sixteen Scottish masonic indentures dated 1573 and between 1660 and 1721 that have been traced, three specifically oblige the master to 'enter' his apprentice in a lodge. One concerns Edinburgh: in 1685 William Fulton, mason burgess, took Alexander Robesone as apprentice for six years and bound himself 'to enter his said prentise at Marys Chappell and that within three years of the dait heirof'.[13]

Once his trade apprenticeship ended the former apprentice became free to seek employment as a wage-earning journeyman or servant, working for a master mason. His achievement of this status was not formally recorded by burgh, incorporation or lodge, though if he took employment with a master of the incorporation he would be 'booked' in its records for the period of his employment. A few years after becoming a journeyman, about seven years after being made an entered apprentice, he would be promoted in the lodge to 'fellow craft' or 'master'. So far as the lodge was concerned he was now a master mason through this initiation to the higher grade: but to the incorporation he remained a journeyman not permitted either to undertake work for a customer himself (except for very small jobs) or to employ others. Finally, after about a year as a fellow craft, those masons who had the right family connections, or who could pay the high fees, would become burgesses and (after their skills had been tested) be admitted as masters of the incorporation.[14] But though now free to undertake work on their own behalf, take apprentices of their own, and employ journeymen, some master masons continued to spend much of their time working for wages for other masters, the successful minority who acted as building contractors.

This complicated zigzag climb of the 'typical' aspiring mason up two overlapping but separate hierarchies may be summarised as follows:

Year	The Public Hierarchy: Incorporation and Burgh	The Secret Hierarchy: Lodge
1	Apprentice	
2	,,	
3	,,	Entered Apprentice
4	,,	,,
5	,,	,,
6	,,	,,
7	,,	,,
8	Journeyman/Servant	..
9	,,	
10	,,	Fellow Craft/Master
11	Burgess and Master of the Incorporation	

There were, however, wide variations in the timing of the various stages of individual masons' careers, and even in the order of advancement in the two hierarchies—in a few cases men became burgesses and members of the incorporation before becoming fellow crafts in the lodge.[15] Moreover some mason burgesses evidently never joined the lodge at all, and there were many fellow craft masters of the lodge who never became burgesses and masters of the incorporation.

As to the general position of the masons in Edinburgh, they formed a fairly small craft group. Few members were very rich, but few were poor either, and the craft has been described as one offering moderate security.[16] It has been estimated that by the end of the seventeenth century Edinburgh had about 2,200 burgesses, about 57% of them craftsmen; and burgesses and their dependents made up only about 30% of the total population.[17] Masons formed less than 1% of the total burgess population. Even within the Incorporation of Masons and Wrights the masons were greatly outnumbered by other trades, and though the numbers of masons remained stable some of the other trades were growing, so the masons comprised a declining proportion of the total membership, as the following figures demonstrate:[18]

	Masons	Wrights	Glaziers	Painters	Slaters	Others	Total
1670	15	46	8	4	8	15	96
1709	14	63	17	15	5	16	130

By custom the masons came first in the title of the incorporation, and their names were written first in the membership lists, reflecting the traditional prestige and pretensions of the craft, but there were three wright masters for every mason in 1670 and their position continued to decline in the years that followed. Presumably the masons had always been in a minority, and the fact that they and the wrights had separate deacons may have been a concession designed to persuade the masons to accept membership of an incorporation in which they would always be numerically weak. But the wrights were increasingly reluctant to accept a secondary position, as was indicated by disputes over precedence which led in 1690 to a decision that the wright and mason deacons should preside at alternate meetings of the incorporation, though the right of the masons to have their names called first was upheld.[19] Having their own deacon to protect their interests was much valued by the masons, but the fact that they also had a lodge indicates that they felt that they also needed an organisation of their own through which they could assert, perhaps more symbolically than practically, their claims to complete control of their own craft, and in which they could perform their rituals and communicate their secrets. And this was accepted in practice by the incorporation, doubtless reassured by the fact that the acceptance by the lodge of the authority of the mason deacon ensured that the lodge would not try to usurp rights belonging it.

In the seventeenth century in Edinburgh as elsewhere the burgh and incorporation performed some of the functions that the Schaw Statutes had assigned to the new lodges, notably booking apprentices and setting and examining the essays or trials of skill of would-be masters. This was not a limitation on lodge activities that developed after William Schaw's death, for the Edinburgh Lodge minutes show no trace of such activities even during his lifetime. The tantalising fact that Schaw's signature is said to have occurred many times in the lost early records of the incorporation suggests that as master of works he claimed the right to supervise in it, and it may be that after the statutes were issued he worked out some division of functions between lodge and incorporation which surrendered to the latter some of the matters the statutes had assigned to the former.

The lodge's minutes contain only one reference to an essay, when in 1683 the nineteen year old son of a deceased former deacon asked to be tested by an essay to qualify himself as a fellow craft master. The masters of the lodge decided that none under the age of twenty-one was qualified to be admitted fellow craft, 'far mor to be admitet to an asaie'.[20] Thus the lodge differentiated the essay from passing fellow craft, regarding the essay as something to be undertaken rather later in the mason's career.

The minute books of the incorporation confirm that the essay was set as part of the process of admission to that body, not to the lodge. David Murray Lyon, the nineteenth-century historian of the lodge, knew of these references to essays, but caused much confusion by citing one of them without adequate explanation. John Hamilton was made a mason burgess of Edinburgh on 6 January 1686, and three days later appeared before the incorporation and petitioned to be admitted to an essay. This was agreed, and his essay was defined as a house 120 feet long, details of which were given. As Lyon indicated that the essay when complete was to be presented to the essay masters for inspection (by Lammas—1 August) he obviously assumed that a scale drawing or model was involved, but his failure to state this clearly, and the fact that the lodge clerk had erroneously written Lammas when Candlemas (2 February) was meant, has led to the minute sometimes being read as requiring Hamilton to build a real house, being given eight months for the purpose.[21] Hamilton's essay was in fact accepted on 6 February, and he was admitted to the incorporation on paying the customary fees totalling £104.[22] That the essays were indeed models is proved by a 1691 act which laid down that masons' essays should be preserved like those of other crafts in the incorporation, instead of being destroyed immediately, as had been the practice previously;[23] and that the models were constructed of pasteboard was indicated in 1706 when Henry Wilson's essay was to make 'ane double House in paisboard' sixty or sixty-six feet long.[24]

The fact that the essay whereby a mason proved his skills was not cutting or laying stone, but an exercise in designing a house to a given basic specification and constructing a scale model of it indicates the extent to which masons had accepted the identification of the mason and the architect. Whether this type of essay had only come into use in the seventeenth century or was much older is unknown. As a test of skill, however, the essay was probably not very demanding. Those who undertook it to qualify for membership had in fact usually already been registered as mason burgesses by the burgh, and no cases are recorded of men's essays being rejected as inadequate.

More detailed study of the later seventeenth century records of the Incorporation of Mary's Chapel will be necessary before its role in regulating the mason trade in the burgh can be properly assessed, but preliminary work indicates that there was little to distinguish it from the other incorporations in the burgh. In Mary's Chapel the masters of the building trades sought to regulate entry to the trade both to limit the numbers working in the trade and to ensure that entrants were properly trained and qualified. Working practices and a variety of routine matters relating to the welfare of the trades were dealt with, and efforts were made at least to limit access to work in the burgh by stranger tradesmen from outside it. Breaches of regulations were punished and attempts made to settle disputes between members. Though only masters were members of the incorporation, it exercised jurisdiction over apprentices and journeymen as well: the latter had to be 'booked' with the incorporation by their masters, and fees paid for them.[25] Some of these journeymen, either because they came from outside the burgh or through some other defect in their training were not eligible for burgess-ship and membership of the incorporation, but it was accepted in 1685 that such men could become apprentices even though previously they had been booked as journeymen.[26] By 1694, however, the incorporation was refusing to accept this practice of allowing an already skilled man to serve a nominal apprenticeship in order to qualify for burgess-ship, and it was supported by the burgh council.[27] Others who had been trained outside the burgh qualified for membership of the incorporation by marrying the daughters of members. Mr James Smith (c.1645-1731), a university graduate (as the 'Mr' indicates) who was to become a notable architect, became a member in 1680 through marriage to a daughter of Robert Mylne, the king's master mason, and through 'haveing been bred a measson myself'—his father had been a mason burgess of Forres.[28] Finally, the incorporation was a benefit society, caring for members fallen on hard times through age or illness, and for the widows or dependent children of deceased members. The accounts of the incorporation provide lists both of pensioners receiving regular help and of one-off payments.

The incorporation also extended its authority over areas outside the burgh but subordinate to it—though not over the Canongate, which had its own burgh council and incorporation. By a contract of 1650 the masons, wrights and coopers of the suburb of Portsburgh agreed to submit five names a year to the Mary's Chapel Incorporation, which would pick one of them to be oversman of the Portsburgh building trades, and to consult the incorporation before they set essays or admitted freemen.[29] Thus the Portsburgh men kept their own guild but accepted its subordination to Edinburgh's. A similar arrangement covered Leith, and from at least 1678 the incorporation appointed three oversmen each year for the masons, wrights and coopers of Leith—but though the incorporation 'elected' them there is an indication in 1690 that the Leith men may have presented their own candidates to the incorporation which then rubber-stamped the appointment.[30]

In regulating the building trades in the seventeenth century the Mary's Chapel Incorporation was probably reasonably effective—but only within the limits set by custom and the burgh authorities. It accepted that men from outside the burgh might be employed within it by Edinburgh masters, and tacitly conceded that major building projects, especially ones undertaken by the burgh council, required more skilled man-power than the burgh itself could provide. Nor could it stop individuals regarded as outstanding in their skills being recruited to play leading roles in such ventures. Thus John Ritchie was the master mason for the building of Parliament House in Edinburgh from 1633, but was not made a burgess until 1636, when he was admitted free by order of the burgh council.[31] It is not certain where he came from, but he may have been the Glasgow mason burgess of that name.[32] In 1633 the masons and wrights complained bitterly that their trades were decaying through lack of work as so many unfree men, resident both inside and outside the burgh, were intruding into their trades,[33] and this may be linked to the fact that there appear to have been labour problems at Parliament House in 1634, with a sudden and sharp decline in the number of masons employed followed by a slow drift back to work.[34] Was this a protest by the Edinburgh masons against the employment of outsiders such as Ritchie, the dispute being partly settled by making him a burgess? William Aytoun, the master mason of Heriot's Hospital from 1631, was a highly skilled carver and expert 'dialer', or maker of sundials (responsible for many of the dials on the hospital walls, and for one erected in the university), as well as being a skilled calligrapher, producing two copies of the National Covenant of 1638 illuminated in gold and proudly signed 'William Aytoun, Maison'. He was a member of the dynasty of Aytoun masons in the Musselburgh area, a number of whom were members of Aitchison's Haven Lodge, and, like Ritchie, only became an Edinburgh burgess years after beginning work in the burgh, being admitted by act of council in 1640.[35]

No doubt Edinburgh masons disliked such prestigious positions as those held by Ritchie and Aytoun going to outsiders, but there was little they could do about it, and in any case though many of the burgh's masons might hope to spend their working lives employed in Edinburgh, some would seek employment elsewhere at times, and it may have feared that insistence on excluding strangers from working in Edinburgh would lead to retaliation against Edinburgh masons in other parts of the country.

On some occasions stranger master masons worked in the burgh for ordinary as well as for official customers, against the wishes of the incorporation through the intervention of public authorities. Masons and wrights seem to have been notorious for trying to extort unduly high wages, as legislation dating back to the early fifteenth century indicates; doubtless the nature of their product put them in a strong bargaining position, as they could suddenly demand a wage increase under threat of leaving their employer with an unfinished but partly paid-for building on his hands. In 1557 Edinburgh council invoked acts of parliament to authorise unfree masons and wrights from outside the burgh to work in it, as the burgh masons had refused to complete work being undertaken for the baxters (bakers) unless paid exorbitant prices: and this act was to be enforced whenever in future the craftsmen made unreasonable demands.[36] Over a century later, in 1675 Thomas Borlands in Kingstables found that the mason who had contracted to build a house for him had failed to pay the mason journeymen employed to do the building, using the money provided by Borlands for other purposes. He therefore brought in four unfree masons, who were promptly arrested and imprisoned in the tolbooth on the instructions of the incorporation. Borlands complained to the privy council, and the unfree masons were released, the mason deacon and two other burgh masons taking their place in the tolbooth in spite of their pleas that for many years the burgh masons had been in the habit of arresting unfree masons found working in Edinburgh or areas such as Portsburgh (where Borland's house was being built).[37]

Officially it was only when burgh craftsmen behaved unreasonably that customers could turn to unfree men, and the burgh council passed acts to this effect in 1677 and 1689.[38] But the incorporation was soon in trouble again. In 1691 it set minimum rates of pay its members should accept, on the grounds that those who worked for less were ruining themselves and becoming a burden to the incorporation as it then had to provide them with financial help. When the council discovered this it immediately ruled the setting of minimum wages illegal.[39]

The incorporation was from time to time torn by internal dispute as well as quarrels with outsiders. In 1671 the unmannerly carriage of some members was denounced. Only one member was to speak at a time, and though he was to be called up to stand before the deacons to do so, he was not to bang on the table to emphasise his points.[40] Members of one trade within the incorporation doing the work of others was a frequent cause of complaint: in 1689 a wright unwise enough to harl walls in Niddry's Wynd, where the incorporation met, was ordered to employ a mason to do the work.[41] The smaller trades sometimes resented the domination of the masons and wrights, and got the court of session to declare that their members should be eligible for election as deacons. But it was not until 1721 that the lesser trades took advantage of this and had one of their number, a glazier, elected mason deacon.[42]

The Incorporation of Mary's Chapel looked after the interests of masons— or at least of mason burgesses—in exactly the same way as it looked after its other trades, and as the other incorporations did their members. What, then, was there left for the Lodge of Mary's Chapel to do in the way of trade regulation? Not much, and certainly not enough to justify the existence of a separate institution. It has usually been assumed that the early 'operative' lodges (defined as ones whose members were entirely or largely working stonemasons) existed primarily to do operative things, regulating the trade like guilds. But though the Edinburgh Lodge minutes do indeed record a trickle of regulatory actions, they are thin on the ground. In acting to control apprentices and journeymen, settling disputes between members, and trying to exclude unfree men, the basic types of operative activity found in its records,[43] the lodge was doing exactly the same sorts of things as the incorporation. Perhaps the most convincing explanation of why the lodge dabbled in such activities when the incorporation could have easily dealt with them is that masons wanted to assert at least occasionally the right to settle on their own matters which solely concerned their trade, without taking them before all the trades in the incorporation and thus having to display (in the case of internal disputes between masons) their dirty washing in public instead of discreetly sorting it out in private. The masons might accept being lumped together with other trades in the incorporation, but with their unique claims for their craft and its ancient traditions they developed and maintained through the new lodges at least a pretence of their autonomy, their freedom from outside control by incorporation or burgh. The incorporation was prepared tacitly to accept this, regarding the lodge in this capacity as acting like an informal subcommittee for mason affairs, presided over by the mason deacon. But in some respects the lodge was of course very unlike a sub-committee. The Lodge did not claim authority derived from the incorporation as its parent body, it was not responsible to the incorporation for its actions, and it did not report to the incorporation.

Moreover, whereas the incorporation was subordinate to the burgh council and other public authorities, the lodge did not claim to derive its right to act from any public authority with the exception of the general warden of the masons, and that authority was abandoned in practice after the death of William Schaw in 1602. Like all other individuals and institutions in the land, the lodge and its members were subject to the king and to the law, but the fact that the lodges were secret bodies with no officially recognised existence meant that their activities were unsupervised—except, in Edinburgh's case, through the mason deacon in effect representing the incorporation. But this autonomy of the lodge was also a source of weakness. As the existence of lodges was not admitted, they could not appeal to higher authorities, in the way that incorporations could turn to the burgh council or the court of session, to uphold their customary rights. In Edinburgh lodge members could only maintain publicly the rights of the masons through the incorporations, and since so far as the incorporation was concerned the lodge had no official existence even this was difficult—as the confusion in the dispute which led to the foundation of the Lodge of Journeymen masons in 1714-15 (considered later in this chapter) demonstrates. Outside the burghs, masons did not have any recognised institution through which they could indirectly uphold the interests of their lodge. And the very secrecy surrounding the lodges was a potential weakness, making discretion rather than effectual action the first priority through fear that public knowledge of their activities would lead to their suppression for trying to exercise a jurisdiction over masons to which they had no legal right.

Edinburgh and the other lodges were social organisations, giving a sense of belonging and opportunities for sociable eating and drinking at annual banquets on St John's Day (27 December), as well as trade regulating organisations and benefit societies. But all these functions they had in common with the incorporations and many other organisations. What made them unique were their 'secrets', their rituals of identification and initiation, and their lore as to the importance and history of the craft. These were vastly more elaborate than those of any other organisation, and were much more secret. They were the true reason for the lodges' existence, and the very fact that the existence of the lodges was kept secret is one indication of the fact that members regarded them in this way. Trade regulation, sociability and relief of members in need did not require secrecy, yet secrecy was of the essence of the lodge.

At least in its trade regulating functions, it has been suggested above, the Lodge of Mary's Chapel may be seen as acting as a kind of irregular subcommittee for masons of the Mary's Chapel Incorporation, but in membership as in other respects already discussed this description is not entirely accurate. All the master masons of the incorporation were eligible for membership of the lodge, but so too were many who were not members of the incorporation. Apprentices and journeymen masons were subject to the incorporation, yet they were not in any meaningful sense members of it. But after the first two or three years of their service apprentices could become entered apprentices in the lodge. As such they were members, and though they were seldom given any say in the running of the lodge (though on two occasions in 1603 new members of the lodge were referred to as being admitted with consent of the entered apprentices as well as the fellow craft masters),[44] they had been initiated to some of its secrets. And the entered apprentices would usually become fellow craft masters of the lodge, before being admitted to the incorporation as masters. Moreover, while membership of the incorporation was limited to Edinburgh mason burgesses, the lodge recruited masons who were freemen of Leith and other suburbs (with the exception of the Canongate), at least some of whom were members of guilds subordinate to the Edinburgh incorporation. Thus there were far more masons in the lodge than in the incorporation. The lodge minutes for 1599 refer to seventeen fellow crafts and twelve entered apprentices, as well as six servants whose status is uncertain (they may not have been members but, as employees of members regarded as subject to the lodge's jurisdiction).[45] It is not known how many masons were members of the incorporation at this time but there were probably considerably fewer of them than there were members of the lodge.

The majority of the seventeenth-century minutes of the Edinburgh Lodge are concerned either with recording details of membership (the admission of entered apprentices, and their subsequent promotion to fellow crafts), or with regulation of the operative trade. The former type of minute greatly outnumbers the latter. In 1629 to 1645 forty-nine meetings of the lodge are recorded, in sixty-four separate minutes, and all these minutes are solely concerned with admissions and promotions.[46] This period is an extreme case, and it is true that the minutes of some meetings have probably been lost, as is suggested by the facts that many promotions to fellow craft are recorded without any previous record of admission as entered apprentice, and many names of members occur without record of either admission or promotion.[47] But the decade 1631-40, lying at the centre of the longest of the periods for which there are no entries dealing with trade regulation, has more meetings recorded than any other decade of the century, suggesting that it is not just chance loss that has led to lack of evidence of 'operative' activity. Another explanation might be variations as to what the clerks of the lodge thought fit to record in the minutes, and it is true that not all lodge activities were recorded. The election of the warden was supposed to take place on 27 December each year, but only in a few cases are the elections recorded in the surviving minutes in the seventeenth century: and in 1599-1630 only four 27 December meetings are recorded.[48] Though they probably took place regularly, with elections of wardens and the annual banquets, it was evidently not regarded as necessary to minute them. But the minutes do suggest that an attempt was made to record regularly admissions, promotions and actions concerning the operative trade (whether general regulations or decisions on individual cases). Thus if references to trade regulation are in many periods rare, it was because the lodge was not seeking to supervise the trade systematically. Moreover the lodge met too infrequently for it to have done so. Surviving minutes indicate that throughout the period 1601 to 1710 the lodge met on average about two and a third times a year. Even if this figure be generously doubled to allow for lost minutes and meetings which were not minuted, there would not have been enough meetings to make possible supervision of the trade on a day to day basis. Yet it is true that in some at least of the cases concerning the trade that the lodge dealt with, it was effective in disciplining erring masons. But while offenders may have been in part ready to submit to the lodge because it could by 'operative' sanctions make it difficult for them to earn a living, it seems likely that its most effective sanction was the threat of exclusion from the brotherhood and rituals of the lodge.

The first minute book of the Lodge of Edinburgh opens with an undated draft minute, evidently dating from late in 1599, followed by a copy of the First Schaw Statutes of 27 December 1598. The earliest minute follows, dated 31 July 1599. In it a mason confessed to working with a cowan: he was not punished, but warning was given that any further offenders would be.[49] The definition of what a cowan was differs somewhat according to context. Basically it was the trade name for the builders of drystone walls, who on occasion may have undertaken more elaborate work with stone and clay. Master masons regarded them as rivals to be shunned—to prevent them learning the practical secrets of the trade and thus breaking the monopoly of skilled work the masons sought to preserve. Doubtless there had long been tension between masons and cowans, but the First Schaw Statutes are the earliest known source to forbid masons to work with them, and from this time the word cowan was evidently sometimes used to describe a man who had not been initiated to the secrets of the Mason Word, whatever training they had received in the mason trade. That the earliest Edinburgh Lodge minute concerns a cowan surely indicates an attempt to enforce this aspect of the statutes. But, as already indicated, in practice the lodge was to enforce discipline only sporadically in the decades ahead (there are no further cases concerning cowans recorded). Schaw had clearly intended his statutes to lead to a thorough reorganisation of the trade, with the new lodges having a central place in enforcing them, but they failed to live up to his expectations.

In one respect, however, Edinbugh Lodge anticipated Schaw's wishes. The Second Schaw Statutes of December 1599 were to specify that each lodge should have a notary public as its clerk, but Edinburgh had such a clerk, Adam Gibson, by the time of its first minute, and he also signed several other 1599 and 1600 minutes.[50] It has been argued that he was a member of the lodge.[51] If this be accepted, Gibson would be the earliest known 'non-operative' initiated into the secrets of the mason craft in the new lodges. Certainly later in the century in a number of lodges (including Edinburgh) clerks were initiated, but as the clerk was only involved in recording aspects of the lodge's activities which were not secret there was no necessity for this. Adam Gibson and his immediate successors are never listed among lodge members present at meetings, and it seems most likely that he was not admitted to his employers' secret rituals. His appointment as clerk probably arose from the fact that in 1599 he was acting as common scribe to the deacons of the crafts.[52]

How long had the Edinburgh lodge existed before the first recorded minute? The question cannot be answered with complete certainty, but it is probable that, while the masons of Mary's Chapel Incorporation may have met on their own from time to time to rehearse the secret lore of their craft and consider problems of operative regulation and discipline, the lodge as a formal body with that name and with elaborate rituals and secrets only came into being as the result of the work of William Schaw. Perhaps the convention of masons which approved the First Schaw Statutes on 27 December 1598 should be regarded as marking the foundation of the lodge. The meeting was held in Edinburgh and probably comprised largely the burgh's own masons. It is true that the first minute records an act of an organisation already in existence, not its foundation, but the second minute, 27 November 1599, suggests the organisation was still in its early stages, or at least that reorganisation was under way, for it dealt with the basic matter of choosing a warden annually. Wardens were the chief elected officials in lodges, and normally presided at meetings (except in cases like Edinburgh Lodge where the incorporation's deacon did so). The minute decreed (as Schaw had done for all lodges) that elections should take place on 27 December and that the general warden should be informed annually of the new warden's name.[53]

The second part of the 27 November 1599 minute also related to the development of lodges at this time, for it ordered that a general meeting of masons be held in St Andrews on 13 January 1600 for settling the affairs of that lodge. All the masters and others under the jurisdiction of the St Andrews lodge, along with two commissioners from every other lodge, were to attend. Moreover the masters of Dundee and Perth were to assemble in St Andrews at the same time. Thus St Andrews already possessed a lodge, but outside intervention was necessary, perhaps because it was just being formed; and it may be that the Perth and Dundee masters were to meet so the first steps could be taken to form or regularise lodges in these burghs. This minute is in the same hand as the Edinburgh copy of the First Schaw Statutes, and some further information is provided by the undated and unfinished minute which is entered immediately before the statutes, for it was evidently a first draft of the 27 November minute. This laid down that the commissioners (presumably those to attend the 13 January meeting) were to be elected at the same time as the warden, and that the commissioners were to convene when and where the general warden commanded.[54] Schaw took the initiative in getting the St Andrews convention summoned, but had the orders for its meeting issued in the name of the Lodge of Edinburgh, which his second set of statutes, issued a month later, was to call the first lodge of Scotland. His intention seems to have been that, as first lodge, Edinburgh should have a degree of authority over other lodges. This is confirmed by the fact that when on 28 December 1599 the commissioner of the Lodge of Kilwinning represented his lodge's interests on the occasion of the issuing of the Second Schaw Statutes he appeared before not just the general warden but the masters of the Lodge of Edinburgh as well. It is not known whether the St Andrews meeting ever took place, but some assembly of masons convened in 1600-1 when the First St Clair Charter was accepted by representatives of five lodges, including three Edinburgh masons.

The close interest Schaw continued to take in the Edinburgh Lodge's affairs is indicated by the fact that on two occasions in 1600-1 John Yellowlees, described as his servitor and clerk general, acted as clerk to the lodge.[55] But in a number of respects the lodge clearly was not interested in Schaw's ambitious plans for its future. After its early years its activity in regulating the mason trade declined notably. Though notaries were occasionally employed as clerks at first—Adam Gibson being replaced by Archibald Gibson in 1600-3 and George Mostede in 1605[56]—this custom soon lapsed. The names of the 'intenders' chosen by entered apprentices to prepare them for initiation as fellow crafts were only recorded in the records twice, in 1606 and 1609.[57] Above all, the lodge showed no interest in maintaining authority over other lodges as the first lodge of Scotland.

Schaw himself soon found fault with the conduct of those running the lodge. On 8 June 1600 he held a meeting of the lodge as principal warden and chief master of masons (titles found nowhere else) at the palace of Holyroodhouse: as the king's master of works he doubtless had rooms there like other officials. Schaw was accompanied by an Ayrshire laird, John Boswell of Auchinleck, and they proceeded to find the warden of the lodge, John Brown, guilty of some offence (which is not specified) and to fine him £40. The fine was the largest ever imposed in the lodge, so the warden's offence must have been regarded as serious, but it was then 'modified' or reduced to £10 by the masters. The main interest of the minute, however, lies in the presence of the laird of Auchinleck. Murray Lyon claimed this as the 'earliest authentic record of a non-operative being a member of a Mason Lodge'. Harry Carr reversed this interpretation, arguing that what took place was not a lodge meeting but a trial, that Auchinleck may have attended to help Schaw in this legal matter, and that the mark Auchinleck appended to his signature on the minute was not a mason mark.[58] None of these arguments are convincing. The twelve master masons of the lodge who signed the minute and appended their mason marks clearly did so in their capacity as members of the lodge, and though Schaw and Auchinleck sat as judges in a trial this took place in a meeting of the lodge. Schaw was exercising the right he claimed as general warden to supervise lodges. The lodge was acting as a court, but there was nothing unusual about that. Finally, Auchinleck's mark may not conform to later artificial definitions of what a mason mark should be, but the same could be said of a number of other marks which were accepted by lodges in the seventeenth century: when Dr William Maxwell joined the Edinburgh Lodge in 1647 his mark was a small flower![59] And if Auchinleck's mark was not a mason mark, what was it? Mason marks were normally taken on initiation but (with very rare exceptions) no particular symbolic or other significance was assigned to them.

There remains the problem of why Auchinleck was present in the lodge, for even if he had been initiated as a mason he was not a member of the Lodge of Edinburgh. It may simply be that he was a friend of Schaw's brought in to support him in acting against the lodge's warden, but another possibility is worth considering. Kilwinning Lodge appears to have been highly sensitive about its status, and evidently had been unwilling to accept being only the second lodge of Scotland when the Second Schaw Statutes had assigned it that rank in 1599. If Auchinleck was indeed an initiated mason, then as an Ayrshire man he probably belonged to Kilwinning Lodge, or had been initiated by masons from that lodge (not all initiations took place in lodges). In view of this, it becomes possible to postulate a scenario in which the warden of Edinburgh Lodge had done something to exacerbate the tension between the two lodges, endangering Schaw's efforts to satisfy the pretensions of Kilwinning. Schaw therefore intervened to punish the warden, and did it in the presence of Auchinleck as a representative of Kilwinning to make sure that the offended party was appeased. This can be no more than guesswork, but it would explain the presence at a meeting of Edinburgh Lodge of a man who evidently was a non-operative mason but was not a member of that lodge.

After William Schaw's death in 1602 there is only a single reference in the Edinburgh Lodge minutes which suggests that the lodge took an interest in the general development of the craft's organisation. This is a tantalising unfinished minute dated Roslin 1 May 1628 recording that Sir William Sinclair did something—but not what. Presumably the entry relates in some way to the Second St Clair Charter, which was accepted by the warden, deacon and two other members of the lodge, but the minutes record nothing further of the matter.[60] Nor, indeed, do the minutes mention anything except admissions and promotions for the following decade and a half. But though the lodge thus appears to have turned its back on supervision of the operative craft in these years, an exciting new development took place during them. The lodge began for the first time to admit non-operatives.

The inspiration for this development came, it appears, from John Mylne younger. Mylne came from a notable family of masons and architects. His father, also John, was appointed master mason to the king in 1631 (though the claims that were soon to be made that the family had served the crown in that office for generations are fictitious), but resigned office in favour of his son in 1636. Three years before this the younger Mylne had been made a fellow craft in the Edinburgh Lodge. There is no record of his admission as an entered apprentice, and it seems likely that he had already attained at least that rank elsewhere, perhaps in the Lodge of Scone. The epitaph erected to the younger Mylne after his death in 1667 expressed with startling clarity the vision of architecture as the discipline that above all others united the highest and the lowest, theory and practice, the scholar or courtier architect and the humble artisan; and the epitaph proclaimed that in his own life Mylne succeeded in combining these extremes to an unusual extent.[61] His influence on the Edinburgh Lodge suggests that for once the praises of a eulogist can be trusted.

On 3 July 1634 William, Lord Alexander, his younger brother Anthony Alexander (the king's master of works), and Sir Alexander Strachan of Thornton were all made fellow crafts of the lodge, their social status carrying them directly to the higher of the two grades of initiate. John Mylne younger was present, but there is nothing in the minutes to prove that he was responsible for introducing the new members to the lodge. Between July 1634 and August 1637 the lodge is recorded as meeting twelve times, and on six of these occasions the three non-operatives were present. The fact that Mylne was also present every time they attended is not significant, as he was present at all but one of the meetings, but the fact that when the four were present their signatures in the minutes are grouped together helps confirm the suspicion that they form a group of friends.[62] Moreover, Mylne was the only member of the lodge in 1634 who was closely linked to the court, through his father being king's master mason and therefore working closely with Anthony Alexander as master of works. It might be argued that as Alexander himself was, as master of works, in close contact with masons, they might well have invited him to join their lodge without the intervention of Mylne. This is true, but it is surely significant that while Alexander had been master of works since 1629, it was only after Mylne joined the lodge in 1633 that Alexander and his colleagues began to enter it.

Assuming that Mylne suggested to this little group of courtiers that they might join the lodge, why did they agree to do so? The answer is doubtless complex. Simple curiosity about secrets and rituals to which they were offered admission is part of the answer, but there would also have been present, to a greater or lesser degree, the influence of the whole complex of ideas which enhanced the status of architecture as central to human knowledge and led men to believe that lost wisdom was to be found in secret organisations, and this linked up with the ideas of artisans having knowledge not known to scholars. There may also have been an element of 'going slumming' in the minds of these aristocrats, penetrating into a secret organisation of the lower orders and there meeting them on their own ground, though doubtless the actual social interaction between them and the operative masons was limited. But an interesting feature of the 'Mylne group' of the 1630s is that its members took a sustained interest in the lodge. Aristocratic non-operatives in Edinburgh and other lodges later in the century are often only recorded as visiting their lodges once, on the occasion on which they were initiated. But the members of the 'Mylne group' made a number of visits, and seem to have only stopped attending through the death of Anthony Alexander (three weeks after attending a lodge meeting) and the disruption caused by the outbreak of the Scottish rebellion against Charles I in 1637.

Moreover several new members were added to the group in its brief existence. In July 1635 its members were present when Archibald Stewart of Hesselsyd was made a fellow craft. Stewart was (or was soon to become) principal master gunner of Scotland, and two years after joining the lodge he witnessed orders issued by Anthony Alexander summoning masons to meet to be organised into companies according to his Falkland Statutes.[63] At the final meeting attended by the group, in August 1637 (a month after riots against royal policy had begun), David Ramsay, described as one of the king's special servants, was admitted, and he was joined in December by Alexander 'Alerdis', who has been tentatively identified as Allardyce of that Ilk. Two months later Henry Alexander, who had succeeded his brother as master of works, also became a member of the lodge.[64]

In the case of some of the 1630s non-operatives in Edinburgh Lodge connections with the mason trade or interest in architecture can be traced. Anthony Alexander had studied architecture, and both he and his brother Henry were masters of work. Archibald Stewart was a gunner, so his skills fell within the Vitruvian definition of architecture. Lord Alexander's personal interests are unknown, but presumably he became involved through his brother. Strachan of Thornton was a distinctly shady character who nonetheless managed to hang on to royal favour, doubtless helped by the friendship with the Alexander brothers, who were the sons of the king's secretary, Sir William Alexander, earl of Stirling. Thornton had caused a major scandal when, not content with seducing the Earl Marischal's wife he had looted his castle as well. Indignant protests had persuaded Charles I not to appoint him to the privy council in 1625, but he managed to get the king to grant him a commission to collect unpaid crown revenues, keeping half for himself. Opposition was strong, and Thornton eventually agreed to surrender his commission—in return for £3,000 sterling compensation.[65] David Ramsay's identity is not clear. There was a gentleman of the privy chamber of that name in the 1620s, but he was at the centre of an astonishing case of alleged treason in 1631. Lord Reay alleged that Ramsay had tried to involve him in a plot whereby the marquis of Hamilton (whose agent Ramsay was) would seize the crown for himself. It was eventually concluded that there was no plot, Ramsay being guilty of wild talk at the very least. Bewilderingly, however, he was not punished, and indeed the king gave him money to leave the country and tried to find him a job abroad. Hamilton was warned to steer clear of the 'pest' Ramsay in future, the king concluding that he had a violent tongue and though not innocent was not guilty of what he was accused of.[66] This was a remarkable end to a major treason panic, which might have been expected to end in a death sentence for the man guilty of stirring it up, and the king's conduct has never been explained. Perhaps his clemency had extended to letting Ramsay return quietly to Scotland a few years later. The final member of the group, if he is indeed Allardyce of that Ilk, was, like Strachan of Thornton, a Kincardineshire laird, and may therefore have been introduced to the lodge by the latter.

This fascinating development of a group of courtier-masons in the Lodge of Edinburgh in the 1630s, men evidently prepared to take a lasting interest in the lodge and by their presence exemplifying John Mylne's ideal of architecture as uniting the top and the bottom of society, was cut short by the collapse of the regime in 1637. In the light of later developments in terminology it might seem highly appropriate that the first known uses of the term 'freemasons' in Scotland occur in the lodge minutes in 1636, but no special significance should be attached to this: the term the 'heall Mesteres frie Mesones' of Edinburgh is simply one of the many variants used to refer to the masters of the lodge, the freemen masons.[67]

Even during the confusion of the civil wars that followed the 1637 rebellion a few non-operatives joined the lodge. The first were Robert Moray and Alexander Hamilton, respectively the quartermaster general and the general of artillery in the army with which the Scots covenanters occupied the north of England in 1640. The two generals chosen for membership of the lodge were both men whose duties involved the application of mathematical and technical knowledge in ways which made them architects in the Vitruvian definition of the term, so their initiation was highly appropriate, and Moray, a professional soldier who became involved in politics during the civil wars but later concentrated on pursuing his interest in science, was unique among seventeenth-century freemasons in several respects. Firstly he regarded his mason mark, the pentacle or five pointed star, as containing deep and complex mystical and symbolic significance, expounding his Stoic-Christian philosophy, a non-doctrinal brand of religion, tolerant in tendency and with love of his fellow men central to it. Secondly, he explained this symbolism, and thus what being an initiated mason meant to him, in letters to a friend. It would be wrong to take Moray to be a typical early freemason and to assume that his values and beliefs were shared by his colleagues in the Lodge of Edinburgh. But the fact that he could without incongruity see his mason mark, the symbol of his initiation, as encapsulating such values suggests that he believed that the ethos he found in the lodge was basically in tune with his philosophy. And Moray's personal attitudes do have close similarities to aspects of eighteenth-century masonic values.

Moray was admitted to the lodge on 20 May 1641 at Newcastle: doubtless Edinburgh masons, recruited into the army as pioneers, came into contact with Moray through working under him on such tasks as constructing camps, and decided to hold a special lodge meeting on English soil to initiate him. Alexander Hamilton was probably initiated on the same occasion: the minute of his entry is dated 20 May 1640, but this is probably simply a slip of the pen (the minutes were presumably written up in Edinburgh some time after the event).[68]

The only other occasion on which Hamilton and Moray were recorded as present in the lodge was in July 1647 when Dr William Maxwell, physician in ordinary to the king, was admitted.[69] Moray's interests included medicine, and

1 Alexander Hamilton
General of the artillery and member of the Lodge of Edinburgh
(Copyright: the duke of Hamilton, Lennoxlove)

possibly Maxwell had been with the king when Charles I had been held captive by the Scots in Newcastle the previous year. If so, Moray may well have got to know him while engaged in the abortive plotting for the king's escape.

On 17 August 1649 the lodge acquired its first merchant member in the person of Hercules Jenking or Jonkin. Though there is no record of his becoming a burgess he was described as a merchant when he married in Edinburgh in 1643 and when he died there in 1675, and there is a reference to his owning a house in the burgh in 1653.[70] Why he was singled out for membership is unknown, but the minute admitting him is of interest in that it describes him as being admitted entered apprentice and fellow craft.[71] This was to become the usual phrase in lodge minutes for the admission of non-operatives, privileged by being admitted to both grades on the same occasion. Previously non-operatives had been described as being admitted as fellow crafts, or simply as being admitted to the lodge. The change in wording probably does not represent a change in procedure but merely a more precise recording of what took place. It is, however, useful to the historian in that it makes it easy to identify non-operatives of fairly humble status who might otherwise be overlooked, for it is quite possible that some of those recorded in earlier minutes as being made fellow crafts without any record of their being entered apprentices were such men. Almost immediately the new precision makes it possible to identify another non-operative, James Thomson, admitted to both grades on 19 December 1649.[72] The name is, however, too common to be able to trace him in the burgh records.

The next non-operative to join the lodge (in or about 1652) gives rise to no problems of identification: 'Mr Edouart Tesine'. This was Hans Ewald Tessin, an architect specialising in military engineering. Tessin, probably Dutch by birth, had come to Scotland to build fortifications for the English, who under Cromwell had recently conquered the country. He designed the citadel built at Leith, his plan of it being dated 1654, and was made a burgess of Edinburgh in 1659. The following year he was admitted to the Incorporation of Wrights and Coopers of the Canongate (which included masons), being described as engineer to the citadel of Leith, but the withdrawal of the English army of occupation on the Restoration of monarchy in the same year was followed by the slighting of his works, and in 1661 he is found at work in Dunkirk.[73] Tessin, whose citadels must have offered much employment for masons, was obviously a valuable friend for them to cultivate, but the lodge was certainly displaying a willingness to swing with political tides in its choice of members, royalist courtiers being replaced by covenanting generals and then by an official of the country's English conquerors.

In 1649 the lodge had for the first time admitted a merchant to its ranks. In 1654 it first admitted a craftsman who was not a mason, though his craft was a closely related one. James Neilson had become a slater burgess of Edinburgh in 1635, and as such must have been a member of the Mary's Chapel Incorporation. In 1643 he achieved membership of the merchant guild, a fairly unusual distinction for a craftsman, and by 1654 was described as master slater to the king (though the English regime had of course abolished the monarchy).

He was admitted brother and fellow of the Edinburgh Lodge at his own request, having been previously entered and passed in the Lodge of Linlithgow. This is the only occasion in the Edinburgh minutes in the seventeenth century in which it is specifically stated that an entrant had previously been a member of another lodge—and is especially valuable as it provides the only evidence for the existence of that lodge.[74]

The next non-operative to join the lodge was Sir Patrick Hume of Polwarth, admitted on 27 December 1667. In 1673 he condemned the regime led by the duke of Lauderdale in parliament (where he sat as a member for Berwickshire), supporting the opposition group led by the earl of Tweeddale. The following year he went to London with the duke of Hamilton to protest to King Charles II about Lauderdale's corrupt and tyrannical government and the persecution of presbyterians. He was imprisoned in 1675-6 and 1678-9 for his outspokenness. Moving to England, he was implicated in the Rye House Plot to assassinate Charles II, and in 1684-5 fled first back to Scotland and then to Holland. In 1686 he took part in the earl of Argyll's unsuccessful rebellion against the Catholic James VII, but survived to support the 1688-9 revolution which overthrew the king. Created earl of Marchmont in 1697, Hume lived on until 1724.[75]

Three other non-operatives followed Hume into the lodge on 24 June 1670. All were lawyers, and probably friends of his. They were led by Mr William Moray, who had been justice depute since 1665.[76] The fact that he took the pentacle as his mason mark combined with his name possibly suggests that he came to the lodge through some kinship link with Sir Robert Moray who had interested him in the lodge; but that can be no more than speculation, and as with a number of the other non-operatives who have no obvious connections with masons or interest in related subjects, it may simply have been chances of personal or professional contacts which brought him to the lodge. In political sympathies the two remaining members of the 1670 group of non-operatives had much less in common with Moray, an official in the regime, than with Hume. Mr Walter Pringle of Graycrook was a younger brother of Sir Robert Pringle of Stitchel. Graduating at Leyden University in 1661, he became an advocate in 1664. In 1674 he took part in a movement demanding that appeals be allowed from the court of session to the Scottish parliament. Politically the point of this was to force the king to summon parliament and thus provide the opposition with a forum in which to denounce the regime. Pringle and about fifty other advocates were, as a result, barred from exercise of their profession, the movement eventually collapsed, and Pringle himself submitted in January 1676. When in 1679 Lauderdale's opponents drew up a list of men who might be suitable for office once the duke was deprived of power Pringle's name was on it, he being described as 'a good countryman; to church indifferent; a friend to England'. Lauderdale was indeed dismissed by the king, but there was no major change in the character of the regime and Pringle remained associated with opposition causes. He represented in court men who had taken part in the 1679 rebellion in the south west, and in 1681 he defended the earl of Argyll on a treason charge. In 1684 and 1685 he can again be found acting for the defence in treason cases, and he died in the latter year. His membership of the lodge is of particular interest through his close kinship to several of the men who were to found the Lodge of Haughfoot in 1702.[77]

The third member of the 1670 group, Sir John Harper of Cambusnethan, was a member of parliament for Lanarkshire in 1669-74 and sheriff depute of the shire. Like Hume he can be identified with Tweeddale's opposition group in 1673. He took part in the 1674-6 attempt to force the summoning of parliament (submitting on the same day as Pringle), and in 1679 he was included on the list of potential office-holders once Lauderdale fell, being described as a good countryman, a presbyterian, 'but changeable of late'. That his basic presbyterian sympathies did not change is indicated by his arrest in 1683 on suspicion of treason through contacts with religious dissidents.[78]

The fact that three of the four non-operatives admitted to the lodge in 1667-70 were subsequently associated with active opposition to the regime could be mere coincidence, but this seems unlikely. But even if their admission to the lodge does indicate some sympathy within it with opposition causes, there is certainly no evidence of the lodge being used to help organise opposition: none of the three attended the lodge again after being initiated. As with the entry of courtiers in the 1630s and covenanting generals in the 1640s, the historian is frustrated by the fact that just as a trend in admission of non-operatives seems to be emerging, the development halts abruptly.

The next entrant does, however, confirm the existence of another trend discernible in the lodge. In the 1630s it had admitted a gunner, whose profession required mathematical skills. This had been followed in the 1640s by two generals with mathematical expertise, and in the 1650s by a military engineer. In 1674 'James Corss mathematician' was added. The number of men with known mathematical interests joining over the decades was only a trickle, but even so it involved far more men than were likely to have become freemasons by chance and thus reflects the identification of mathematics with architecture.

James Corss, evidently a Glasgow man, had received permission in 1658 to open a school in Edinburgh teaching arithmetic, geometry, astronomy 'and all uther airts and Sciences belonging theirto as horometrie Planimetrie, Geographie Trigonometrie and siklyk'.[79] A great advocate of the usefulness of mathematical skills, he published a number of almanacs and other works in Edinburgh and Glasgow which included astronomical information but also described the construction and use of instruments, and gave practical instructions about weighing and measuring. They also lamented the neglect of mathematical studies in Scotland, only saved from oblivion by John Napier, inventor of logarithms and 'the Generalissimo of all wise men'.[80] Though Corss urged nobles and gentry to become patrons of mathematics the main market for his publications and teaching lay lower in society. His *Practical geometry or a manual of mathematical recreations* (1666) was addressed to 'Artificers, Massons, Wrights' and other craftsmen (including engineers, surveyors and gunners), and would have delighted any mason embued with the traditions of his craft as it extolled geometry as having originated in Egypt and as having priority over all other sciences through its infallibility. The burgh valued his services enough to admit him as a burgess in 1664.[81]

After 1674 the thin trickle of non-operatives into Edinburgh Lodge which had begun forty years before ceased for quarter of a century. The lodge records contain no explanation of this (any more than they explain why non-operatives had previously been accepted), but it may be connected with the fact that the lodge was experiencing internal difficulties and external threats in these last decades of the century. When recruitment of non-operatives began again in 1700 there was a change in the type of new member admitted. Previously no members of the Incorporation of Mary's Chapel who were not masons had been admitted to the lodge, with the single exception of the slater James Neilson who had been admitted because he was already a member of another lodge. But most of those admitted in the decade after 1700 were members of the incorporation, were connected with it in some way, or belonged to other incorporations. Thus many of them were themselves craftsmen, though 'non-operatives' in the context of the lodge in that they were not stonemasons.

First, on 27 December 1700, the lodge recruited Patrick Anderson, the wright deacon, and the boxmaster (treasurer) of the incorporation.[82] In 1706 Mr William Marshall, the clerk of the incorporation since 1696, was admitted to the lodge, which he was to serve as clerk without payment in return for the honour. On the same occasion Sir Samuel McClellan (lord provost of Edinburgh), William Neilson (dean of guild), John Wardrop (wright deacon) and Robert Mowbray (wright and boxmaster of the incorporation) were admitted.[83] When William Marshall died in 1709 his successor as incorporation clerk, Robert Alison, was admitted to serve the lodge as clerk on the same terms as his predecessor.[84] The year 1710 saw the admission of Mr Alexander Nisbet (a surgeon-apothecary who was deacon convener of the crafts), Mr Alexander McGill ('architector'), William Elphinstone (wright), Mr John Clerk younger of Penicuik (advocate and one of the barons of the exchequer), and John Duncan (dean of guild).[85]

McGill was an architect who was working on Yester House with James Smith, a longstanding member of the lodge (though Smith was not present when he was admitted) and was later to repair and extend Greyfriars Church, and build a new parish church at Newbattle, dying in 1734.[86] Clerk of Penicuik was a successful lawyer with antiquarian interests whose membership of the lodge may have arisen from business dealings he had had with the Mary's Chapel Incorporation the previous year: he had arranged to buy lodgings in Edinburgh from the incorporation, though in the end the property was evidently sold to someone else.[87]

Up to 1700 the records of the Lodge of Mary's Chapel had carefully ignored the Incorporation of Mary's Chapel to which the lodge was so closely related. Other members of the incorporation must have known of the existence of the lodge, and some doubtless would have liked to have been admitted to its secrets out of curiosity if nothing else. But even when, in the 1630s, the lodge began admitting men who were not operative masons, it seems to have deliberately avoided recruiting members of the incorporation, perhaps fearing that having such members would strengthen links with that organisation in ways which might weaken the lodge's autonomy. But then in the first decade of the

2 Sir John Clerk of Penicuik
Member of the Lodge of Edinburgh
Copyright: Scottish National Portrait Gallery

eighteenth century the lodge changed direction, and showed itself willing not only to recruit leading members of the incorporation and to share a clerk as well as a deacon with it, but to admit powerful merchants holding the highest offices in the burgh. Two reasons may be suggested for this change. Firstly, the lodge may have reacted to a decline in its power and prestige by swallowing its pride and accepting the need to win the patronage of men of influence in the burgh in order to revive its fortunes: if the surviving minutes can be trusted, the lodge had met fewer times in 1691-1700 than in any other decade in the period 1601-1710. Secondly, by 1700 public knowledge of and interest in freemasonry was spreading fast both in England and Scotland, so there may well have been pressure from burgh worthies seeking admission to the lodge.

Yet though 1700-10 saw such a dramatic concentration of non-operative admissions, this trend was not sustained. Two wrights joined in 1711,[88] but then there was a full decade without new non-operatives appearing. Then, in 1721, the admission of Dr John Theophilus Desaguliers, one of the leading figures in the spread of freemasonry in England, took place. He had asked to meet the Edinburgh masons and they, after finding him fully qualified in all the points of masonry, received him 'as a Brother into their societie'. The next day Desaguliers was present when the provost of Edinburgh, two baillies, the treasurer, the deacon convener and the clerk to the dean of guild presented a supplication (which was accepted) asking to be admitted to the lodge. As Desaguliers was in Edinburgh as consultant engineer to the burgh authorities on plans to improve the burgh water supply it looks as though he had interested his employers in joining the lodge.[89]

The visit of Desaguliers to Edinburgh was, it seems, responsible for this sudden interest in the lodge by leading burgh officials, and his visit may be taken as a sign of the way in which London had emerged in the previous few years as the most active centre in the development of freemasonry. Much of the masonry practised south of the border might be Scottish in origin, but now, through men like Desaguliers, masonry as adapted in England was beginning to influence the Scottish lodges.

The position of the Mary's Chapel Lodge was also changing in other respects. Up to the later seventeenth century it was the only lodge in the urban area controlled by the burgh of Edinburgh, though a few masons in the Canongate belonged to another lodge, that of Aitchison's Haven. By the second decade of the eighteenth century there were four lodges in the area, two of the three new ones having been founded in direct defiance of Mary's Chapel. In 1677 the masons of Canongate, where the Lodge of Mary's Chapel had no jurisdiction, had founded their own lodge. In 1688 the Leith masons had followed suit, and then in the years after 1708 a bitter dispute within Mary's Chapel Lodge led many journeymen to break away and found an organisation of their own which soon began to operate as a separate lodge. Far from being the 'first lodge' of Scotland in the sense of exercising a measure of authority over all other lodges in the land, as William Schaw had planned a century before, the Edinburgh Lodge could not even enforce its will on its own doorstep.

The Lodge of Canongate Kilwinning

The burgh of Canongate, adjoining Edinburgh on the east, developed as a burgh under the control of the abbey of Holyrood. After the Reformation, it was erected into a burgh of regality within the barony of Broughton (which included North Leith) with the Bellenden family as feudal superiors. Edinburgh naturally sought to gain control over these neighbouring communities, especially the thriving Canongate, and finally succeeded in 1636. The lands were then in the hands of the earl of Roxburgh, and both he and the king were in debt to Edinburgh. An arrangement was therefore reached by which the feudal superiority of the Canongate, Broughton and North Leith was transferred to Edinburgh in settlement of these debts.[90] The burgh had long been governed by its own council, though this had been subordinate to the burgh's feudal superior, and this arrangement continued after Edinburgh acquired the superiority. Soon the Edinburgh council came to chose the baillies and some of the councillors of the Canongate, but no attempt was made to make the craft incorporations of the Canongate directly subordinate to those of Edinburgh, in the way that the craft organisations of South Leith and Portsburgh were.

The Incorporation of Wrights and Coopers of the Canongate received a seal of cause or letter of licence from the lord of the regality, William Bellenden of Broughton, in 1612, and this was ratified by the king in 1626 and confirmed by a seal issued by the burgh council in 1636.[91] The fact that the masons were one of the lesser trades in the incorporation, not mentioned in its title, indicates that they had not been as successful in asserting their primacy among the building trades as the Edinburgh masons had been— though Canongate masons were listed first among the lesser trades in the incorporation's records.

The Canongate Incorporation acted much like that of Edinburgh, though on a smaller scale, in regulating the building trades, and controlled the trades in North Leith and elsewhere in the barony of Broughton as well as within the burgh itself.[92] Its minutes, beginning in 1630, provide earlier evidence than that from Edinburgh proving that a mason's essay involved the skills of the architect rather than the stonemason: in 1651 Patrick Brenche's essay was a pasteboard model of a house.[93] In earlier years only once is the essay defined in the minutes: in 1648 John Johnston had been set a 'clay hous of Tua hous hicht',[94] and this may indicate that clay models, presumably cruder than the later pasteboard ones, had been standard in earlier times. Of twenty-five masons listed as being admitted to the incorporation in 1625-60 only ten can be traced in the Canongate burgess register, but this probably reflects poor record keeping rather than anything else. The tendency was for a man to join the incorporation before being admitted as a mason burgess[95]—the reverse of the situation in Edinburgh, but an arrangement that at least would have made it easier to fail an essay and refuse a candidate admission, though there is no sign of this ever actually happening.

The Canongate incorporation was unusual, though not unique, in that it licensed cowans to work within its jurisdiction, though they were not admitted to membership. The earliest example is in 1636, and cowans or cowaners were licensed quite frequently in the 1650s and 1660s. They were permitted to work with stone and clay but not lime, except that they could use it to 'cast' timber door and window frames and clay chimney heads. This is the most detailed of the surviving definitions of the limitations placed on cowans, and indicates that they were free to construct the houses of the poor but not more substantial or permanent buildings.[96] Whether the masons were prepared to work alongside or employ the cowans, or refused to do so as William Schaw had ordered, is not spelt out in the minutes. Nor is it clear whether the cowan was limited in the work he could undertake through lack of skill, or lack of formal training and qualifications, or lack of the Mason Word, or, indeed some combination of these factors.

It is, however, likely that the Canongate masons disapproved of the incorporation granting cowans a recognised status, though they were not influential enough to prevent it. Whether the Canongate masons had their own lodge parallel to the incorporation as in Edinburgh, in which they tried to take a harder line on cowans, is unknown. There is no evidence for any lodge in the Canongate before 1677, but as knowledge of the existence of many early lodges depends entirely on the chance survival of lodge records there probably were some lodges which have vanished without trace. Only in a few exceptional cases are Canongate masons known to have attended the two known lodges in the vicinity (Mary's Chapel and Aitchison's Haven), so either the Canongate men did without a lodge entirely, or they belonged to some vanished lodge. When in 1660 John Johnston, mason freeman in the Canongate and North Leith, undertook to see that his apprentice James Temple received the Mason Word and was admitted to Johnston's lodge,[97] which lodge was meant? Johnston had been admitted to the Canongate Incorporation in 1648,[98] but he was not a member of either Mary's Chapel Lodge or Aitchison's Haven Lodge. A further indication that there may have been an earlier Canongate lodge is that when a new lodge was founded there in 1677 those who founded it were not the leading master masons of the burgh. Either the latter already had a lodge to satisfy their needs, or they had no lodge and still did not feel the need for one.

On 20 December 1677 the members of the Lodge of Kilwinning resolved that, considering 'the love and favour' shown to them by 'the rest of the brethren of the caningate in edinbroughe ane part of our number being willing to be booked and inrolid', the Canongate masons should be given power and liberty to enter and pass (that is, to admit as entered apprentices and pass as fellow crafts) any qualified persons they thought fit, in name of and on behalf of the Lodge of Kilwinning. Fees for admissions were to be sent to Kilwinning, and a commissioner from the Canongate was come to Kilwinning annually: if necessary, Kilwinning would send a commissioner to Canongate. The names of the eleven Canongate men involved in the approach to Kilwinning were then listed.[99]

The records of Grand Lodge in 1737 state that this act was passed on the petition of the masters and brethren of the mason lodge in the Canongate 'Representing that as they were part of the Company belonging to Kilwinning Lodge, And in regaird of the former Correspondence betwixt our said Lodge and them', humbly craving authority to enter and pass masons.[100] While doubtless there was a petition by the Canongate men, this account of it adds to the problems of interpretation posed by the Kilwinning minute itself and it may be that in 1737 the paraphrase of the petition was slanted in order to 'prove' that the lodge that came to be known as Canongate Kilwinning was not created in 1677 but already existed. If the Canongate men only then gained authority to admit members, how could they have constituted a lodge in the past?

If, then, it is assumed that a new lodge was being created by the 1677 minute, why did the Canongate men go to Kilwinning for permission? Seeking authority from an existing lodge to establish a new one is not a procedure found anywhere else in the period under consideration. Kilwinning and Canongate masons had no doubt made personal contacts when working together on buildings in different parts of the country, but there is nothing in the Kilwinning minutes indicating that the lodge as such had contacts with Canongate before 1677, and there is no sign of later contacts between Canongate and Kilwinning masons. Moreover, who were these Canongate masons who appeared at Kilwinning? None of them appear in the burgess register of the Canongate, and none of them are listed as members of the Canongate Incorporation of Wrights and Coopers. Robert Prentice was doubtless the mason of that name who married in Edinburgh in 1673, and John Wilson, mason, had been married in the Canongate in 1665. William Cochrane may have been the mason admitted as burgess of Edinburgh free (to reward him for his services to the town) in 1676, but he was not admitted to either the Incorporation or the Lodge of Mary's Chapel. Thomas Gib is recorded as a servant to a mason burgess of Edinburgh in May 1677.[101]

The failure to trace most of the founders of Canongate Kilwinning in the Canongate records makes it clear that they were not the leading masons of that burgh. As they were not masters of the incorporation most were probably journeymen, and it is perhaps plausible to suggest that, as in Edinburgh in the late seventeenth century, a split was developing between the master masons and the journeymen, employers and employees. On this hypothesis, it is possible that the journeymen were splitting away from an incorporation (or an older Canongate lodge) which they no longer regarded as serving their interests, as the Edinburgh journeymen were to do a few decades later. It is interesting that the name of William Cochrane, the only one of the Canongate men listed in the Kilwinning minute who can be plausibly identified as a burgess (of Edinburgh), heads the list, as this suggests that he was the ringleader. Defiance of the incorporation or of an existing lodge would explain why the authority of Kilwinning was invoked to establish the new lodge; members of the new body might feel the need not just to organise themselves but to seek to legitimise what was an act of rebellion against an established authority. Kilwinning would then be the obvious place to turn to, as it had (in theory) a territorial jurisdiction far wider than any other lodge, and probably already in the seventeenth century claimed precedence over all other Scottish lodges. Kilwinning Lodge in turn would be happy to give its blessing to the new lodge as this would strengthen its traditional claims by showing that masons from a distant part of the country recognised it's pretensions, and a further incentive would be that the petition of the Canongate men allowed Kilwinning to exercise its authority on the doorstep of its rival for primacy, Mary's Chapel Lodge. That the claim that the new lodge was really part of Kilwinning Lodge was a convenient fiction, helping justify the demand that entrance fees be sent to that lodge, is indicated by the silence of the Kilwinning records as to the Canongate Lodge thereafter. Once back in the Canongate with their 'charter' the Canongate men needed no further contact with the Ayrshire lodge.

The founding of Canongate Kilwinning has usually been presented as a major blow to the Lodge of Mary's Chapel, as a direct challenge to its jurisdiction.[102] As Mary's Chapel had never had jurisdiction covering the Canongate this was not so, but nonetheless the development must have been unwelcome. For Kilwinning to authorise a lodge just outside Mary's Chapel's sphere of influence was cheeky and provocative, especially if some Edinburgh masons were involved; and if the new lodge, as postulated above, arose from a rebellion in an existing lodge that too must have been seen as a worrying event, likely to set a bad example to others. When in August 1679 a fellow craft of Mary's Chapel, John Fulton, two entered apprentices and 'other omngadrums' (a word indicating a miscellaneous assembly of people) entered and passed several gentlemen in Ayrshire as members of Mary's Chapel Lodge, it is tempting to interpret this as Edinburgh striking back by poaching in Kilwinning's territory. But if this was so it was a free-lance retaliation undertaken without the permission of the Edinburgh Lodge, for this irregular conduct was severely punished.[103]

That masonic organisation in the Canongate continued to be in a state of confusion in the years after the founding of Canongate Kilwinning is suggested by the fact that only in the 1680s can Canongate men be traced in the lodges of Mary's Chapel and Aitchison's Haven. In 1683 the apprentices of two Canongate mason burgesses were received as entered apprentices by Mary's Chapel,[104] and in 1684 John Johnston was made an entered apprentice at Aitchison's Haven, his master being Alexander Baxter, mason in the Canongate.[105] Was controversy between rival lodges in the Canongate leading some masons to look elsewhere for a lodge rather than choose between them?

The question cannot be answered. The Kilwinning minute of 1677 is the only direct evidence relating to the Lodge Canongate Kilwinning before its surviving minutes begin in 1735, so it is not even certain that the lodge had a continuous existence in the years between. It is not even known whether the lodge's title, provocative through the inclusion of the word Kilwinning, dates from 1677 or was only adopted later.

The Lodge of Canongate and Leith, Leith and Canongate

The Canongate had the status of a burgh of regality, and though ultimately subordinated to the royal burgh of Edinburgh it retained its own council and incorporations. Leith (or more strictly South Leith) by contrast was, like North

Leith, a community without the status of burgh. Leith's subordination to Edinburgh had begun centuries before and was complete by the late sixteenth century. Relations between Edinburgh and Leith were frequently strained, for while the port of Leith represented Edinburgh's greatest commercial asset, if Leith had been allowed to develop unhindered it might soon have overtaken Edinburgh in wealth. After gaining the superiority in 1570 Edinburgh took measures to emphasise its complete control over Leith, and these included suppressing the craft incorporations which had been granted seals of cause by previous superiors.[106] But though at first the intention appears to have been to destroy all craft organisation, in time it became accepted that Leith could retain incorporations provided they were subordinate to the relevant Edinburgh incorporation.[107] It has been stated that the masons of Leith were included in the Incorporation of Hammermen,[108] but it is more likely that they were teamed up with the wrights as in Edinburgh. References in 1657 to coopers, masons, wrights and slaters acting together to build a new seat for themselves in the parish church, and in 1663 to the same four trades sharing a loft in the church with the fleshers, seem to confirm that the building trades were linked.[109] As has already been indicated, when the records of the Incorporation of Mary's Chapel begin in the later seventeenth century it can be seen controlling the election each year of oversmen for Leith, who acted as deacons in the incorporation there—and indeed are sometimes referred to as deacons. Thus the Leith craftsmen were supervised by the Incorporation of Mary's Chapel, but were not admitted to it as members. By contrast some masons from Leith did become members of the Lodge of Mary's Chapel, and it regarded all Leith masons as being under its jurisdiction. Thus in 1600 two Leith masons were disciplined for disobedience to their deacon and oversman in Leith—a matter which it might have been expected that the Incorporation of Mary's Chapel rather than the lodge would have dealt with, as it supervised the appointment of the oversmen.[110]

The Leith masons were at least better off than other craftsmen; they could not become members of the Edinburgh Incorporation, but they could join the parallel trade organisation, the Edinburgh Lodge. But they must still have smarted at the restrictions placed on them through Leith's subordination to Edinburgh, and they may have been encouraged by the upheaval in the mason craft in the Canongate which led to the appearance of the Canongate Kilwinning Lodge in 1677 to think that though by law any incorporation in Leith that they belonged to would be subordinate to Edinburgh, forming a lodge could provide them with an autonomous organisation. As a lodge had no legal status it would be hard for Edinburgh masons to claim a right to control it. In this they were evidently encouraged by Canongate masons unable to find a lodge to suit them even now that Canongate Kilwinning existed.

On 27 December 1688 the deacon and masters of the Lodge of Mary's Chapel denounced the contumacious deserting schism, as they called it, of five masons in Leith and four in Canongate and North Leith, and their adherents. Contrary to all customs, law and reason, and contrary to the mason law itself, they had presumptuously met, and entered and passed masons within the precincts (jurisdiction) of Mary's Chapel. They had erected a lodge without royal authority or the general warden's. Therefore none of the deserters were to be allowed to work as journeymen within the freedom of Mary's Chapel until they submitted and were punished.[111]

The first two of the five deserters listed as masons in Leith, Alexander Barr and George Rankin, can be identified—as Canongate masons! Rankin had become a Canongate burgess and member of the incorporation there in 1670, having formerly been apprenticed to Barr.[112] Thus the division between Canongate and Leith masons was not clear cut; masons working as wage earners doubtless moved around a good deal in the Edinburgh area. Eight of the nine Canongate and Leith masons who 'deserted' to form the new lodge can be traced as members of the Mary's Chapel Lodge, but its efforts to make them submit were ineffectual. Only one man (not named among the original nine deserters so presumably one of their 'adherents') submitted, confessing (in December 1689) his fault 'in going from this Company and passing himselfe in Chanongat loge'[113]—and even here the reference could be to Canongate Kilwinning Lodge rather than to the new Canongate and Leith Lodge.

Thus another new lodge emerged in the Edinburgh area. Though action was not taken by Mary's Chapel Lodge against the upstart until the end of 1688, it produced records before the Grand Lodge in 1738 which were accepted as proving that it had been constituted on 29 May 1688, and had met regularly since then.[114] As with Canongate Kilwinning, it is not certain that the title Canongate and Leith, Leith and Canongate goes back to the lodge's foundation, but this is likely, the peculiar form being adopted to emphasise that the masons of neither place accepted the other as having precedence.

The minutes of Mary's Chapel Lodge had contained no protest at the foundation of Canongate Kilwinning, indicating acceptance that that was beyond the lodge's legitimate jurisdiction even if it was irksome. Canongate and Leith, by including South Leith masons, did infringe Mary's Chapel's traditional rights, and the indignant minute denouncing the deserters should not be read as evidence of a sudden attempt by Mary's Chapel to extend its rights over the Canongate, for the penalties imposed would only effect Canongate masons if they sought work with Edinburgh masters who were members of the injured lodge. The creation of the new lodge indicated the weakness of Mary's Chapel, for all its futile bluster about the mason law and establishment of lodges requiring either royal consent (which in reality no lodge had) or permission from the general warden (an office which had become extinct). The 1688 schism doubtless owed something to the desire of Leith masons to escape to some extent Edinburgh's heavy hand, but it is notable that the Incorporation of Mary's Chapel was not brought into the dispute: if the Edinburgh masons tried to get its support they failed, the incorporation presumably taking the attitude that as its own authority was not being directly challenged the quarrel was not its concern.

Yet the schism probably reflected in part at least developments in the operative mason trade which were leading to growing conflicts of interest between those working as masters employing others on the one hand and journeymen employees on the other. The Mary's Chapel Lodge minute condemning the 1688 deserters ended by ruling that for journeymen or other members of the lodge to complain or appeal against its decisions to the civil magistrates was against the mason law. This, it was proclaimed, was an old act now being renewed. The reference was evidently to some dispute about wages, but the position of the minute strongly suggests that it was linked with the Canongate Leith schism.

The third of the new lodges in the Edinburgh area, the Journeymen Masons, certainly did arise from a sectional dispute among the masons of the burgh, and on this occasion both the incorporation and civil magistrates were ultimately to become involved.

The Lodge of Journeymen Masons, Edinburgh

A full explanation of the problems of Mary's Chapel Lodge in the late seventeenth century will not be possible until the economic history of the building trade in the burgh is written, but some of the main trends can be discerned. There was a notable growth in building activity in the first decades after 1660, but not all members of the mason trade benefited equally from this. In the Medieval ideal of craft organisation a man would progress from apprentice to journeyman, and then eventually to master. Thus though men at different stages in their careers might well have conflicting interests, all would be following the same basic pattern and expecting to reach the same goal. An apprentice or journeyman might be frustrated by the power of master or employer over him, but he would look forward to being a master himself one day. However, this ideal was not always maintained in practice, and a common type of distortion led to a situation in which many apprentices and journey-men found that they had little or no hope of becoming masters. This could arise from a number of different circumstances (or combinations of them): general economic difficulties in a craft leading to stagnation or decline after a period of expansion; the admission of too many apprentices; and changes in structure leading to the craft being dominated by a few masters. Whatever the reason, the result was for the perceptions of journeymen to change; they were less likely to identify with the interests of masters now that they had no chance of themselves becoming masters and would spend their lives as wage earning employees. The result was often the emergence of fraternities or guilds composed exclusively of journeymen, set up to represent their interests as these now conflicted with those of the masters who dominated the traditional guilds. Such organisations can be traced in the late Middle Ages in England and elsewhere. Among masons such journeymen organisations emerged in France as the *companonnages* with their own secrets and rituals.[115]

In the mason trade in late seventeenth-century Edinburgh distortions of this sort were present. Expansion in building activity evidently led to masters taking increasing numbers of apprentices, old rules limiting the numbers of apprentices a master could take being abandoned to increase the labour force. The First Schaw Statutes had been remarkably restrictive in limiting apprentice numbers, ruling that a master could only have three in his entire career. Mary Chapel Lodge in the first half of the century had attempted to control apprentice numbers, but thereafter some masters seem to have taken apprentices freely, restrictions collapsing or being evaded.[116] Moreover, much of the work generated by increased building activity seems to have been monopolised by a relatively small number of masters; outstanding among them were successful architects and businessmen like Robert Mylne and James Smith, employing substantial numbers of journeymen (and, indeed, other masters). Many in the growing labour force created by the expansion in apprentice numbers came to realise that they had little hope of becoming masters. To become mason burgesses and members of the incorporation was an expensive business: the fees for joining the Incorporation of Mary's Chapel alone amounted to £104, which was of the order of six months' full-time wages for a journeyman, and work was often irregular. Even if a journeyman did manage to become a master in the incorporation, with the trade dominated by a small number of well-off masters he was likely to find himself still having to work for wages for one of them. Thus strains within the trade were growing even when times were good for the industry, and these were greatly exacerbated when economic stagnation in the 1680s was followed by the disasters of the 1690s, with the decline of overseas trade and widespread famine. For the journeymen and lesser masters the problem may no longer have been resentment at having to remain a wage earner, but the difficulty of making a living as one.

If, however, it was basically a widening gap between the interests of different groups within the ranks of the masons which led to disputes and schisms in the late seventeenth century, why were these feuds fought out in the lodge rather than the incorporation? It was the latter that had legal power to regulate the trade, and it has been argued above that the role of the lodge in supervising the operative trade was sporadic and limited. The answer lies in the fact that the incorporation consisted only of masters, whereas many journeymen were members of the lodge. Thus the lodge provided the journeymen, whether entered apprentices or fellow craft 'masters', with a forum in which to express their grievances.

The signs of widespread discontent among journeymen first came to the surface in lodge minutes in the 1680s. There had been an earlier incident in 1670 when a fellow craft, Thomas King, was accused of making mutiny among his fellow journeymen,[117] but King seems to have been a quarrelsome individual rather that the ringleader of journeymen grievances, and as he soon became a master of the incorporation and, in 1679, mason deacon he was clearly not experiencing problems in advancing in his trade. By 1681, however, the lodge was complaining about a tendency emerging among journeymen. Some of them were refusing to become fellow crafts, being prepared to remain entered apprentices indefinitely. The reason for this is not stated, but it seems likely that these were men who saw no prospect of becoming masters of the incorporation, and therefore felt that there was no point in becoming fellow crafts as part of the ascent of the normal masonic hierarchy. If they were to be wage earners all their lives, why go to the expense of becoming fellow crafts? This suggests that respect for the lodge, and in particular for the secrets revealed during initiation as fellow crafts, was low: the fees for promotion in the lodge were relatively small, so it is unlikely that motives for refusing promotion were primarily financial.

Refusal should therefore perhaps be seen as a deliberate gesture of contempt for what the lodge stood for. It was as if the journeymen were saying that the lodge's talk of fraternity and its pretence that all fellow crafts were equal as masters of the lodge was a sham, for it was obvious that many in their working lives remained journeymen. The lodge's response was to rule that entered apprentices were only to be employed by masters as journeymen for two years after they had finished serving their apprenticeships. After that, they would have to become fellow crafts to qualify for employment[118].

The boycott of promotions, financially damaging to the lodge in that it was deprived of the fees involved, was probably part of a wider problem; there were increasing numbers of journeymen working in the burgh who were not members of the lodge at all. In 1682 the lodge ordered that all such journeymen should pay twelve shillings yearly for the privilege of being employed by freemen of the lodge. The reason cited for this enactment, the great necessity of the lodge's poor, was hardly likely to reconcile the journeymen concerned: why should they have to pay to help support old and sick members of a lodge to which they did not belong?[119] Moreover they already had to pay booking money to the incorporation to qualify for employment, so there were now two organisations dominated by the masters screwing money out of them.

Thus by the 1680s the Lodge of Mary's Chapel was in financial difficulties and finding it impossible to enforce on journeymen masons either membership of the lodge or promotion within it. Mismanagement was probably partly to blame for the former problem. The minutes contain no mention of lodge accounts until March 1688 when they were evidently in some confusion. The accounts were kept by the warden, Hugh Liddell, but he confessed that 'seuerall acoumpts has eskaped his memore'.[120] Less than three months later the Lodge of Canongate and Leith was formed. It is possible that exasperation at the confusion in the internal affairs of the Lodge of Mary's Chapel had something to do with the schism, and, as already indicated, the discontent of journeymen was also involved.

In 1693 Mary's Chapel Lodge admitted partial defeat over the issue of forcing entered apprentices to pass as fellow crafts, for the former were to be permitted to work as journeymen indefinitely provided they, like the journeymen outside the lodge, paid twelve shillings a year for the privilege.[121] In 1698 however, the full penalties of the 1681 act were reimposed, eleven entered apprentices being named as being in breach of it. This time the lodge had some success; four of the transgressors became fellow crafts in 1699-1700, one in 1704.[122] But financial problems continued, and it was to be these that brought about a new schism in 1708. In the 1690s it became usual for the warden's accounts to be examined and approved periodically by the lodge, sometimes annually, sometimes two or three years' accounts being approved together. But not all members of the lodge were allowed to take part in scrutinising the accounts. Not only were entered apprentices excluded, so were many of the fellow craft masters. The privileged lodge élite allowed access to the accounts was composed of the deacon and other fellow crafts who were also masters of the Incorporation of Mary's Chapel. This is not always clear from the wording of the minutes, but in 1695 it was stated that the accounts had been audited by 'the deacone masters and remanent breathering of the Incorporatione of the meassons' of Edinburgh, and a similar phrase occurs in 1696.[123] Thus power in the lodge was concentrated in the hands of what might be called the 'real' master masons, burgesses and members of the incorporation as well as fellow crafts, to the exclusion of the 'honorary' master masons, those fellow crafts given the title of master in the lodge but in practice only permitted to work as journeymen. It is hardly surprising that entered apprentices saw little point in becoming fellow crafts if they would still be excluded from power in running the lodge of which they had supposedly become masters.

Not only were the incorporation masters in the lodge altering its nature by monopolising power at the expense of the other fellow crafts, they could also be seen as binding the lodge much more closely to the incorporation than in the past, endangering its autonomy. The mason deacon of the incorporation had always been accepted as deacon in the lodge. This involved tacit acceptance that the incorporation had the right to keep an eye on the lodge's activities; and indeed it gave the masons who were masters of the incorporation a special role in the lodge, for they were the men who chose the presiding officer of the lodge in that they (along with the masters of some of the lesser trades) elected the mason deacon of the incorporation. But now the masters of the incorporation were claiming that they alone could audit the accounts, and this was close to saying that the incorporation had the right to audit lodge accounts. The 1695 and 1696 lodge minutes were the first ever to mention the existence of the incorporation. The 1698 act concerning promotions in the lodge mentioned the masters of the incorporation as those who were not to employ the recalcitrant. From 1700 deacons of wrights and other non-mason masters of the incorporation were admitted to the lodge. From 1706 the lodge accepted clerks of the incorporation as its own clerks.

The trend was clear. Those who claimed the monopoly of power in the lodge as masters of the incorporation sought much closer links than in the past between lodge and incorporation, perhaps in order to consolidate their power in the former. The other members of the lodge fought back to protect their interests, maybe seeing the growing links with the incorporation as a threat to the traditional autonomy of masonic lodges. On 18 November 1708 no fewer than forty-four masons met in Edinburgh and recorded that 'Here we journeymen Masons in Edinburgh convened and agreed amongst ourselves' that they would each contribute a 'small penny' for 'our distressed poor who stand in need thereof'. Amounts given ranged from twelve shillings to £1. 16s. 0d.[124]

The journeymen had not at this point, it should be emphasised, formed a new lodge. Rather they had reacted to being refused access to the lodge accounts by demonstrating that they did not believe that the interests of journeymen and their dependants were being looked after properly by forming a benefit society of their own. That a few of the 'journeymen' involved were in fact masters of the incorporation indicates that some of the lodge elite and not just those excluded from the incorporation were unhappy about the way the lodge was being run.

The new journeymen society was intended to be permanent, and the fact that many journeymen contributed to the society's funds who were not members of the lodge shows that the establishment of the former was not merely an attempt to bring pressure on the ruling group in the lodge to allow some power to the journeymen within it. But this last motive was undoubtedly present, and the ploy was successful. On 27 December 1708, on the petition of some fellow crafts that they had no say in inspecting the accounts, it was resolved that the warden's accounts should be overseen in future by six of the most sober and descreet craftsmen, 'whereof two entered for the freedom and four Journeymen', though they were to be appointed by the deacon. 'Entered for the freedom' meant masters of the incorporation, but that the name of that body was thus evaded suggests a return to the tradition whereby it was never mentioned in lodge records. That the six inspectors who were appointed were all men who had contributed to the funds of the new journeymen's society the previous month demonstrates that the journeymen had brought about a major shift of power within the lodge.[125]

The new arrangements for appointing auditors continued until 1712, though arguments in the lodge continued: the 1709 auditors were commissioned also to consider the 'pretensions of the remanent brethren'.[126] But then in 1712 the controversy came into the open again. On 29 August the lodge determined that because of the great numbers of journeymen in the burgh that were not members of the lodge, such men were to pay £1 Scots to the lodge annually to qualify for employment. As the act ended by ordering that the widows of former members of the lodge should be visited and given charitable help if necessary, it seems that the act was intended, like its predecessors, both to encourage masons to join the lodge and to boost the lodge's funds.[127] The regulation did not effect journeymen who were members of the lodge, but some of them at least probably resented the act as an attack on journeymen in general. Along with journeymen outside the lodge who were being penalised, the fellow craft journeymen belonged to the new journeymen benefit society and had been contributing regularly to its funds, and thus would be inclined to take up the case of the former in the lodge. Why when the journeymen outside the lodge were supporting their own poor should they also have to support the lodge's?

At the St John's Day meeting on 27 December 1712 bitter dispute rather than brotherhood predominated. The journeymen probably protested against the levy on non-lodge journeymen being increased to £1, but their opponents triumphed and annulled the 1708 act for appointing auditors for lodge accounts. Rather than submit to power being again monopolised by the incorporation masters, all the journeymen except two walked out (or perhaps, on an alternative reading of the minute, they had refused to come to the meeting in the first place). At the suggestion of William Smellie it was resolved that none of the deserters would be allowed back into the lodge until they gave satisfaction, and that any entered apprentices assisting them would be expelled from the lodge.[128] The mason deacon, James Watson, may have attended the St John's Day meeting, but if so he soon withdrew in protest against what was being done, for on 9 February 1713 the lodge denounced him for having deserted and joined the journeymen, and for entering entered apprentices and passing fellow crafts in 'a publicke change house'—an ale house or inn.[129]

Not only had the journeymen converted their benefit society into a masonic lodge, by initiating members as entered apprentices and fellow crafts, but they had been led in this by the deacon of the masons. Deacon Watson's motivation is obscure. Though he presumably had genuine sympathy for the journeymen his action may be linked with another controversy in which he was involved: he was engaged in a bitter quarrel with the wright deacon. It was concerned with the voting of deacons in burgh council elections and so had no direct bearing on the issues involved in the lodge's problems,[130] but it may be that Watson had found little sympathy for his side of the argument in either the incorporation or the lodge, and had partly joined the deserting journeymen in fury at this. Certainly the incorporation showed no sympathy with him, electing William Smellie, who had taken a lead against the journeymen in the lodge in 1712, to be mason deacon in his place in 1713.[131]

As the deserters showed no sign of submitting, Mary's Chapel Lodge tried to put pressure on them in December 1713 by ruling that entered apprentices and fellow crafts created by the journeymen in 'publicke ale houses' should not be employed by the masters of the lodge until they gave satisfaction.[132] More significantly, the master masons also enlisted the support of the incorporation. In March 1714 Deacon Smellie and other masters presented it with a complaint against James Watson for 'deserting his brethren and protecting unfreemen to work within the priviledges of this Incorporation' and for, along with the other journeymen masons, 'keeping a Common box and making Lawes amongst them selves to the prejudice of her majesties Leidges'.[133] The fact that the deacon of the wrights, James Brownhill, had himself been admitted to the lodge in 1711 no doubt helped to persuade the incorporation to become involved in the dispute that had originated in the lodge: the complaints were referred to a committee, and its report was considered by the incorporation on 26 June. What measures were proposed is unknown, except that the incorporation rejected the idea of banning Watson from working as a mason, but the committee's work had in any case been overtaken by events.

In March 1714, shortly after the incorporation had become involved in the case, Deacons Smellie and Brownhill had attempted to take action against the journeymen on their own. They had gone to the journeymen and demanded that they hand over all their books and papers relating to their activities in collecting money for their box. A lead in resisting them was taken by William Brodie (himself a master in the incorporation) and Robert Winram, and the row culminated in the deacons having them arrested by the city guard for offering them indignities and scurrilous language. The champions of the journeymen were soon freed from the tolbooth, however, and they brought an action for wrongful imprisonment against the deacons before the court of session. Whether the journeymen were just out for revenge or saw in this procedure a means of bringing the controversy before the courts in the hope of having their right to organise themselves recognised is unknown, but certainly the move proved in the end to be of great benefit to them.

The accused deacons worriedly reported this legal action against them to the incorporation, and it agreed to pay the expenses of defending the case. But the fact that neither of the old deacons was put on the leet for electing new ones in September may reflect a feeling that they had acted unwisely— or at least a feeling that it would be better for the incorporation's reputation if they were no longer deacons if they were convicted.[134]

The court of session decided sensibly that the whole dispute should be investigated, not just the March confrontation between the deacons and the two journeymen. The matter should, moreover, be settled by arbitration. By a deed of submission the parties agreed to this in November. Smellie and Brownhill nominated a former deacon of the goldsmiths as an arbitrator; the journeymen picked a former deacon of the surgeons; and the deacon convener (a glover) was choosen by the court as 'oversman' of the arbitrators. Their decision, to be registered by the court as a decreet arbitral, would be binding on both parties.[135]

In their judgement, dated 8 January 1715, the arbitrators ruled that Smellie and Brownhill had been justified in ordering the arrest of their two opponents, as they had been provoked by the insolent and rude language of Brodie and Winram and by the 'indignity alleadged offered by them'. But, on the other hand, the journeymen's representatives had been put 'under greater restraints than their crime did deserve', and for this Smellie and Brownhill were to pay them £100 compensation, and the journeymen's books were to be returned to them. So far what is happening was perfectly clear, but what followed reveals something quite remarkable: the arbitrators were not aware of the existence of the Lodge of Mary's Chapel, though it was a dispute in the lodge that had led to the court case. Two other interpretations of the evidence are conceivable. The arbitrators might have known of the lodge but nonetheless not known that it (as opposed to the incorporation) was a party to the case. Or, though they knew of the lodge's existence and involvement in the case, the arbitrators might have suppressed all mention of it deliberately. The first explanation, however, seems by far the most likely. Both parties in putting their cases to the arbitrators had conspired to present the issue as a conflict between journeymen and incorporation rather than journeymen and lodge, so that secrecy as to the existence of the latter could be maintained. As a result, the decreet arbitral never mentions the lodge.

The decreet therefore absolved the deacons and masters of the *incorporation* from having to account to their journeymen for the money the *incorporation* received for giving the Mason Word. Lodge funds, which were what the quarrel was really about, were largely made up of fees paid by entered apprentices and fellow crafts for initiation, the rituals of which had at their centre the giving of the Mason Word, and that the funds were connected with the Mason Word could be admitted because the existence of the Word was well known. But the conspiracy of silence about the lodge transferred these funds (so far as the arbitrators and the court were concerned) from the lodge to the incorporation, the public front behind which the lodge lay concealed.

To prevent further disputes, the decrees ruled that the incorporation must record in its books an act allowing 'the said Journeymen Massons... to meet together by themselves as a Society for giveing the Masson Word', receiving both fees for this and voluntary contributions. But the meetings of the Journeymen Masons were only to be concerned with giving the Word and collecting contributions. They were not to attempt to regulate the mason trade, they were to keep proper records of money collected, keep the money 'in a common purse', and use it only to support their poor and sick and bury their dead. Their books and money were to be kept in a box with two locks. One key would be held by a master of the incorporation chosen by it from a leet of three names put forward by the journeymen, the other by a man elected by the journeymen. The first of these key keepers would attend the journeymen's meetings to see that the restrictions on their conduct were observed, and their books were to be inspected twice yearly by the incorporation.[136]

The decreet arbitral came only a few weeks after the Lodge of Mary's Chapel had taken further action against journeymen who convened among themselves and admitted entered apprentices and fellow crafts 'in manifest contempt of this societie', by forbidding any journeymen involved in setting up a rival lodge or society in the city to work within it. Acts of 1679 against a mason who had admitted members outside the lodge and of 1693 ordering payments from journeymen who refused promotion to fellow craft were renewed.[137] Even without the decreet arbitral these acts would have been unenforceable, yet even after the decreet was issued the incorporation and lodge were reluctant to back down. The incorporation referred the matter to a committee when in April 1715 Brodie and Winram demanded that the decrees be implemented, and in May it was conceded that the incorporation boxmaster should pay the £100 compensation due to the journeymen. But the incorporation was to be reimbursed for this by getting 'bills due to the Societie of Measons' assigned to it. Thus the incorporation would pay up, as the decrees had ordered, but the money would be recovered from the lodge or society of masons which was hidden behind the incorporation.[138] Payment was delayed, however, perhaps because the lodge refused to agree to reimburse the incorporation, and in July the journeymen obtained letters of horning demanding implementation under threat of legal penalties.[139] On 27 July Deacon Smellie asked the lodge whether it would implement the decrees by passing the required act authorising the existence of the journeymen's society and by agreeing to pay the £100, or whether a suspension or delay in execution of the horning should be sought. The lodge unanimously resolved not to submit and to seek a suspension.[140]

There, so far as the lodge's records are concerned, the matter rested. The accounts of the incorporation for 1713-15, however, reveal that it paid the £100, plus £95. 4s. 0d. in legal expenses and money spent in taverns and coffee houses in connection with the case.[141] Neither the Lodge nor the Incorporation of Mary's Chapel implemented the decreet by passing an act recognising the new Lodge of Journeymen Masons of Edinburgh; nor did they appoint masters to supervise the journeymen's activities. Needless to say the journeymen did not press for fulfilment of these parts of the decreet. On the one hand they now had the authority of the court of session to support their right to form their own society. On the other hand Mary's Chapel, by proudly refusing to give any form of explicit recognition to the journeymen's lodge, failed to exercise its right (granted by the decreet) to make the journeymen's organisation subordinate to their own.

In the years that followed the bitterness died down. In 1718 the Lodge of Mary's Chapel repealed the act expelling the deserters as part of a wider settlement whereby four journeymen (including William Brodie) were to act jointly with the deacon, warden and masters to 'oversee the affairs' of the lodge. A few of the deserters had already been allowed back, and others followed. In 1719 James Watson was elected mason deacon of the incorporation, and as such led the lodge—though it is noticeable that in the lodge he presided under the title of 'preses' or president, not deacon. Then, from 1721, though the deacon still sat in the lodge a separate preses took the chair. The potential dangers of having the same man as leader of the lodge and one of the two leaders of the incorporation had been recognised.[142] The incorporation had also learnt a lesson from the dispute. By 1717 a journeymen wrights' box had appeared, and by 1721 a journeymen slaters' box, each supervised by a master of the incorporation.[143] The incorporation of masters now had to show more concern than in the past for the interests of the journeymen, for fear that they follow the example of the journeymen masons.

The journeymen masons had started out by establishing a benefit society. Because the Lodge of Mary's Chapel had refused to accept their right to do this they had gone on to convert it into a lodge. It was unique among the Scottish lodges of the day—and probably among all those established since as well—in having its right to exist based on a decreet with the authority of the court of session behind it, even though that decreet had never used the word lodge. It was also unique through not having any element of trade regulation in its activities, this being banned in the decreet. Though in its membership of working journeymen it was an entirely 'operative' lodge, in functions it was entirely 'non-operative', existing only to bestow the Mason Word through ritual initiations and to provide benefits for members fallen on hard times, carefully recording the contributions made by members at quarterly meetings (of which in fact there were at first only three a year).[144]

Among the lodge's prized possessions today is a red silk purse, said to have been given to the lodge to keep its money in by the lords of session in 1715.[145] The story is impossible to authenticate, and though it is hard to imagine the judges taking such a personal interest in a very minor case which they referred to settlement by arbitration (quite apart from the fact that such a gift would have been a display of partiality blatant even for the period), it may well be a gift presented by some well-wisher when the lodge won the right to exist in 1715, and its nature nicely symbolises the remarkable origins of the lodge in the demand of journeymen to control their own funds.

3 Geometria
Carving in the garden of Sir David Lindsay, Lord Edzell, at Edzell Castle, Angus, which is dated 1604. Geometry was often equated with masonry - the stonemason's work was to apply the rules of geometry to stone. Geometria is shown here measuring the world, with her foot resting on the books that teach her skills, and the tools of her art around her. Behind her, within the arch, was originally carved an ashlar wall, stressing geometry's role in masonry, but wear to the stone means this is no longer clear.
Copyright: Bob and Yvonne Cooper

3

THE LOTHIANS

The Lodge of Aitchison's Haven

Both the Lodge of Aitchison's Haven and the settlement which gave it its name have long disappeared.[1] The lodge served the masons of a fairly heavily populated area to the east of Edinburgh, and the extent of its influence is indicated by the places at which it met:

> Musselburgh, a burgh of regality at the mouth of the river Esk.
> Fisherrow, lying across the Esk from Musselburgh.
> Prestonpans or Pans, a burgh of barony on the coast a few miles to the east of Musselburgh.
> Inveresk, just south of Musselburgh.
> Dalkeith, a burgh of regality a few miles south of Musselburgh.
> Aitchison's Haven itself, a tiny port between Musselburgh and Prestonpans.

The history of the port of Aitchison's Haven is obscure. It was evidently founded by Newbattle Abbey with the name of Millhaven, and lodge minutes refer to it by that name in 1600. In 1713 a meeting of the lodge was held in Morrison's Haven, and this may be a third name for the same place.[2]

Two explanations of why the lodge took its name from so insignificant a place may be suggested. Firstly, as the lodge drew its members from several burghs, to name it after one might have aroused jealousies, by implying that it was superior to the others (a type of dispute which led later to the odd name of the Lodge of Canongate and Leith, Leith and Canongate). Aitchison's Haven Lodge (or simply Aitchison's Lodge, as it was often called in the mid seventeenth century) may thus have chosen to meet at the Haven as it was neutral both as a place and as a name. Secondly, a number of lodges chose to meet in, and sometimes took their names from, places beyond burgh jurisdiction, doubtless to emphasise their autonomy and perhaps to help to preserve secrecy.

The fact that Aitchison's Haven lay between Musselburgh and Prestonpans also made it a convenient place to meet, as most members of the lodge evidently came from these burghs. The minutes usually fail to specify where the lodge met, and in such instances it probably met in Aitchison's Haven itself. When a location is given Musselburgh and Prestonpans were by far the most common. Thus in 1693-1707 the lodge held its most important meeting, that on 27 December, alternately in Musselburgh and Prestonpans, though this regularity is unusual. Meetings in Inveresk, Fisherrow and Dalkeith.[3] were relatively uncommon. Perhaps they were exercises in 'showing the flag' to emphasise that the lodge claimed authority in such places, and to keep masons resident in them happy, but rather inconvenient for most members. That Dalkeith was on the fringes of the lodge's influence, at least by the end of the century, receives confirmation from poll tax rolls. The rolls for Dalkeith and Inveresk for 1694 and 1698 respectively survive, and eight masons are listed in each.[4] All the Inveresk masons can be identified as members of Aitchison's Haven Lodge, whereas none of the Dalkeith men can be traced in the minutes. But three of the Dalkeith men can be traced as members of Melrose Lodge, having (judging by their surnames) close family connections with Melrose masons. In one case at least a Dalkeith mason was initiated as an entered apprentice of Melrose Lodge in Dalkeith itself.[5] Which lodge a Dalkeith mason joined was probably a matter of his own or his master's family connections as much as anything else.[6] Two of the three Dalkeith members of Melrose Lodge were Meins, members of the family that dominated that lodge—though there were also Meins in Aitchison's Haven. Kinship probably also accounts for a case in which Aitchison's Haven recruited a member from outside its normal territory: in 1626 John Aytoun, mason in Dumfries, 'bookit himself' by consent of the brethren of the lodge, an ambiguous phrase whose alternative meanings will be considered below.

Like Melrose, Aitchison's Haven was dominated to an unusual extent by a few dynasties of masons, if the surnames of members can be trusted. The list of fellow crafts in the lodge for 1598 contains twenty-three names, of which five are Aytouns.[7] Even more strikingly, among about sixty-four members named in the lodge records in 1598-1612, there are three Ables, four Peddens, nine Petticriefs and twelve Aytouns.[8]

References to the buildings the lodge met in are very rare, but twice in 1601 it met in the parish church of Inveresk, and twice in 1601-2 in the church of Musselburgh,[9] which indicates that the lodge was on good terms with local ministers. Meetings were probably usually held in the houses of members, or perhaps in inns.

Aitchison's Haven's main claim to fame is that its minutes are the earliest known for any masonic lodge. The first is dated 9 January 1598 though the fact that the new year in Scotland up to 1600 (and in England up to 1752) did not begin until 25 March means that the true date by modern reckoning was 9 January 1599. Thus the first Aitchison's Haven minute predates that of the Lodge of Mary's Chapel by about six months. More importantly, the minute comes just ten days after the First Schaw Statutes had been issued, and as in Edinburgh the keeping of written minutes was doubtless a response to the Statutes, which were themselves copied into the minute book.[10] Again as in Edinburgh, the first Aitchison's Haven minutes reveal a lodge which already existed, but which had probably only come into existence recently.

Unlike the Mary's Chapel Lodge minutes, the early records of Aitchison's Haven regularly record the choosing of intenders or instructors to prepare candidates for initiation, as the First Schaw Statutes had ordered: but whereas the statutes only referred to intenders in the context of initiation of fellow crafts, the lodge appointed them for both would-be entered apprentices and fellow

4 William Aytoun, 'Measter Meason to Heriot's Vork,' and his wife
This double-portrait celebrates his work on George Heriot's Hospital (a school for
poor children) in Edinburgh in the 1630s and 1640s. Aytoun was a member of the
Lodge of Aitchison's Haven
Copyright: George Heriot's Trust, Edinburgh

crafts. Though the minutes are often confusing and inconsistent in their wording, they also record in some instances the earliest of all the stages of a mason's career, his becoming an apprentice. In Edinburgh this had been a process supervised by the burgh and incorporation, but the masons of Aitchison's Haven had no incorporation paralleling the lodge, and came from several burghs as well as rural areas. There may have been incorporations or societies of masons, or including masons, in some of the burghs in the area, but if so none had a close relationship with the lodge.[11] Therefore the lodge took on the function of 'booking' apprentices, recording their names and (usually) the names of their masters, as the First Schaw Statutes had ordered all lodges to do. As 'booking' meant simply recording an event, the word was used also when admitting entered apprentices to the lodge, which is confusing, but it is clear that two different types of booking were involved— and indeed there was a third, for recording promotions on entered apprentices to fellow crafts was often called booking.

In June 1599 Andrew Patten paid twenty shillings to record the terms of his apprenticeship: he had already served six years and had another two to serve.

Thus he was registered or booked with the lodge. But he was not really a member of it until in January 1600 he was again booked, this time as an entered apprentice, and paid another twenty shilling fee and presented each master with a pair of gloves. Had he been the son of a member, the fee in each case would have been ten shillings. Presumably those who were resident in burghs would also have had their apprenticeship registered or booked there, and would hope ultimately to become burgesses, but the two parallel and clearly distinct hierarchies of the mason's career found in Edinburgh are in Aitchison's Haven often partly run together.

Patten booked himself after he had already served most of his apprenticeship. In May 1599 John Petticrief booked himself some weeks after his apprenticeship had expired, and he may well have been made an entered apprentice at the same time. Certainly he was of that grade by 1600, and was a fellow craft by the end of 1612. Both these men booked the terms of their apprenticeships and became entered apprentices unusually late in their careers, suggesting perhaps that the lodge had been established very recently so they had not had an opportunity to be initiated earlier.

Though the 'booking' of the apprentice with the lodge, registering the length of his apprenticeship, is sometimes separable in the minutes from his 'booking' on admission to the lodge as an entered apprentice, in most cases only one booking of an apprentice is recorded, and while this may partially reflect lack of consistency in recording the two types of an apprentice booking, another explanation is possible. The two things may often have been combined on a single occasion, either because at Aitchison's Haven it was accepted that an apprentice could become an entered apprentice as soon as he began his service to his master, or because registration of the fact that a lad had become an apprentice was delayed until after he had served enough of his apprenticeship to be qualified to become an entered apprentice. Even in major burghs the booking of an apprentice with the burgh authorities sometimes did not take place until years after his service had begun, and when registering the apprentice was undertaken by a lodge which sometimes met only once a year delays in booking were inevitable. It is, however, hard to prove that there were such delays, as the Aitchison's Haven minutes record how long apprentices were bound to their masters for, but very seldom specify when their terms of service had began. Nor, in the early minutes at least, is the term indenture used; in some cases there may have been written indentures, but it is possible that in rural areas and small burghs they were far from universal. The length of service was the core of the agreement between apprentice and master, and it may be that registration with the lodge was the only formal written record of the agreement. In Aitchison's Haven, where kin ties between members were unusually common, many of the apprenticeships registered involved a son serving his father, a circumstance in which an indenture is not to be expected.

A minute of 20 November 1600 (St Andrews Day, which the lodge also planned to meet on in 1601) may also reflect an early stage in the evolution of the new masonic lodges, cryptic though it is. 'The quhilk day the dewisioun of ye ludg was maid betwixt Milhaven [Aitchison's Haven] and Newbottle'.[12]

Nothing further is heard of the matter, and different interpretations of the minute are possible, but it looks very much as if a split to form two separate lodges was contemplated. It is interesting that the proposed new lodge in the south of the Aitchison Haven 'territory' was to be called Newbattle rather than by the name of the largest burgh in the vicinity, Dalkeith: again a small settlement was favoured over a large one in naming a lodge. William Schaw had summoned a meeting in January 1600 to take order with the Lodge of St Andrews; the First St Clair Charter of 1600 seemed uncertain about whether Dunfermline and St Andrews were two lodges or formed a single lodge, suggesting that what had originated as a single Fife lodge soon divided in two. It may thus be that as his reorganisation of the trade proceeded Schaw encouraged subdivision of the units he had originally established. While no complete split took place at Aitchison's Haven, there are some indications that sectional or branch meetings may sometimes have taken place. In 1670 it was recorded in a minute that is partially illegible that the whole company, convened at Prestonpans, 'hath chosen Alex. Baxter Deacon for Musselburgh and Prestonpans Lodge' and Thomas Calderwood warden for Prestonpans, 'and the samen Lodge to continue for ane yeir'.[13] Was Baxter deacon for the whole lodge, with Calderwood leading a branch in Prestonpans? Possibly, though the fact that the following year the two men are referred to simply as deacon and warden of the lodge may indicate otherwise.[14]

Like the minutes of the Lodge of Mary's Chapel, most of those of Aitchison's Haven are concerned with recording changes in status, though initial booking of apprentices is added to (or combined with) admission of entered apprentices. Fellow crafts are passed, becoming masters of the lodge. The diversity of the area over which the lodge sought to exercise its jurisdiction, including both rural areas and burghs, placed severe restrictions on the lodge's ability to enforce trade regulations. So too did the fact that many of its members probably spent much of their working lives elsewhere; that so many masons lived in the area doubtless reflected its proximity to the Edinburgh-Canongate-Leith complex, the largest urban area in the country, as well as the availability of work within the area itself. Study of the early minutes reveals that many members are only mentioned on one or a few occasions, and that others disappear for years before reappearing again. The membership of the Lodge 'thus seems to have been very transient, with a small nucleus that was relatively permanent'.[15]

The activities of the lodge as a funeral benefit society are revealed by references to mortcloths, the velvet cloths used to cover coffins during funerals. They are also mentioned in the records of a number of other lodges, and probably in all lodges one of the duties of members (as for members of most craft organisations and religious fraternities) was that of honouring deceased members by attending their funerals. The use of the mortcloth was a sign of the status and worth of the deceased, adding dignity to the occasion. Aitchison's Haven had a keeper of the mortcloth by 1624. In 1630 a voluntary collection for buying a new cloth was arranged, and individuals appointed to collect money in Prestonpans, Musselburgh and Edinburgh. The first two places specified confirm that these coastal burghs and the area between them was the core of the lodge's territory, while the third indicates that many lodge members were working in the Edinburgh area—the Edinburgh collector was William Aytoun, the eminent member of the lodge who was soon to be appointed master mason of Heriot's Hospital. By 1666 however the lodge was without a mortcloth, and arranged to buy one from the seamen of Fisherrow, who had their own society or incorporation, for £122.18s. 0d. The following year the lodge possessed two cloths, small and large, one of which was provided with a new fringe in 1669. In 1702 a new large mortcloth was purchased—but only those members of the lodge who contributed to the cost were to have the use of it.[16]

The fining of a member in 1599 for taking an apprentice without permission of the lodge, and of another in 1660 for keeping company with a cowan, suggests an early zeal for enforcing the First Schaw Statutes: in the latter case the offender was also instructed to go to the master of works to be put in ward (custody), but it is not stated whether William Schaw himself, or a local master of work supervising the project the mason was working on was meant.[17] But the silence of the records thereafter may indicate declining enthusiasm for adhering to the statutes (as in the Lodge of Mary's Chapel, where the only fine relating to cowans was imposed in 1599). But there is one unique piece of evidence indicating that even generations later the Lodge of Aitchison's Haven still looked on the statutes as a code which it respected: in 1661 the lodge inserted an alteration to one of the statutes into their copy.[18]

The lodge also transcribed in its records the Falkland Statutes of 1636, agreeing to accept them in the presence of Sir Anthony Alexander as warden to the king and general master of works (a title betraying confusion, as it should of course have read master of works to the king and general warden) at Aitchison's Haven on 14 January 1637.[19] On the same day Sir Anthony and the lodge appointed George Aytoun, notary public, clerk of the lodge; but subsequently the minute was crossed out and his appointment was instead recorded a year later.[20] On 17 March 1638, the lodge met in Musselburgh in the presence of Sir Anthony's brother and successor, Henry Alexander (getting the names of the offices right this time), and again the lodge agreed to uphold the Falkland Statutes. Some reorganisation of offices in the lodge was carried out at the same time. George Aytoun was admitted as clerk, James Witherspoone, burgess of Musselburgh, became deacon, and James Petticrief, indweller in Prestonpans, became warden depute. Aytoun was to be clerk permanently, while the other two men were to remain in office until the normal time for annual elections.[21]

Why did the two Alexander general wardens impose their Falkland Statutes, seeking to reorganise all the building trades, on the Lodge of Aitchison's Haven but not on the Lodge of Mary's Chapel, when both men belonged to the latter lodge and not the former? There is no trace of the statutes in the Mary's Chapel minutes. The answer doubtless lies not in what the Alexanders wanted but what they could get away with. The statutes specified that they should not prejudice the rights of existing incorporations, but both the Incorporation of Mary's Chapel and the burgh authorities would have been disturbed at a royal official trying to reorganise their crafts, seeing this as a threat to their authority, and they and the lodge would therefore have resisted the statutes. The Lodge of

Aitchison's Haven, on the other hand, would have had no such powerful allies in resisting imposition of the statutes, and indeed may well have been flattered by having great men coming to consult with them and take an interest in their affairs. So they registered the statutes—and thereafter ignored them.

The appointment of intenders to prepare candidates for initiation as entered apprentices and fellow craft indicates the imparting of the secret lore and rituals of masons to them, though the fact that intenders were chosen and the subsequent initiations took place at the same meeting shows that the amount of information involved was limited. A late reference (27 December 1722) complained that it was a great loss that entered apprentices were not 'tried' every St John's Day. In future the warden was to do this on the morning of each 27 December.[22] That this was the revival of an old custom is suggested by the fact that similar references appear in the minutes of other lodges. But what were the entered apprentices tested on? Possibly on practical craft skills, but that seems unlikely. Nor is it plausible to think that anything directly related to the additional secrets of the Mason Word imparted to fellow crafts were involved, because these were only communicated immediately before initiation and thus could not have been tested annually. The most likely explanation is therefore that the warden coached and tested all entered apprentices each year in the lore contained in the Old Charges, probably reading or reciting it to them: perhaps also, as William Schaw had ordered, some version of the art of memory was involved in the tests.

That secret written documents were used to help preserve the rituals and lore of the Aitchison's Haven masons, and not merely the art of memory, is indicated by a cryptic act made at Inveresk on 28 December 1646 ruling that 'if ony copies sall be found with ony person that keipis the said booke after this tyme' he should be fined £40 and 'be depryved of all Societie within the said compane'.[23] It is likely that the item which was not to be copied was a version of the Old Charges, though the lodge's surviving version of the charges was not written until 19 May 1666, when it was inserted into the minute book by the lodge's clerk, John Auchinleck.

Aitchison's Haven minutes reveal the presence of very few non-operatives in the lodge. The first that can be identified has already been mentioned, George Aytoun. The cancelled minute of 14 January 1637 which admitted him to be lodge clerk calls him brother of craft as well as notary public, the former being an alternative term for fellow craft. The fact that his successor as clerk, John Auchinleck, was permitted to copy the Old Charges probably indicates that he too had been initiated. Certainly William Smith, clerk of Musselburgh, was initiated as a member of the lodge when he was admitted as lodge clerk in 1677, and so was William Young from the Canongate who succeeded him in 1682.[24]

Apart from the lodge clerks only four non-operatives can be traced in the lodge in the period up to 1710, and only two of them can be identified. On 23 March 1672 Alexander Seton, brother of the fourth earl of Winton, was initiated to both grades. Alexander had been born in 1644 and was dead by December 1673; the family history records that 'Nothing is known of him', which is not much help in trying to ascertain his motives for joining the lodge.[25] A William

Sandilands was admitted to both grades in 1677, on the same day as the clerk, William Smith, and presumably he was a non-operative. Mr Robert Cubie, admitted as entered apprentice and fellow craft on 27 December 1693, was described as a 'student and [*illegible*] preacher of the Gospell'. The 'Mr' proves that he was a graduate (master of arts), and he was doubtless training for the ministry. Another man, whose name is illegible, was initiated in both grades on the same day.[26]

Like Mary's Chapel Lodge, Aitchison's Haven suffered problems towards the end of the century. On 27 December 1700 members meeting in Musselburgh considered the disorders of the lodge, they being 'contrary to the most ancient, orderly, and well constituted laws in all the Lodges' of Scotland, dishonouring the lodge and threatening to bring it to nothing. This was a 'great disgrace on our Craft of Masonry, which has been so much honoured in all ages for its excellent and well-ordered laws'. These laws, established by 'the first planters of Lodges' were so well founded on reason that no one honest could object to them. To restore the unity and peace of the lodge a code of regulations was passed which reveals what the problems were. Members were not attending meetings. Entered apprentices were taking work of all kinds 'without ever qualifying themselves', by which refusing promotion to fellow craft (the problem which was also worrying the Lodge of Mary's Chapel) was meant. Fellow crafts encouraged the recalcitrant by continuing to employ them as journeymen so they had all the benefits of being fellow craft without being promoted to that grade. This would 'bring all law and order, and consequently the MASON WORD, to contempt'. Another abuse was that some members were admitting whoever they wanted as entered apprentices when and where they liked, 'which practice has ever been the cause of keeping our Box so low and an effectuall way to destroy it'. The company would not be able to support its poor if fees were not collected for initiations.

To remedy these abuses members were to attend meetings regularly and 'pay their quarter counts'. No entered apprentices were to work as masters, and fellow crafts were to refuse to work with those who refused promotion. If such entered apprentices 'get [employment with?] Masons of other Lodges' redress would be sought from these lodges. None were to be entered or passed in the lodge except on the day of the general meeting (27 December), and all their fees were to be paid to the box. Those who refused to obey the old laws and the new regulations would be excluded from the lodge, for 'as we are all Brethren incorporated in one Corporation, we all wish and desire that we may live in love, peace, concord, and agreement one with another, which will always be to the great credit and advantage of our Company in Atchison's Haven.[27]

Attempts to tackle the types of difficulty listed in 1700 can be traced earlier. An act of 1655 had ruled that admissions to the lodge could only take place on St John's Day; entered apprentices had been ordered to behave according to their duties in 1670: and in 1688 financial problems arising from the fact that many members paid their dues in 'tickets' or bonds instead of cash were highlighted.[28] Thus the problems of the lodge were long standing, and the close parallels between them and those experienced by the Lodge of Mary's Chapel indicate that neither in town nor country, in Scots terms neither to burgh nor to landward, were the masonic lodges nearly as effective in enforcing discipline in the mason trade as they wished. Throughout the seventeenth century the pretence that they could limit exercise of the craft to their members, enforcing Medieval ideals of craft organisation, had not fully conformed to reality. But by the later decades of the century the gap between ideal and reality was becoming more and more obvious, and it was feared that this was leading to increasing devaluation of the greatest privilege the lodge had to offer, access to the secrets of the Mason Word.

The Lodge of Haddington

The area from which the Lodge of Aitchison's Haven recruited its members straddled the border between Midlothian and East Lothian, and the latter shire also had a lodge centred on its largest burgh, Haddington. Masonic organisation in the burgh can be traced back to 1530, when it was agreed that the wrights and masons were to have an image of St John the Evangelist in the parish church to be their patron provided they maintained his altar and worship at it.[29] The date on which a seal of cause was first granted to the Incorporation of Wrights and Masons of Haddington is unknown: when a new seal was granted in 1647 it was said that its predecessor incorporating them as two free crafts had been lost 'past memorie of man'.[30] A code of ordinances survives from 1606, and minutes begin in 1616.[31] As in the Incorporation of Mary's Chapel in Edinburgh, the Haddington building crafts were led by two deacons, of wrights and masons, within one incorporation, the lesser trades being divided between the two. And, as in Edinburgh, the lesser trades came to resent their subordinate position. After two years of disputed elections it was conceded in 1674 that slaters or plasterers might be elected as mason deacons, coopers as wright deacons, and so on.[32]

The little that is know of the early history of the Lodge of Haddington has to be gleaned almost entirely from three isolated fragments from the lodge records which survived long enough to be described by nineteenth-century writers but which have since been lost. The first known minute book of the lodge, which began in 1713, could have given an indication of its nature just after the period this study is concerned with, but it also has been lost. The earliest of these lost documents was noted by William Laurie in 1859. Though largely illegible, it recorded a meeting of the lodge in the church of Gullane (lying on the coast seven miles north of Haddington) in 1599.[33] Laurie is by no means the most reliable source for masonic history, but it is hard to imagine why he or anyone else should have invented this isolated and inconsequential reference. Assuming it to be trustworthy, it adds Haddington to Aitchison's Haven and Mary's Chapel as lodges which appear to have begun to keep minutes in the months immediately following the issue of the First Schaw Statutes. The meeting place suggests that though centred on Haddington, the lodge included masons from surrounding parishes, as Aitchison's Haven did, and sometimes met in such outlying districts. An alternative interpretation might be that the meeting at

Gullane indicates that Haddington was one of the burgh lodges which deliberately met outside the burgh's jurisdiction, but this is unlikely—seven miles would be inconveniently far for Haddington masons to travel regularly to meet.

Confirmation that the lodge existed by the beginning of the seventeenth century is provided by the fact that three of its representatives assented to the First St Clair Charter in 1600-1. One of them, P. Campbell, appears from his signature to be the Patrick Campbell who was deacon of the incorporation when their minutes begin in 1616, and again in 1624-9.[34] After 1600-1 there is a long silence as to the lodge: like Aitchison's Haven, it is not recorded as assenting to the Second St Clair Charter.

On 2 February 1682 John Anderson, mason burgess of Haddington, granted a bond to the lodge promising to pay it £6.[35] Two years before, on 27 December 1679, Anderson as former apprentice to William Douglas had appeared before the Incorporation of Wrights and Masons, producing his indenture of apprenticeship and a discharge indicating that he had completed his service. He was instructed to draft a house as his essay (a phrase suggesting a drawing rather than a model) by 25 March, but he was not in fact admitted as a member of the incorporation until 11 September 1680.[36] It seems likely that the £6 he owed the lodge in 1682 represented a fee due on being passed as a fellow craft. But whether it was usual in Haddington for a mason to become a master of the incorporation before becoming a fellow craft master of the lodge, reversing the order usual in Edinburgh, is uncertain.

The example of Anderson as a member of both incorporation and lodge is, however, valuable, for the two lodge members mentioned in the only other fragment of seventeenth-century evidence cannot be traced in the minutes or accounts of the incorporation. On 29 May 1697 a contract and agreement was made between Archibald Dawson, mason in Nungate (a suburb of Haddington) and deacon of the mason lodge of Haddington, and John Crumbie, mason in Stenton (a settlement seven miles east of the burgh). By the contract Crumbie undertook not to work with or keep company with any cowan at any manner of building or mason work. While he remained an entered apprentice he would only work for daily wages or contract to do minor jobs worth not more than £6. If he failed to observe these limitations, or contravened the rights and privileges of the lodge in any other way, he was to be liable to a £40 fine. In return Dawson and the other members of the lodge accepted and received Crumbie as an entered apprentice.[37] While it is possible that the Lodge of Haddington regularly made such formal agreements with new members, it seems more likely that this was an unusual case, Crumbie being a fully trained mason from an outlying area who had decided to join the lodge, perhaps because he was finding it difficult to get employment as he lacked the Mason Word. In these circumstances a formal contract with an adult entered apprentice who had no master as he was not serving an apprenticeship, would have been appropriate.

That Crumbie, coming from a country district, should not have been a member of the incorporation is no surprise. But it is puzzling not to be able to trace Dawson. Though he is described as deacon of the lodge, he was not the mason deacon of the incorporation in 1696-7: that post was held by John Jack.[38] Thus the Edinburgh custom of the lodge accepting the incorporation deacon as its own deacon evidently did not prevail in Haddington, perhaps because the territorial jurisdictions of burgh and lodge did not coincide, the latter including surrounding rural areas.

The opening entry of the lost lodge minute book recorded the election of deacon and warden, and the passing of a fellow craft, on 26 December 1713, thus confirming that like most lodges it had both deacon and warden, and that it held its annual meetings and elections on St John's Day (though avoiding 27 December in 1713 as it was a Sunday).[39] The records of the incorporation show that it also frequently met that day, which must thus have been a busy one for local masons.

The Lodge of Linlithgow

On 2 March 1654 James Neilson, master slater to the king and a member of the Lodge of Linlithgow, was admitted to the Lodge of Mary's Chapel.[40] That is the total of information that has survived about the Linlithgow Lodge in the seventeenth century. As the shire town of West Lothian it was, like Haddington in East Lothian, an obvious place for a lodge, and it had an added interest for masons in that it was the site of a royal palace, attracting many masons from a wide area during periodic repairs and rebuilding up to the early seventeenth century. Representatives of all the other lodges known in Edinburgh and the Lothians before the 1670s—Mary's Chapel, Aitchison's Haven and Haddington—accepted at least one of the two St Clair Charters, but Linlithgow is notable by its absence. This may indicate that the Linlithgow Lodge was not created until well into the seventeenth century. The 1654 reference proves that it was admitting non-operatives, but Neilson was an operative in a building trade closely related to that of the masons and would thus be of similar social status to other members—though the fact that he was the king's slater shows that he was very successful in his trade.

The Lodge of Linlithgow was involved in the creation of the Grand Lodge of Scotland in 1736, but there is no certainty there had been continuity between this lodge and that mentioned in 1654.[41]

4
THE WEST

The Lodge of Kilwinning

To adapt a famous slogan coined by George Orwell, all the early Scottish masonic lodges were unique, but some were more unique than others. The prize for the 'most unique' lodge belongs to Kilwinning, with its determined claims to be 'more equal' than other lodges. In later generations these pretensions led the lodge to acquire the odd title of Mother Kilwinning, and the ambiguous privilege of being 'No. 0' in the list of lodges affiliated to the Grand Lodge of Scotland. Thus, at the price of being formally designated a nothing, Kilwinning can claim precedence over the other formerly squabbling lodges which follow it on the list with the peculiar numbering No. 1 (Edinburgh), No. 1^2 (Melrose), and No. 1^3 (Aberdeen).

The uniqueness of Kilwinning rests in its claims to precedence above all other lodges as the original source of masonry in Scotland, and to possess a far wider territorial jurisdiction than any other lodge in Scotland. The claim to a special position among the Scottish lodges was first made explicitly in a surviving source by a minute of 1643 referring to the lodge as 'the ancient ludge of Scotland',[1] but the claim does not appear in the sources thereafter until the mid eighteenth century. That it had nonetheless been present much earlier is however indicated indirectly by events. The Second Schaw Statutes of 1599 appear to have a dual function. On the one hand they supplemented the regulations contained in the First Schaw Statutes: on the other, they were addressed specifically to the Lodge of Kilwinning, and seem to have been designed to go at least some way towards meeting the lodge's objections to the earlier code of statutes. William Schaw showed himself willing to accept Kilwinning as 'head' (whatever that meant) and second lodge of Scotland, and to recognise it as having authority over a wide area in western Scotland. But the fact that Kilwinning never publicised this status, officially awarded to the lodge by the general warden, suggests that the Second Schaw Statutes had not given the lodge all it wanted. If being declared second in precedence was not enough, obviously the Lodge of Kilwinning must already have been claiming to be first.

That Kilwinning had sent a commissioner to the meeting at Holyroodhouse in 1599 at which the Second Schaw Statutes were issued indicated a willingness to negotiate with Schaw about the status of the lodge: but the fact that the lodge apparently then rejected them, and failed to accept either of the St Clair Charters suggests a general unwillingness to accept the authority of either the general warden or the Sinclairs of Roslin over the mason trade as they would not confirm the lodge's claim to primacy.

The extent of Kilwinning's claims, and the high status Schaw was willing to grant the lodge, may indicate that even though many of the other early lodges were created, or virtually created, by Schaw, who thus gave masonic lore and ritual an institutional vehicle which they had previously lacked or only found uneasily within an incorporation, the masons of the west had had some form of organisation—or at least a tradition of former organisation—based on Kilwinning which was strong enough for them to resist William Schaw's plans as incompatible with their past.

Kilwinning, the village which had grown up round the abbey of the same name, lay in northern Ayrshire, three miles north of Irvine and sixteen miles north of Ayr, the two royal burghs in the shire. The Second Schaw Statutes accepted that the Lodge of Kilwinning had jurisdiction over the Nether Ward of Lanarkshire, Glasgow, Ayr and Carrick. This list is a peculiar one. Carrick was the most southerly division of Ayrshire, and presumably the other two, Cunningham (in which Kilwinning lay) and Kyle, were comprehended in 'Ayr'. The Nether Ward was the northern division of Lanarkshire, and Glasgow (the largest burgh in the west) lay within it, twenty-four miles north east of Kilwinning. The puzzle is that the lodge never in practice tried to exercise its authority in Glasgow (which had its own lodge), the Nether Ward, or Carrick—or at least if it did so it very quickly backed down, for there is no trace in the minutes from 1642 of attempts to assert authority in these areas. A few Glasgow masons were members of Kilwinning Lodge, but they were all men with close family links with masons in Ayr and Renfrew, and some owned land in these shires: but there was no general attempt to recruit Glasgow masons. On the other hand many of the lodge's members were from Renfrewshire, not mentioned in the Schaw Statutes but lying much closer to Kilwinning than the Nether Ward or Carrick.

Ayr had its own guild for the building crafts, the Incorporation of Squaremen, which had existed since at least the mid-sixteenth century. Two of its members signed the Second St Clair Charter, the only men to sign either charter who did not do so as representatives of a lodge. The presence of their signatures might suggest that the Incorporation of Squaremen acted as a lodge for its mason members, imparting the Mason Word to them, and a glance at the early seventeenth century minutes of the incorporation might seem at first sight to support this, for they record men being admitted as fellows of craft. Closer inspection, however, reveals that the term was used interchangeably with freemen of the craft to record the admission of masters of the incorporation. It thus has no particular significance, though it is interesting (as is the use of the word 'entered' to describe the admission of some masters) as indicating that the specialist terminology of the lodges, with the entering of apprentices and passing of fellows crafts, was created from terms already used by the craft incorporations but given new definitions in the lodges. That the Ayr signatories of the Second St Clair Charter were not representing a masonic lodge is, moreover, also indicated by their crafts. In signing the charter Hew Duok or Dowok described himself as deacon of the masons and wrights of Ayr, George Liddell as deacon of the squaremen and now quartermaster. Both were in fact former deacons, Dowok being a wright and Liddell a glazier, and in 1609 Liddell had been elected deacon on the same day that Dowok was admitted as a master of the incorporation.[2] Many members of the Ayr incorporation can be found later in the century among the members of the Lodge of Kilwinning, but it seems likely that the two Ayr signatures on the Second St Clair Charter indicates that Kilwinning Lodge, still pursuing its claims to a special status, refused to give its consent to the charter, whereupon Sir William Sinclair had to make do with the signatures of two men who were not masons but as former deacons of the squaremen had previously been the leaders of the Ayr masons. Evidently he regarded this as better than nothing, giving an impression that he had support in the west for his claim to be patron of the mason craft.

The other royal burgh that came within Kilwinning Lodge's actual rather than theoretical sphere of influence was Irvine. Craft organisation in the burgh can only be traced back to 1646, when after complaints by craftsmen about their treatment the burgh council issued seals of cause to seven incorporations, one of them being the squaremen or wrights. This probably included masons along with the other building crafts from the first, though evidence of their presence only appears later.[3]

The first minute book of Kilwinning Lodge begins on 20 December 1642, twenty-six men being present. The very date is an indication that the lodge claimed to be different from the rest of the Scottish lodges. The Second Schaw Statutes had specified that the lodge's warden should be elected on 20 December, and the minutes show it meeting and holding elections on that day with great regularity. What the date's significance was remains a mystery (it was not St Wynnyn's Day, so does not commemorate the patron saint of the abbey): perhaps its main importance to Kilwinning was that it set it apart from all other lodges whose main annual meeting was on St John's Day.[4]

The 1642 minute simply recorded that those present 'Inrollit thame selffis in the said Ludge' and agreed to submit themselves to it and to its acts and statutes. This wording suggests that some reorganisation or revival of the lodge was taking place, and this impression is reinforced a year later, in December 1643. A notary from Irvine, James Ross was appointed clerk to the lodge (though there is no mention of his being initiated), and a number of regulations were passed. The meeting referred to itself as the court of the Lodge of Kilwinning, and this phrase or variants of it were used frequently in the years that followed. This should not, however, be interpreted (as has sometimes been done) as indicating that the lodge's meetings were somehow different in nature from those of other lodges: in that all lodges tried offenders, all acted as courts. That Kilwinning's minutes call it a court merely reflects the legal training of the clerk. More inclined to formality than most lodge clerks, he frequently recorded the affirming, or formal constituting, of the court and the calling of suits before it. The 20 December meeting was sometimes referred to as the head court, the most important meeting of a court which all owing suit to it were bound to attend.[5]

The December 1643 meeting was held in the upper chamber of the dwelling house of Hew Smith at the Cross of Kilwinning, and meetings are frequently recorded there up to December 1661. Smith was not a member of the lodge, and it has been surmised that he ran an inn or ale house. Support for this is provided by the fact that he can probably be identified with Hew Smith, cooper, in Byres of Kilwinning: when he died in March 1661 money was owed to him for malt that he had supplied, suggesting that he was involved in brewing.[6] Closure of the inn after his death would explain why the lodge ceased to meet there.

The 1643 regulations, passed in Hew Smith's chamber, asserted the right of the warden, deacon and fellow crafts of Kilwinning, the ancient lodge of Scotland, to exclude from their ancient company those who failed to conform to its ancient statutes. No fellow craft was to be admitted unless six fellow crafts and two entered apprentices were present. The names of those present at the initiation were to be recorded, together with those of the intenders who prepared the candidate for promotion. No man was to be admitted without an essay and trial of his skill and worthiness in his vocation. All members were to assemble at Kilwinning on 20 December each year on pain of fining. Penalties were specified only for members in Cunningham and Renfrew, those in the former area paying twice as much as those in the latter, presumably because the Renfrew men would have further to come so non-attendance was less blameworthy. Small quarterly payments were to be made by all members, these being collected by quartermasters. Two quartermasters were elected for the quarters of Inchinnan and Dumbarton, two for the 'heights' of Renfrew and Paisley, and two for Cunningham. This provides a useful definition of the area from which the lodge drew most of its members: Renfrewshire, Dumbarton on the north side of the inner Clyde estuary, and northern Ayrshire. Moreover the lodge was to convene once a year in Renfrewshire, meeting at Kilbarchan each July—penalties for non-attendance on these occasions being less for Cunningham masons, more for Renfrew ones. Finally, the 1643 minutes record the election of a warden and deacon. The former was at first the senior office, the runner-up in the election of the warden becoming deacon, but for reasons unknown from 1646 the order of precedence was reversed, the deacon presiding. Concern to build up membership was indicated by three fellow crafts being ordered each to enter an apprentice. The wording indicates that it was not the case that these men had apprentices serving them whom they had failed to have admitted to the lodge. When they obediently entered apprentices the following year the new members of the lodge were their servants or journeymen, men who had completed their apprenticeships—or perhaps in rural areas had not served a formal apprenticeship—and that they were being brought into the lodge at this late stage in their career again suggests that the lodge had been dormant or in decay in previous years and was now being resuscitated.[7]

The 1642-3 minutes indicate in several ways that the lodge was in part at least seeking to conform to the Schaw Statutes—as in choosing a notary as clerk, and in the rules for numbers to be present at admissions, for the appointment of intenders, and for setting essays. Practice never lived up to good intentions, however. Intenders are never recorded in the minutes in the seventeenth century, and there is no sign of essays being set. Nor were the efforts to institute regular meetings outside Kilwinning and to have quartermasters collecting dues from masons over a wide area successful. There was a meeting at Kilbarchan in 1644, but no later meetings are mentioned.[8] In January 1647 the lodge met in Ayr, and in 1659 it was ordered that annual meetings to deal with transgressors be held in Ayr and Renfrew. These were to be attended by the deacon and the warden and by two fellow crafts and one entered apprentice from each quarter. The same 1659 meeting confirmed that the lodge regarded its authority as limited to the two shires of Ayr and Renfrew by appointing four quartermasters for Renfrew, Cunningham, Kyle and Carrick, and in each quarter there was also to be an officer to assist the quartermaster.[9] But this ambitious scheme to hold courts regularly in the north and the south of the lodge's territory and increase the efficiency of the quartermasters had little effect. There is no evidence of any of the court meetings taking place, and though quartermasters and officers continued to be appointed, if rather sporadically, for some decades there is no indication that they were effective. As in many lodges, absenteeism was a major problem. Long lists of absentees from 20 December meetings were sometimes recorded, though 1693 must have been a record when nine men attended the meeting and ordered the fining of fifty absentees.[10] There was of course the consolation that absenteeism could be good for lodge funds—provided the fines imposed could be collected. Another problem, shared by at least two other lodges (Mary's Chapel and Aitchison's Haven), was that many entered apprentices failed to pass as fellow craft as they saw no advantage in it unless they had an opportunity to set up as master masons instead of remaining journeymen.[11]

Full analysis of the membership of the Kilwinning Lodge in the seventeenth century would be difficult since, as with some other lodges (particularly Aitchison's Haven and Melrose), many surnames occur repeatedly with only a narrow range of christian names between them, and often no further identification apart from the name is given. The twenty-six men listed in 1642 as lodge members include four Fultons, three Caldwells, two Crawfords and two Alisons. But sometimes additional information is given, and from this a general picture of membership can be constructed. The lodge contained masons from most if not all the burghs of Ayrshire and Renfrewshire, though it is highly unlikely that all the masons in them belonged to the lodge. A very substantial part of lodge membership comprised, however, rural masons, and many of these combined their craft with work on the land. Where in the records a mason is referred to as 'in' a place this usually means that they were tenants of land there (unless the place was a burgh, in which case it is just an indication that they resided there). Of the twenty-six names given for members of Kilwinning Lodge in 1642 nine, a third of the total, are 'in' somewhere, and only in one case is the place a burgh. Further, a few of the stonemasons of Kilwinning Lodge are revealed by their designation as being landowners. Whereas most of Scotland outside the burghs was divided up into fairly substantial estates, in some districts (especially in the west) land had been very much subdivided, creating groups of small feuars, men who farmed their own land but had legal ownership of it by feu charter, unlike the vast majority of the country's tenant farmers. In Renfrewshire and Melrose some of these 'bonnet lairds' were masons as well as farmers. As to why so many masons lived in the countryside instead of urban areas, only in the largest burghs was there enough demand to give regular employment to a substantial number of masons. Thus even if they lived in burghs they might regularly have to leave home to seek work. Living in the country brought no disadvantages, and was cheaper than living in burghs. Moreover, retaining a hold on the land, as tenant or owner, must have provided security for bad years when employment as a mason was hard to find. Much more investigation is needed, but the evidence suggests that rural masons did whatever work they could find locally, but often set out in spring in search of work (other members of their families looking after the farm in their absence) and returned each autumn at the end of the building season. Nor did the members of the little dynasties of rural masons that can be identified simply set out on random wanderings when seeking work, for they were not cut off from the craft in the countryside. While some may have been trained locally, others had served apprenticeships in burghs, perhaps with members of their families who had become burgesses. Networks of family relationships existed which must have kept masons in touch with where work was to be found. The Caldwells and the Fultons, prominent families in Kilwinning Lodge, were also major mason dynasties in Glasgow and Edinburgh respectively. John Carruth elder, portioner of Risk (that is feuar of part of the lands of Risk) in Lochwinnoch parish in Renfrewshire, became a Glasgow burgess in 1643 after serving his apprenticeship with Mathew Caldwell, but his burgess-ship was cancelled in 1655 as he had left Glasgow and settled elsewhere, and he died in 1665. He can be traced in the Kilwinning Lodge records in the 1640s and 1650s, along with his brother Robert, a tenant in Risk. John Caldwell younger in Risk and John Caldwell portioner of Risk are also recorded in the lodge in the 1640s. In 1695 there was still a mason portioner at Risk, James Orr.[12] The example of Risk indicates that not only were there isolated masons scattered in the countryside, there were in some cases groups of masons. Lochwinnoch was particularly richly endowed, with Caldwell mason portioners at Beltrees and Auchingown as well as Risk who were members of Kilwinning Lodge: one of the latter built Kelburn Castle in the 1690s. Lochwinnoch was perhaps particularly attractive to masons through the fact that it contained good limestone and sandstone deposits, providing additional employment for them as quarriers, but it is far from unique in containing substantial numbers of rural masons. The poll tax records for Paisley in Renfrewshire list only two masons and one apprentice in the burgh, but six masons and two apprentices in the landward areas of the parish.[13]

As with other lodges, it is hard to see the 'operative' Lodge of Kilwinning as being an effective instrument of control of the mason craft. It might have some degree of control over masons who wanted to belong to the lodge, but even this was probably limited, and there was no way in which it could really exercise supervision over two shires. The pretence was kept up, a few offences punished in what looks more like occasional symbolic gestures to show it still claimed to be regulating the trade rather than systematic action. Masons who were not members doubtless from time to time came across members who refused to work with them, but it can hardly have been this that attracted many men into the lodge. The real motive was surely to make themselves part of the great heritage of masonic lore and ritual, gaining access to the secrets of the Mason Word. The Kilwinning minutes contain no evidence relating to the esoteric side of the lodge's activities (except in the sense that any admission to one of the two grades of membership implies a ritual initiation). But this does not mean that it was unimportant, merely that (as elsewhere) it was not recorded in writing (just as the fact that the lodge's copy of the Old Charges dates from the later seventeenth century does not prove that its lore was unknown before then).[14] Even in the imparting of secrets, however, the lodge did not have an effective monopoly. In 1686 the lodge enacted that admitting entered apprentices and fellow crafts should only be done in the lodge, and only on 20 December.[15] Some lodges made provision for groups of members to admit new ones away from the lodge, as at Dumfries, Dunfermline and Haughfoot, but Kilwinning joined Mary's Chapel and Aitchison's Haven in seeking to keep direct control over entry to masonic secrets. A well known Kilwinning minute of 1705 defined a cowan as someone 'without the word', indicating a determination to boycott those who would not seek entry to the lodge: the concession that a master might employ a cowan if no mason with the Word could be found within fifteen miles indicates that here at least cowans were not regarded as lacking professional skills, but esoteric knowledge. It has been said that cowans were 'a recurrent source of trouble' to Kilwinning Lodge, but so far as the seventeenth century is concerned this is not so. Action against those working with cowans is recorded in 1645-58, but otherwise the minutes are silent.[16]

Non-operatives arrive in Kilwinning Lodge in a remarkable burst of activity in the 1670s. As in other lodges, the motives of both lodge and non-operatives are unclear. The first non-operative has been claimed to be Walter Turke, a Glasgow burgess admitted fellow craft in 1671, but his case is doubtful. He cannot be traced in Glasgow records, and indeed the only man of that surname in the burgess register is John Turke, burgess in 1629, licensed by the Incorporation of Masons to undertake painting and plastering in 1630.[17] Given the rarity of the surname it is likely that John and Walter were related. Thus Walter probably had a family connection with the building trades, and may well have been initiated as an entered apprentice somewhere else before being promoted to the higher grade at Kilwinning.

The next entry requiring discussion was certainly that of a non-operative, but it raises other problems. In the midst of what are otherwise routine minutes for 20 December 1672 it is recorded that the earl of Cassillis 'wes chosen to be deacon'. His name does not appear on the list of members present, nor on the leet from which the deacon was supposed to have been chosen: the successful candidate from the leet was subsequently described as depute deacon. Nothing is said about Cassillis being initiated as a member of the lodge. It has indeed been argued that Cassillis was not even present on this occasion, but certainty is impossible—unfortunately it was not customary at Kilwinning, as it was at some other lodges, for those present to sign the minutes. Possible alternative interpretations are many: that Cassillis had already been initiated elsewhere, and was now admitted to Kilwinning Lodge and through his status made deacon; that he was initiated by Kilwinning masons but not at a meeting of the lodge; or that he was initiated at a lodge meeting but this was not recorded for some reason. Harry Carr inclined to the view that not only was Cassillis not present, but that it was only after he had been elected that the lodge approached him asking him to be deacon, as it felt the need for a powerful patron to protect its interests.[18] But it seems unlikely that the Kilwinning masons would have ventured to elect an important nobleman even honorary head of a craft organisation without having any previous contact with him. Moreover if the lodge had been seeking a leading establishment figure as a patron it would not have chosen Cassillis. In 1670 he had been the only man in parliament to dare to vote against an act designed to suppress conventicles, the meetings of the presbyterian dissidents whose main strength lay in the south west. In 1678-9 he was in trouble for failing to act against conventiclers, being regarded in the latter year as being himself a presbyterian.[19] In making Cassillis deacon in these troubled times the lodge was surely indicating its religious and political principles. There are signs of difficulties being experienced by the lodge around this time. In 1670 it had failed to hold its 20 December meeting, and when it did meet the following February existing officials were confirmed in office without a new election;[20] and the meeting which elected Cassillis was evidently not attended by the the deacon and warden. This may indicate that holding lodge meetings was awkward, perhaps even dangerous. Armed rebellion in the south west had been crushed in 1666 by the king's army, and during the continuing persecution thereafter masons travelling to secret meetings in mid winter could be mistaken for those engaged in seditious conspiracies, and secret lodge meetings themselves could look like conventicles. There may also have been divisions among members themselves over religious issues, culminating in the more radical members getting their way by electing a noble known to have some sympathy with the conventiclers to be deacon.

The entry of a single non-operative, who may not even have been initiated, in 1672 was followed by four or five non-operatives on 20 December 1673. The doubtful case was James King, assumed to have been a non-operative because he was admitted as entered apprentice and fellow craft on the same day, but in spite of this oddity he may well have been an operative, perhaps the Kilbarchan mason of that name.[21] The other four admissions were Sir Alexander Cunningham of Corsehill and Joseph Cunningham of Carlurg, two local landowners, David Stewart, and Alexander Galt in Stewarton.[22] Stewart was a brother of Sir Archibald Stewart of Blackhall, and his sister was married to Corsehill. Galt lived in the barony of Corsehill, his name often appearing in its court book,[23] and his entrance fees to the lodge were paid by Cunningham of Corsehill, suggesting that he had accompanied the laird either as a friend or a servant.

Corsehill and Stewart were no sooner admitted than they were put on the leet for deacon along with Cassillis and three operative masons. Corsehill was elected by nine votes to one, Cassillis receiving the only dissenting vote, perhaps indicating disappointment that he had not shown an interest in the lodge by attending the meeting. Corsehill chose an operative to be depute deacon under him, and two wardens were elected, perhaps to balance the two deacons.

More non-operatives appeared almost immediately. Just a month later, on 20 January 1674, the lodge met again. Corsehill was absent, but wrote authorising the lodge to act in his absence; and he was present the following day when the earl of Eglinton and Lawrence Wallace, an Irvine merchant who was a younger brother of the laird of Shewalton, were admitted entered apprentices and fellow crafts.[24] Eglinton took little part in public life, but when his political sympathies emerged in the following decade they lay with the opposition to the regime.[25] From this point onwards the lodge minutes are in the handwriting of Robert Fergushill, who was later said to have been appointed clerk by Corsehill when he had been deacon. Fergushill, a notary public, had become clerk to the baron court of Corsehill the previous year, and thus now served the laird both in his own court and in the lodge which he presided over as deacon.[26]

There was now an established demand by non-operatives seeking to enter the lodge, and on 11 February 1674 a meeting made up entirely of operatives decided to cash in on this. In future gentlemen seeking to be fellow crafts were to pay £40 besides other dues and presenting gloves to the existing fellow crafts.[27] It may also be that some, alarmed by the sudden transformation of the lodge, hoped that the high fee might serve to deter entrants. If so, they were disappointed, for non-operative domination of the lodge continued to grow. Only one new non-operative appeared in December 1674, John Smith at the Kirk of Stewarton, who may be classified as belonging to the Corsehill group.[28] But on this occasion all the names on the leet for deacon were non-operatives), and one of them, David Stewart, was also on the leet for warden. Eglinton and Stewart were elected to office (the former unanimously), and operative deputes were appointed for both offices. Cassillis was not on the leet for deacon on this occasion, but Lord Cochrane was, though as with Cassillis there is no indication that he had been admitted to the lodge. Like Cassillis he was a man unhappy at the way the country was being ruled, protesting against the persecution of dissidents in 1678 and being regarded the following year as one of those suitable for office if Lauderdale fell from power. In the controversy over church government he was said to be indifferent rather than positively presbyterian, but his presence on the leet may have been brought about by those in the lodge who had made the gesture of electing Cassillis two years before.[29] Lord Cochrane is also of interest in linking the other two nobles who appear in the lodge in the 1670s. He was Cassillis' uncle by marriage, and in 1676 his daughter was to marry Eglinton's son.

The spate of non-operative activity in the lodge continued in December 1675, with all those on the leets for warden and deacon being non-operatives. Eglinton was retained as deacon, being preferred to Corsehill and Lord Cochrane, while David Cunningham younger of Robertland became warden—having, presumably, been admitted fellow craft. His grandfather had been master of works to James VI, his uncle a member of a secret fraternity of Scots courtiers under Charles I, but there is no indication that these previous family interests had any influence on the fact that he joined Kilwinning Lodge. He appears again in the Kilwinning minutes in December 1676 as Sir David Cunningham of Robertland, having presumably succeeded his father in the intervening year. He was then elected warden, with Eglinton as deacon.[30]

Then, in December 1677, the lodge seems to have changed direction completely. Operatives were elected warden and deacon, the deputes disappeared, and no non-operatives were present. The most important item on the agenda in 1677 was the granting of permission to the deputation of Canongate masons to form their own lodge, nominally a branch of Kilwinning.[31] The involvement of non-operatives in this process was evidently felt to be inappropriate, so the Lodge of Kilwinning had hastily converted itself back into a conventional 'operative' lodge, with only stonemason members, for the occasion.

In 1678 Eglinton and Lord Cochrane were elected deacon and warden respectively with operative deputes, and a new non-operative was admitted John Ker of Breakenhills). Thus it looked as if operative domination of the lodge was being resumed. In fact the brief age of the non-operatives was about to end as abruptly as it had begun. There was some argument at the 1678 meeting which led to Fergushill being replaced as clerk. No election of office holders was recorded for 1679, and when the lodge met on 20 January 1680 the operatives who had been elected deputes in 1678 were referred to as deacon and warden. The meeting lamented the lack of order among members of the lodge, and ordered that old records be searched and lawyers be consulted about such abuses and disorders, and as to how they could be corrected and the guilty punished.[32] None of the gentlemen non-operatives were present, and none were to hold office in the lodge for half a century. Clearly some major upheaval had taken place, a counter-revolution restoring control of the lodge to the operatives. Chance had something to do with the change: Lord Cochrane died in 1679, and Eglinton transferred his estates to his son and went to live in England at about the same time. But obviously this is not the whole explanation. Nor does it seem that the local gentry simply lost interest, fascination with masonic secrets having been a passing fashion in the area: it was in 1678, it will be recalled, that a mason of Mary's Chapel Lodge initiated some Ayrshire gentlemen.[33] It is indeed conceivable that the non-operatives, their appetites whetted by initiation at Kilwinning simply withdrew from the craft organisation they had joined in order to practice their rituals in their own lodge. Political considerations may also have played a part. In 1679 a major rebellion took place in the south west, and was crushed at the Battle of Bothwell Bridge. In the atmosphere of fear and suspicion that followed the gentry could have decided that dabbling in a secret society of the common people was potentially dangerous as it could be seen as seditious.

Whatever the reason for the withdrawal of the gentlemen non-operatives, the fact that generations were to pass before such members were again admitted to the lodge suggests that the operatives were not sorry to see them go. Though at first they may have been flattered to have men of rank wishing access to their secrets and rituals, the operatives had found that once their social superiors had got into the lodge they quickly took it over, changing its nature. The working masons probably wanted control of their lodge back, and got it after 1678. It is quite likely, however, that admission of another type of non-operative continued, men of fairly humble status who were not themselves stonemasons but through some personal, family or working relationship came into contact with masons. There may, indeed, have been such non-operatives in the lodge before the 1670s, impossible to detect as only their names are given in the minutes. But from the 1670s there is an intermittent trickle of men whose only distinction from other members is that they were admitted entered apprentice and fellow craft on a single day. One of these, on 20 December 1686, was John King in Kilbarchan, evidently the King who had acted as clerk of the lodge since 1680. On the same occasion James Tarbet, perhaps a friend of King and identifiable as a merchant in Kilbarchan, was admitted.[34] Even men only admitted to one grade at a time might not be stonemasons: James Montgomery was made only an entered apprentice in 1706, but was a wright in Kilwinning.[35]

Most of the gentlemen masons of the 1670s in the Lodge of Kilwinning were friends and acquaintances of each other before joining the lodge. Corsehill seems to have been at the centre of group, and probably his influence brought a number of his acquaintances to the lodge. The three nobles do not seem to have any strong connection with Corsehill, and thus form a separate group. Several of the gentlemen masons were out of sympathy with the regime's political and religious policies, but too little is known about most of them to generalise about their outlooks and characters. Corsehill himself seems to have been of a sociable nature—in the 1680s he was on several occasions among visiting lairds entertained with wine by the magistrates of Irvine, Lawrence Wallace also being present on one of them.[36] In choice of friends Corsehill was not, however, always well advised. His fellow member of Kilwinning Lodge, Cunningham of Robertland, was suspected of having tried to murder his father, and was such a spendthrift that he not only ruined himself but Corsehill as well, for the latter had become a surety for his debts.[37] More sober-minded were Cassillis and Lord Cochrane, but it is not even certain that either actually attended a lodge meeting. Eglinton, the third of the nobles, must have been present in 1674 when initiated, but though elected deacon several times thereafter he may not have appeared again.[38] The Lodge of Kilwinning had tried to create a new identity for itself by admitting non-operatives from the upper ranks of society, had (it seems) not liked the results, and hastily drawn back. But the lodge's effectiveness (never very great) in its older role of regulating the operative mason craft was in decline. Attendances at meetings, always low compared to total membership, seems to have decreased even further. Quartermasters might still sometimes be appointed but even the pretence that they were effective in collecting dues from masons throughout Ayrshire and Renfrewshire was impossible to maintain. As with Mary's Chapel Lodge, there is a feeling of loss of direction within the lodge by the end of the seventeenth century, of falling morale and reduced interest among masons in general in the value of the lodge and its secrets.

The Lodge of Glasgow

The masons, wrights and coopers of Glasgow received a seal of cause in 1551, but in 1569 the coopers split off to form a separate incorporation, and in 1600 the wrights and their associated minor trades also seceded. The reasons cited by the wrights in petitioning the burgh council for permission to form their own incorporation was that the trades of mason and wright were so different that members of one were unable to judge the work of the other.[39] This explanation is distinctly weak, for in many other burghs the two trades managed to work together. It may simply be that, perhaps through personal antagonisms, the normal degree of tension and rivalry between masons and wrights within one incorporation had become too intense in Glasgow to be contained in a single organisation. But the timing of the separation is intriguing: is it possible that it was connected in some way with William Schaw's reorganisation of the mason craft in the years immediately before 1600? No Glasgow representatives signed the First St Clair Charter in 1600-1, but if a lodge was emerging in Glasgow for the masons in the Incorporation of Masons and Wrights, with the masons asserting the right to meet on their own, excluding other trades and conducting secret rituals, then it is conceivable that the wrights and others felt they were becoming second class citizens in the incorporation and therefore demanded their own incorporation.

The events of 1600 left the masons of Glasgow forming their own incorporation, though it had jurisdiction over slaters as well as masons.[40] A lodge is first heard of a few years later, and the reference to it occurs in the minutes of the incorporation. Several other entries in the same source appear to refer to matters usually dealt with by the lodge, indicating that lodge and incorporation were very closely linked. As the masons had an incorporation to themselves, not shared with other tradesmen (except a few slaters), it and the lodge were doubtless almost identical in membership. The mason deacon of the incorporation also presided in the lodge as deacon—and was to continue to do so up to the mid nineteenth century.[41] These connections, and the fact that the lodge possesses no seventeenth-century records, has led to the assumption that incorporation and the lodge formed a single organisation, with the incorporation's minute books recording the transactions of both.[42] This is very unlikely. Though there are references to lodge-type activities in the incorporation minutes they are rare and usually ambiguous. Several reasons for their occurrence may be suggested. The two bodies may well have shared the same clerk, who on occasion got confused as to what should be recorded where, especially in the early years when the lodge was establishing its separate identity and the specialist terms 'entered apprentice' and 'fellow craft' had not yet become the exclusive preserve of the masonic lodges.

It has already been argued that references in the minutes of the Incorporation of Squaremen of Ayr to fellows of craft should not be seen as implying masonic initiation, and the same is true in Glasgow. Thus when on 9 February 1620 Malcolm Snodgrass was admitted and received freeman and fellow of craft with the masons he was in all probability simply becoming a master of his incorporation like any other tradesman; he had become a mason burgess only a few days before.[43] Similarly when two apprentices were 'ressavet and enterit prenteiss' in 1618[44] it may be assumed that they were simply being 'booked' (the usual word in the minutes) or registered, not that they had been singled out from all the other apprentices for initiation. As for the claim that the early Glasgow incorporation minutes, very unusually for Scotland, use the term freemason,[45] in all the instances cited a check with the manuscript minutes reveal that simple misreading is involved: in every case the word is clearly 'freeman'.[46] Moreover, though the first reference to the Lodge of Glasgow occurs in the incorporation minutes, the entry implies that lodge and incorporation were not the same thing.

In 1620 an item was inserted in the minutes headed 'Intrie of prenteiss to the Ludge of Glasgow'. It recorded that on 31 December 1613 John Stewart, deacon of the masons, had signified to David Slater, warden of the lodge of masons, that he was going to enter John Stewart his apprentice (and son) in the lodge. This had then been done on 1 January 1614, in conformity with the acts and liberties of the lodge.[47] John Stewart had begun his apprenticeship on 27 October 1613, he having then been booked at the Trades House (the Glasgow equivalent to being booked in the burgh register of apprentices) and ordered to begin his service,[48] and some months later had been admitted to the lodge as an entered apprentice. Why, seven years later, this latter fact should have been so carefully recorded in the incorporation's minutes is obscure, but it may be that the lodge had not kept a proper record of his admission as entered apprentice and that in 1620, as his term of apprenticeship drew to a close, doubts had arisen as to his status. Perhaps the lodge was refusing to accept he had joined it as an entered apprentice, having failed to record his admission, but his father somehow in the course of the dispute managed to get the incorporation to record it instead.

The only other reference to a lodge in the incorporation minutes occurs in 1622, when one of the masters of the incorporation was accused of employing a cowan. In his defence he alleged that the the cowan 'was entered in a Lodge, and had a discharge of a Master in Paisley with whom he is entred'.[49] His argument thus was that his employee was not a cowan, being an entered apprentice in a lodge. This implies that the definition of a cowan as a man without the Mason Word, rather than as a man lacking professional skills, was accepted in Glasgow at this early date. By taking action against a mason alleged to have associated with a cowan, the incorporation was doing something usually done by lodges. But, on the other hand, the incorporation did not (like the lodges) shun cowans entirely. In 1623 a cowan was licensed to work in the burgh, building walls up to an ell in height provided he did not use hewn stone or sand and lime[50]—and, presumably, provided he did not work for or with masons.

The Lodge of Glasgow gave its assent to the Second St Clair Charter in 1627-8, the names of the deacon and two other masons appearing on it. A full half century of silence follows, and during this period an act of the incorporation suggests that it may have again been involving itself in what were normally lodge matters elsewhere. On 15 February 1667 an 'Act anent Entrit prentiss' ordered

That all entrit prenteiss keip meiting with the deacon and Maister wpon ilk first tuesday of January yeirlie ilk yeir till they be friemen.[51]

This immediately recalls the meetings of entered apprentices with the warden of the lodge held on St John's Day by Aitchison's Haven Lodge, at which, it has been suggested above, apprentices were taught and tested in the traditional history of masonry, and perhaps exercised in the art of memory and secret rituals as well. Was the incorporation in Glasgow concerning itself with such matters, thus acting as a lodge? No certain answer is possible, but it may well have been doing so, perhaps taking action in a period in which the lodge itself was in decline or even abeyance. On the other hand, the deacon could have been meeting with apprentices ('entered' only in the sense of having been booked) in connection with teaching them the practical skills of the craft.

Evidence that incorporation and lodge were indeed separate organisations in the later seventeenth century, each controlling admission of its own members, survives in an unusual form: two wooden boxes. In October 1678 Alexander Thom, 'architectour', was granted liberty to reside in Glasgow 'and exerce his imployment and calling in architectorie, or in measonrie' until Candlemas 1680.[52] He was not made a burgess, however, and subsequent events suggest that it was probably only through the patronage of the archbishop of Glasgow, Alexander Burnet, that Thom was granted permission to work in the burgh. Thom stayed on working in Glasgow after 1680, and perhaps in an attempt to regularise his position the archbishop and others put pressure on the Incorporation of Masons in 1683 to admit him. The issue was controversial, and the incorporation held several meetings on 3 September 1683 on the subject. Eventually, at the archbishop's express desire, the incorporation gave way. Thom was tried 'to be a fellow craft' (in the sense of master of the incorporation), submitted an essay, and was admitted as a freeman. On 2 June 1684 it was further accepted that Thom should pay his freedom fine or fee 'by ane new carvit box to the said trade'.[53]

Thom specialised in stone and wood carving,[54] and the splendid box or charter chest he gave to the Incorporation of Masons still survives. Inscribed 'God save the King and the Masons Craft 1684' it is decorated with elaborate carvings including the tools of the trade (compass, plumbline, level and square).[55] But there was also a second box, inscribed 'God save the King and St John's Lodge 1686'. Infuriatingly it has proved impossible to confirm that it still exists, let alone to inspect it, but in all probability it was also carved by Thom.[56] If so, it surely indicates that Thom was initiated into the lodge two or three years after his entry to the incorporation, and again paid his entry fees with an example of his craftsmanship designed to become the lodge charter chest—which he would hardly have done unless the lodge's records were separate from those of the incorporation.

The affairs of the lodge and incorporation in Glasgow remained closely entwined up to the nineteenth century. The overlap and confusion between the two indeed led at one time to the lodge possessing the 1684 box originally given to the incorporation, while the incorporation had the 1686 box inscribed with

5   Charter chest of the Incorporation of Masons in Glasgow.
Presented by Alexander Thom. Masonic tools are carved on the top, and on the front
the inscription 'God save the King 1684 and the Mason Craft'
Copyright: Glasgow Museums, Glasgow City Council

the lodge's name and used it as its deacon's box.[57] Nonetheless the few tantalising fragments of evidence which have survived suggest that, in the seventeenth century at least, it makes more sense to regard lodge and incorporation as linked but separate institutions, rather than as a single one. Most of the members of the one may also have belonged to the other, and this may have occasionally led to confusion, but they were nonetheless distinct bodies. A cricket club and a golf club may contain the same members, and as a result the affairs of one may sometimes be discussed on the premises of the other, but this does not make them a single institution.

The 1686 box is also of interest in that it demonstrates that the Glasgow Lodge had taken the name of St John as far back as the seventeenth century. As such its annual meeting was doubtless 27 December, a day on which the incorporation also occasionally met. As a St John's lodge it represented the majority tradition in Scotland, and thus there is no sign that it was in any respect an off-shoot of Kilwinning, with its rival meeting date of 20 December, in spite of the fact that Glasgow lay within the jurisdiction claimed for Kilwinning in the Second Schaw Statutes. Some Ayrshire and Renfrewshire masons who served apprenticeships in Glasgow but later returned to their homes were probably members of both lodges, but it is impossible to know whether they would have found significant differences in rituals between the lodges.

So far as is known, the Lodge of Glasgow did not admit any non-operatives before the nineteenth century. Its refusal to broaden its membership led to the foundation of a rival Glasgow lodge in 1729.[58] That Glasgow St John was prepared to see this happen rather than change its ways indicates a strong prejudice against non-operatives, but the lack of seventeenth-century minutes means that it is conceivable that it had, like Kilwinning, experimented with admitting such members at some point before reverting to being exclusively operative in membership.

The Lodge of Dumfries

In Kilwinning the earliest surviving lodge minutes seem to mark a reorganisation and revival of the lodge. In Dumfries the first minutes make it explicit that this is the case. On 20 May 1687 the 'honourable Company of Masonry being mett togither for setling of ane Lodge belonging to the burgh of Dumfreis' appointed a master and warden of the lodge, and five fellow crafts. Thus an organisation called the 'Company of Masonry' already existed, and had decided to convert itself into a lodge. The company had evidently experienced a period of decline and disorder, for the 20 May minutes include a resolution that the company, considering the abuses 'done by them at some of ther Meetings and the dishonour done to God by cursing and swearing' would fine any member swearing or taking God's name in vain.[59]

The Lodge of Dumfries grew out of an existing body which was not regarded as a lodge. Later, this lodge was to take the name Lodge Dumfries Kilwinning, which might suggest that it (like Canongate Kilwinning) owed its legitimacy to a licence granted by Kilwinning Lodge, but there is no evidence to support this in the early Lodge records. Nor, in spite of quotations from the early minutes published by the lodge's historian, did Dumfries call itself 'the old lodge', suggesting a claim to antiquity: he erroneously read 'sd.' (the abbreviation of 'said') as 'old', making references to 'the said lodge' into 'the old lodge'—though in other contexts he read 'sd.' accurately.[60]

Dumfries had possessed since at least the early seventeenth century an Incorporation of Wrights or Squaremen which included all the building trades,[61] and most members of the lodge were probably members of this body. But of the three men listed in the first minute of the lodge who can be readily identified only one was a mason. Hugh Barton was a wright in Dumfries.[62] Robert Anderson was a wright who was deacon of the incorporation.[63] With James Selkrig a mason at last appears—but not a Dumfries one, for he lived at the Kirk of Twynholm, twenty miles away in Kirkcudbrightshire.[64] A sample of three is hardly convincing, but it seems probable that there were as many wrights as masons in the lodge, or even more. This is, however, easily explicable. In many country areas and small burghs it was common for men to undertake both wright and mason work. Indentures of apprenticeship can be found (Dumbarton 1663, Lanarkshire 1670, Kinross 1683, Rutherglen 1712) in which the apprentice was bound to both trades, and in 1663 James Robertson described himself as a cowan, mason and wright burgess of Paisley, a combination of trades which would have horrified the purist.[65] Even in a large burgh like Glasgow some men were given special permission to work in both trades when the wrights and masons split into separate incorporations in 1600, as up to that time it had evidently been accepted that men could work in both.[66] James Johnston, elected warden of Dumfries Lodge in May 1687 and later deacon of the incorporation, can be traced in 1699 contracting to build a mill using both stone and timber.[67] Thus in many areas outside the largest burghs wright and mason were not mutually exclusive trades, and most if not all of the 'wrights' in Dumfries Lodge would also work as masons.

The Dumfries Lodge was evidently connected to the Incorporation of Wrights, but the links between the two institutions were not nearly so close as in Edinburgh and Glasgow. The deacon of the incorporation did not preside *ex officio* in the lodge. The latter's presiding official was sometimes called deacon, sometimes master, but whichever title was used it referred only to his position in the lodge. Thus on 20 May 1687 the lodge elected James Tod as master and James Johnston as warden, while the incorporation deacon, Robert Anderson, was merely listed among the fellow crafts of the lodge. On 27 December the same year James Selkrig was elected to preside in the lodge as deacon, but he was not incorporation deacon. It was, however, usual for the incorporation deacons to be at least members of the lodge, and the hasty initiation of Robert Newall, wright, as both entered apprentice and fellow craft on the same day in 1704, a privilege usually not accorded to craftsmen, seems to have come about because he had been elected deacon of the incorporation but had not previously been a lodge member. Moreover, though the incorporation deacons were not as such lodge officials they seem to have been regarded as occupying a special position in the lodge. This is indicated by the fact that the lodge frequently met in the house of the incorporation deacon: the 1704 meeting which initiated Deacon Newall took place in his house. Sometimes leadership of the lodge and the incorporation may have been combined under a single deacon/master, but further analysis (which will be hindered by the lack of incorporation records) is needed to confirm this.[68]

The business of 'settling' the lodge on 20 May 1687 included a ruling that no member of the lodge should enter apprentices or pass fellow crafts within twelve miles of the lodge.[69] Mary's Chapel, Aitchison's Haven and Kilwinning legislated to prevent their members initiating men to the Mason Word outside the lodge. Dumfries, struggling to assert its authority, felt it could go no further in enforcing its monopoly rights over admission to the Word than claiming exclusive rights within the immediate vicinity of the burgh. Beyond this it accepted that even its own members could do as they liked. They were not even bound to inform the lodge of such initiations carried out elsewhere.

Finally, at its first recorded meeting, the lodge appointed a clerk, William M'George of Inglistoun, a notary who was later to become keeper of the Dumfries register of sasines and baillie depute of the barony of Sweetheart. It was not specifically stated that he was initiated as a member of the lodge, but it is likely that he was.[70]

That the lodge had no objection to admitting men who were not craftsmen was demonstrated by a minute of 2 June 1687 which laid down separate fees for 'mechanicks' entering the lodge and those who were 'no mechanicks': the entry is incomplete but doubtless the intention was that the latter should pay more. The first such member was admitted on 7 May 1688: Lieutenant John Livingstone was entered and passed. Edward Sinclair, a dragoon in Captain John Strachan's troop, was admitted on 11 May, followed on 31 May by another dragoon from the same troop, Robert McAlexander—though he was only made an entered apprentice.[71] That the lodge's published history does not mention this notable group of non-operatives is understandable: their membership subsequently became an embarrassment, for they were soldiers engaged in suppressing the religious dissidents of the south west. Years of persecution had driven some presbyterians into taking up extreme positions disowning the king, and attempts to suppress them had led to the two major rebellions of 1666 and 1679 being followed by prolonged guerilla warfare in which (as so frequently happens in such cases) troops frustrated by inability to identify and crush elusive enemies who hid within the peasant population were provoked into sporadic cruelty and atrocity. The previous year Dumfries burgh council had entertained Strachan, Livingstone (both of whom were regarded as guilty of ordering summary executions of dissidents) and other officers with wine and tobacco, to the disgust of a later local historian who commented 'here is a pretty batch of bloodstained Bacchanalians'.[72] The council's welcome to the officers does not necessarily indicate support for what these officers were doing. Entertaining notable visitors, especially those in the burgh on official business, was routine, and to have failed to welcome the king's officers could have been interpreted as a deliberate insult arising from lack of support for the regime. Whether the lodge's admission of three of the officers represents positive support for their work of repression cannot be known: a possible alternative interpretation might be that the lodge had come under suspicion as a secret organisation in an area in which sedition and conspiracy were being ruthlessly sought out and punished, and that the lodge initiated Lieutenant Livingstone as a way of proving that its rituals and other activities were harmless. But whatever the motives of the lodge, its timing was bad. Within a few months the 1688-9 revolution swept the Catholic James VII from the throne and led to the restoration of presbyterianism in Scotland. In subsequent local mythology— based on fact— the 1680s became the killing times, in which humble, godly men had been hunted down, tortured and murdered by the corrupt and bloodthirsty dragoons.

Not surprisingly, perhaps, after this unfortunate episode the lodge only admitted craft members for nearly twenty-five years—except that John Newall, a writer in Dumfries who was admitted as clerk in 1705 after the death of M'George, may have been initiated.[73] Moreover, even among existing members interest in the lodge was waning. Early enthusiasm led to six meetings in 1687, four in 1688. Thereafter a single annual meeting on St John's Day became normal, though this is not in itself a sign of unusual weakness: a number of lodges only met once a year (or only recorded meetings once a year, for it is always possible that some meetings were not minuted). Instructions to members to assemble quarterly to receive instruction were issued in 1688 and 1692, but if the extra meetings ever took place they were not recorded. Definite signs of problems in the lodge soon appear. In 1693-5, 1698-1700 and in 1714-16 inclusive not even St John's Day meetings figure in the minutes. The last of these gaps was certainly due to troubles within the lodge, for in December 1717 it was recorded that James Johnston, the last master of the lodge, had prevented meetings being held for several years.[74]

Just before this interruption, the lodge had begun again to admit non-craft members. In December 1712 Francis Maxwell of Tinwald, a local laird, was admitted to the two grades. A Dumfries innkeeper, Mr George Camick, followed in 1713, William Sutherland (land waiter and searcher of customs), Robert Beck and John Younger (writers), Alexander Agnew (glazier) and Alexander Frog (tidesman) in 1717. These last members were admitted 'considering their good qualification to Christianity', a rare indication of the religious orthodoxy of candidates being checked.[75]

The Lodge of Dumfries was dominated by craftsmen, masons and wrightmasons. But the early minutes show no sign whatever of it acting as an operative lodge in the sense of regulating the mason trade in the area—fining a member for working when he should have been attending the lodge is hardly evidence of an attempt to control the trade in general.[76] It therefore existed entirely for ritual and social purposes. In 1711 it was ordered that each member pay monthly twelve pennies to the warden to uphold St John's Day and other meetings.[77] Presumably the money was spent on drink and the annual banquet. At another meeting in 1711 one member certainly carried his enjoyment to excess. The minute book at this point is disfigured with great splashes of ink, and the indignant clerk has recorded that John Fleming, mason, drunk and swearing in presence of the fraternity, had grabbed the book, swearing that he would 'rype the book all in peices'. In doing so he upset the inkhorn, causing the blots which so offended the clerk's pride that he minuted the fact that they were not his fault.[78]

The early minutes of the lodge combine their lack of interest in trade regulation with an unusual number of hints at the activities of the lodge relating to its lore and ritual. When quarterly meetings were ordered in 1688 members were to attend 'there to be examined quhereby every man may be taught quhat is just'. When the act was renewed in 1692 it was so they could 'receave instructione of what already they have not receaved'.[79] This is irritatingly vague, but it does show that continued teaching of (and no doubt testing in) masonic lore was intended to take place not just for entered apprentices but for fellow crafts as well.

Though there is no evidence that quarterly meetings were actually held, the fact that the lodge possesses no fewer that four copies of the Old Charges, one of them including a catechism, dating from the late seventeenth and early eighteenth centuries does suggest a close interest in studying the traditional history of the craft: no other Scottish lodge has more than one copy. The minutes prove, moreover, that these documents were brought to meetings of the lodge. In November 1696 the clerk, William M'George, was instructed to give 'ther institutions in parchment' to the deacon, Robert Anderson younger, wright, to keep with the minute book until St John's Day, and on St John's Day in 1705 and 1706 a parchment belonging to the lodge was delivered to the warden for safekeeping, presumably after being used at the meeting.[80] This can be identified as the Dumfries No. 3 Manuscript, as the lodge's other copies of the Old Charges were all on paper.[81] In 1718 the minutes refer to the 'Constitutions of the said Lodge in parchmentt with two coppies therof',[82] and though this is the first reference to the paper versions one at least must have existed by 1704 if, as has been claimed, the Dumfries No. 1 Manuscript is in the handwriting of William M'George who died in or before that year.[83] Finally, when Francis Maxwell of Tinwald was admitted to the lodge in 1712 it was recorded that the lodge had 'been easie to him in respect of his quallity'.[84] This is unique as an indication that the elements of ritual humiliation, the boisterous horseplay, that were part of the initiation ceremonies of the Mason Word might be toned down out of respect to those from the upper ranks of society. It is likely that such tact was widespread. A gentleman might want to be admitted to the secrets of the craft, but nonetheless be unwilling to subject himself to humiliation by social inferiors—and, indeed, they might hesitate to inflict it on him except in a token form.

The Lodge of Kirkcudbright

The evidence that an early lodge existed in Kirkcudbright is a single late reference. In 1741 the lodge then existing in the burgh explained to the Grand Lodge that all documents proving its antiquity had been lost, but that its oldest members testified that it had been constituted upwards of fifty years before 'in a singular manner'. Grand Lodge accepted this, and granted the lodge precedency from before 1691.[85]

While this cannot be held to be conclusive (the Grand Lodge was no fool when it came to adjudicating on claims to antiquity) it could not disprove the frequent claims by lodges of Medieval origins (usually related to the building of local abbeys or cathedrals), any more than the lodges could prove them, but when it came to the delicate matter of granting precedency such extravagances were simply ignored. That Grand Lodge accepted Kirkcudbright's claim therefore suggests that the testimony of the lodge's oldest members revealed a consistent and convincing tradition, not just the assertion of a vague and pious belief. The strange phrase 'in a singular manner' is impressive but unhelpful, and the taking of the round number of fifty years as representing the approximate age of the lodge is worrying. It may be that the lodge itself claimed greater antiquity but that Grand Lodge would only accept that the evidence proved foundation at least fifty years previously. The name St Cuthbert Kilwinning adopted by 1741 may indicate belief that masons formerly connected with Kilwinning Lodge founded the lodge but (as with Dumfries Lodge) this probably reflects the popularity of the legend of Kilwinning as the mother lodge in the eighteenth century rather than historical fact.

The question of other forms of organisation of the mason craft in Kirkcudbright is almost as obscure. The burgh council had authorised the crafts to choose deacons in 1598, but the fact that it agreed in 1681 that incorporations should be formed as the crafts were disorganised and often produced poor quality goods indicates that little progress had been made by then.[86] John Fleming, wright, was a deacon in the burgh in 1697, and may well have been the same John Fleming who had been a deacon (craft unspecified) in 1684 and 1699.[87] Thus there must have been an incorporation including wrights, and it is likely in such a small burgh to have embraced all the building trades.

The unsatisfactory inconclusive conclusion is, therefore, that by the late seventeenth century Kirkcudbright probably had an incorporation including masons, and they probably had a lodge.

The Lodge of Hamilton

All, it seems, that has ever been said in print about the origins of the Lodge of Hamilton is that it had once had a minute book beginning in 1695 but that this had been lost.[88] This is one case, however, in which investigation has happily turned regret at carelessly lost early masonic records into delight, for the minute book was rediscovered some years ago (in Australia), and is now back in possession of the lodge; and the lodge also possesses other papers beginning in 1695.

The minutes begin on 27 December 1695, and open with a statement that the members of 'the Lodge of Hamilton having esta[blished ours]elves in a Incorporation' had obliged themselves to obey all the acts and ordinances of 'the masters of the Society' for the government and unity of the lodge. The names of the thirteen masters present were then listed. This minute seems at first sight to record the foundation of the lodge, but things are not as simple as this, for at the meeting the boxmaster of the lodge, James Hinschaw, presented his accounts for the preceding year.[89] Moreover, the oldest document in the lodge's possession is a bond dated 27 March 1695 whereby John Steill, son to John Steill, wright in Hamilton, promised to pay £10 to James Naismith, wright in Hamilton, with John King, wright, acting as cautioner for Steill.[90] James Naismith was named first in the December 1695 list of masters of the lodge, and both John Steill and John King were to be listed as entered apprentices in 1696.[91] Thus the bond very probably represents a payment of fees by Steill at his admission to the lodge: perhaps Naismith (who was elected boxmaster for 1695-6) had paid Steill's fees for him, or perhaps the fees were payable to him as he had been acting as master of the lodge.

Though the lodge was thus in existence before December 1695, its previous history was probably very short. Since the early 1680s the little town of Hamilton had been a hive of building activity as Anne, duchess of Hamilton in her own right, systematically rebuilt Hamilton Palace stage by stage to designs by Mr James Smith, the well known Edinburgh architect (and member of Mary's Chapel Lodge). Not only was the palace itself rebuilt, the burgh of Hamilton was moved to a new site from its old one near the palace so the latter could stand alone amidst its parks and gardens.[92] Many members of the lodge were involved in this work over the years, and some of the non-operatives it admitted were servants of the duchess. It may therefore plausibly be suggested that the lodge emerged from this great building project, as masons and other building workers settled in Hamilton to take up the opportunities for employment it offered, joining craftsmen already resident there. Pride in their craft would have been strengthened as the splendid new palace took shape, reviving interest in the legends and rituals of masonry, leading to the foundation of the lodge–or, more likely, to its evolution, as masons talking informally of the craft's lore and perhaps admitting men to the secrets of the Mason Word gradually coalesced into an institution with officials and fees. In an evolutionary process of this sort it is probable that no precise foundation date for the lodge would emerge even if records were copious. 27 December 1695 is, however, perhaps the point at which it may be said that the process has been completed, with the lodge deciding to keep formal minutes and declare itself an incorporation—not meaning a guild with a publicly recognised place in the social structure of the burgh, but simply a corporate body, an institution rather than a collection of individuals.

All the members of the lodge mentioned in the bond of March 1695 were wrights: as in Dumfries the trades of wright and mason were not rigidly separated. Nonetheless, it is notable that even in the context of a masonic lodge these men called themselves wrights rather than masons, indicating that though they might undertake mason work they were primarily wood workers. At least three of the thirteen masters listed in December 1695, however, could not claim to be even part time operative masons. John Naismith was a surgeon, John Baillie of Woodside and Arthur Naismith were clerks. Baillie of Woodside was also a small local landowner, and can be traced in 1712 being appointed a parish overseer of highways.[93] Arthur Naismith, a writer in Hamilton, was much employed by the duchess of Hamilton, being regarded at the palace as honest, faithful and intelligent. He was town clerk of the burgh of Hamilton (of which the duchess was superior) at the time of his death in 1697.[94] A third clerk, John Robertson, was probably a member in 1695 though as he was not a fellow craft his name was not recorded until December 1696, when the first list of entered apprentices appears. By 1700, when he was promoted to fellow craft, he was sheriff clerk of Lanarkshire (the duchess being sheriff principal), and by 1709 he was baillie depute of the regality of Hamilton.[95] In December 1698 the duchess's secretary, David Crawford, became an entered apprentice, being promoted to fellow craft (along with John Robertson) on 24 December 1700.[96] The son of an Ayrshire laird, Crawford was Duchess Anne's leading legal and business adviser and administrator. He combined his duties in Hamilton with a thriving legal business in Edinburgh, where he held the office of clerk to the admission of notaries, and he became a burgess of the Canongate. His twin careers brought him both prestige and wealth. His house in Hamilton was designed, like the palace, by Mr James Smith, and he became a laird through possession of the estate of Allanton, perhaps given to him by the duchess. Appointed a justice of the peace in 1716, he lived on until 1736. No wonder the lodge was happy to initiate so eminent a local worthy, and promote him to fellow craft, free of any payment.[97]

Just three days after Crawford became a master of the lodge, on St John's Day 1700, another lawyer was admitted to it as an entered apprentice: John Hamilton of Barncleuch, sheriff depute of Lanarkshire.[98] In 1704 the lodge turned to industry instead of the law for a recruit, admitting James Loudoun, 'manadger of the woollen manufactory' as an entered apprentice (free, as he had been 'beneficial' to the lodge). But the fact that he was referred to as Baillie Loudoun when promoted in the following year indicates that he too was active in local government, presumably being baillie of either the burgh or the regality of Hamilton.[99] William Cullen of Sauchs, admitted as an apprentice in 1705 (free, but he paid thirteen shillings and four pence on taking a mason mark and gave a dollar for the poor) also fits into this closely knit group, of lawyers and administrators in the lodge. In 1708 he was described as clerk of the regality of Hamilton, notary public, and a procurator before the sheriff court.[100] Another minor laird, John Miller of Watersaugh, was admitted (with his brother William) in 1708, and promoted to fellow craft in 1712 or 1713.[101] In 1710 the lodge recruited a member involved in national as well as local affairs, Sir James Hamilton of Rosehall, who was a justice of the peace and represented Lanarkshire in parliament in 1710-15 and 1735-50. His brother, Mr Archibald Hamilton, and James Hamilton of Dalyell (later a justice of the peace) also joined the lodge at the same time as entered apprentices.[102]

This impressive roll-call of local power and influence was further strengthened in the years that followed: John Cunison, town clerk of Hamilton, and Mr James Boyle, secretary to the earl of Selkirk (the son of Duchess Anne), were entered in 1715.[103] But the lodge also admitted more humble non-operatives, such as a maltman in Bothwell and Thomas Smith, miller in Old Milne, in 1698.[104] There were probably many other such non-operative members who were craftsmen or tenants but cannot be identified, as only their names are given in the records.

However, though the lodge from its inception included many non-operatives drawn from different levels of society, it was actively 'operative' in the sense of supervising the mason trade in Hamilton. Moreover, the records give the impression that such activities were not mere token gestures at asserting authority which in reality the lodge did not possess, as seems the case with some other lodges, but something fairly effective. A startling indication of the realism of the lodge was its attitude to cowans. Every other lodge that mentions them does so only in the context of ineffectually denouncing masons who worked with them (though Kilwinning grudgingly conceded in 1705 that a cowan might be employed if no mason was available). Hamilton Lodge, on the other hand, simply accepted cowans as one of the categories of men legitimately concerned in the building trade, if in a lowly position. This is shown by a scale of fees set down in 1696. Each master of the lodge was to pay it six shillings Scots annually. Entered apprentices were to pay twelve shillings if they worked in the town, and a different (doubtless lesser) sum if they worked outside it. Any mason not belonging to the lodge who worked for a month or more in a year in Hamilton (as a journeyman employed by a master of the lodge) was to pay the lodge eighteen shillings; and any cowan similarly employed was to pay two shillings and six pence.[105] The 1696-8 lodge accounts confirm that it was thus quite acceptable for Hamilton masons to employ cowans. The list of James Mack's journeymen is made up of six masons and four cowans; James Bryson's list has one mason and three cowans.[106]

When a code of statutes and acts for the lodge was drafted in 1701 this toleration of cowans was continued (though the scale of payments was different from that of 1696). It was stressed that no mason or 'workman cowan' from out of town was to be given work until after it had been offered to town masons, but that was the only discrimination against the cowans. In other ways too the 1701 statutes confirm the impression of a lodge run on unusually realistic and business-like lines, for they carefully defined a number of things generally not mentioned in lodge records—partly, no doubt, as this was a new lodge which felt the need to legislate rather than rely on lodge traditions. The warden was to be chosen annually on St John's Day, and was to summon all meetings and preside at them. In running the lodge he was to be assisted by a boxmaster and five other masters. Only they and the warden were to have votes in managing lodge affairs. This is the earliest known reference to the formal establishment of a lodge management committee. The lodge was to meet each quarter as well as on St John's Day. Entered apprentices on admission were to pay £10 and a pair of gloves to the warden, unless they were 'not Masons to their Imployment' whom it nonetheless pleased the lodge to admit. But such non-operatives, whether admitted free or after payment of fees, were not to be recruited unless they were men who had been 'beneficiall to the trade or may bring reputation to the Lodge'. Here for the first time a lodge defined in writing its attitude to the recruitment of non-operatives. Such members must be men who had helped the lodge or its members, or whose membership would enhance the status of the lodge (and, it was doubtless expected though not stated, had influence they could exercise in its favour). On promotion to fellow craft each apprentice was to pay £4 and give each fellow craft present a pair of gloves; but no apprentice was to be promoted who owed money to the lodge. Every entered apprentice was to register his mark, those who took marks without doing this being fined. Finally, after specifying annual payments due to the lodge from different categories of members and non-members, the statutes repeated one of the oldest and most basic of trade regulations: no mason was to take work over another's head, that is undertake work begun by another mason whose employer wanted to replace him. But even this regulation has a sensible exception: if the original mason lacked 'Cunning', the skill to finish the work adequately, another might perfect it.

Given the legal and administrative talent of the lodge's non-operative members it was hardly surprising that the statutes were clear and realistic. Moreover, the lodge had the advantage that, unlike most burgh lodges, it did not exist in parallel with an incorporation. Thus it was the only body claiming the right to regulate the mason trade, and did not have to go through the usual little farce of pretending to ignore the existence of a related incorporation while at the same time being careful to avoid action which might offend it.

David Crawford, the duchess' secretary, was by this time acting as lodge clerk, and he was on the committee which drafted the statutes. They were accepted unanimously by the lodge, and all the masters of the lodge signed the copy written out by Crawford, new masters adding their signatures in the years that followed. It was also agreed that the statutes should be read out to the masters every St John's Day. But only relevant sections of the statutes were to be read to the entered apprentices, and they were not to sign the statutes themselves but a separate sheet of paper, so they could not see the complete text. This is a rare indication that entered apprentices were excluded from some parts of lodge meetings. Obviously they must have been kept out when the secret rituals for admitting fellow crafts were performed, but here at Hamilton they were not even allowed to know the full contents of the statutes, though there was nothing of an esoteric nature in them.[107] Hamilton Lodge still possesses a Bible inscribed 'This Bible was gifted to the Masons of the Lodge of Hamilton By David Crawford, one of that Society. Anno 1701', and the date of his gift makes it tempting to link it with the statutes. Perhaps it was provided so that members could swear to the statutes on it.[108]

Though the lodge was relatively efficiently run the statutes were not adhered to in all respects. Quarterly meetings were sometimes held, but as elsewhere enforcing attendance proved difficult—in November 1702 few or no members appeared to pay dues to the lodge. Even the St John's Day meetings were sometimes poorly attended. In 1699 few met and, as the boxmaster had not got his accounts ready for auditing, he was penalised by being appointed boxmaster for the following year as well.[109] The 27 December meetings were nonetheless the highlight of the lodge's year, with the annual dinner or banquet. These meetings were sometimes held (like quarterly meetings) in the houses of members, on other occasions probably in inns or ale houses. Thus in 1705 and 1706-8 the dinner was held in John Kennedy's house. He does not appear to have been a member of the lodge, and the likelihood that this was a commercial establishment is increased by the fact that when a dinner on the occasion of the admission of Rosehall, his brother, and Dalyell on 2 January 1710 was held there it was referred to as being held at Mrs Kennedy's. In 1709 the St John's Day dinner was at the house of Cullen of Sauchs.[110] The lodge also considered acquiring its own premises, judging by a tantalising isolated reference in the 1712-13 accounts to the expenses of a meeting 'about building the Masons house': the six shillings then spent, like the small sums recorded for other meetings, doubtless provided the ale necessary to facilitate the conduct of business.[111]

Unlike some other lodges where most non-operatives only attended meetings once, when they were admitted, a considerable number of the Hamilton non-operatives appear to have taken a continuing interest in their lodge. Hamilton was also highly unusual in that if they were to become fully initiated fellow craft masters they had to be present at least twice. The almost universal practice of initiating non-operatives to both the masonic grades at a single meeting was not adopted, giving an impression that the lodge expected all those it recruited, operative or non-operative, to take initiation seriously. Ironically it was the new Lodge of Hamilton which resisted the sacrifice of masonic tradition to expediency that older lodges had made in their eagerness to oblige non-operatives.

The lodge minutes also record care being taken to determine the masonic status of operatives admitted to the lodge. In 1701 John Hamilton 'called Gray John' was accepted as an entered apprentice 'In respect he was formerly admitted a prentice of another Lodge' for £2 instead of the usual £10. Andrew Paton was entered free for the same reason in 1710, but the most interesting of these references is to John Nicolson in 1702. He was admitted free as he was formerly entered in another lodge, 'and having gone out with his Attendar He was called in againe and examined and found sufficiently qualified. Therfor they also received him ffellow of Craft', for which he paid £4. Two years later there is another mention of 'attenders': the non-operative James Loudoun choose two on the occasion of his entry to the lodge.[112] These were obviously the intenders of the First Schaw Statutes, attending and instructing candidates for initiation, but they are rarely mentioned in minutes.

Some of the founders of the Lodge of Hamilton may have been men with the Mason Word but not members of lodges. Others had probably been initiated in lodges elsewhere, and members were subsequently recruited from other lodges. It is impossible to know for certain how older lodges reacted to the emergence of a new lodge. They may have had no objection provided the new lodge did not threaten an existing one's authority, in the way that Canongate-Leith and Edinburgh Journeymen Masons had infringed the rights of Mary's Chapel. There being no known lodge recruiting members in the Hamilton area, the new lodge may not have been treading on anyone's toes. But as it lay within the Nether Ward of Lanarkshire it was within the jurisdiction allocated to Kilwinning Lodge in the Second Schaw Statutes, though the Kilwinning minutes contain no indication that that lodge sought to uphold this right. What is to be made, however, of the item in the Hamilton Lodge accounts in 1710 'Spent by the Master with Thomas Stevenson Boxmaster of the Ludge of Kilwinning', £2. 9s. 8d?[113] The 'Master' was presumably the warden (or perhaps masters is meant, a term sometimes reserved at Hamilton for the lodge management committee), and Stevenson can be traced as deacon of Kilwinning Lodge in 1704-5 and 1707, and as warden in 1711.[114] Was Stevenson just passing through Hamilton, or was he working there, and Hamilton Lodge thought it appropriate to wine and dine a leading member of a lodge which claimed to be the ancient lodge of Scotland? Or had the Kilwinning boxmaster come as representative of his lodge to claim authority over Hamilton Lodge and fees from its members as it lay within the Nether Ward? The latter seems quite likely, as lodge funds were spent entertaining him. If this was so, however, he was treated respectfully but then sent home empty handed, and not surprisingly Kilwinning Lodge did not record this failure to assert its traditional rights for posterity.

6 The stonemason supreme among the building crafts
This engraving is taken from a painting celebrating the work of the craftsmen of the Incorporation of Mary's Chapel, Edinburgh, in the rebuilding of Holyrood Palace in the 1660s and 1670s. The stonemason, representing the most prestigious of the crafts, is shown in the centre, flanked by the lesser trades of the incorporation. The craftsmen, from left to right, are sievewright (maker of sieves), slater, glassinwright (worker in glass) cooper (barrel maker), mason, wright (carpenter), bowmaker, painter, plumber, and upholsterer.
From R.S. Mylne, *The master masons to the crown of Scotland*, 1893.
Photo copyright: Bob and Yvonne Cooper

5
FIFE AND TAYSIDE

The Lodge of St Andrews

The Lodge of St Andrews is first mentioned in the Mary's Chapel minute of 27 November 1599 ordering that a general meeting be held in St Andrews on 13 January 1600 for settling and taking order with the affairs of the lodge there. All masters and others within the lodge's jurisdiction were to be summoned to attend.[1] It has been suggested earlier that this marks a stage in the formation of a St Andrews Lodge, William Schaw perhaps intending to complete its establishment at the meeting. Confirmation for such an interpretation may be provided by the notorial attestation subjoined to the First St Clair Charter in 1600 or 1601 on behalf of masons who could not write. In this Thomas Robertson is described as warden of the lodge of Dunfermline and St Andrews, and as accepting the charter himself and on behalf of his brethren of the mason craft within these lodges, and on behalf of the commissioners of these lodges. (three of whom were named for each lodge). Thus first there appears to be a joint St Andrews and Dunfermline lodge, then immediately thereafter the same document talks of two lodges, but with the same man as warden of both.[2]

These references may indicate that the First St Clair Charter appeared while Schaw was in the middle of reorganising the mason trade in Fife, part of his task consisting of dividing a single lodge in the shire into two, Dunfermline for the west and St Andrews for the east. Certainly by the time of the Second St Clair Charter in 1627-8 the two lodges were completely separate, three men (one being the warden, Thomas Wilson) attesting on behalf of St Andrews Lodge and two on behalf of Dunfermline Lodge.[3]

The Edinburgh minute and the St Clair Charters provide both the beginning and the end of the known history of St Andrews lodge in the seventeenth century. A lodge is known to have existed in the burgh in 1720, when it had thirty members,[4] but there is no evidence for (or against, for that matter) continuity between it and the earlier lodge. It is possible that the early lodge collapsed through the unsuitability of St Andrews as a location. William Schaw may have been attracted to it through its traditional status as the ecclesiastical capital of Scotland, with a great cathedral as a monument to the achievements of the mason craft. But the cathedral was falling into ruins, the burgh itself was small, isolated and decaying. Masons in eastern Fife must have found most of their employment in the thriving little burghs to the south and were perhaps reluctant to travel long distances to St Andrews Lodge—though it is true there is no sign of a rival lodge having emerged in the region to serve their needs.

The Lodge of Dunfermline

The Lodge of Dunfermline is first heard of as a party to the First and Second St Clair Charters, references which have been noted already in examining the origins of the Lodge of St Andrews.[5] There are no further references to the lodge until 27 December 1673, the date of an obligation signed by members whereby they undertook to attend the lodge each year. This document is now largely illegible, but it was evidently in similar terms to another obligation dated 27 December 1688. In this the subscribers, masons in the Lodge of Dunfermline, calling to mind 'the antient love familiaritie and correspondence that hes bein amongst our predecessors massons', resolved to continue this by meeting each St John's Day. Failure to do so was to be punished by a fine of £10, payable to the deacon or warden of the mason craft of Dunfermline. The members also undertook not to enter apprentices or pass fellow crafts without consent of these officials. Persons thus entered and passed became members of the lodge, and therefore were obliged to attend the lodge on St John's Day.[6]

The 1673 obligation has over fifty signatures on it, including those of at least three lairds: the signatures are partly illegible, but they appear to be those of James Mudie younger of Ardbickie, Henderson of Fordell, and James Carmichael, perhaps of Balmeadow. The later 1688 obligation musters over a hundred signatures, but there are no immediately identifiable non-operatives among them. In neither case, however, do these signatures represent attendance at a single St John's Day meeting, for many signatures were added by new members (or ones absent when the documents were first signed) for many years after the dates given on the documents.

The minutes of the lodge begin on 27 December 1698, and the long lists of members absent then recorded confirms the evidence of the 1673 obligation that the lodge was already admitting non-operative members in the later seventeenth century.[7] Fellow crafts absent include the earl of Kincardine and a number of local lairds: Sir William Preston of Valleyfield, James Carmichael of Bamblea, James Moultray of Rescobie, Robert Betson of Killerie, and the laird of Evelick. The most intriguing of these is the third earl of Kincardine, for he was the son of Alexander Bruce, second earl of Kincardine, the friend to whom Sir Robert Moray (Mary's Chapel Lodge) had, in the 1650s, explained the elaborate symbolism of his mason mark. It is very notable in the correspondence that though Moray went into great detail about his mason mark, he said nothing whatever about other aspects of freemasonry. Yet if he had been talking to an outsider who knew nothing of the lodges and rituals, it would surely have been necessary to preface his references to his mason mark with some explanation (though constrained by his oath of secrecy). That he does not do so raises the possibility that he did not need to, as the second earl was himself an initiate, and the discovery that his son the third earl belonged to Dunfermline Lodge increases the plausibility of this suggestion.

If the names of the non-operative absentees in the 1698 lists are interesting, those of the operative absentees are astonishing, and serve to distinguish Dunfermline in patterns of membership from all other early lodges about which relevant information survives. Many of the masons lived outside Dunfermline in western Fife (North Queensferry, Inverkeithing, Largo, Milton of Balgonie, Tulliallan, Burntisland), Kinross-shire (Kinross), Clackmannanshire (Alloa) and eastern Stirlingshire (Airth). But there were also members from much further away, two from Edinburgh and one each from St Andrews, Dundee, Perth and Ayr. Thus not only did the lodge recruit from a whole region around Dunfermline, it had members from widely scattered places in southern and central Scotland, a much greater geographical spread than Kilwinning Lodge, for all its pretensions. The most plausible explanation for this unique pattern is found by linking it to information contained in the obligations signed by lodge members. These show that Dunfermline Lodge members could initiate men into the craft wherever they liked, provided they had permission of the deacon and warden and registered those initiated as members of the lodge. This was a very different attitude from that displayed by other lodges, which sought to ban such 'out-entries', as at Edinburgh, or at least limit them, as at Dumfries (where no initiations were to take place within twelve miles of the lodge and the lodge showed no interest in recruiting as members those initiated outside this radius). Dunfermline masons working far from home seem to have recruited new members for their lodge, registering their names on returning home. But it may well be that many of the distant members never attended lodge meetings in Dunfermline, the inclusion of their names on lists of absentees being a formality as there was no real expectation that they would ever attend. The lodge benefited from their nominal membership by pocketing their entrance fees and obtaining an enhanced sense of its own importance by greatly increasing its nominal membership.

The 1688 obligation mentions the warden and the deacon of the lodge, and the 1698 minutes record the elections to these two offices. The fact that the lodge elected the deacon suggests lack of an incorporation containing masons in Dunfermline. But this does not seem to have been the case. A late sixteenth-century list of the crafts of the burgh does not include masons (though they could have been comprehended in the wrights), but there is mention of the deacon of the masons among the other craft deacons in 1680,[8] and in 1719 a new seal of cause was granted to the Incorporation of Masons, as their ancient gift of privileges was almost illegible through its antiquity.[9] Thus there was an incorporation in Dunfermline, separate from the lodge. But as elsewhere the two institutions were doubtless very closely linked, and the lodge's 'election' of the deacon may have been a formality, an acceptance of the incorporation deacon's right, as in Edinburgh, to preside in the lodge. On the other hand it is possible that here the relations of the two institutions was the other way round. The lodge minutes give leets from which the deacon was elected, and it may be that this really was where the deacon was chosen, he subsequently being accepted by the incorporation—which would, after all, be largely composed of members of the lodge.

The Dunfermline minutes are, as elsewhere, mainly concerned with admissions and promotions, but they also record miscellaneous information about its organisation and activities. A committee was often appointed to audit the annual accounts, five masters undertaking this in 1698, and membership of this committee probably reflected the tendency for real control of lodges to fall into the hands of a small group of masters as a management committee evolved.[10] Enforcing attendance at lodge meetings was a universal problem, and as already indicated the lodge can hardly have really expected to enforce attendance or payment of fines from its far-flung members. Indeed according to the 1688 obligation those who admitted new members outwith the lodge were responsible for payment of their entrance fees, which were presumably collected on the spot when the initiation took place from members who might never come to Dunfermline. Nonetheless, on 18 January 1699 the clerk was ordered to pursue all absentees 'the gentilmen excepted'. 'The haill gentrie' and other members who were not 'actual! workmen' were expected instead of attending to pay the lodge £3 a year.[11]

Like Mary's Chapel, Aitchison's Haven and Kilwinning, the Lodge of Dunfermline experienced the problem of men failing to seek promotion, so it was ordered in 1700 that entered apprentices should become fellow crafts after three years, those failing to do so being banned from undertaking any work worth over ten merks.[12] The lodge initiated non-operatives to the two masonic grades on a single occasion, as most lodges did. Thus James Richard, messenger in Dunfermline, was entered and passed in 1700 free on undertaking to serve the lodge as messenger without pay.[13] The early minutes contain only one item that might relate to the lodge's esoteric activities. In 1701, at a meeting in Alloa (the lodge, or at least its accounts committee, sometimes met outside Dunfermline, in the homes of officials), James Somerville, one of the leading members of the lodge, gave it 'ane brass squar for the use of the ludge'.[14] Presumably its 'use' was a symbolic one in the lodge's rituals.

As was common outside the largest burghs, many members of Dunfermline Lodge had probably not served a full seven year apprenticeship, and did not work exclusively as masons. When John Thomson younger, mason in Kinross, took an apprentice in 1683 his service was only to be three years, and Thomson undertook to teach him the wright as well as the mason trade. John Lyall became apprentice on 15 February 1712 to James Moreis, mason in Milnathort, for three years, plus one year additional service for meat and fee. Lyall's is one of the rare indentures in which the master obliged himself to enter an apprentice in a lodge, in this case the Lodge of Dunfermline.[15] Moreis was in fact warden of the lodge at the time, and Lyall was duly entered in the lodge on 18 November 1714.[16]

Interest in the burgh in the developments which were taking place in freemasonry in England is indicated by the granting of burgess-ship to Dr John Desaguliers on 26 August 1720.[17] He was not present, for his burgess ticket was ordered to be sent to Captain Halket in London. As Sir Peter Halket of Pitfirrane was provost of Dunfermline at the time it looks as if some Halket family connection with Desaguliers was responsible for this honouring of one of the leading figures in the early development of the Grand Lodge of England.

The Lodge of Dundee

The fact that the master masons of the burgh of Dundee had been ordered to come to the convention planned at St Andrews in January 1600 may indicate that William Schaw had then been seeking to organise them into a lodge,[18] but the first reference to the lodge is in 1627-8, when the names of five of its members appear on the Second St Clair Charter. The Dundee masons evidently had no recognised guild in the burgh, though they made several attempts to obtain one. By a grant under the privy seal dated 6 March 1592 James VI gave liberty, freedom and power to all masons, wrights, slaters and other craftsmen in Dundee 'that wirkis be square reule; lyne; or compass under the airt of geometrie' to elect annually a deacon and hold courts and assemblies as freely as any other craft, and as the crafts did in Edinburgh. But there is no evidence of any attempt by Dundee trades united by the practice of geometry to implement this unusual royal grant. Indeed the fact that it existed was soon forgotten, for in 1629 the masons and wrights of Dundee petitioned Charles I for the right to elect a deacon and thus form an incorporation, making no reference to the 1592 grant. The representative of the masons and wrights in the 1629 approach was John Mylne, burgess of Dundee and soon (1631) to be appointed king's master mason. The fact that the crafts sought a grant from the king suggests that their aspirations had met opposition locally, and this is confirmed by the outcome of the affair. The privy council referred it to the convention of royal burghs, which ruled against the petitioners. They had tried to argue that their crafts had the right to choose deacons in all royal burghs, but the convention supported the magistrates and council of Dundee. Only they had power to grant the right of appointing deacons. Moreover, such a grant to the masons and wrights of Dundee 'micht not onlie induce sum alteratioun in thair quyet state of government' but might prove prejudicial to the burgh. The crafts once organised might make 'combinatiounes and quiett pactiounes for thair awin proffeit' as they were mainly men of mean substance. Experience elsewhere showed that giving the building crafts liberties was neither convenient nor expedient. Perhaps the same sort of opposition by the burghs had thwarted James VI's grant a generation before.[19]

The traditional bad reputation of the building crafts (for attempting to push up wages unreasonably, and through the relative poverty of their members) was thus used to prevent an incorporation emerging. The wrights nonetheless maintained an unofficial guild or society, the earliest legible entry in their book being dated 1628, and the slaters were electing a deacon by 1654.[20] But nothing further is heard of a lodge or any other organisation of masons in Dundee until 1659. In that year six masons petitioned the burgh council complaining that they were being ruined through stranger masons working in the burgh, there being nothing to prevent this, and requesting that as in other well governed burghs some settled order be established among them and encouragement given to them. This time the burgh authorities looked more favourably on the masons—perhaps because their ambitions had been scaled down since the 1629 debacle. When they could afford it, the Dundee masons were to become burgesses—something that had evidently not been permitted previously.[21] Hours of work and pay for masons were fixed by the council, and if there were too few masons in the burgh to meet its needs the council was to have power to compel the masons to admit extra members 'to their company'—and indeed power to impose any regulations on the trade that it thought fit. The company or society was to have the right to do all things conducing to its good, controlling entry to the trade; and no cowan was to be employed in the burgh except for building dry stone dykes.[22]

So far the situation is clear. The masons were to have a society or company, a guild. In one sense it was an incorporation, a corporate body, but it was not to have that title or equality of status with the major craft incorporations which had a recognised place in the government of the burgh. Instead, this new society was to be directly dependent on the burgh council, subject to its orders. Such bodies, craft guilds with official recognition but limited in their powers and privileges, can be found emerging in many burghs in which the long established incorporations were unwilling to accept lesser trades as their equals.

The 'lockit book' (minute book) of the mason trade of Dundee opens with the heading 'Acts and Statutes'. Under this comes a brief invocation or prayer, followed by a minute dated 11 March 1659. The date of invocation and minute may be taken to be the same, a point which becomes of some importance when it is realised that the invocation was taken from the opening of a copy of the Old Charges. This is the earliest firmly dated direct evidence that proves that the text of the Old Charges was known in Scotland. Further, among the miscellaneous records of the Society of Masons of Dundee is a complete text of the Old Charges.[23] The 11 March minute calls the organisation 'the Lodge of Dwndie', naming as its masters and freemen the same six masons who had petitioned the burgh council for permission to organise. They had, it was related, procured an act from the council giving them privileges, since in the past they had sustained great injury through not having a 'community'. The statutes which follow reveal that this organisation, licensed by the burgh council and subject to its control, was operating as a lodge as well as a society. Thus it was ordered that each 'entered' apprentice serving a master mason in the burgh was to pay forty shillings before he 'enter' to work for him. This was payment of what was usually called booking money, at the start of a trade apprenticeship, and not becoming 'entered apprentice' in the sense of being initiated to a lodge. The regulations make this clear by proceeding to state that 'at his entred prenticeship' the apprentice was to pay £8, a pair of double gloves to every master of the lodge, a pair of single gloves to every entered apprentice, and other dues. Thus the second type of entering was joining the lodge. Next, each fellow craft on promotion was to pay £10 Scots and other dues. Finally no man serving a free master (that is, no fellow craft employed as a journeyman) was to become a freeman until he had paid £20 'with the wine'.

What has happened in Dundee is that the two parallel hierarchies normally ascended by burgh masons, of lodge and incorporation (as described for the Lodge of Mary's Chapel and the Incorporation of Mary's Chapel) have here been fused into a single hierarchy within a single institution. Successively the Dundee society or lodge admitted a mason as booked apprentice; entered apprentice; fellow craft master; and finally, freeman master.

The statutes of March 1659 also detailed fees to be paid by stranger masons and journeymen, and set down other regulations relating to admission to the trade and taking mason marks. Four general meetings were to be held each year. The officials of the organisation mentioned in these minutes were the deacon, the clerk and the officer.[24] But another version of the proceedings on 11 March 1659 was entered in a separate book (which has become known, misleadingly, as the register of journeymen masons). This lacks the invocation, but in introducing the statutes gives two of the six masons who had got the burgh's approval for the organisation official positions. John West was referred to as master of the lodge, Andrew West as its warden.[25]

A first reaction to this keeping of two sets of records is that a distinction was being attempted between the proceedings of lodge and society, but this does not stand up to examination, for both refer to the institution as a lodge and the later entries in the two books overlap bewilderingly. Why two books, both essentially minute books, were kept remains a mystery. However, the fact that two of the masons involved in the events of March 1659 already held offices in the lodge makes it possible to construct a plausible interpretation of what was going on. A lodge had already existed in the years before 1659, probably identical with that mentioned in the Second St Clair Charter. But, in the absence of any organisation with rights granted by the burgh authorities, the lodge was ineffectual in protecting the economic interests of its members. The 1629 attempt to get an incorporation had failed, but at last in 1659 a masons' society had been recognised. The campaign to get recognition for the society had probably, to all intents and purposes, been undertaken by the lodge. But this was not made public, for lodges were secret organisations. The lodge officials and other members had petitioned the burgh council as individual masons. So what happened in 1659 was not so much that a completely new society was founded as that a deacon and privileges granted by the council were grafted onto an existing lodge, without the council being aware of this.

The lodge/society is next recorded as meeting on 27 December 1659. The lockit book records that the masters, having met together and desiring the blessing of God, had decided that a deacon should be chosen. But the name lodge is no longer used: now and in the succeeding decades the references are to the master and freemen masons of Dundee, or the mason craft, or even to the Incorporation of Masons.[26] The first deacon was elected at this December 1659 meeting—John West, previously described as master of the lodge—but there is no mention of a warden. Indeed the term warden disappears (like that of lodge) entirely until the early eighteenth century. It is not the case that after initial confusion lodge and society have separated, nor that lodge activities have lapsed; what had happened is simply that they are not referred to explicitly in the minutes. The entries relating to admissions contain many references to entered apprentices, and sometimes at least seem to use the term in the lodge sense of an apprentice initiated to some of the secrets of the Mason Word.[27] But the terminology is so varied that this is not conclusive, and there are no references to men becoming fellow crafts. When, however, an act of 1677 refers to the exorbitant price of the gloves that masons have to give 'at their entrie and fallowshipe' it seems certain that this refers to initiations.[28]

Only one non-operative can be traced in the mason lodge/society of Dundee in the later seventeenth century. Patrick Kyd of Craigie was admitted a free master in December 1669 and was deacon in 1677.[29] While it is possible that he was merely admitted to the public 'society' side of the organisation it seems much more likely that he was initiated. This must surely be the case in the opening years of the eighteenth century when a minor flood of non-operatives appears, reflecting the fast-growing knowledge of and interest in masonic lodges. In 1705 Mr James Dundas, merchant, was admitted to the society along with a clock and watch maker. In December 1706 Dundas was elected deacon and another merchant and a writer were admitted, and four more merchants joined the following May. In December 1707 Dundas was again elected deacon, and he chose a warden and two boxmasters.[30] Thus the existence of a warden was admitted in the records for the first time since 1659.

This burst of non-operative activity was not sustained, however, in the years that followed, perhaps because the dual nature of the lodge/society, in one aspect an independent organisation, in the other subordinate to the burgh council, made it difficult to adapt to such radical changes in membership. It may also be the case that at Dundee as elsewhere admission of non-operatives was for a time accepted as flattering and profitable for the lodge, but soon led to tension and resentment as the operative masons felt that the new members wanted to take over and change the organisation, resulting in determination not to admit any more non-operatives.

The Lodge/Society of Dundee was a strange hybrid. Having lodge and incorporation existing separately in burghs raised problems both at the time and for historians, as their functions overlapped confusingly. But joining the two into one as at Dundee was equally awkward, creating a body claiming independence in some respects but accepting subordination to higher authority in others. Yet if there are problems in trying to understand what was happening in Dundee, they pale into insignificance when attention is turned to Stirling.

6
CENTRAL

The Lodge of Stirling

The recorded history of the Lodge of Stirling begins by indicating that it was a lodge of major importance, but then there follows over a century of obscurity and confusion. The Second Schaw Statutes of 28 December 1599 described it as the third lodge of Scotland, though it is not clear whether this indicates acceptance of some existing claim of Stirling masons, or was a new status awarded them by Schaw intended to give them jurisdiction over other lodges in central Scotland? Possibly Stirling, like Kilwinning, was not happy with the status assigned to it, for it was not a party to the First St Clair Charter of 1600-1.

Two Stirling men signed the Second St Clair Charter in 1627-8, and a third signed with the aid of a notary as he could not write. This was John Service, who was described as a master of the crafts in Stirling. This is an unusual description, and in view of the problems of interpreting the situation in Stirling in the 1630s it is worth stressing that the three Stirling men were all masons. Service can be traced working at Edinburgh, Dumbarton and Stirling Castles and at Linlithgow Palace. In 1616 he was the warden of a masons' lodge at Edinburgh Castle, being in charge of the other masons and responsible for testing the quality of their work—this being a lodge in the Medieval sense of a shelter or building for masons to work and perhaps sleep in. He provided a sun dial for the town clerk of Stirling's house in 1635, and in 1643-4 prepared the first designs for a statue of John Cowane which was made by the younger John Mylne. He died in 1645.[1] James Rhynd worked at Stirling Castle in the 1620s, and in the years following 1637 built Cowane's Hospital to the designs of the younger John Mylne.[2] John Thomson can also be traced working at Stirling Castle and he died in 1643.[3]

As mason burgesses of Stirling the three men were all evidently members of the Omnigatherum (Omnium Gatherum; Omnigadrum). This marvellously descriptive name was used in Stirling to describe a loose organisation of miscellaneous trades which were not included in any of the established craft incorporations. Its early history is obscure. In the 1590s it was conceded that it should have four members on the town council; but this was soon reduced to two, and by 1614 the omnigatherums were prohibited from meeting. But the organisation survived with a recognised corporate existence, though without the full status of an incorporation. It was thus similar in some respects to the Society of Masons which was to emerge in Dundee, but its character was very different in that it was a catch-all for trades of low status which had not found a place in any other organisation, dominated by the litsters (dyers) and the building trades. From 1643 there are a number of references to donations being made for the stipends of ministers by the mechanics on the one hand and the rest of the omnigatherum on the other, indicating that the orgsanisation was dividing into two parts.[4] By 1660 the mechanics and the omnigatherum had separate seats in the parish church, and a petition relating to the seating of about the same date was presented by a wright, a cooper, a litster, a mason and a slater in name of the rest of the mechanics—who thus seem to have included all the more important trades in the omnigatherum.[5]

Fitting a number of references which occur in the records of the mechanics in the late 1630s into the context of these developments is not, however, easy— especially as the manuscripts concerned are damaged and partly illegible. On 27 April 1637 Sir Anthony Alexander as general warden held a court in Stirling Castle, and the 'luge' of Stirling was mentioned,[6] and it was probably on this occasion that a copy of Alexander's Falkland Statutes of October 1636 was acquired by the mechanics.[7] On 15 May 1637 another court was held in the castle, this time by Alexander Cunningham, deacon, and John Service, 'wardane of the companye of Stirling'. In the same month a mason was recorded being admitted to the lodge and company, and a meeting was held in the presence of Service as warden of the lodge and company of Stirling. A few minutes of meetings in the months that followed record several cowans undertaking not to do the work of masons, by abstaining from the use of lime and mortar.[8] Then on 5 November, in presence of Cunningham (now identified as a wright) as deacon and Service as warden of the lodge and company, the Falkland Statutes were formally accepted.[9]

On 7 March 1638 all this activity reached a climax with a court held by Henry Alexander, who had succeeded his brother as general warden. He nominated Cunningham, wright, as deacon and Service, mason, as warden 'to us within the ludge and company of Stirling'. A procurator fiscal, an officer and a dempster 'within the said ludge', and two clerks were also appointed.[10] An isolated minute of 1642 records that the two dominant figures in the organisation had by then swapped offices: Service was deacon and Cunningham was warden.[11]

What was happening? What was the nature of the organisation? At first sight things look fairly simple: Sir Anthony and Henry Alexander were attempting in Stirling, as at Aitchison's Haven, to adapt an existing masonic lodge into one of the companies of building crafts envisaged in the Falkland Statutes, and they had some success in that the lodge had agreed to call itself the lodge and company. But if this was the case, it seems that the lodge in Stirling was a peculiar one, for its deacon (and later warden) Alexander Cunningham was a wright, making this by far the earliest record of the presence of a wright in a masonic lodge. Moreover the deacons who appear in burgh lodges were almost invariably deacons of the relevant incorporation or guild. Was Cunningham deacon of the omnigatherum, or (if it had already differentiated itself sufficiently to have its own deacon) of the mechanics? The fact that John Service had been described as a master of the crafts in the Second St Clair Charter may suggest that he had been a leader of the mechanics (or of the whole omnigatherum) in the late 1620s, the title deacon not yet having been adopted, so it may be that the term 'mechanics' was interchangeable with 'lodge and company'. On the other hand though no litsters are mentioned in the scanty records of the 'lodge and company' of 1637-42, they were evidently included in the mechanics. It is not impossible that the word 'lodge' is used in Stirling to describe a trade organisation which lacked the esoteric side to its activities normally associated with the seventeenth century lodges. The few records that survive never mention entered apprentices or fellow crafts. But if this was the case then the Lodge of Stirling, recognised as third lodge of Scotland by William Schaw, had evolved in ways unknown elsewhere.

There are no further references in the seventeenth century to a Stirling Lodge, but that one did continue to exist in some form is indicated by the fact that the lodge in Stirling in the eighteenth century possessed a copy of the Old Charges dating from the middle of the previous century. This copy is unique in having appended to it the texts of two certificates or testimonials which were supposed to be given to masons. In one the signatories were intended to testify that a mason had been trained in Stirling, had always behaved honestly, and had always finished the work he had begun: there was therefore no impediment to allowing him to work as a master mason. In the other satisfied employers were supposed to testify that the mason concerned had always completed satisfactorily whatever houses, castles, abbeys and other buildings he had undertaken and thus was fit to work as a master mason.[12] Apart from the deliberate anacronism of mentioning abbeys to recall the great achievements of masons in previous centuries, the certificates could have served a practical purpose as 'references' for masons to show to potential employers, but there is no evidence of their actually being used.

When in 1671 the Society of Mechanics obtained additional powers from the burgh, masons were not involved.[13] Their abstention from these negotiations with the council may be a sign that they were unhappy with the limited concessions the council was prepared to make. That they were not alone in being discontented was shown in 1674. In April John Morison younger, cooper, deacon of the trades 'incorporat under the name of mechanicks' met with others to consider the great damage they suffered through lack of the liberties and privileges enjoyed by other trades. They therefore resolved to seek a remedy for this in the same way as the Dundee masons had in 1629, by petitioning the king for a gift of privileges. Morison and John Buchanan, mason, were chosen to undertake this task.[14]

The enterprise collapsed, however, as soon as the burgh council found out what was going on. In August it passed a furious denunciation of the masons, wrights and other mechanics who, factiously led by John Buchanan, had without the council's knowledge sought power to elect a deacon who would have a seat on the council and control the admission of men to the trades. This, it was stated, would prejudice all who had houses to build or repair: the old reputation of the building trades as being unusually prone to extortion from customers if given a chance was thus revived. Buchanan, as chief contriver and promoter of the scheme was called before the council and told to abandon it. He boldly—or arrogantly and insolently according to the council—refused, saying he would do all he could to advance his plans. For this he was deprived of his rights as a freeman burgess of the burgh.[15]

In spite of Buchanan's defiance nothing more was heard of the plan for promoting the mechanics to equality with the seven main incorporations of the burgh. In 1687 some additional privileges were granted to the masons on the same lines as those granted to the other mechanics in 1671,[16] but in general the council was determined to keep the mechanics in their place. In 1705 they were refused permission to erect their own loft in the church, and in 1708 it was confirmed that they did not share the privileges of the seven incorporated trades.[17] Grants in 1726 and 1729 finally gave full official recognition to the mechanics, but their rights were still limited, they like several other groups (the omnigatherum, maltmen and barbers) being excluded from the seven incorporations, being rather condescendingly known instead as Tolerated Communities.[18]

Whether the Lodge of Stirling existed continuously throughout the mid and later seventeenth century is uncertain. It has often been stated that the lodge which still exists in Stirling was founded, or refounded, in 1708; or alternatively that it first admitted 'speculative' members in that year.[19] These are misinterpretations of the the only scrap of evidence that remains. In 1738 a number of masons who had seceded 'from an old Lodge kept at Stirling' approached the new Grand Lodge of Scotland and desired that they be erected into a new lodge. Grand Lodge's verdict was that it was contrary to its constitutions and to those of masonry in general that any masons should separate from their original lodge, but it ordered its secretary to write for a list of the Stirling brethren who had seceded, and of any who had joined them from other lodges.[20]

It appears to be this list that was entered in the records of Grand Lodge as containing the names of Stirling masons who owed no dues to it as they had been admitted to the craft before Grand Lodge had been founded. The dates on which these men had entered their lodge are given, ranging from 1708 to 1734. Thus 1708 represents no significant development in the Lodge of Stirling, but is merely the earliest time at which someone had been admitted to it who was both still alive in 1738 or 1739 and had joined a group who had seceded from it! Nonetheless, in the absence of other evidence this is in itself important, demonstrating that the lodge was active in 1708. Further the fact that the man admitted to it in 1708 was John Gilfillan, cordiner (shoemaker), and that a soldier in Stirling Castle was admitted in 1714, shows that the lodge was already admitting non-operatives, though ones of fairly humble status.[21]

The Lodge of Scone (Perth)

The master masons of Perth were summoned to the meeting held at St Andrews on 13 January 1600,[22] but if this indicates (as has been suggested in the case of the Dundee masons) that William Schaw had plans to organise them as a lodge, there is no evidence as to whether or not he was successful. But by the middle of the century Perth not only had a thriving lodge but one which had the confidence to make grandiose claims as to its own importance. These were set out in the contract or agreement of the masters freemen and fellow crafts masons resident in the burgh of Perth, dated 24 December 1658.[23]

They and their predecessors as masons had had, since the building of the temple of temples (Solomon's Temple), 'ane uniforme communitie and unione throughout the whole world'. From this temple 'proceided one in Kilwinning in this our nation of Scotland, and from that of Kilwinning many moe within this kingdome Off which thir procieded the Abbacie and Lodge of Scone buill[t] of men of Art and Architectorie wher they placed that Lodge as the second Lodge within this nation which is now past memorie of many generationes'. This lodge had been upheld by the kings of the Scots at Scone, at the old city of Bertha, and now at Perth, for about 465 years in all.

This opening section of the Perth agreement of 1658 contains three notable firsts. It contains the first explicit reference in Scotland to the myth of Solomon's Temple as the source for the later skills and achievements of the craft. There is also here the first exposition of Kilwinning Lodge's claim to be the source of all Scottish masonry, and of the claim that the next lodge to be founded was Scone, which was thus the second lodge of Scotland. The willingness of the Perth masons to accept the pretensions of Kilwinning indicates that the latter's mythology was already well established and had spread widely, for clearly the Perth men felt deriving from Kilwinning conferred honour on them. Finally, this first section of the 1658 agreement calls the Perth Lodge that of Scone. The siting (in name alone or in reality) of a number of early Scottish lodges reveals a tendency to favour the sites of great medieval ecclesiastical buildings, especially monasteries. Such buildings were regarded as the greatest achievements of the mason craft, and there was present an implicit claim of the descent of the lodge from the masons who had built these remarkable structures. Now this is spelt out: the Lodge of Scone had originated with the building of the Abbey of Scone.

The sections of the agreement which follow also make important claims relating to the lodge's past. The members of the lodge had always maintained their liberties. Their names had nearly all been lost, but it was known that there had come from the north country a mason called John Mylne, who became master of the lodge and king's master mason, and he was succeeded by his son John, king's master mason under James VI. In all, Mylne's had for several generations been both masons to the king and masters of the Lodge of Scone, the last of them dying in 1657.

The Mylne family had indeed produced prominent masons for generations, but there is as much mythology as fact in this account of them. Of the three John Mylnes mentioned, the first was in fact Thomas Mylne, and he was not the king's master mason. Neither was his son John (died 1621). The son of this John did become king's master mason and did die in 1657, so here at last the Perth agreement reaches solid ground. It may be accepted that he had been master of the lodge, but in view of the document's taste for invention it cannot be held to constitute firm evidence that his father and grandfather had also presided in the lodge. But the Mylne legend was now established, and was soon to reach its apogee. The inscription commemorating the John Mylne who died in 1667 (son of the former master of the Lodge of Scone) claimed him as

> ... by descent from Father to Son
> Sixth Master Mason to a Royal Race
> Of seven successive Kings...[24]

The fact that the John Mylne who died in 1621 had not been the king's master mason is important because it helps in assessing the next startling claim contained in Scone's 1658 agreement. This is that King James VI, at his own request to Mylne (who was both his master mason and the master of the lodge), had been made freeman mason and fellow craft of the Lodge of Scone, thus making it '(iff weell ordered)' the most famous lodge in the kingdom. Kilwinning might be recognised as first lodge, but Scone could claim precedence in this respect. A first reaction, influenced by the absurdities of later masonic historians in claiming that practically every king had been a mason, is to dismiss Scone's claim out of hand. But in view of James' well known intellectual curiosity, and the fact that he was the first king of Scots to condescend to be made a burgess—and that in Perth (1601)[25]—indicates that the idea of his being intrigued by the idea of a craft organisation which hinted that it possessed esoteric knowledge is not totally unthinkable. Even if his master mason was not master of the lodge, his master of works in earlier years, William Schaw, was the man who had been responsible for the sudden transformation of the craft around 1600, and Schaw had linked the craft to the art of memory, a subject in which James is known to have taken an interest. Nonetheless, the fact that the assertion that James VI entered the lodge occurs in a passage creating the fabulous history of the Mylnes, quite apart from other considerations, makes the story of James VI's initiation implausible.

The first statement in the 1658 agreement that may be accepted as factually accurate is that the John Mylne who died in 1657 had been master of the lodge, for the agreement was apparently drawn up as part of a reorganisation of the lodge following his death. It may well be that his father had also been master, for his greatest achievement as a mason was the building of the eleven arch bridge over the Tay at Perth. Completed in 1617, it was swept away by the river in 1621, the year of his death. There may, indeed, be a connection between the work of the Mylnes in Perth and the earliest mention of the Mason Word. This occurs in a long and tedious poem written in about 1630 by a Perth man, Henry Adamson. One theme of the work was the destruction of the bridge over the Tay at Perth, and Adamson invoked the brethren of the rosy cross (the Rosicrucians), the Mason Word and the Second Sight, all connected with the ability to see the invisible, to support his assertion that the bridge would be rebuilt: it was 'seen' rebuilt with King Charles I's name on it, for 'By skilfull art this cleerlie we behold'. Later Adamson reverted to the theme, and taking up the conceit which saw the work of the mason as imitating God's building of the universe, referred to the bridge's 'heaven-like arches' and continued

> Even so the arches of this bridge proclaime
> And shew the building of the starrie frame;
> But now all lost, needs Archimedes' skill,—
> Oh! if it were supplied by Master Mylne!

Thus the demolished work of old John Mylne should be restored by his son. So far it might be merely that, like any Perth citizen, Adamson had a strong interest in the rebuilding of the bridge, but there is another piece of evidence that may link him more directly to the Mylnes. The epitaph of John Mylne the bridge builder is in rhyming couplets that closely resemble Adamson's style and thus may have been composed by him, ending

> Seven foot of ground clay floor clay wall
> Serve both for chamber now and Hall
> To Master Mill whose squirbuily braine
> Could ten Escurialls well containe
> Whill he breath'd lyfe, yet in his Sonne
> And Sonn's Sone he lives two for one
> Who to advance Mill's Art and Fame
> Make Stocks and Stones speak out his Name.[26]

If Adamson heard of the mysterious Mason Word locally, then it was probably through masons of the Lodge of Scone (assuming it existed $c.1630$), and may well have been from the lodge's most distinguished members, the Mylnes, with whom he was probably acquainted.

The master of the lodge having died in 1657, Thomas Craich, warden, and six mason freemen and fellow crafts met on 24 December 1658 to deliberate on the future of the lodge.[27] As the lodge could not stand without a master, James Roch was elected master of the lodge for life, Andrew Norie warden for life— or as the masters found convenient. In appointing officials for life the lodge was almost unique, though in Aberdeen wardens were supposed to be permanent officials. Scone Lodge seems, up to this point, to have been dominated by the Mylnes, who had acted as masters for life, thus establishing a tradition varying from the annual elections held in most lodges.

Having elected officials, the members, all residents of Perth, bound themselves to abide by the acts made by their predecessors, some of which were then narrated. Members were not to go to any other lodge or make a lodge among themselves, as their lodge was the 'principall within the shyre'. Any member who did join another lodge would be heavily fined and made to renounce it before being readmitted to the Lodge of Scone. All fellow crafts passed in the lodge were to pay £16 plus dues, present gloves to the masters, and pay £3 at their first coming to the lodge. Entered apprentices were to pay twenty merks plus dues, and forty shillings at their first coming to the lodge. After a number of acts regulating the working relations of masons, the agreement ends with the signatories undertaking to uphold the liberties of the lodge as 'an ancient frie lodge ffor entring and passing within our selves.... And that soe long as the Sun ryseth in the East and setteth in the west' and as they wished the blessing of God. This recalls the way in which the masonic catechisms dating from the end of the century describe rituals involving symbolism of the rising and the setting of the sun, and probably indicates such rituals were already practised in Perth in 1658.

The lodge was the Lodge of Scone. But the meeting which drafted the 1658 agreement was held in Perth, and the document itself repeatedly describes the lodges members as the freemen masons resident in Perth. In all probability in spite of its title the members did not travel the two miles or so from Perth to Scone for their meetings, having chosen the name Scone simply to associate themselves with the former abbey there. Forty signatures are appended to the agreement, headed by those of the new master and warden: surprisingly of the other five men named in the text as present at the meeting only one signed. Moreover, most of the signatures were added later, sometimes decades later, as the records of the Incorporation of Wrights of Perth and other sources show. Thus the number of signatures does not indicate the size of the lodge in 1658.

That the masons of Perth were members of an incorporation of wrights and not, as often elsewhere, an incorporation of wrights and masons indicates that they were not equal partners but very much a subordinate trade in an incorporation dominated by wrights. The incorporation existed by 1519, and a decreet arbitral of 1569, following on earlier disputes, had laid down that masons might belong to the wright calling, but could not hold any office above that of boxmaster.[28] This, incidentally, was why the Lodge of Scone had a master and warden rather than the deacon and warden usual in burgh lodges: the incorporation's deacon was always a wright. The weakness of the masons' position was shown by the fact that the incorporation admitted cowans as freemen, the only known instance of this happening (though some other incorporations licensed cowans to work, as did the Lodge of Hamilton). This was stated in an act of 1670, and in 1671 a 'fail' or journeyman was booked to a cowan as his master 'for what belongs to ane cowane' only. The admission of cowans may have been an innovation, however, for a month later the incorporation referred the debates between the masons and the cowans to the convener court. The result of the dispute is unknown, but in 1673 the masons petitioned successfully that all former acts in their favour should be confirmed, suggesting continuing worries about their status.[29]

Among the masons admitted freemen of the incorporation were Andrew Norie (son of the warden of the lodge elected in 1658) in 1669, Robert Strachan in 1687, and John Watson in 1695. Watson was excused payment of a football as part of his dues (the Perth equivalent of the usual gloves) 'for reasones knowen to themselves'.[30] These three men all signed the lodge's 1658 agreement, showing that it was (as with documents of the Dunfermline and Hamilton lodges) customary over a long period for those admitted to the lodge to sign it.

The records of the incorporation also demonstrate that not all those who signed the 1658 agreement as lodge members were masons by trade. Lawrence Chapman, deacon of the incorporation in 1665 and re-elected in 1671, was a wright.[31] Chapman later became a baillie of Perth, as did another of the 1658 signatories, Thomas Craigdallie. Serving as baillie and treasurer of the burgh on a number of occasions in the 1670s, he was a litster or dyer by trade.[32]

There are no direct references to the Lodge of Scone for forty years after 1658, but then a group of bonds dated between February and April 1698 confirms that the lodge was actively recruiting members. In the most explicit of these it was recorded that John Wilson, weaver in Perth, owed £16 to Thomas Roch, mason, 'and the rest of the lodge of measons att Perth',

> conforme to use and wont of these that desire to be incorporat among the said measons and also I obldige me heirby not only to pay the rests of the ordinary deues by and attour the payment of the foirsaid soum but also l heirby obldige me to be in the will of the said lodge when or all that tyme any offence by me is given to them.

The bond was witnessed by Alexander Donaldson, officer in Perth and John Milne, wright there.[33] Wilson's name does not appear on the 1658 agreement but those of the two witnesses do, and (judging by the scale of fees laid down in the 1658 agreement) Wilson's debt to the lodge was the fee he should have paid on becoming a fellow craft.

By another bond Mr William Dobie acknowledged that he owed Thomas Roch (master of the lodge) and the rest of the lodge of masons of Perth £20, the witnesses being two Perth merchants, James and John Whyte.[34] The signatures of both James Whyte and Dobie are on the 1658 agreement— though the latter has always been read in the past as 'Mr L. Dobie'. A third bond acknowledged that Mathew Borland, glover, and Andrew Tosoch, slater, owed £10 to Thomas Roch as master of the lodge of masons of Perth. Borland's name is on the 1658 agreement as are those of both the witnesses, Alexander Donaldson (again) and David Cochrane.[35] The same witnesses, now described as sergeants in Perth, appear on the bond of Alexander Hasilton, slater, who owed Roch and the whole brethren of the masons in the burgh £10.[36] The lodge is not specifically mentioned on this occasion but it may be assumed the debt was owed to it. Finally, David Archibald, tailor, owed £6 to Roch (master of the lodge) and the other members of the lodge, payable between midsummer and St John's Day, the witnesses being David Cochrane, now identified as a maltman, and Henry Brown, notary.[37]

This fascinating little group of bonds shows the lodge (now called that of the masons of Perth, not of Scone) sorting out its financial affairs, taking bonds for debts due—some probably longstanding, others (like John Wilson's) probably fees due from newly admitted masons. The fact that no fewer than seven of the forty signatures on the 1658 agreement can be identified as those of men who were members in 1698 may indicate that the lodge was being revived and expanded at this time; and the registration of the bonds may itself indicate a reorganisation of the lodge. But of course the main interest of the bonds lies in the range of occupations of members revealed: they and the incorporation's records show that there were litsters, maltmen, town officers, merchants, wrights, glovers, slaters and weavers in the lodge, as well as Mr Dobie (whose title reveals him as a university graduate) and perhaps a notary (Henry Brown).[38] The 1698 bonds do not of course provide a full list of the lodge's members in the 1690s, but it is nonetheless remarkable to find that of all those mentioned in the bonds only the master, Thomas Roch, was actually a stonemason. The lodge might not be admitting gentlemen non-operatives (so far as is known), but by the later decades of the seventeenth century a wide variety of men who were not masons by trade had become members, and may well indeed have formed a majority in the lodge.

The Lodge of Dunblane

The first minute of the Lodge of Dunblane, a little cathedral town a few miles north of Stirling, is dated 28 January 1696. It lists members, appoints officials, sets times of meetings, specifies entry fees, and enjoins secrecy about the acts passed by the court, or to be passed hereafter.[39] In the absence of any indication to the contrary, this brief but comprehensive settlement of the basic points necessary for the administration of the lodge may be taken as recording its creation. Two specific points strengthen the case for the lodge being a new one. Firstly, in referring to the lodge's acts there is no mention of old laws and statutes such as was almost universal in such a context in older lodges. Secondly, offices are assigned to ten or eleven of the thirteen members present, two of the others evidently being guests who never attended again. This inventiveness with offices to provide jobs for all the boys surely indicates that the non-operatives who dominated the lodge were not having to fit into the framework of a long established institution but were free to shape the lodge as they liked since they were creating it. The date April 1695 appears in fragmentary and largely illegible accounts in the minute book, and this may indicate that the first moves to found the lodge were being made by then, perhaps with those who were to form the lodge being initiated in advance to the secrets of the Mason Word by members (operative or non-operative) who had already been initiated elsewhere. But the January 1696 meeting may be regarded as the occasion on which the lodge formally constituted itself as, according to the heading of the minute, the mason's court of Dunblane, held by the society of masons.[40]

The social range of the members of the lodge present at this first meeting, and the offices to which they were elected, are indicated by the following list:

> William Drummond, Lord Strathallan (master).
> John Cameron, younger of Lochiel.
> John Pearson of Kippenross (warden in absence).
> Alexander Drummond of Balhaldie (warden).
> Alexander Cameron, John's brother.

John Grahame younger in Dunblane (procurator fiscal).
William Caddell of Fossochie (treasurer).
James Grahame, lorimer in Dunblane.
Thomas Muschett, mason in Dunblane (eldest fellow craft).
Robert Duthie, mason in Dunblane (officer).
John Duthie, mason in Kippenross (eldest fellow craft in absence).
William Baxter, mason in Kilbryde (officer in absence).
James Turner, writer in Dunblane (clerk).[41]

'In absence' indicates that the men concerned were to act if the person initially appointed to the office concerned was not present at a meeting.

Of thirteen members only four were operative masons, and seven were gentlemen non-operatives (John Grahame, as will be seen shortly, comes into this category). In looking at the latter it is immediately evident that the lodge had a strongly Jacobite political bias. Lord Strathallan, hereditary baillie of the regality of Dunblane (which included the burgh), was married to the daughter of his kinsman John Drummond, earl of Melfort. Melfort had been one of the leading Scottish advisers of the dethroned James VII and had been in exile with him since the 1688-9 revolution had driven him from his thrones. Strathallan himself had been imprisoned in 1689 on suspicion of supporting the rising led by Lord Dundee which attempted to restore James, and though he made his peace with the new regime of King William probably at heart he remained committed to the Stuart cause.[42] The Cameron brothers were the sons of one of the greatest Jacobite heroes, Ewen Cameron of Lochiel. John (to whom Ewen transferred his estates in 1696) had missed the brief moment of Jacobite glory in 1689, the victory at Killiecrankie, but had joined the army shortly thereafter with Cameron reinforcements.[43] Allan Cameron was to become a gentleman of the bedchamber to James VII's son, James 'the Old Pretender' (otherwise the Chevalier de St George), and landed in Scotland with him in 1716 just as the 1715 Jacobite rising was collapsing.[44] John Pearson of Kippenross' family evidently also had Jacobite sympathies, though his elder brother, James, had been killed in 1685 by Cameron of Lochiel's men, who had been involved in suppressing the earl of Argyll's rebellion against James VII and had mistaken James for one of his supporters.[45]

Drummond of Balhaldie had a happier connection with the Camerons, having married Lochiel's eldest daughter. His family had long been one of the most important in the Dunblane area, having had the name of MacGregor until it was proscribed early in the seventeenth century. In his long career as a Jacobite Balhaldie fought at both Killiecrankie in 1689 and Sheriffmuir in 1715, and it is said that he entertained Prince Charles Edward during the '45 rising.[46] There is no sign, however, that the lodge as such was actively connected with Jacobite political activities, with the intrigues and conspiracies endemic in the period. Similarity of political views were an added bond to kinship and friendship in binding together many members, but the lodge was not used to advance these views.

Little is known of Caddell of Fossochie and his connections with the other landowners in the lodge, but the presence of the clerk of the lodge, James

Turner, can be explained as arising from his professional links with Lord Strathallan. In 1701 he was described as baillie depute of the regality of Dunblane, and he probably already served Strathallan in that or some other capacity by 1696.[47] The only other member of the lodge in 1696 who was not a tradesman, John Grahame younger, was the son of the commissary clerk of Dunblane, a notable local figure who had presented two silver communion cups to the cathedral the previous year. The family was successfully climbing the social ladder, and the younger John ended up as a laird, holding the lands of Glendoick.[48]

The January 1696 meeting of the Dunblane Lodge stipulated that it should meet five times a year: quarterly, and on St John's Day. This proved too ambitious, and was cut in 1698 to twice a year, in May and on St John's Day, with five members as a quorum.[49] Nonetheless, the lodge managed to hold a total of thirty-two meetings in its first twelve years, and though fining absent members was the only business recorded on eighteen of these occasions[50] this does not indicate that the lodge was in a parlous state, struggling to survive by enforcing attendance. Here as with other lodges the most significant business that brought members together, the dining together and performing of rituals, makes little or no impact on the minutes. It is true that the St John's Day meeting in 1699 was adjourned through low attendance, but in general the minutes give an impression of a stable and compact lodge. With the exception of the Cameron brothers, most of those present at the first 1696 meeting attended repeatedly in the years that followed, and many rose to hold leading offices in the lodge. Though the first minute had made provision for recruiting new members, including men who had already been initiated elsewhere, the core of the membership remained men who lived in or within a few miles of Dunblane— the only exceptions to this in 1696 having been, again, Balhaldie's Cameron brothers in law. The reason for the slow rate of recruitment in the lodge's early years (only fifteen admissions in the first fifteen years)[51] might be simply lack of interest in joining, but it looks more like selectivity, the small core of founder members carefully controlling admissions of both operative and non-operative members. A number of sons and other relatives of existing members were among those admitted, and many if not all of the others may have been friends or acquaintances.

Though operative masons were admitted as members of the lodge, there is no indication in the minutes of it trying to act as a guild regulating the mason trade in Dunblane until 1703, when it was ordered that any operative member of the lodge who took an apprentice pay twenty shillings 'entry booking money' and pay the lodge clerk to write the indenture. This was the booking of apprentices at the beginning of service rather than on admission to the lodge as entered apprentice. Not until 1710 and 1714 are there references to booking money actually being paid.[52] Yet there are indications that in the second and third decades of the eighteenth century the lodge came to regard itself as, and be regarded as, a craft incorporation, thus taking on a public role it had not previously had. One sign of this is that in these decades the term deacon is used instead of, or interchangeably with, that of master to describe the presiding officer in the lodge.[53] On 27 December 1722 the lodge approved the payment of contributions for mortcloths 'for the use of this and the other Corporated trades in this City', and the terms of this arrangement 'entred into by the other incorporated trades' were ordered to be produced before the lodge. It was in connection with the mortcloths that the lodge was again referred to as an incorporation in 1728. The kirk session of Dunblane complained that the six incorporated trades of Dunblane, the masons being one of them, had three mortcloths (two velvet and one plush) and that these were not only being used by members but were being hired out to others. This was being done at far cheaper rates than those at which the kirk session could afford to hire out its own mortcloth, and this competition was leading to a serious drop in the income which the church was able to devote to supporting the poor. The deacon and boxmaster of the Incorporation of Masons mentioned in the dispute (William Muschett and Christopher Finlayson, merchant) are the men holding these offices in the Lodge of Dunblane,[54] indicating that the two names denote a single institution. This was confirmed in the final settlement of the dispute in 1732 by the trades agreeing to surrender their mortcloths and leave the church with a monopoly. Four of the trades which were parties to this agreement were represented by deacons. The masons involved were described as John Duthie, late master mason, and Robert Duthie, clerk and treasurer of the Lodge of Dunblane: but the mason's organisation concerned was then referred to as an incorporation[55].

Several explanations of this evidence are possible. It could be argued that there was an Incorporation of Masons in Dunblane, which though otherwise totally unknown had existed before the lodge was founded. But, as in other burghs, lodge and incorporation were closely linked, and what happened in the 1720s was that members of the two bodies got confused as to which functions belong to which organisation.[56] However, in the absence of any evidence whatever as to the existence of an Incorporation of Masons except for the 1722, 1728 and 1732 references which identify lodge and incorporation, this interpretation is implausible. Another scenario is that the institution which emerged in 1696 had from the start been intended to be both lodge and incorporation. But the problem with this is that an incorporation in the sense of an institution with a recognised part in craft administration would normally have its authority recognised and ratified by a higher authority. In Dunblane in the 1690s this would have been Lord Strathallan, as hereditary baillie of the regality. Thus in 1697 he issued a charter confirming the privileges (officially recognised since at least 1649) of the Incorporation of Hammermen of Dunblane.[57] But where the masons' lodge is concerned Strathallan in 1696 was not its superior granting it rights, but the elected master of a voluntary association; and he took the title of master and not deacon. Moreover, the lack of activity in regulating the mason trade suggests the lodge had at first no pretensions to be a craft incorporation—and the very fact that its boxmaster in 1728, when it was called an incorporation, was not a mason but a merchant demonstrates this.

Further analysis of membership and office-holding in the lodge is needed, but what seems to have happened is that in the later 1710s and the 1720s the non-operative members of the lodge were less dominant than usual in the running of the lodge. The operatives took advantage of this to try to upgrade the public status of their trade by calling the head of the lodge by the title generally used for the head of a craft, deacon. And when it came to the business of the mortcloths they were happy to call the lodge an incorporation, giving the masons equal status in negotiations with the other five trades. But apart from the mortcloths affair the lodge made no real attempt to assert itself as a trade regulating body under either name. It is, moreover, in these very years that the minutes first reveal explicitly that the organisation was a body concerned with rituals and secrets above all else, in other words a lodge. In 1719 Mr Robert Renton, surveyor of the excise, was admitted as an entered apprentice and the same day, after instruction and trials of his knowledge, passed fellow craft 'with all the usual Solemnites'. In 1723 a member promoted from entered apprentice to fellow craft was described as having been 'past from the Square to the Compass', and that the strong influence of developments in freemasonry in England were being felt was shown in 1723 when the warden, William Caddell of Fossochie, presented the lodge with a copy of James Anderson's *Constitutions of the Free-Masons* published in London that year. Again in 1729 two entered apprentices from the Lodge of Kilwinning were admitted after examination had proved them to have 'competent knowledge of the secrets of the Mason Word'.[58] It was esoteric knowledge that counted, not craft skills.

At first it was quite common for non-operatives to be admitted to both grades on a single occasion. This happened with Mr David Pattoun (who was admitted free, being 'governor Balhaldies childe', whatever that means) in 1699, and Charles Stirling of Kippendavie in 1703. But in 1716 it was ruled that no one should be entered and passed at the same time 'Except such Gentlemen who cannot be present at a second dyet'.[59] The reference displays both a desire not to devalue initiation by rushing it, and acceptance of the fact that though most of those admitted were local men who were expected to attend regularly it was also legitimate to initiate men who (like the Cameron brothers) were only temporarily present in Dunblane.

Early references to the social side of the lodge's activities are completely lacking in the minutes, except for an isolated entry in 1697 when Pearson of Kippenross, then master of the lodge, was fined for absence at a previous meeting, the penalty subsequently being converted into paying for 'the present treat'.[60] Only twice was it recorded where the lodge met: in 1696 members assembled on two occasions in William Caddell's house in Dunblane. This was probably not a house belonging to Caddell of Fossochie, the member of the lodge, but a well known local inn where refreshment, liquid and otherwise, would be readily available for 'treats'[61].

The lodges of Hamilton and Dunblane, both first heard of in 1695, have a number of similarities. Both start life with a mixed membership of operatives and non-operatives, and in both a significant number of the non-operatives did not just appear on a single occasion to experience initiation (as was so common in older lodges) but attended meetings over a number of years. But there was a difference in the balance between operative and non-operative members and activities in the two lodges. In Hamilton traditional functions of trade regulation were important, and indeed the need for a body to provide such regulation when the number of masons in the area grew rapidly had been one of the motives for founding the lodge. In Dunblane, by contrast, though there were operative masons in the lodge, and they on occasion rose to its highest offices, only occasional gestures were made towards this traditional type of activity. From its inception, the Lodge of Dunblane was built on sociability and love of secrets and rituals, shared by operatives and non-operatives alike.

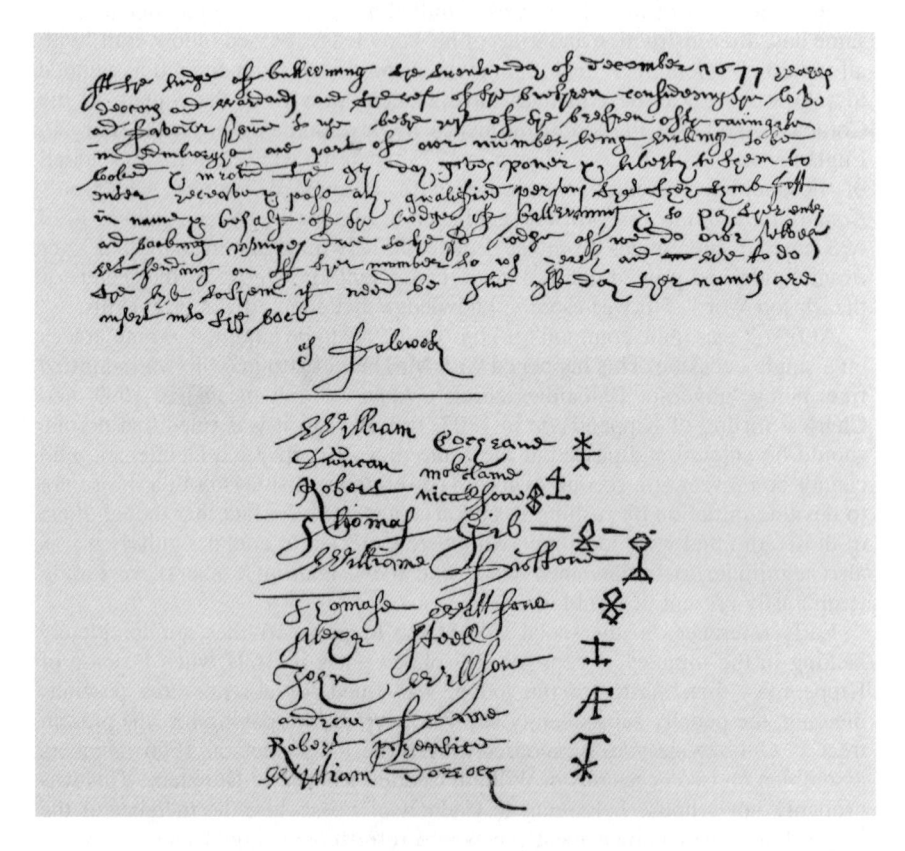

7   Minute of the Lodge of Kilwinning, 20 December 1677
Here the Lodge of Kilwinning ('At the fudge of Kullwinning') authorises the masons of the Canonsrate Edinburgh to admit members to their lodge. Thus in the absence of a Grand Lodge, an old lodge gives legitimacy to a new one, The Lodge of Canongate Kilwinning. The names and marks of the eleven Canongate masons involved are listed after the minute
From D. M. Lyon, *History of the Lodge of Edinburgh*. Photo copyrighy: Bob and Yvonne Cooper

7

THE BORDERS

The Lodge of Melrose

As with many lodges, the records of the Lodge of Melrose begin at a time when reorganisation was taking place. On the first four days of December 1674 'A.M.' (almost certainly Andrew Mein) transcribed the Old Charges for the lodge's use, taking the text (directly or indirectly) from an English version dated 1581.[1] It is possible that the version being copied was already in the lodge's possession, but more likely that it had been borrowed: certainly the fact that a 1581 text was copied does not provide evidence that the lodge had existed almost a century earlier. Later in the same month, on 28 December 1674, the first entry was made in the lodge's minute book. This ordered that, by the voice of the whole lodge, no master should take an apprentice for under seven years, and that when any apprentice was entered he must pay the lodge £8 for meat and drink, £2 for the box, and 'sufficient gloves'. When an entered apprentice was 'mad frie mason' he was to pay £4 plus gloves. No one was to be admitted to either grade except on St John's Day.[2]

These resolutions were then included in an agreement of 29 January 1675, where it was explained that a three or four year apprenticeship produced a mason 'not able to serve as a perfyt workman by reason of his small insight in the trade of meason craft'. By the agreement all members obliged themselves to meet on St John's Day and not to take on work begun by other masons. The document was dated at Newstead (a mile from Melrose) though it refers to the lodge as that of Melrose, and it was written by Andrew Mein, mason, portioner of Newstead. There follow about eighty-five signatures, of which no fewer than thirty-two are those of Meins, and another fifteen those of Bunzies.[3]

Certain families were strongly represented in the membership of some other lodges—Aitchison's Haven and Kilwinning, for example—but nowhere was there anything rivalling the domination of the Meins and Bunzies at Melrose. As in the case of the similar obligations or agreements signed in other lodges (Scone, Dunfermline and Hamilton, for example), the Melrose agreement almost certainly includes the signatures of members who joined in the decades after it was first signed in 1675. Thus though the lodge in the years after 1675 seems to have been a fairly large one, it had nothing like as many members as the number of signatures on the agreement might seem to imply.

The Lodge of Melrose met at Newstead not just because it was a convenient place just outside the burgh of Melrose's jurisdiction but because there was a remarkable concentration of masons actually living in Newstead—led by, inevitably, the Meins and Bunzies. In analysing Kilwinning Lodge's membership families of masons were found scattered in rural locations, combining practice of their craft with farming as tenants or proprietors of land. In Newstead there existed a larger and more stable community dominated by masons. When it originated is unknown, but it was consolidated by the breakup of the great church estates in the sixteenth century through the granting of feu charters, which in effect transferred permanent possession of the land. In some cases the land was feued out in small parcels to the existing 'kindly' tenants, and this happened on parts of the estates of Melrose Abbey, creating a series of 'feuar touns' in the Tweed valley, little islands of peasant ownership in the sea of great estates farmed by tenants. Newstead was one of these, the crown confirming feus to thirty-two feuars in 1586.[4] A charter of 1564 named six Meins holding land in Newstead,[5] and a 1606 charter of confirmation to the feuars of Newstead listed twelve Meins among the thirty-three feuars.[6]

A list of the proprietors who comprised the suitors of the head court of the regality of Melrose several generations later, in 1682, demonstrates the stability of this little community. It named the thirty-three feuars or portioners of Newstead, of whom twenty-one were Meins and five Bunzies.[7] How many of these were masons, spending the winter with their families on their lands and then spreading out through the country in the spring to work as masons, is impossible to say: the records are not consistent in giving trades, and with so many Meins and Bunzies and a limited range of Christian names there is a good deal of confusion. But it is clear that a substantial number of the feuars were masons, and Mein masons can be traced at work throughout southern Scotland. Thus, for example, in 1615 Andrew Mein and three other masons were paid for the transport of their workloms (tools) from Melrose to Edinburgh Castle, and similar payments were made to Robert Mein and two masons a year later. When the burgh of Peebles wanted its bridge repaired in 1635 it first sought masons in Lanarkshire, but ended up employing Robert and Alexander Mein and their two sons from Melrose.[8] In Newstead itself Robert or Richard Mein built himself a house in 1613 and there is a strong tradition that the lodge met in this house until the meeting place was transferred to Melrose in 1743.[9]

Already by the 1670s the Lodge of Melrose was admitting men who were not operative masons, but relatives and neighbours of members who were. Thus signatures on the 1675 agreement include John Mein, maltman, portioner of Newstead; Andrew Bunzie, weaver; and John Mein, osler (innkeeper). Thus the non-operatives in the lodge were men of similar social status to the operatives. A few members are recorded in the first decade of the eighteenth century with the title 'Mr' indicating that they had university degrees, but their names indicate that they were relatives of existing members—Mr Andrew Mein (1703-5), and Mr Nicol Mean and Mr Andrew Tait (both admitted in 1706).[10]

Not all the members of the lodge were resident in Newstead, but those who came from further afield were usually connected to Newstead men by blood, friendship or service. When John Houlet in Dalkeith became an entered apprentice in 1680 his master was David Mein, mason in Dalkeith. The following year James Mein, son to James Mein in Dalkeith, was entered in that burgh rather than in Newstead, but this was regarded as an irregularity.[11]

The 1675 agreement mentioned the offices of master and warden of the lodge, and when the holders of these offices were first named, in 1680, both were, predictably, Meins, Andrew and Alexander respectively. A clerk was first mentioned in 1694—John Mein 'Wynd' (nicknames or places of residence were often given to help distinguish between men of the same name). With the Old Charges copied, the minutes started and the agreement signed, all within two months of each other in 1674-5, the Lodge of Melrose was clearly being put on a sounder footing than in the past—if indeed, this activity does not mark its creation. The fact that the lodge had a master and not a deacon indicated that it neither claimed to be an incorporation nor was linked to one. That there was no incorporation of masons in Melrose is confirmed by the fact that the lodge itself undertook a task which an incorporation would normally have seen to. The masons and portioners of Newstead petitioned (for themselves and in name of other masons depending on the Mason Lodge of Melrose) the earl of Haddington, as patron of the parish of Melrose, for permission to erect a loft for the trade in the parish church. They had in fact previously begun to erect such a gallery, but the earl's baillie had stopped them. Haddington agreed, and the loft was then built at a cost of nearly £250.[12] No other Scottish lodge in the seventeenth century is known to have publically admitted its existence, let alone displayed its membership like the Melrose masons in their loft in the kirk each Sunday.

The Melrose minutes are mainly concerned with finance—payments made or due, and lists of money or bonds held in the box. Arrangements for the annual St John's Day banquet are frequently detailed. In 1685 John Mein, osler, was paid 'for meat and Drink and making of it readie', and in 1688 'for our dener and his paines for making it redie'. In 1687 tobacco was added to food and drink.[13] In 1698 a member was dispatched to Melrose 'about the flesh and the bread'. Agnes Philp was paid for ale and 'beare' (barley), and for 'making the meat ready', while William Brown was paid for two legs of mutton, a pound of tobacco, pipes, white bread and salt.[14] Perhaps it was after ale had been consumed more freely than usual that the lodge voted in 1690 that any mason who took his place in the kirk before his elder brother (presumably those who had been admitted fellow crafts before him) 'is a great ase'.[15]

Traces of the ritualistic side of the lodge's activities occur occasionally in the minutes. On 27 December 1694 Richard Mein (warden) and John Mein 'Wynd' (clerk) were chosen 'to examin the wholl tread of measons.... And that upon the selfe sam questions that the first man is examined on And that before witnesses of the tread'.[16] Some of the text has been lost, or perhaps the entry itself is garbled, but it is evident that the holding of annual examinations, presumably relating to esoteric knowledge and the contents of the Old Charges, was established at Melrose as in some other lodges. The three men who paid four shillings each in 1696 'for not being perfyt' were perhaps being fined for failing the examination (an alternative explanation might be that they were entered apprentices who had refused to 'perfect' themselves by being promoted to fellow craft, though the fines were perhaps too low for this).[17] 'An Commpt of them that hath bein examined And is to pay in anno 1701' lists seven names with the sum of £2 marked against five of them. This also suggests the fining of those deficient in knowledge.[18]

The minutes of the lodge are so sparse that it is hard to reach any conclusion as to how seriously it took its role as a body regulating the mason trade in the area. Certainly it went through the usual motions. In 1702 entered apprentices were forbidden to take work worth over £2 for themselves, and both they and fellow crafts were forbidden to work with cowans.[19] But the fact that having resolved to buy a mortcloth in 1698 and again in 1710, the lodge was still without one in 1716[20] hardly suggests efficiency, and as the lodge (if the minutes can be trusted) only met once a year it was hardly a suitable body for dealing with routine trade disputes.

Though the Lodge of Melrose built itself a loft in the parish church in the early 1680s, not all its members were willing to accept the episcopal established church of the period. The regality court of Melrose's list of those fined for attending house and field conventicles, taking part in irregular baptisms and marriages and withdrawing from their parish churches in 1682-4 included James Mein 'Byres' and James Mein 'Townheid', both identifiable in the lodge minutes, along with their wives and many other Meins, Bunzie's and others from Newstead.[21] They must have welcomed the Revolution of 1688-9 and the subsequent restoration of presbyterianism in 1690. In that year three Meins became elders. Another became kirk officer or beadle, and a fourth Mein elder appeared in 1692.[22] The evident strength of religious dissent at Newstead in the years before 1690 makes it remarkable that the lodge was permitted to meet freely to hold its banquets and secret rituals without persecution as a potentially seditious meeting or conventicle.

It seems that Melrose Lodge can claim the distinction of supplying America with one of its first known initiated masons. John Cockburn signed the 1675 agreement and it appears that he was the mason of that name who arrived in East Jersey in 1684 and wrote letters home the following year designed to encourage others to emigrate. To his uncle, a Kelso shoemaker he wrote 'I am very well in this land of America.... I am working at my work daily, and have very good encouragement among the old Planters'. More significantly another of Cockburn's letters was addressed to his uncle George Faa or Fall, mason in Kelso. Fall was a member of Melrose Lodge, being a signatory of the 1675 agreement and of minutes in the 1680s.[23] Cockburn recalled that his uncle had been very angry with him for emigrating, but stated that he had not repented. He had abundance of work and 'I am at the building of a great Stone house in New Perth, with another Scotsman'. This was evidently the first stone building in Perth Amboy, and Cockburn stressed that there was plenty of work for masons. Those who emigrated would get good wages and do far better for themselves than if they remained in Scotland. In later years Cockburn can be foumd working in Newark and New York.[24]

The Lodge of Kelso

The Lodge of Kelso's minutes begin on 27 December 1701 with a confidence that at first sight suggests that the lodge has long existed, but closer examination makes it quite likely that it was only just being formed. The minute recounted that the company of the Honourable Lodge of Kelso, under the protection of St John, had considered all former 'sederunts' (meetings) and found that the terms of office of the master, warden and treasurer had expired. After deliberation whether to 'continou the first ofisers, or elect nou' the existing officials were continued in office. Later there are references to 'all former fines', and a 1702 minute referred to an obligation which would have been dated 2 June 1701 and signed by all members—if the committee appointed to draft it had not failed to do so.[25]

Taken together, these references indicate that the lodge was just coming into existence in December 1701, with the previous meetings referred to having been held to make preliminary arrangements for its foundation by electing provisional office holders and drawing up an 'obligation', a mutual oath for members binding them to the lodge. The reference to all former sederunts seems impressive—but if meetings had been taking place for years why would there be a need to search all records of them to check on when office holders should be elected? If the only meetings to have taken place previously were recent ones, preliminary planning meetings concerned with defining the constitution of the new lodge, about which there was still confusion, then checking on the decisions taken makes sense. That the treasurer was instructed to keep a register of all subsequent sederunts in a book again suggests an institution just being organised, and the officials whom it was decided to retain in office were called 'the first ofisers', which surely must mean the first men to hold office. That the lodge failed to announce that it was a recent creation is hardly relevant: none of the early lodges do, and in an age when antiquity gave respectability it would be surprising to find a lodge admitting to being a novelty.

The other business of the December 1701 meeting also points to a new lodge drafting its rules. Payments for entrants were defined, those of 'all the gentlemen who are honorary members of the companie' being differentiated from those of ordinary members: the distinction was later defined as between honorary members and mechanics. Meeting times were set—St John's Day and the first Tuesday of June. Fines and other funds were to be distributed to indigent persons then and on other occasions by the lodge officials.[26]

The minute of December 1701 does not name any of the members of the lodge, but the next meeting, in June 1702, recorded that the master of the lodge, had died. This was none other than George Faa or Fall, the member of the Lodge of Melrose who had signed that lodge's minutes in the 1680s and had been addressed as mason in Kelso in 1685 by his emigrant nephew (though this information has been concealed by the erroneous transcription of Faa's name in the published extracts from the Melrose minutes).[27] Moreover, the first recorded treasurer of the lodge (1702) was Alexander Mein. He may well have been not only a member of Melrose Lodge but a former master of it, for Alexander Mein in Maxwellheugh (a suburb of Kelso) had been elected master of Melrose Lodge in 1700.[28] This is the only instance in which some of the founder members of an early lodge can be identified as members of an older lodge. The new Lodge of Kelso evidently acquired its esoteric knowledge from operative members of the Lodge of Melrose. There may also have been a feeling that having a few such operative members served to give the new institution legitimacy, by providing a direct link to the mason trade, for the Kelso Lodge was at first dominated by gentlemen non-operatives (a type of member completely absent from Melrose) and it was probably these members who had taken the initiative in the founding of the lodge.

Faa's successor as master of the Lodge of Kelso can also be linked, though less directly, to another lodge. This was Sir Robert Pringle of Stitchel, whose uncle Walter Pringle had been admitted to the Lodge of Mary's Chapel in 1670. Walter had died in 1685, but it is possible that he had passed an interest in masonry to his nephew.[29] As the Kelso minutes in the first few years give no lists of members or entrants it is impossible to know precisely when various members joined: often they are first mentioned when elected to office or fined for being absent. But as the following list indicates many gentlemen non-operatives were recruited in or soon after 1701. Robert Pringle of Clifton, Thomas MacDugall of Stodrig and Walter Scott, merchant, are first mentioned in 1702, followed in 1704 by Andrew Kerr younger of Greenheid, William Scott of Thirlestane (an advocate), Andrew Don of Smailholm, Gilbert Kerr of Banf Miln, William Bennet of Grubet, Kerr of Chirtrees, Cornet Drummond and Lieutenant Bennet. Dr Brown was a member by 1705. In the same year the minutes at last provide a full membership list of forty-one names. About a third, those named above, can be classified as gentlemen non-operatives: how many of the rest were stonemasons and how many craftsmen in other trades or other humble non-operatives is impossible to know, for only one (a wright) is given any description.[30]

Judging by this membership list the lodge was in a thriving state, and this seems to be confirmed by a codification of rules made since 1701 which were inserted in the minutes at this point. But then something seems to have gone wrong. There is a minute for 1706, then nothing until 1709 when it was agreed that the 'stent' or annual payment collected from honorary members was too high, stopping people from joining the lodge. It was therefore reduced from a crown to half a crown. But this made no difference, suggesting that the problem was not merely a financial one. The next minute, dated 31 December 1716, reveals a sorry state of affairs. The members declared that they had found their box confused by containing unnecessary papers. The reason for this was that none of 'our honorary party' had attended the lodge for so long. The lodge had been waiting for them year after year without attempting to sort things out. As none of the honorary members had returned to the lodge, the remaining members had purged the box of unnecessary papers between 1706 and 1716. They had spoken to some of the honorary members, who had advised them to do this. Some minutes had been kept of meetings in the intervening years, on loose sheets of paper, but these were such a mess—nothing 'but blloting of peper and conffosion'—that it had been decided by the 'sosity' (society) that it was 'unesory' (unnecessary) to record them in the minute book.[31] In the absence of the gentlemen members there was no-one in the lodge sufficiently literate to keep proper records, as the spelling in the minute demonstrates convincingly.

After 1716 the minutes were entered with reasonable regularity (and somewhat improved spelling), but the post 1716 lodge was very different from that of 1701-6. The gentleman masons have gone, leaving the lodge to the artisans. Probably tensions between gentlemen and artisans had grown after the first years of enthusiasm had passed, with the two types of member wanting different things from the lodge. Masonry might claim to unite men from all levels of society, but in practice it may have been found that they had different outlooks and interests. In 1718 the artisan lodge, as it now was, complained that some of the entered apprentices and fellow craft 'were not so dilligentt in proveing of ther lessons as could satesfie the lodge'. Time was therefore to be spent every St John's Day in examinations, and those found not to be qualified were not to be passed as fellow craft.[32] Was there a feeling that under the gentlemen masons the lodge had been too slack in preserving masonic lore and ritual—or indeed that the gentry in their zeal for their new hobby of masonry had proved altogether too inventive in such matters, shocking conservative minded operative members? No certain answer can be given, but Kelso provides an interesting example of a lodge probably begun through the initiative of gentlemen, though with a strong artisan presence from the start, shedding its gentry members—or possibly having them secede to form a new gentry lodge of their own. In the Lodge of Haughfoot a similar process can be observed taking place more gradually, but in the end achieving a greater change, for the artisan presence in Haughfoot when it was founded was weak.

The Lodge of Haughfoot

The Lodge of Haughfoot has been described as the first non-operative lodge to be founded in Scotland, in that it made no attempt to control the operative mason trade, was founded by non-operatives, and existed almost exclusively for ritual and social purposes. It would, however, be a mistake to see it as an entirely new type of lodge. In many respects it was very similar to the Lodge of Kelso, and differed from it in degree rather than kind. Both were innovatory in that they owed their foundation to gentlemen non-operatives, though it is true that this was more clearly the case in Haughfoot than Kelso. Neither lodge took an interest in trade regulation in any meaningful sense, but in Haughfoot as in Kelso the operative element among members became strong enough to take over the lodge in time, excluding or losing the gentry but still remaining essentially social and ritual organisations.

The little settlement of Haughfoot lay at the south east corner of the shire of Midlothian, twenty-three miles from Edinburgh and a mile south of Stow,[33] but the lodge's character and the fact that its location lay deep in the southern uplands of Scotland makes it appropriate to consider it in the Borders group of lodges rather than in the Lothians group. The siting of the lodge probably arose from the fact that Haughfoot lay just half a mile or so from Torsonce, the residence of one of the two lairds mentioned in the first minutes (1702), and about four miles from Gala, the residence of the other. The very obscurity of Haughfoot may have made it attractive, in keeping with the tradition (enshrined in the masonic catechisms) that lodges were supposed to meet secretly, well away from any burgh.

That the lodge was unusual is suggested immediately by the fact that the first words to survive in its minute book are the closing words of a masonic catechism, the previous pages having been torn out. While other lodges may have possessed written copies of catechisms by the end of the seventeenth century, their secrets were guarded so carefully that no other surviving text can be associated with a lodge. The founders of Haughfoot, by contrast, did not scruple to write a catechism into their minutes. But the fact that it was later removed indicates that not all were happy at this, and it may be that it was destroyed as soon as the members of the new lodge were confident they could remember the rituals without the help of a written text.[34] The appearance of a written catechism may reflect the fact that the lodge was not founded by a mixture of operative masons (skilled in the craft's esoteric lore) and gentlemen, as was the case with the Kelso Lodge, but by men all of whom may have been beginners, only admitted to the secrets of the Mason Word shortly before.

The catechism was apparently written on the same day as the first minute, 22 December 1702. On that day the following gave in petitions earnestly desiring to be admitted to the society of mason and fellow craft:

Sir James Scott of Gala or Galashiels.
Thomas Scott, his brother.
David Murray in Philiphaugh.
James Pringle in Haughfoot.
Robert Lourie in Stowtounheid.
John Pringle, wright.

After their desires had been 'maturely considered ... they each of them by themselves were duely and orderly admitted apprentice and ffellow Croft', and made payments to the box. The impression given here is of a lodge which already existed admitting members. But there is evidence in the minute of the presence of only two other men, John Hoppringle or Pringle of that Ilk (or of Torsonce) and Andrew Thomson, and later minutes reveal no other members of the lodge (apart from those admitted subsequently), with the sole exception of James Pringle, a brother of Pringle of that Ilk, who first attended a meeting in 1704: as he was then listed as senior to Thomson in the lodge he must have been a member by 1702. It looks as if Pringle of that Ilk, Thomson, and perhaps the former's brother had already been initiated into the secrets of the Mason Word, and as if it was they who initiated the six men listed above, founding the lodge in doing so. After this had been done, it was resolved that the lodge should meet every year (at Haughfoot) on St John's Day. Pringle of that Ilk was to decide the date of the next lodge meeting and inform members of it. This suggests that he was presiding over the lodge, a fact that is confirmed in later years when he is referred to as master or preses (president). Similarly Andrew Thomson, who was ordered at this first meeting to buy a book in which to record the lodge's business is soon called boxmaster of the lodge, a position he occupied until 1717.[35] The lodge was highly unusual in that it did not have a warden, again demonstrating that though Haughfoot was not a completely new type of lodge it did differ in some respects from its predecessors.

Pringle of that llk and Andrew Thomson may have previously been members of another lodge, but equally they may have been initiated to the Mason Word without becoming members of a lodge, a practice of which many traces survive. The fact that the head of another branch of the Pringle family, that of Stitchel, had played a leading part in founding the Kelso lodge the year before was doubtless more than mere coincidence, and again Pringle involvement in establishing a lodge may owe something to the fact that Walter Pringle, Stitchel's uncle, had been initiated in Edinburgh in 1670. Walter Pringle had been a witness at the marriage of Pringle of that Ilk in 1681— and the bride on that occasion had been a sister of Sir James Scott of Gala, who was to be initiated by his brother in law at Haughfoot in 1702.[36]

Scott of Gala and Pringle of that Ilk were major figures in powerful local landowning families: the former represented Roxburghshire in parliament in 1698-1702. With Pringle married to Scott's sister, and each of the two men having a younger brother in the lodge, the gentry element in the lodge formed a closely knit family group. The other members in 1702 can only be identified by the information given in the minutes. Thomson, acting as treasurer and clerk, must have been a man of some education, and perhaps served Pringle of that Ilk in some capacity in administering his estates. John Pringle was a wright, probably a mason wright in the rural tradition. Certainly he was the closest the lodge got at first to having a genuine operative mason as a member. David Murray, Robert Lourie and James Pringle probably came from a similar level in society, being tenant farmers or artisans (or, of course, combining the two). Though the lodge was essentially the creation of gentlemen, having an artisan element in it appears to have been regarded as important (here as in Kelso) in giving the organisation validity as a genuine mason lodge, and at the same time doubtless exemplifying the claims of the mason craft to unite men from different levels of society.

That the lack of a 'real' mason in the lodge was felt to have been a weakness was perhaps indicated by the action of the next recorded meeting, on 14 January 1704. William Cairncross, mason in Stockbridge, petitioned to be allowed to associate himself with the lodge. When he was examined the lodge was satisfied 'of his being a true entered apprentice and fellow Croft' and admitted him as a member. Thus Cairncross had previously been initiated to the secrets of masonry before joining Haughfoot Lodge. Whether he came from the Stockbridge near Edinburgh or from the one in Berwickshire is not known. Both were well over twenty miles from Haughfoot, but he may have found employment in the area and the fact that he attended the lodge for many years suggests that he had settled there. His son George, who was admitted to both grades at the same meeting, evidently being initiated for the first time (as he, unlike his father, had to make a payment to the box), was later referred to as a mason in Galashiels.[37]

The January 1704 meeting continued Pringle of that Ilk in office as master, elected Andrew Thomson as boxmaster, and fined absentees. It also gave commission to any five of its members to admit qualified persons to be members of the lodge, either as entered apprentices or as fellow crafts, in the coming year. This power was to be renewed regularly in the years that followed, and was widely used to admit new members.[38] Such recruitment provided a steady trickle rather than a flood of new members, entrants being a mixture of gentry, their servants, and men of tenant or artisan status. Most of the latter cannot be positively identified, but the gentry and their associates confirm the pattern of personal and kin connections determining membership.

William Borthwick, younger of Falahill and Walter Scott, a servant of Pringle of that Ilk, joined on 27 December 1704. Alexander Young, surgeon in Galashiels followed in 1705, and in 1706 the admission of Scott of Gala's brother John (an army surgeon with the rank of captain) was reported to the lodge—the first example of an admission outside the lodge by a commission of five. Alexander Baillie of Ashiestiell, and John Younger (writer in Edinburgh) were also admitted in 1706, along with another genuine stonemason, John Young, mason in Stow. He was evidently initiated by the lodge into the masonic secrets, but George Gray 'in ffaims Lonend' was accepted in 1707 as already a true entered apprentice and fellow craft. William Craig, servant to the laird of Torwoodlie was also admitted to both grades in 1707, but this practice, universal since the foundation of the lodge, was now changed, it being ruled that except in special circumstances a year at least must pass between being made an entered apprentice and passed a fellow craft.

By 1709 the lodge could boast twenty-six members, eighteen of them being present at the St John's Day meeting, and three new members were admitted on that day. Two were only admitted entered apprentices in accordance with the 1707 regulation, but James Pringle of Torwoodlie was admitted to both grades. As elsewhere, gentry tended to be excluded from the rule about separating initiations to the two grades. John Mitchelson of Middletoun, an Edinburgh advocate, was allowed the same privilege in January 1711 when five members initiated him to the Lodge of Haughfoot at a ceremony held in Edinburgh.[39]

From the middle of the second decade of the eighteenth century, however, a change came over the Lodge of Haughfoot. The last members to be admitted that can be categorised as gentry or their associates were John Donaldson (a servant of Scott of Gala, and probably the man of that name who was baillie of Galashiels a few years later) in 1711, and Hugh Scott younger of Gala and John Borthwick (a servant to the laird of Torwoodlie) both recruited in 1714.[40] Hugh Scott was elected preses or master in 1718 and 1728, but otherwise all the masters of the lodge after 1716 were non-gentry, whereas up to 1716 only gentry had held the office.[41] Some lairds continued to attend meetings into the 1720s, but thereafter the lodge was left in the hands of the artisans. The process was gradual, not abrupt as at Kelso, and there is no sign in the records of tension or ill feeling between gentry and artisans, but the end result was the same.

Once the local lairds had left the lodge, Haughfoot became an awkward place to hold meetings (as, indeed, Baillie of Ashiestiell had complained back in 1710). Therefore in 1739 it was resolved that thereafter the lodge should hold its annual meetings alternately at Stow and Galashiels. No Stow meetings are recorded, and in 1741 'the Masons of Galashiels seperat from the Brethren at Stow'. Whether the Stow masons, no doubt regarding themselves as the true Haughfoot Lodge (as that place lay only a mile away), continued to meet is unknown. The Galashiels masons took over the minute book and met there until 1754 when, through further changes in membership, their lodge began to meet alternately in Galashiels and Selkirk. The last minute in the book was dated 1763, and thereafter all trace of the lodge vanishes.[42]

The Haughfoot minutes are in some ways even less informative than those of most other lodges, as it had no operative functions of the sort which would have been recorded. With rare exceptions the early minutes were confined to recording those present, fining absentees, financial matters, and admissions. On the admission of two members in 1710 it was noted that they had received 'the word in Common form', the only hint of the performance of the rituals described in the missing catechism that had prefaced the minutes.[43] There are, however, two entries which indicate an effort to preserve secrecy by punishing loose-tongued members. In 1708 James Frier was reproved for 'Some rash Expressions he had in relation to admission to the Society' and in 1714 Thomas Frier was reprimanded for his fault (which is not defined) and had his mason oath of secrecy administered to him 'of new'. As he expressed sorrow he was not fined.[44] The only hint of the sociable aspects of the lodge occurs in 1711, when it was resolved that absentees should not only be fined but made to pay 'their Share of the Reckoning'. Thus at Haughfoot (unlike Hamilton and Melrose) the annual dinner was not paid for out of lodge funds. In the same year comes the first reference to the lodge's charitable functions, payments being made to the widows of two artisan members.[45]

However frustrating the impossibility of penetrating behind the bland facade of the Haughfoot minutes may be, it is only through them that anything at all is known about the lodge. It is a fascinating lodge in that, like Kelso and (to some degree) Dunblane, it reverses the expected pattern of development. Instead of an 'operative' lodge being taken over by gentleman non-operatives, a lodge founded by the gentry but admitting operatives moved 'down-market', becoming entirely the preserve of artisans—and it looks as if the numbers of these who were actually stonemasons increased in the later decades of the lodge's known life. There is no sign that the gentlemen members resented or resisted the change. Either the gentry members died off or lost interest in time, or it is possible that (as suggested at Kelso) they hived off to form a new exclusively gentry lodge. In either case, the result was that the lodge was left to their social inferiors.

8

THE NORTH

The Lodge of Aberdeen

The organisation of the mason craft in sixteenth and seventeenth-century Aberdeen is obscure. A 'lodge' existed in the 1480s and the 1490s connected to the parish church of St Nicholas, as both a place of work and an institution with its own regulations controlled by the burgh. The lodge building must have been a fairly substantial one, for it still existed in 1605, though in a ruinous condition. The burgh council then ordered that 'the hous callit the kirk ludge at the north vest end of the kirkyard' be repaired and divided into three 'houses' for three schools.[1] The Medieval semi-permanent site lodge attached to a major church had disappeared, probably in the decades of decline of the Catholic church before 1560.

In 1527 the burgh council had granted a seal of cause to the wright, cooper and mason crafts, which were to maintain the altar of St John the Evangelist in the parish church, but whether the intention was that there be one incorporation with three deacons or three incorporations which acted together to uphold the altar cannot be determined. A new seal issued in 1541 added the crafts of carvers, slaters and painters to those previously mentioned, and appears to indicate that all six crafts had their own deacons (though the burgh council's ratification of the gift fails to mention the slaters). It may be possible to conceive of three deacons in a single incorporation (after all, the Mary's Chapel Incorporation in Edinburgh had two) but five or six sounds like a recipe for chaos. Thus it seems likely that separate organisations were envisaged, sharing the same altar. In the same year the wrights and masons were assigned the altar of St John the Baptist (perhaps the same as that of the other St John). But after this the place of the mason craft in the burgh becomes difficult to determine. By the seventeenth century the wrights and coopers shared a single incorporation, the deacon being chosen from each craft alternately.[2] The masons were no longer linked to these crafts, and though it has been asserted that they had a society or guild of their own (which later developed into the lodge),[3] there appears to be no evidence whatever of the existence of such a body.

There is, however, evidence that something peculiar happened that changed the status of the masons in the burgh at about the time that the second seal of cause was granted. Two masons had been admitted as burgesses of Aberdeen in 1478. A long gap ensued (though the records are probably not complete), and then in 1533-41 four mason burgesses appear.[4] Given the small population of Aberdeen, and the fact that many masons resided outside burghs, only a handful of masons would have been qualified for burgess-ship, and it looks as if they may have begun to become burgesses after the issue of the first, 1527, seal. But after the year of issue of the second seal, which should have consolidated their position in the official hierarchy of burgh society, masons disappear completely from the burgess rolls until after 1700.[5] Accounting for this is difficult, but one interpretation possible is that the masons, perhaps through some tradition of protecting their craft's autonomy, rejected the offered 'privilege' of incorporation under a seal of cause as it would strengthen the hold of the burgh authorities over them: and that in retaliation the burgh excluded them from the right to become craft burgesses. Yet, to add to the confusion, a deacon of the masons is mentioned (along with those of the wrights and coopers) in 1554, suggesting that the masons were still regarded as one of the incorporated crafts.[6] It is possible that some masons were created simple burgesses, with a lower status than craft burgesses and very limited privileges, without any reference to their craft being made: the John Ronald or Roland made a simple burgess in 1655[7] may be the mason of that name who was later a member of Aberdeen Lodge. And a few Aberdeen masons in the seventeenth century were licensed to brew and sell ale, beer and aquavite,[8] an additional right sometimes given to craft burgesses. But these were the only formal rights in the burgh a mason could aspire to.

The burgh's determination not to make any mason a burgess was seen in 1622. John Mylne, the well known Dundee, Perth and Edinburgh mason, had come to Aberdeen to advise the council about building a new tolbooth. In these circumstances most burghs would have honoured him by making him a mason burgess free of charge. Aberdeen virtually did this, but carefully avoided the word burgess in doing so, to avoid setting a precedent: Mylne was thus made 'frieman of his craft, allanerlie' (only).[9] Masons were a recognised craft, they may still have had some organisation of their own, but they were not permitted to become craft burgesses. Thomas Watson, the mason who built the burgh a new wardhouse (prison) in 1616, prospered and branched out into the business of dealing in and importing grain. This was a privilege reserved for merchants, and in 1623 he was admitted as a merchant burgess: as a mason he had not been qualified for the lesser status of craftsman burgess, and he now had to renounce the mason trade.[10]

It may be that the anomolous position of masons in Aberdeen was connected in some way with a development revealed by a grant under the privy seal in 1590. In this, James VI confirmed the right of a minor Aberdeenshire laird, Patrick Copland of Udoch, to act as warden and justice of the masons in the shires of Aberdeen, Banff and Kincardine.[11] The position was a hereditary one, though confusingly it was also stated that most of the master masons of the area had elected him to office. Nothing more is known of the Copland wardens or their attempts to exercise jurisdiction over masons in the North East of Scotland, but it is possible that the loyalty of Aberdeen masons to their hereditary wardens had come into conflict with the exclusive loyalty members of a mason incorporation would have owed to the burgh authorities.

Such a conflict of loyalties possibly deprived Aberdeen masons of the right to have an incorporation and become burgesses, but there is no sign of an alternative organisation based on their hereditary wardens emerging, and when evidence for the existence of a masonic lodge in Aberdeen appears late in the seventeenth century there is no mention of the lairds of Udoch or their supposed jurisdiction.

Assessing the nature of the Aberdeen Lodge in its early days presents major problems. To the usual tantalising problem of records being incomplete or lacking is added the peculiar frustration of records existing but inaccessible at least to the present author, as access is denied to those who are not freemasons. Luckily past writers on the lodge have published substantial portions of these records (which makes secrecy about the remainder distinctly pointless), but it is clear that significant material remains unpublished.[12] This is especially unfortunate in that the earliest and best known record of the lodge, the so-called Mark Book, is clearly not quite what it claims to be. It bears the date 1670, but what purports to be a list of members in that year is quite clearly not genuine. It needs only the most cursory examination to establish this, yet none of the masonic historians who have examined it have expressed doubt about it—or at least they have not ventured to do so in print.

The difficulties raised by the Mark Book are intensified by the fact that in 1748 the Lodge of Aberdeen decided to have it rebound and, at the same time, to detach the least valuable pages and insert fresh ones. The boxmaster, to whom this task was entrusted, unfortunately went further: he bought an entirely new volume, into which he pasted some pages from the old one, the rest being destroyed. The extent of this wanton destruction by the lodge of its own history is indicated by the fact that twenty-eight pages were preserved, but the old pagination on some of them indicates that the original volume had had at least 147 pages.[13]

The surviving pages consist (it appears from published accounts of them) of a page illustrating the tools of the mason trade; a title page and list of members of the lodge and their marks in, supposedly, 1670 (these items being elaborately decorated and illuminated in gold leaf); names of members who joined subsequently; laws and statutes of the lodge; part of the Falkland Statutes; and a version of the Old Charges.[14] The title page of the Mark Book announces that

> This Account Book Appertaines to ws the Maister Measones And Entered Prenteises of the Honourablle Lodge off Aberdein, Wherin is Contained the wholl Lawes and Articles of the Meason Craft to all Succeeding Generationes in that airtt, Be ws who are the authores and subscryuers of this Book.
> And Lykwayes all the Debts we shall be Resting To others Is Contained in this Book As after ffolloweth wreattin be James Anderson Glassier and Measson and Clerk to our honourablle Lodge.[15]

This title indicates one type of record contained in the pages destroyed in 1748—financial records. Beyond this it is only possible to speculate as to the contents of the lost pages. One possibility is that they included a copy of a masonic catechism, perhaps destroyed (like that at Haughfoot) to preserve secrecy. A surviving paper shows that in 1699 the lodge paid for the printing of a broadside 'concerning the Measone Word', a description that makes it all but certain that it was a catechism which was thus printed.[16] If the masons of Aberdeen Lodge were prepared to have their secrets printed (though of course only for lodge members) in 1699, then they may well have been ready to commit them to paper in the Mark Book some years before. Financial records and a catechism, however, would have taken up relatively few of the minimum of 119 pages destroyed in 1748. Many of them may have been blank, but sadly many items were probably lost whose nature it is impossible even to guess at.

The most remarkable item in the surviving pages of the Mark Book is that which gave it its name, the list of lodge members and their marks. This is the earliest list claiming to give the complete membership of a Scottish lodge, and it is highly impressive, totalling forty-nine masters and eleven entered apprentices. Nor is it only in numbers that the list is remarkable: so too is the social range of its members, as the following summary of the fellow craft masters of the lodge demonstrates:

Landowners, 7 (4 nobles, 3 lairds)
Professional men, 5 or 6 (2 or 3 ministers, 1 preacher, 1 professor, 1 lawyer)
Merchants, 10
Craftsmen, 26 or 27 (6 hammermen, 3 wrights, 4 barber-surgeons, 10 or 11 masons, 3 slaters).[17]

The names of the masters are said to be those of the authors of the book, 'in order, according till our ages, as wee wer made fellow craft (from which wee reckon our age'. The first name is that of Harry Elphinstone, tutor of Airth, collector of customs in Aberdeen and master of the lodge. This immediately makes it impossible that the list of names was written in 1670.

Harry Elphinstone was the younger son of Sir Thomas Elphinstone of Calderhall. His eldest brother Richard married the heiress of the estate of Airth, Jean Bruce. She died in March 1683, and Richard followed her in June. They left an infant son, Charles Elphinstone of Airth, and Harry Elphinstone became the tutor or guardian of his young nephew, thus becoming tutor of Airth.[18] Thus the '1670' list in the Mark Book cannot have been written before 1683 as it decscribes Elphinstone as tutor. Other names confirm the dubious nature of the '1670' list. Mr Alexander George, described as an advocate in Edinburgh, did not become a member of the faculty of advocates until 1676.[19] Mr George Liddel, professor of mathematics, pushes the date of the list forward to at least 1687, as only then did he succeed his father in the chair of mathematics at Marischal College, Aberdeen.[20] The evidence so far cited, however, only proves that the '1670' membership list could not have been written in 1670. It could still be argued that it represents membership of the lodge in that year 1670 accurately though, being written later, it assigns occupations and titles to members which they had not possessed in 1670: perhaps an old list had been updated and elaborated. Again, however, on examination the 1670 list provides the evidence of its own invalidity. George Liddel was a third year student at Marischal College in 1683-4,[21] which means he would then have been in his mid teens: unless Aberdeen Lodge accepted infants as fellow crafts he could not possibly have been a member in 1670. If it be assumed that he could not have become a master until aged about say, twenty, then he could not have been listed as a master until the late 1680s.

Moreover, if the list records the names of members arranged according to their order of admission as masters (as it claims to do), all those listed after Liddel must have reached that grade after him. As his name is twenty-second on the list, twenty-seven of those listed as '1670' masters could only have became masters in or after the late 1680s. But this cannot be the case. John Skene, merchant (no. 27 on the list) emigrated to New Jersey in 1682 and is not known ever to have returned to Scotland. Mr George Seton, minister of Fyvie was evidently dead by 1685.[22] The very common names of many of the merchants and craftsmen on the membership list makes tracing their careers with certainty difficult, but the general impression is that though some were adult by 1670, many only reached an age and status at which they were likely to have become lodge members in the 1670s or 1680s.

For all the attention the Aberdeen Mark Book has received, the few simple questions about members which show that its '1670' list is invalid appear never to have been asked—though the extreme terms in which at least one assertion of its authenticity is phrased suggests an attempt to counter doubts about its dating while refusing to admit that any doubt could exist.[23]

A full analysis of the list and study of it alongside the unpublished lodge records is required to throw further light on its status, but this is for the present impossible through the inaccessibility of the records. The easiest solution to doubts about the list's status would be simply to dismiss it as fabrication, a forgery by James Anderson, the enthusiastic lodge clerk, designed to glorify his lodge and having no value at all as evidence. This would, however, be too drastic a reaction to the list's obvious implausibility. It is hard to imagine that Anderson would have come up with the remarkable mix of names on the list by pure invention: while there are some names of powerful men on the list, surely he would have been tempted to add more influential figures from in and around Aberdeen itself. As it is, the list contains several interesting groupings which its author would have had no reason to create artificially, but which make sense if, at Aberdeen as elsewhere, members brought friends and acquaintances to a lodge once they themselves had been admitted. The earl of Dunfermline (no. 31), John Gray younger of Crichie (no. 33) and George Rait of Mideple (no. 35) were all landowners in the parish of Fyvie,[24] and Mr George Seton (no. 34) was minister of the same parish from 1672. Moreover the other member who appears on the list in the midst of these names, the earl of Erroll (no. 32), owned most of the parish of Slains, where Mr William Fraser (no. 17) was minister from 1665 until 1699 (though frequently in trouble for neglecting his duties and eventually resigning under suspicion of having poisoned his wife).[25] If William

8 Patrick Whyte, hookmaker
Member of the Lodge of Aberdeen
Portrait dated 1704
Copyright: Dr Guild's Managers, Aberdeen

Fraser joined first, as his position in the list suggests, had he introduced Erroll to masonry, who in turn influenced the 'Fyvie group' through Dunfermline? Though the order of members on the list is not in general an accurate guide to when members joined the lodge, the fact that the names of Erroll and the Fyvie group are closely bunched together may suggest they joined at about the same time, in one of those sudden influxes of gentlemen non-operatives seen in Kilwinning and other lodges.

Turning to the craftsmen on the list, grouping of a similar sort can be observed. Members of only two of the burgh's seven incorporations were represented on the lodge list: it contained six hammermen (one armourer, one cardmaker, one hookmaker, one smith and two glaziers) and three wrights. As these incorporations included members of building trades this seems logical, and the hammermen and wrights seem to have stood up for each others interests. The hammermen were recognised as first in precedence among the incorporations, and in 1682 they conspired with the wrights to try to usurp second place for the latter, ousting the baxters (bakers): two of the wright members of the lodge took a leading part in the affair, and the deacon of the hammermen was Alexander Paterson, armourer and lodge member.[26] But most of the hammermen in the lodge had nothing to do with building, and neither had the four barber-surgeons (two wigmakers and two surgeons), who had a society which was not recognised as a full incorporation.[27] The three slater members of the lodge also lacked an incorporation: the only burgess among them, Alexander Forbes, thus had the status of simple burgess, being neither a merchant or craft burgess.[28] At least seven of the men described on the '1670' list simply as masons were operative stonemasons traceable in local records; the same is probably true of three of the other four, but the final 'mason', Mr Alexander Irvine (no. 23), is an exception. While it was not entirely unknown for seventeenth century stonemasons to have university degrees, these were men who would more accurately be described as sculptors or architects, well known men who are easily identifiable. Irvine is not in this category, and thus was probably a graduate who was described as mason (meaning a member of the lodge) as he had no other title or trade at the time. Possibly he was the Alexander Irvine who had a chequered and unsuccessful career as a parish minister. After graduating at King's College, Aberdeen he was a minister in Edinburgh in 1672-4, an assistant to the minister of Logie Buchan in the early 1680s (where he was regarded as careless and frequently absent), and minister of West Kilbride from 1688 to 1689 when he was driven from his parish by the 1688-9 revolution which overthrew episcopacy.[29] If this was the lodge member, presumably the '1670' list was compiled at one of the times when he was 'resting' between parishes.

It is hard to imagine James Anderson inventing the pattern of membership revealed by the list, at once wide ranging and including distinct groupings. If he was simply creating a fictitious membership in order to bring glory to his lodge, surely he would have been more systematic and ambitious: if seen as pure invention, the '1670' list displays remarkable restraint. As a working hypothesis, therefore, the '1670' members list is best regarded as an attempt by James Anderson, probably in the late 1680s, to list those who were, or had been, members of the lodge. He attempted to list them in the order in which they had become fellow crafts, but through lack of information and defects of memory often got muddled. It seems a coincidence that after the supposed '1670' members there is no trace of any new members being admitted to the lodge until 1687, when one new member appears, followed by no fewer than eleven in 1688.[30] The admission records are, admittedly, incomplete, but it looks as if the lodge may have been reorganised in 1687-8, the Mark Book then being compiled and recording the names of former and existing members, those of new members then admitted to strengthen the lodge being added subsequently.

It might be argued, in defence of the honour of James Anderson, that his list of the authors and subscribers of the Mark Book does not itself explicitly claim to represent lodge membership in 1670. Not only does the date 1670 at the head of the list create ambiguity as to whether the date refers to the whole list or only the year in which it was started, the date may have been added later, as it is squeezed in below a line as if added after the rest of the page had been written.[31] But references to the membership list in the laws and statutes of the lodge, which evidently preceded the list in the original Mark Book, undermines this defence. The statutes are dated 27 December 1670 in the title, and in the text it is recorded that the masters and entered apprentices of an honourable lodge held in Aberdeen on that day had established a box or fund for the support of their poor. It is plain that the authors and subscribers of the book mentioned in the statutes were supposed to be those named in the membership list. Yet, as already shown, some of those listed could not possibly have been lodge members in 1670. Thus the Mark Book is, to some extent at least, a deliberate forgery: either it lies in dating the statutes 1670, or if they were indeed drawn up in 1670 it lies about who were involved as authors and subscribers. James Anderson thus belongs to the long and fascinating tradition of men who elaborated on the truth to add to the glory and antiquity of institutions which they valued. But even this does not entirely explain the Mark Book. If he was really writing in the late 1680s, Anderson again showed remarkable restraint in only pushing the history of his lodge back to 1670. It may well be that it had existed then, and that Anderson himself had been a member (he would then have been twenty-one years old).[32] Perhaps a poors' box had indeed then been established (in one of the periodic reorganisations after a period of decline which can be detected in many lodges) but no proper records of this had been kept. Anderson might then have seen himself as retrospectively providing a suitably dignified record of a real event, an important turning point in the lodge's history which had not been properly marked at the time. As no record or memory of precisely who had been in the lodge in 1670 survived Anderson listed as authors of the statutes all the lodge members, past or present, whose names he knew. It has been asserted that in 1680 or 1682 the statutes (or something very like them) were printed,[33] and this may point to the true date of the statutes, Anderson later conflating them with some other development which had taken place in 1670. It is notable that a lost lodge minute book is said to have begun in 1679,[34] suggesting some reorganisation of the lodge at that time.

The statutes themselves[35] provide no evidence as to their true date. They open with a vow by all members of the lodge, repeating that made at their entry to the lodge 'when we receaved the benefit of the Measson word', to attend lodge meetings unless they were out of town, sick, or had some other lawful excuse.

132　　　　　　　　　THE FIRST FREEMASONS

9   The Pillars of Solomon's Temple - perhaps

(a) Detail from portrait of
Patrick Whyte, 1704
Copyright: Dr Guild's Managers,
Trinity Hall, Aberdeen

(b) Detail from portrait of
Alexander Paterson, c.1704.
Member of the Lodge of Aberdeen
Copyright: Dr Guild's Managers,
Trinity Hall, Aberdeen

The master of the lodge was to judge all faults of members and quarrels between them, but in doing so he was to take the 'voice' of the other members, a word that often means vote but here may mean merely that the master should consult the members. Those who refused to pay fines were to have their workloums (tools) or other goods seized by the officer of the lodge. If a rebellious member appealed to the courts of the land, the master and members were to go to the judge of that court 'and will mack him ane perjured man', meaning that they would tell the judge that the offender had broken his oath as a lodge member to submit to it. The offender would then be expelled from the lodge: neither he nor his children would have any claim on the lodge's charitable fund, and no member of the lodge would employ him. Attempts would also be made to prevent him getting employment elsewhere 'far or near in so far as we Can hinder'.

In the lodge the warden was to be 'the next man in power to the maister'. If the master was absent from a meeting the warden was to take his place, someone else being chosen to act as warden: the fact that it was necessary that at least acting holders of both offices be present suggests that they each had some essential role to play in the lodge's rituals. The lodge's warden was to hold office permanently, unless he resigned or was removed by members for some major offence, but the master was to be elected annually on St John's Day— though the old master might be re-elected. A boxmaster was also to be chosen annually. He held one key to the box, the other two required to open its three locks being in the hands of the master and the warden. The clerk similarly was only elected to hold office for a year, while the lodge's officer was to hold office until a new member entered the lodge. Thus in Aberdeen as sometimes elsewhere the officer, a sort of general errand boy, was the youngest (most recently entered) entered apprentice.

No lodge was to be held in any dwelling house in which people were living, 'but in the open fieldes except it be ill weather, and then Let ther be a house chosen that no person shall heir nor sie ws'. Later the statutes laid down that 'all entering prentisses be entered in our antient outfeild Lodge in the mearnes [Kincardineshire] in the parish of negg [Nigg] at the scounces at the poynt of the ness [Girdleness]'. It is hard to believe that the Aberdeen masons really met regularly not only outside the burgh (as the early catechisms required) but in the open air. The exposed point of Girdleness, jutting out into the cold North Sea just south of Aberdeen across the River Dee, was not a suitable place for performing solemn rituals in the open air—especially at the time of the most important meeting of the year, 27 December. Perhaps it had become accepted that in practice the theoretical obligation to meet outside would automatically be over-ruled by the 'weather permitting' clause. The sconces at Girdleness were earthwork fortifications guarding the entrance to Aberdeen Harbour, and it may be that the masons had there some shelter with a roof in which to perform their rituals, though if the annual banquet was also held there it must have been a pretty basic affair.

The statutes then move on to 'Lawes for our box for the poor never practised heirtofoir in Aberdeine'. The box and its contents have a central place in the

'1670' statutes, and the impression is given that the functions of the lodge as a benefit society was more central in Aberdeen than in most other lodges. The main benefit of possession of the Mason Word becomes eligibility for support from the box. Lodge members swore by 'all the oathes wee receaved at our entrie to the benefit off the measson word that wee shall own and mentaine the Measson box of Aberdeine and of this our lodge'. Money put in it was to be put to no other use than maintaining 'our destressed brethren especiallie those of our own lodge' suffering through injury, age or fire. The fact that masons with the Mason Word who did not belong to the lodge were entitled to help, in theory at least, is notable, though there were limits. Non-members were only to receive occasional, not regular, help even if they lived in Aberdeen, and lodge members were to have first call on the limited funds available. Members who indulged themselves in drunkenness and other debaucheries, however, or who could work but would not, were not to receive help—except for burial expenses. Virtuously inclined children of deceased members were to be educated and found a trade by the lodge, out of Christianity and respect for their parents.

Exceptions were however made to the rule that the fund existed for charitable purposes. Money from it could be used to 'give a treat to any nobleman or gentleman that is a measson' or for other lodge purposes. But the 'stock' or capital fund of the box was to be maintained, only interest earned on it being spent, and any excess 'spending money' was to be devoted to increasing the capital fund. The 'authors' of the charitable box strictly commanded their successors to maintain it. Any who used the money 'wee mortifie for pious uses' for other purposes 'is to be accounted a perjured man not keeping covenant a breacker of all just Lawes and the malediction of our poor to light wpon him till he restor two fold'.

Next the statutes turned to the main source of lodge funds, admission fees. Each entered apprentice on admission was to pay four rix dollars (about fifty shillings Scots) in 'composition', plus a linen apron and a pair of good gloves for every 'person concerned' in the lodge. If he could not afford aprons and gloves, he was to pay two more rix dollars, and (like, presumably, all entered apprentices) for a dinner, 'ane speacking pynt' and his contribution to the box. Finally, the new entered apprentice had to pay a merk (thirteen shillings and four pence) on taking a mason mark, and a merk to the officer 'for calling a Lodge'—an indication that special meetings of the lodge might be summoned if candidates for initiation appeared. On promotion to the grade of fellow craft a candidate was to pay for a dinner, a pint of wine, or whatever members pleased! Strangers who were masons in other lodges and wanted to become masters of Aberdeen Lodge were to pay two dollars, speaking pints, and their contributions to the box, or (in the case of a gentleman) whatever members thought fit.

The contributions to the box required were very substantial. Entered apprentices who were actual craftsmen were to pay 'only' fifty merks as well as the other dues already specified, though again this was subject to variation by the lodge in individual cases. If an apprentice could not pay this, he was to serve his master for three years without any fee or wage, in return for his master paying the lodge the fees due. This suggests either that Aberdeen did not make masons entered apprentices until the completion of their trade apprenticeships, or that the three extra years bound to a master were not served immediately but after their ordinary apprenticeship expired, perhaps several years after they had entered the lodge. If a mason would, in effect, consider extending his unpaid apprenticeship for three years in order to gain entry to the lodge, then membership must have been expected to bring very substantial benefits indeed, in opportunities for employment and the security provided by the lodge as a benefit society. But three extra years of service seems punitive, recalling the condition in some indentures whereby an apprentice guilty of fornication had to serve his master for three extra years without fee (a penalty which was in danger of making immoral apprentices highly profitable for the masters).[36] It may indeed be that the provision for poorer apprentices paying for joining the lodge by extending their unpaid service was deliberately intended to impose a burden out of all proportion to the advantages of membership. Though lack of records make it impossible to know whether the lodge actually admitted any members through such arrangements in the late seventeenth century, the craftsmen who can be traced in the lodge were mainly fairly substantial figures whose families would have been able to help them pay entrance fees. Was the lodge, while seemingly holding out opportunities for poorer craftsmen to join, in fact ensuring that they could not do so? The poorer the lodge member, the more likely it was that in time of illness or other misfortune he would have to turn to the lodge for support, not having savings of his own to draw on. Thus in insurance terms poorer craftsmen were a bad risk, and may have been deliberately discouraged from joining the lodge.

Of the fifty merks' fee for entered apprentices at least half was to go to the lodge box; the other half might join it or be spent in other ways as the lodge decided. Eldest sons of members were to be privileged, having 'the benefit of the measson word' free of dues except for the speaking pint, a dinner, a pint of wine (presumably for each member), payment for a mason mark, and a contribution (unspecified) to the box. Those marrying members' eldest daughters were also to be admitted 'if they be found qualified' without providing aprons and gloves. Many lodges exacted gloves from entrants, but the same is true in incorporations of both masons and other crafts, so they may not have been the heavy working gloves of stonemasons (especially necessary to protect the skin when handling wet stone) but ornamental gloves. Now, for the first time, aprons are also mentioned in the context of a masonic lodge, and the fact that they are linen rather than leather may again suggest that they were not working aprons used by masons. There is no direct evidence of late seventeenth-century Scottish masons wearing gloves and aprons in lodge rituals, but as the masonic catechisms show that in the lodge masons were symbolically put to work it would have been appropriate to wear them for their rituals.

The final financial obligation of every lodge member was to pay twelve shillings on St John's Day, which was to be kept as a 'day of rejoysing and feasting with on another', and the statutes now at last turned away from money to other aspects of lodge membership. The statutes themselves were to be read to every entered apprentice joining the lodge so he could not claim ignorance of them. Though the statutes do not say so, the Old Charges were probably also read at every meeting: the copy in the Mark Book is entitled 'A discourse hade before A Meeting of Meassones Commonly caled the Measson Charter'.[37] No-one in the lodge was to teach or instruct an entered apprentice until he had been perfected by his intender: presumably this was so the candidate could be instructed systematically. But when his intender and 'Maate' (perhaps an error for 'Master'?) 'Gives him over as being taught then any person hath libertie to teach him any thing he forgates'. But if when 'he is interrogat at our publics meetings' the candidate forgot anything he was to be fined—unless he could show that his intender had failed to teach him, in which case the intender would be fined. This public meeting was evidently the ritual of initiation itself, and the rule that immediately follows, 'that non of our number presume to taunt or mock on another at our meetings' but love each other as brothers reads like a an attempt to prevent the interrogation and ritual humiliation of the candidate getting out of hand.

The statutes ended by making provision for the safekeeping of 'this book of Lawes'. It was to be kept locked in the box except when it was taken out and carried to the place where an entered apprentice was to be admitted (an indication that the box itself was not carried out to Girdleness or elsewhere for meetings). The lodge was to have a special care of the book. Not only was the clerk only to have it in his possession when he was writing in it, but the three keymasters (master, warden and boxmaster) were to be present while he was doing so. All the succeeding generations of masons were commanded not to blot out any of the names of the authors of the book, but to uphold them 'to all generationes as yor Pattrones', for there had never been a 'poores box' among the Aberdeen masons 'since the Memorie of Man' until they had established it. They had all convened on 27 December 1670 (so it was claimed) to set up the box, and each had contributed at least a rix dollar to it. The authors hoped their successors would follow their example: 'let not your poor have occatione to curse yow', was the 'heartie wish of ws all who ar the authoires therof: farweell.'

As indicated earlier, it seems that the statutes of the lodge were probably written into the Mark Book in the late 1680s, though they may well have enshrined the essence of rather earlier acts, 1670 or 1679-80 being likely dates. If the statutes reflect accurately the interests and activities of the Lodge of Aberdeen, then it was a lodge in which benefit society functions were unusually prominent. Ritual and social activities were inextricably linked with the box, but there is no sign of interest in regulating the working lives of masons (except insofar as having the Mason Word was regarded as a qualification for employment). This is perhaps surprising, as lodge's in burghs without mason incorporations tended to take over some of the functions normally performed by the latter. On the other hand if the Mark Book membership list records accurately the composition of the lodge, then it becomes clear that it was not a body suitable for supervising the trade, being dominated by landowners, merchants and craftsmen other than masons.

The problem of dating the '1670' list makes analysis of the membership

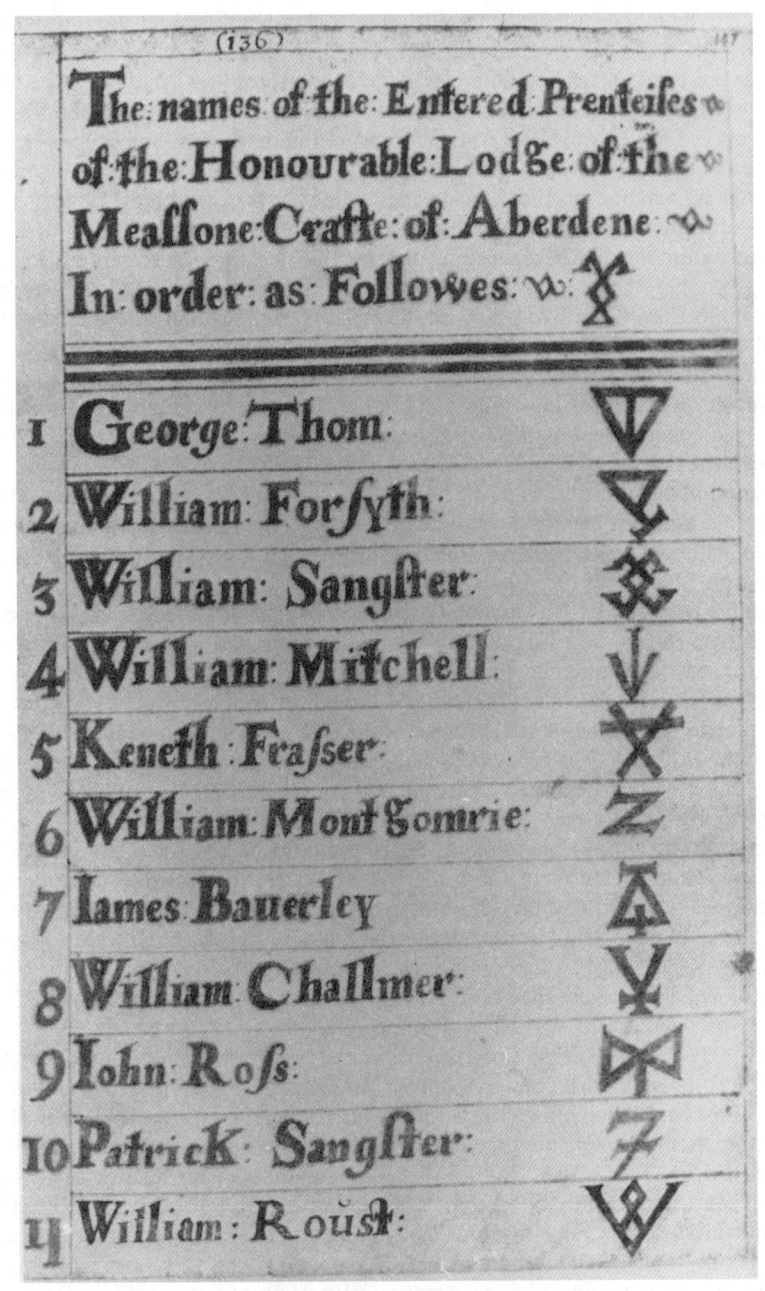

10 Aberdeen Mark Book
First page of the list of the entered apprentices of the lodge
(Miller, *Lodge of Aberdeen*)

difficult even in the case of the nobility. The earl of Dunfermline could be either Charles, the second earl (1622-72) and son of William Schaw's friend the first earl; or the third earl, Alexander (1672-7); or the fourth earl, James (1677-94). Similarly the Erroll listed could be the eleventh earl, Gilbert Hay (1636-74) or the twelfth, John Hay (1674-1704). The earl of Findlater was James Ogilvie, the third earl (1659-1711): through his marriage to a daughter of the eighth earl of Eglinton he was the brother-in-law of a member of Kilwinning Lodge.[38] The final noble member, Alexander Forbes, second Lord Pitsligo (1636-90) held land in a number of Aberdeenshire parishes. Of the three lairds in the lodge, little is known of George Rait of Mideple and John Gray younger of Crichie (later ninth Lord Gray, 1711-23), but their lands in the parish of Fyvie suggest (as already explained) a link with the earl of Dunfermline.

The third of the lairds, Harry Elphinstone, tutor of Airth and laird of Melgum, is a much more interesting figure. His father Thomas, inspector general of the army, had been made a burgess of Aberdeen in 1671, and in 1676 Harry himself was made an honorary burgess.[39] He probably already occupied some post in the collection of customs duties in the burgh, as a collector was made burgess at the same time as he was, and the following year (1677) Harry was acting as one of two collectors of customs in Aberdeen, and making himself very unpopular with the burgh authorities by illegally using his position to trade on this own account.[40] By 1680 he was evidently sole collector in Aberdeen.[41] He still held the post in 1687,[42] and was also in the 1680s tacksman of the imposition on wine, brandy, and aquavite for the burgh: he paid the council a fixed sum in return for the right to collect the duties—though in 1687 on giving his word as a gentleman that he had paid far more for the tack or lease than he had collected the council agreed to a repayment being made to him.[43] Harry also retained connections with Edinburgh, where he had become a burgess (by right of his father) in 1677, and he was buried there on his death in 1695.[44]

Through his commercial interests Harry Elphinstone was linked to one of the most fascinating features of the Lodge of Aberdeen: the fact that it contained several Quakers, and that they were active in the colonisation of New Jersey in the 1680s. When in 1685 it was announced that an English ship, the *Henry and Francis,* was to call at a number of Scottish ports to pick up passengers for New Jersey, local agents were listed for would be emigrants to get in touch with. One of the Aberdeen agents was Harry Elphinstone.[45]

In the 1660s New Jersey had been granted to Charles II's brother, James, duke of York. He in turn granted it to two Englishmen, who in the 1670s divided it into East and West Jersey. Soon afterwards East Jersey was sold to twelve Englishmen, mostly Quakers seeking a refuge from religious persecution. But it proved difficult to attract English Quaker emigrants, who tended to favour Pennsylvania as a destination, so the twelve proprietors agreed to transform the scheme into a largely Scots venture. They bought in twelve new proprietors, and though only half of them were Scots they soon proved the most active and successful of the twenty-four proprietors.[46] By 1684 twelve of the proprietors were Scots, and many had sold parts of their East Jersey lands to others: there were more than fifty Scots 'fractioners'.[47] Many of the Scots proprietors and fractioners came from the North East, and most of the Scots emigrants (700 or more) were from the same region. Most of the emigrants were orthodox in their religion, but a significant number were Quakers, both the geographical and religious biases arising from the fact that the driving force behind Scots involvement in the venture was the acknowledged leader of the Scots Quakers, Robert Barclay of Urie, whose estates lay some miles south of Aberdeen. In 1682 he was recognised as governor of East Jersey.[48]

The Quaker sect had spread to Scotland from England during the English military occupation of the 1650s. Its success was generally very limited, but by the 1660s and 1670s Aberdeen had emerged as its most important centre in Scotland. Quakers constituted only a tiny proportion of the population, but there were little groups firmly established in the burgh and in a few rural areas where lairds—like Barclay of Urie—had been converted. The burgh authorities of Aberdeen were, it seems, the most active in the country in persecuting their Quaker citizens, incensed by their non-conformity in general and by their occasional provocative actions—testifying to the truth (as they saw it) in public, sitting in church with their hats on, or walking through the streets dressed in sackcloth (as Barclay did in 1672). Persecution of Quakers in Aberdeen reached its peak in the 1670s, becoming increasingly intense until it suddenly ceased in 1679. During this decade 'the tolbooth was seldom without its complement of humble Quakers content to suffer for their convictions', arrested when their meetings were broken up or their dead exhumed from the graveyard they tried to establish.[49] Fear and hatred of the Quakers was increased by the strange alliance which emerged between these protestant sectaries and Catholic interests. Both were persecuted minorities, and Robert Barclay became a friend of the Catholic heir to the throne, the duke of York, the two men respecting each other's sincerity. The two faiths were often coupled together by their persecutors, as when in 1675 men of both convictions were banned from becoming burgesses in Aberdeen—an act hastily rescinded in 1686 after the duke of York had become King James VII and proved ready to protect Quakers as well as his own co-religionists.[50] By that time, however, several Aberdeen Quakers had emigrated to New Jersey or become involved in other ways with the scheme to colonise the province. That is understandable: they hoped for a new life in the new world, free from persecution. What is astounding, however, is that some of these men were also members of the Lodge of Aberdeen.

If a list were to be compiled of the main ways in which late seventeenth-century Quakers differed in their outward conduct from other men, very high places on it would be accorded to their refusal to swear oaths (which involved them in endless legal difficulties), and their rejection of ceremony and ritual of all sorts. How, then, did they get into a masonic lodge, initiation into which involved elaborate rituals and blood-curdling oaths of secrecy? And why did they want to be members of a lodge, an organisation at the centre of which lay the performance of rituals? Further, how was it that when Quakers tried to hold their own meetings they were forcibly broken up, but they could meet with others in the masonic lodge quite freely? One answer to these questions might be that the only evidence that these men were masons comes from the Mark

Book, and that it cannot be trusted. This solution is tempting in its simplicity, immediately solving all problems by rejecting the evidence. But it has already been argued that the membership list is plausible in other respects, even if it is not a list of members in 1670. Realisation of the true date of the list partly solves some problems: some of the Quaker members may not have joined the lodge until the early 1680s, when local persecution of Quakers had died down.

Moreover, some of them may not have been active Quakers when initiated (certainly they could not have been orthodox ones). Their support for Quakerism indicated a willingness to do unconventional things, and it could be that joining the lodge was part of the same readiness to try something different, undertaken before they became Quakers or (more likely) during some estrangement (temporary or permanent) from Quakerism. In spite of the huge gap between Quakers and masons over outward things like ritual and oaths, there were some underlying similarities between Quaker convictions and some of the ingredients of emergent freemasonry. In his emphasis on all true knowledge coming from divine revelation directly to the individual, Robert Barclay's thought was related to that of the Cambridge Platonists with their stress on personal religion making churches and their rituals unnecessary. His advocacy of religious toleration and lack of interest in argument over doctrinal niceties led some to accuse him of Deistic tendencies.[51] This strongly recalls Sir Robert Moray's outlook, and like him some Aberdeen Quakers (or ex-Quakers) may thus have found that early freemasonry fitted in well with some of their views. The origin of the lodge's exclusion of the overtly religious from its activities may have originated (as was suggested earlier) in the need to avoid poaching on the preserves of the church. But it led to an emphasis in freemasonry on a morality based on religion yet free from doctrinal content: and the rituals of the lodge could perhaps fill a Quaker's need for a ritual dimension to life without conflicting with rejection of ritual as inadmissable in the worship of God.

How many men who were at some point in their lives Quakers appear in the Mark Book '1670' membership list is uncertain, as all those involved were merchants or craftsmen difficult to distinguish from other local men with the same names. John Cowie (no. 42), merchant and lodge treasurer at an unspecified date, was almost certainly the merchant of that name imprisoned as a Quaker in 1676 and 1677. It was evidently the same John Cowie who, having graduated from Marischal College in 1669, took part in a debate with the divinity students of the college in 1675. The previous year he had cheekily handed the bishop of Aberdeen a tract he had written denouncing the use of excommunication against Quakers. His copy of one of Robert Barclay's works (*Les Principles de la Verité,* Rotterdam 1675) survives.[52] Rather more doubtful is the case of Alexander Paterson, armourer (no. 19), who was to be master of the lodge three times in the 1690s. He may have been the student recorded attending Marischal College in 1672 and upholding the Quaker cause in the debate with divinity students three years later.[53] The fact that he later became deacon convener of the incorporated trades indicates that (if indeed the two Alexander Patersons are identical) he must have lived down his youthful

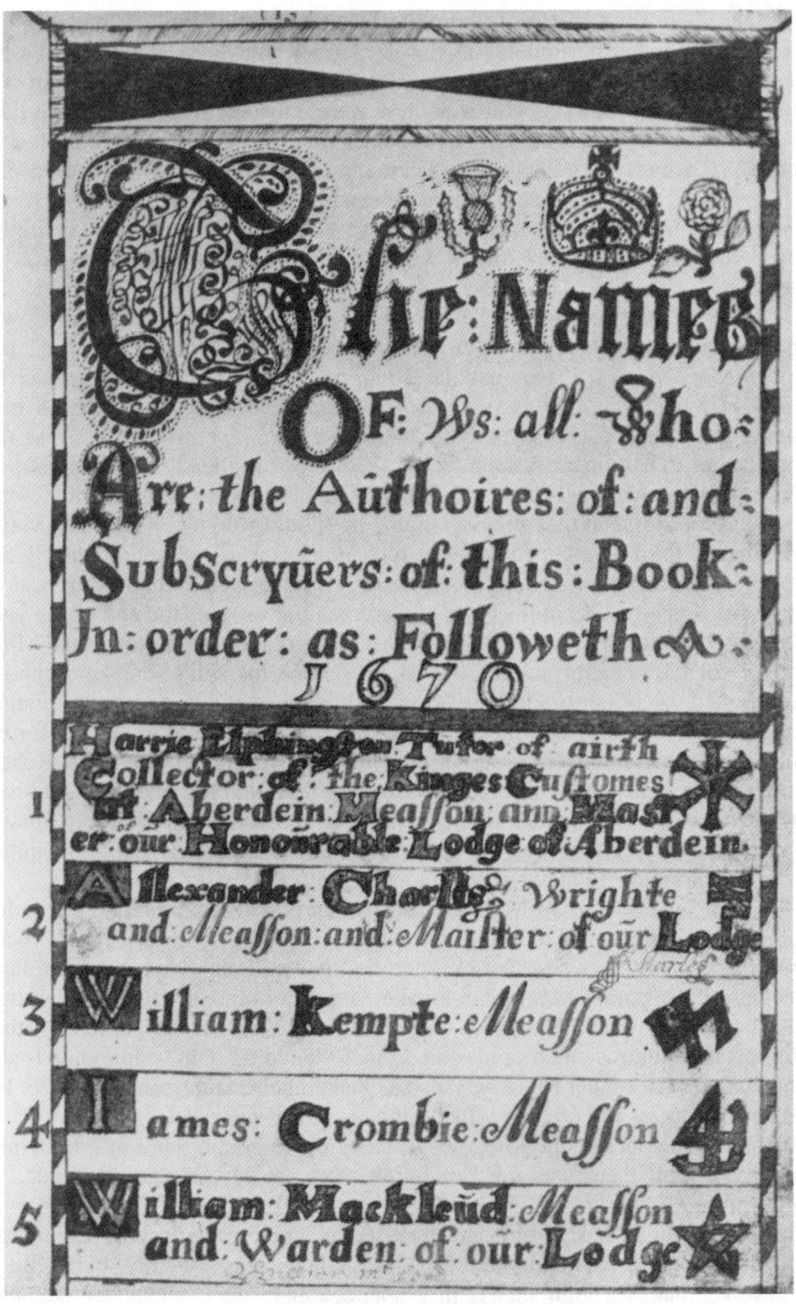

11 Aberdeen Mark Book
First page of the list of the masters of the lodge
From Miller, *Lodge of Aberdeen*

religious aberrations, perhaps finding a substitute for them in the lodge. In the background of his portrait, as in that of Patrick Whyte (a hookmaker) who joined the lodge in 1690, two mysterious pillars appear. In the absence of any other explanation, it is probable that these were intended to represent the pillars of Solomon's Temple, whose Biblical names provided the secret words (Jachin and Boaz) which were central to the rituals of the Mason Word. Thus coded references to the masonic connections were smuggled into portraits of Aberdeen freemasons. Whyte's portrait bears the date 1704, and Paterson's is so similar (they are by the same artist) that it was probably painted within a few years of that date.[54]

Neither of the two possible 'Quaker masons' already discussed, John Cowie and Alexander Paterson, have any known connection with New Jersey, but Robert Gordon (no. 39) bought land in East Jersey. Luckily, as he had so common a name, he had an unusual trade, that of cardmaker (maker of iron combs or brushes used for combing wool fibres or brushing cloth to raise the nap or pile) to help identify him. In 1674 Gordon was already a Quaker, but he was a poor lad without a trade. His fellow Quakers discussed how a job could be found for him, and they concluded that he should work for Alexander Mure, hookmaker, until he attained some insight in drawing wire (manufacturing the wire used for making fish hooks and 'cards'). If he proved diligent Mure was to 'give him some Insight in his trade of Cardmaking' towards the end of the year Gordon was to serve. As a member of the Incorporation of Hammermen Mure should not have taught anyone but an apprentice his skills, but here charity outweighed such considerations as a full apprenticeship was not thought appropriate. Gordon evidently put the training he received to good use, for by 1683 he had purchased from one of the Quaker East Jersey proprietors, Robert Burnet of Lethenty, 1/32 of the latter's 1/24 share of the province. He sold half his estate in 1686 and apparently never himself went to the province; but his son Daniel can be traced there in the 1690s, with power of attorney from his father (who then owned 250 acres in Monmouth County).[55]

The Alexander Mure or Moore who gave Gordon his training had begun his career in Montrose, becoming an Aberdeen burgess in 1657. He was, presumably, a Quaker like Gordon, and he may well also have been a fellow freemason. Alexander Moore, hookmaker, appears in the '1670' lodge list (no. 43), though it is impossible (given the problems of dating the list) to tell whether this was the Montrose man or his son, as they shared the same names and trade. The younger Alexander Mure was also a Quaker, being imprisoned in 1676. He became a burgess in 1682, by which time his father was dead.[56]

Another member of the Lodge of Aberdeen who bought land in East Jersey but never went there was the Edinburgh advocate Mr George Alexander of Peffermiln. His father, Mr John Alexander of Peffermiln, an Edinburgh man, had married an Aberdeen girl and practised as an advocate in both Edinburgh and Aberdeen. He was appointed clerk of the latter burgh in 1660 but died the following year. Through this family connection George Alexander attended Marischal College in Aberdeen (in the late 1660s).[57] Like Gordon he bought a 1/32 share of Burnet of Lethenty's land in 1683, but he is the odd man out among the Aberdeen Lodge men with New Jersey interests, as he was not, it seems, a Quaker.[58]

John Forbes, merchant, (no. 36) was one of the two lodge members who not only bought land in New Jersey but settled there. He was the son of Alexander Forbes of Boyndlie (in northern Aberdeenshire), who had been tutor of Pitsligo during the minority of the second Lord Pitsligo, and John's mother was Harry Elphinstone's sister. Thus he had close family connections with at least two other members of the Lodge of Aberdeen. More than one John Forbes can be traced among local Quakers, but there is no evidence identifying any with the freemason—one was a merchant, but in Ellon, not Aberdeen. However the fact that his father was heavily fined, and evidently detained after the Restoration of monarchy in 1660 on account of his covenanting past, suggests that the family was regarded as suspect in its religious or political loyalties. John Forbes emigrated in 1684, making a last-minute decision to go after being infected by the enthusiasm of friends who were about to sail. He landed at Perth-Amboy with three servants and bought land—again from Burnet of Lethenty. But in 1686 he can be traced appointing an attorney as he was returning to Scotland. He subsequently succeeded his brother as laird of Boyndlie, being called Captain Forbes: when he had acquired this military title is unknown.[59]

The final Quaker mason emigrant of Aberdeen Lodge was John Skene (no. 27), and unlike the others his activities lay in West rather than East Jersey. John's father was a prominent Aberdeen merchant, Alexander Skene, who served as a baillie in the burgh and bought the estate of Newtyle in the parish of Foveran. John was admitted as a burgess in 1659, and was studying at Marischal College in 1662-3 (though it is not known whether he graduated). Both father and son became Quakers, thorns in the flesh of the authorities. In 1674 John was in trouble for sitting through a church service in Foveran with his hat on and then addressing the congregation. The following year he was one of the Quakers who debated with divinity students. In 1676 he wrote to the provost of Aberdeen denouncing religious persecution, and he and thirty-three other Aberdeen Quakers were fined. He was also ordered to find caution not to pray or preach at meetings, or to undertake 'to remove out of the kingdom'. One of those involved in persecuting him at this point was the twelfth earl of Erroll, who may himself later have been a member of the lodge. John Skene was in prison again in 1677.[60] Sometime after this he decided to take the hint and emigrate. The date is uncertain. It is asserted that he sailed from Aberdeen with his wife and family on the *Golden Lion*, arriving at Delaware in October 1682,[61] but he may in fact have been the John Skene who landed at Burlington in 1678 and was in Pennsylvania in about 1681.[62] Possibly he returned to Aberdeen after an initial visit to the colony, to collect his family. In June 1682 he bought the estate of Peachfield in Burlington County, the Quaker form of dating the deed indicating that he was still true to that faith. In 1683 he was elected to the West New Jersey Council, and though 'divested of office' through his opposition to the governor, he was by 1685 himself deputy governor of the colony, a post he held at least until 1687 and possibly until his death. John Skene of Peachfield made his will in 1690 and died soon afterwards.[63]

144   THE FIRST FREEMASONS

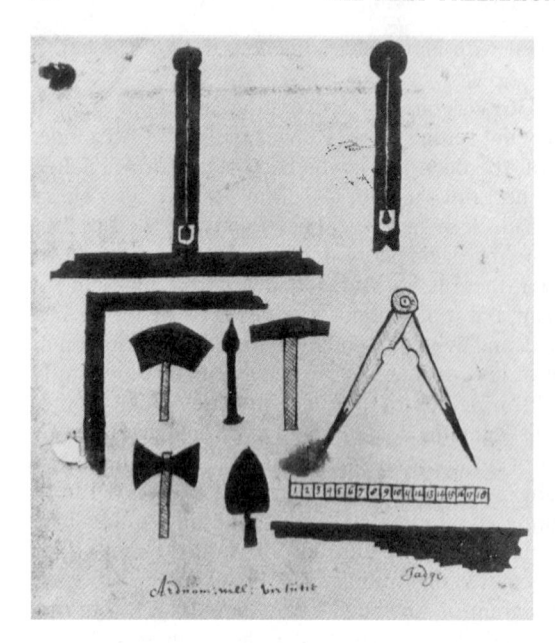

12   Aberdeen Mark Book
     Masons' tools
     From Miller,
     Lodge of Aberdeen

13   The Aberdeen Mark Book
The date given in the text of the book,
1670, cannot be the true date it was
compiled, and it was probably written
about two decades later. It was written by
James Anderson, the lodge's secretary -
and the father of Dr James Anderson, the
author of the famous
Constitutions of the Freemasons
of 1723
From Miller, *Lodge of Aberdeen*

Skene has been hailed as the 'First Freemason to Become a Citizen of the Western Hemisphere',[64] and certainly there are no known earlier examples of an ininiated mason emigrating. He was closely followed in 1684 by John Forbes (though he did not settle permanently) and John Cockburn of Melrose Lodge. As Skene had emigrated before some of those named on the '1670' list could have joined the Lodge of Aberdeen the forty-nine masters there recorded can never have met together. Some, like the nobles and lairds, probably only attended once, when they were initiated on some occasion when public or private business brought them to Aberdeen. Analysis of the masters has raised many problems in understanding what was going on in the lodge. Turning to the eleven entered apprentices on the list reveals a new problem. That they were all, so far as they can be identified, operative masons is explicable if (as in most lodges) other types of member were admitted to both grades in quick succession and thus were entered apprentices only briefly. Nor is it surprising that they can be traced in the late 1680s and 1690s rather than earlier, for if the membership list was really drawn up in the late 1680s that is to be expected: the entered apprentices would be among the most recently joined members. But why is it that of the seven entered apprentices who can be identified only one was from Aberdeen, all the other six coming from the small burgh of barony to the north, Old Aberdeen?[65] By contrast only one of the forty-nine masters of the lodge, David Murray (no. 8), was resident in Old Aberdeen: he was a mason burgess there.

It looks very much as though Old Aberdeen masons had in the past been deliberately excluded from the lodge, but that a recent decision had been taken to admit them. Such a move would have much strengthened the operative mason element in the lodge, for though Old Aberdeen was a tenth or less of the size of Aberdeen there were about the same number of masons in each of them. The poll tax records of 1696 contain the names of six masons resident in Aberdeen, while Old Aberdeen could claim five, plus the widow of a mason and four more masons in the rural parts of the parish of St Machar. As in other areas, many masons felt the restrictions and burdens of dwelling in royal burghs outweighed the advantages. Residing elsewhere also allowed them the freedom to combine the mason trade, subject to major fluctuations in local demand, with other occupations. One of the Old Aberdeen entered apprentices, James Baverley, was the tenant of farmland at Sunieside and also worked as a cordiner (shoemaker) as well as a mason, an odd combination. He was made a burgess of Old Aberdeen in 1696 for working on the burgh's market cross.[66] Others had less respectable additional occupations: two Old Aberdeen masons were banished in 1698 for shop-breaking. One, William Montgomery, was a member of the lodge. By 1705 he had sneaked back into the burgh, and was banished again for threatening the shopkeeper concerned and his family.[67]

In the years after the true date of the '1670' membership list (the late 1680s) the lodge continued the practice, suggested by the '1670' list of entered apprentices, of relying mainly on operative stonemasons for new recruits. Many new members are not identified, and the record of admissions is not complete, but most of those admitted seem to have been in this category. Moreover, when other types of member joined they came from the merchant and craftsman level of society. Four slaters joined between 1687 and 1706, along with a wright, a hookmaker (Patrick Whyte, seven times master of the lodge) and a tailor, this last being the first member of an incorporation other than the hammermen and wrights to be found in the lodge. Three merchant members include a London merchant (Thomas Lushington, 1688) and a merchant who through possession of land was also a small laird (William Forbes of Tulloch, 1701). A junior army officer joined in 1706 (Ensign George Seton), a writer in 1711 (John Deans).[68] But the upper end of the social scale found in the '1670' list had disappeared from the lodge entirely. There are no more nobles, lairds, ministers, or professional men (unless the writer be counted as such). A few such figures appear in the second decade of the eighteenth century: Alexander Jaffray of Kingswells, a member of the prominent local Quaker family, joined in 1718; and George Gordon, 'Master of Arithmetick', in 1717 became the second mathematician to join the lodge. It was probably just a coincidence, but his mathematical predecessor, George Liddel (master of the lodge 1710-12, 1713-14) was deposed from his professorship in Marischal College in 1717—after a previous attempt to depose him in 1706-7 for fornication and other offences had failed on legal grounds.[69] If Liddel left Aberdeen at this point, was George Gordon brought into the lodge to replace him, it being felt a lodge of mason/geometers ought to have a mathematician in its ranks?

Men like Jaffray of Kingswells and Gordon were the exception rather than the rule among the recruits to the lodge in the 1710s and 1720s; most new members were stonemasons from the burgh or neighbouring areas. Thus Aberdeen fits into the pattern found in a number of other lodges, which admitted non-operatives of high rank in society for a time in the late seventeenth or early eighteenth centuries, but then deliberately excluded them in favour of stonemasons and other working men. The fact that the lodge's records are not accessible makes it impossible to know whether this development was accompanied by an attempt by the lodge to become 'operative' in the sense of controlling the mason trade in the area. Minutes of 1701 show that the lodge then still required members to pay twelve shillings a year to the lodge's box, as the '1670' statutes had laid down, and in 1720 the dues payable by a new entered apprentice were established as £12 Scots, fees for the lodge clerk and officer, speaking pint, and dinner. Those who had not served an apprenticeship, not being stonemasons, were to pay £16.[70] It has been said that the lodge records frequently refer to essays being set for entrants. If this was really the case the lodge was highly unusual, but as the authority for this wanders off into totally irrelevant references to Edinburgh essays in other trades without giving a single Aberdeen example the accuracy of the statement is doubtful.[71]

Not having an incorporation to supply a deacon, the Lodge of Aberdeen was presided over by a master. In 1696-1700 the lodge had two wardens,[72] after which there was only one; that the practice of having two prevailed before the minutes begin in 1696 may be suggested by the fact that the '1670' list calls John Roland or Ronald 'the first Warden of our Lodge'. A nineteenth-century list of office holders lists 'tylers' from 1698. Tylers (the origins of the word are obscure) appear in masonic lodges from the mid eighteenth century, acting as guards at the door to make sure that no person who had not been initiated entered while rituals were being performed,[73] and if Aberdeen Lodge records do indeed record tylers from 1698 these are by far the earliest references known to such officials.[74]

According the the '1670' statutes Aberdeen Lodge met at Girdleness. In 1700 it evidently acquired a building for its meetings much closer to the burgh. Lodge historians are confused as to quite what happened in 1700. One states the lodge bought land at Futtiesmyre or Footismyre (lying between Aberdeen and the little fishing village of Futtie or Footdee) and built a croft on it,[75] others add that part of the ground bought by the lodge was then leased to the father of James Gibb.[76] In fact the Gibb concerned in the transaction was James himself, not his father (Patrick or Peter), and he was the seller of the croft. Peter Gibb, an Aberdeen merchant, had lived at Futtiesmyre. He died sometime between 1696 and 1699.[77] In 1700 his son James sold the croft of Futtiesmyre—not to the lodge, but to one Alexander Duncan and his wife. Perhaps Duncan acted as an agent for the lodge, however, for the lodge treasurer's accounts for 1699-1700 reveal that he paid out £400 as part of the price of Futtiesmyre, and that ten shillings had been spent at a meeting with James Gibb about the transaction.[78] The building the lodge thus acquired is shown on a view of Aberdeen dated 1732, identified as 'The Lodge of the Free Masons'. A two-storey structure, it stands on its own, more isolated than any other building shown, which was presumably why it appealed to the lodge. It would be easy to be sure that rituals were not observed by the uninitiated, and though within the burgh's jurisdiction it was 'outside' the burgh in the sense of not being in the built-up area. There must have been a house on the site before 1700, as the Gibbs lived there, and James Gordon's mid seventeenth-century plan of Aberdeen appears to include it. Thus the lodge building was probably not built by the lodge, which took over and adapted an existing one.[79]

The purchase of a special building for the lodge to meet in is of itself of considerable interest. But there is added interest in the transaction through the identity of the seller. The Gibbs were a Catholic family, and though James Gibb may have attended Marischal College in the late 1690s his religion would have prevented him from graduating there. On his father's death he sold the family croft because he was resolved to seek his fortune abroad. After spending some time in the Netherlands he entered the Scots College in Rome to train for the priesthood, but left before being ordained. By 1707 he was studying architecture, and after returning to Britain he became one of the foremost architects of the age in England, anglicising his name to Gibbs.[80] As so often in this book's attempts to squeeze sense out of recalcitrant sources, there is a danger of seeing meaning in what may merely be coincidence. But by some accounts Gibb had displayed an unusual talent for drawing before leaving Aberdeen in 1700. Is it just possible that as well as furnishing itself with a very suitable new meeting place the lodge saw itself as helping a youth with promising architectural skills on his way in life?

Consideration of the early days of Aberdeen Lodge can be ended, however,

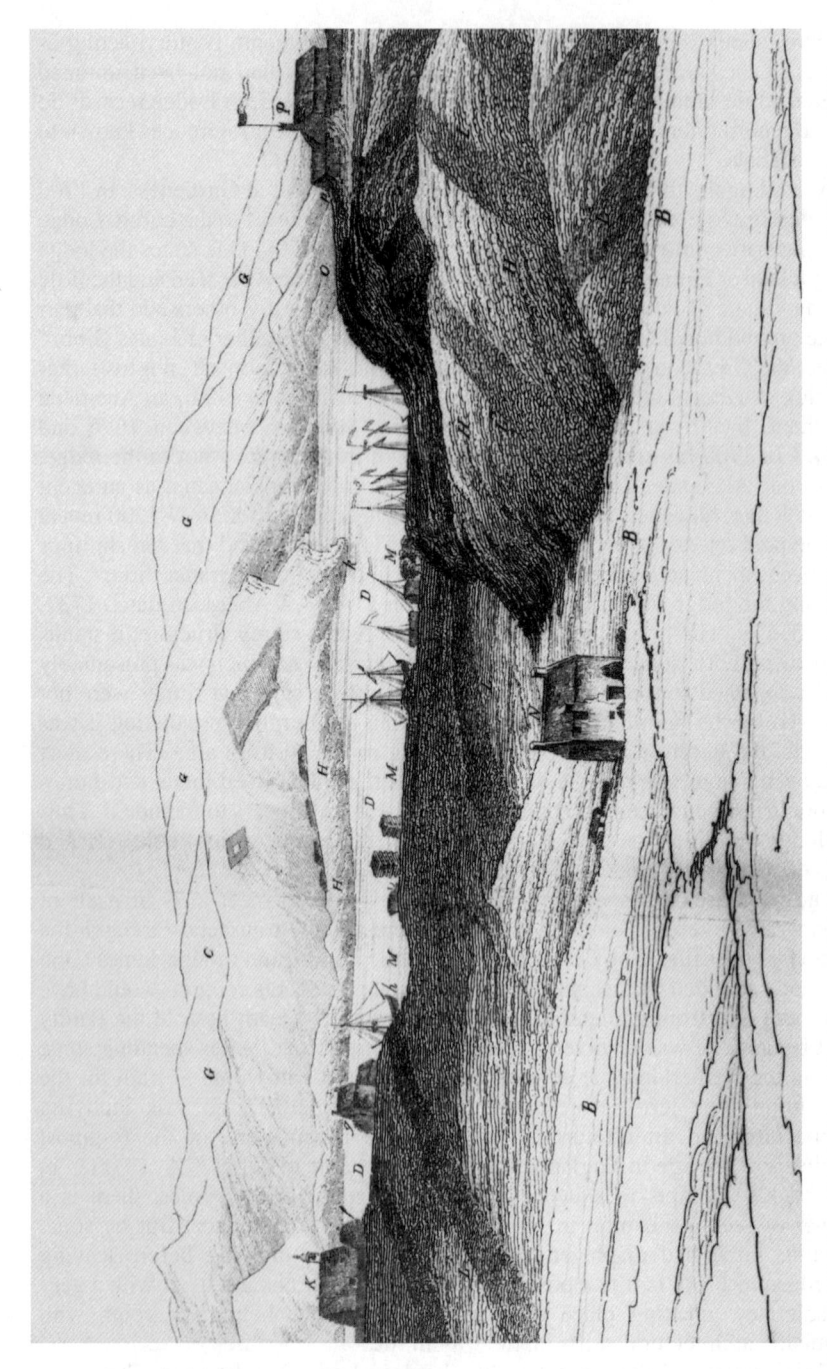

14 The Lodge of Aberdeen, The house at Futtismuir bought by the lodge in 1700 (Gregory Sharpe, *East prospect of Aberdeen*, 1732).

with a link with developments elsewhere which certainly is not mere coincidence. James Anderson, glazier, whose compilation of the Mark Book with its false date has at once provided the only evidence of the early history of the lodge and created great confusion about it, had a son and namesake who continued the family tradition of simultaneously informing and misleading those seeking the origins of freemasonry. Moreover, where the father had modestly confined himself to invention relating to a decade or two of the history of a single lodge, the son's creative imagination ranged over the centuries and concerned the whole masonic movement.

The younger James Anderson was born in 1679, and attended Marischal College in the late 1690s.[81] He studied theology after taking his arts degree, but instead of entering the parish ministry in Scotland he moved to London, and became successively the minister of a dissenting (presbyterian) congregation. The fact that he ultimately received the degree of doctor of divinity from Marischal College indicates that he retained some ties with Scotland, but nothing further is known of these. Nor is it known whether he had been initiated into the Aberdeen Lodge before leaving Scotland, the records of admissions being incomplete. But even if he was not, he may have become acquainted with the lore of the masons through his father and have studied the Mark Book (in its original, much extended, form). In 1723 his *The constitutions of the free-masons. containing the history, charges, regulations, etc. of that most ancient and right worshipful fraternity. For the use of the lodges* was published in London under the auspices of the new Grand Lodge of England. A revised version followed in 1738, *The new book of constitutions of the antient and honourable fraternity of free and accepted masons*. These works were more influential than any others in shaping British freemasonry in the eighteenth century. Through them many of the traditions of the Scottish lodges of the previous century were popularised in England, mixed with the lore of the Old Charges and more recent English inventions. Something so basic as the grades of entered apprentice and fellow craft 'were introduced to the English Craft generally' by the 1723 Constitutions.[82] Admittedly Anderson did not state that such elements were being introduced to England from Scotland, and his grandiose name-dropping sketch of the 'history' of masonry has much to say about supposed English royal masons and very little of their Scottish royal counterparts. But the reasons for this are easy to see. The Scots in general were very unpopular in England for much of the eighteenth century. To admit that much of freemasonry, which the *Constitutions* sought to popularise in England, was derived from her despised northern neighbours would have discredited it. Moreover, Anderson was creating a mythology for the English, and it was therefore appropriate and proper to fill past centuries with eminent English freemasons and thus create a much far more acceptable and respectable past than a Scottish dominated masonic one could ever have been. Scottish masons had their myths to give them pride in their craft, but these national myths could not serve the same purpose in England.

The two James Anderson's, father and son, bridge the gap between the Scottish lodges of the seventeenth century and the English Grand Lodge of the eighteenth, but their talent was as much for mystification as enlightenment of their readers.

The Lodge of Inverness

That anything at all is known about the early history of the Lodge of Inverness is due entirely to the splendidly informative petition it submitted to Grand Lodge in 1737 in seeking a charter from it. This related that according to the tradition of its oldest members the lodge had kept its minutes 'in an irregular manner' on loose sheets of paper up to 1678. These had been lost, but in 1678 William Mackintosh, brother of the laird of Mackintosh, had been chosen master of the lodge and had given the lodge a book in which all their subsequent meetings and transactions had been recorded. The petition then proceeded to give a complete list of all appointments of office-holders in the lodge from 1678 to 1736, compiled from this minute book—fortunately, as it has since been lost.[83]

The petition recorded fifteen meetings in 1678—1736. Obviously only meetings at which office-holders were changed were included in the summary, but even so the record is not impressive. There were no meetings at all recorded in 1703 to 1715 inclusive, for example, and if the lodge had been continuously active in these years it would have been very surprising for it not to need to change any of its four officials in twelve years. Thus it may well be that the lodge was only intermittently active—or entirely inactive— in these years.

On 27 December 1678, at the first recorded meeting of the lodge, William Mackintosh of Elrig was elected master, with Alexander Nicolson as senior warden, Andrew Ross as junior warden and Donald Ross as boxmaster. Inverness is the first lodge in which the offices of senior and junior warden appear: perhaps there were two wardens as the master was a non-operative up to the end of the century, recalling the way Kilwinning elected deputes to the non-operative deacons and wardens of the 1670s. Mackintosh of Elrig was the brother of Lachlan Mackintosh, chief of his clan. Elrig died in about 1691, when John McBean, probably the man of that name who had become junior warden in 1684, was involved in settling his affairs.[84] His successor as master, elected on 27 December 1692, was James Barbour, evidently the laird of Aldowry. Barbour served until 1699. Thereafter all the masters until the 1730s are listed just by Christian name and surname, making identification difficult but indicating that these were ordinary folk rather than gentry with territorial titles. The same is true of the holders of the other three offices in the lodge in these early years. Few can be identified with confidence, but those who can were masons. Alexander Nicolson (senior warden 1678-92) had a contract with the burgh council in 1678 to 'outread and finish the peir at the water syd'.[85] Andrew Ross (junior warden 1678-84, boxmaster 1684-1701, senior warden 1701-2) worked with Robert Nicolson (junior warden 1699-1701) on repairing 'the back of the tounes hous at the water syd' in the 1670s.[86] James Dick (master 1701-16, senior warden 1716-18) contracted to build the tolbooth steeple in 1688, and

Andrew Scott (master 1716-19) built the laird of Macleod's tomb in the burgh in 1720-1.[87]

Whether the lodge really had existed before 1678 must remain uncertain. If it did, that date may be important in the lodge's development not just because it acquired a minute book but because it marked the point at which gentlemen non-operatives entered the lodge and insisted on better record keeping—though judging by the list of office holders non-operatives lost interest in the lodge for the first few decades of the eighteenth century. In the 1737 petition to Grand Lodge the lodge called itself Old Inverness Kilwinning, but there is no evidence of any real connection with Kilwinning, and the name was probably adopted later because it was felt to bestow status and a claim to antiquity.

As the fact that the Lodge of Inverness was presided over by a master rather than a deacon indicates, Inverness possessed no mason's incorporation. But though not given the name incorporation the lodge was regarded, at least by the 1730s as the equivalent of an incorporation (as Dunblane Lodge was, briefly, at about the same time). The burgh possessed six craft incorporations, but the lands and other property of the crafts were divided into seven equal parts held by the six incorporations and the lodge. The arrangement was evidently an uneasy one. In the 1750s the lodge unsuccessfully sought to be incorporated, but later it abandoned this ambition and instead in 1780 it sold its seventh share of the property to the other six trades.[88]

The Lodge of Banff

The Lodge of Banff used to possess a minute book which began in 1703, but sadly this was destroyed by fire some years ago. It is said that it included references to older documents, but all that is known of its contents is the text of two minutes dating from 1708 and 1773.

On 27 December 1708 nine men 'being Measons' met, including Alexander Mill, master for the coming year, and Alexander Forsyth, warden. They resolved that each of them, and the rest of the trade, should pay four shillings to a box to be kept by the warden, and that subsequently the money should be lent out to earn interest. Two other members are mentioned who were evidently not present.[89]

Four of the members can be readily identified. Two were masons by trade. Alexander Mill, the lodge's master, lived at Mill of Alvah just a few miles south of Banff, and was a well known and experienced mason: the burgh council consulted him about rebuilding the tolbooth in 1710.[90] In 1708, the same year as the surviving minute, the council paid James Bennet for building a well in the burgh.[91] The other two identifiable members, Alexander Forsyth, warden, and his son of the same name, were glaziers. In 1701 they were granted a fee of £6 a year for life for keeping the windows of the church of Banff in good order. When the elder Forsyth died in 1724 he was living at Colleonard just outside the burgh.[92] From the scraps of evidence provided by the 1708 minute it looks as though the Lodge of Banff, like other lodges in rural areas and small burghs, drew its members from a mixture of building crafts and not just from masons—almost inevitably, as many craftsmen in such areas would undertake work in several related trades in a way forbidden in the larger burghs where each trade jealously guarded its exclusive preserves. There is no sign in the lodge either of gentry non-operatives or of craftsmen from non-building trades. That the lodge was only just establishing a box in 1708 suggests that either it had not been in existence very long or that it was just reorganising after a period of decline.

The Lodge of Kilmolymock (Elgin)

The 'Roll of Lodges' published by the Grand Lodge of Scotland, normally a reliable guide to the earliest dates at which lodges can be traced in authentic records, assigns the Lodge of Kilmolymock the date 'From 1687'.[93] But the reason that this date was accepted appears to have been forgotten, the earliest known reference to the lodge now being the date of the first surviving entry in the lodge's first minute book, 1704.

It seems, however, that the lodge was then well established and thriving, so its foundation date may well be considerably earlier. The first four pages of the minute book have been lost, and the first surviving page begins in the middle of an entry (concerning the collection of 'quarter pennies' from members). The first complete minute records that 'the whole Masons of Elgin Lodge having mett', in Elgin on 27 December 1704, elected their officials. The first official mentioned is unique: John Gordon was voted to be 'Mr [Master] Speaker'. No official of this name is known in any other lodge, and there are no other references to a speaker in the minutes of the lodge (at least in their early years). Otherwise the lodge has the officials which were fairly standard in lodges without deacons: master mason, warden, boxmaster, keymasters (one keeper of the outer key and two of the inner keys, the latter presumably holding keys to locks which only became accessible once the outer lock was opened), clerk and officer. In addition a number of members of the lodge were appointed councillors; in 1704 two men were added to the existing councillors.[94] Similar additions took place in 1705 and 1706, but then in 1708 eight men were named as 'masters' and councillors of the craft. In 1710 ten men were chosen as councillors by the master mason.[95] Thus here as in a number of other lodges by this time a select group of fellow crafts joined the officials in managing the lodge's affairs, and, though these appointed councillors only served for limited periods and there is no sign of ceremonies associated with their appointment, the fact that they were sometimes referred to as masters in a way which differentiated them from the rest of the fellow craft masters may point the way ahead to the emergence of the trigradal system in which master was a separate and higher degree than fellow craft.

The masons of Elgin probably did not belong to an incorporation. In 1700 an agreement between the burgh and the trades recognised five incorporations with deacons. This was, it was said, a restoration of 'the old deaconrie' settled in 1657, which suggests that the organisation of the trades had decayed and that this was now being rectified. One of the five trades was the wrights,[96] but there is no evidence that masons were comprehended in that incorporation. In view of this it seems likely that the lodge occupied a position similar to that of Inverness, having no officially recognised status in the burgh—and thus no formal subordination to the burgh council—but nonetheless being regarded as the unofficial equivalent of an incorporation. The authority the lodge claimed extended well beyond the burgh's limits. In 1713 it described itself as 'The Lodge of Masons in and about Elgin'.[97] In January 1706 it met in Kirkton of Duffus, four and a half miles north west of the burgh, in January 1707 at Quarrywood, two and a half miles west of Elgin, and in 1716 in Plewlands, near Duffus.[98] Many, probably most, of the lodge's members were working stonemasons. When in 1709 the burgh signed a contract with three masons for rebuilding the tolbooth (which had been burnt down in 1700 by a lunatic imprisoned there) the masons were John Ross, mason in the Kirkton of Duffus, James Ross, and George Ogilvie, masons in Elgin. At that time the three held the positions in the lodge of master mason, keeper of the outer key, and warden respectively.[99] At least one member belonged to a closely related trade: James Forsyth (a keeper of an inner key in 1705-6) was a glazier, paid an annual fee for maintaining the windows of the burgh's churches and chosen as a burgh constable in 1708.[100] James Winchester, who joined the lodge as an entered apprentice in 1704 and became a fellow craft in 1708, was described as a merchant in 1719 when he borrowed 100 merks from lodge funds in addition to 200 merks which he already held.[101] William Crombie, the lodge clerk, may also have been a merchant,[102] and in January 1706 Mr John Kennedy, schoolmaster in Duffus, entered the lodge. As the following December he became a councillor it looks as though his social status had allowed him to be initiated as both entered apprentice and fellow craft on the same occasion.[103] Certainly Michael Anderson in Kirkton of Duffus was both entered and passed as a fellow in January 1707, and in December the same year Francis Brodie was admitted as a freeman of the craft, 'having given Evidence thereof in his entrie and Fellowship'.[104] The wording of this last entry is obscure, but it may be that Brodie was a stonemason who proved that he had already been initiated elsewhere, and that he was thus not only received immediately as a fellow craft but was accepted as a freeman in the sense of being able to work as a mason in Elgin.

Though the lodge had a few non-operatives of fairly humble status among its members, its character was predominantly operative. Its early minutes are largely confined to recording elections and initiations, but the few exceptions show that it was also seeking to regulate the mason trade and the relations of individual masons in a traditional manner. Thus the first such act referred to a function central to guilds: in 1707 it was enacted that when any member was called by death all others should attend his burial, on pain of a fine.[105] From 1705 some of those admitted to the lodge are described as servants to members of the lodge, and these may not just have been journeymen employed by the members but their former apprentices. An act of 1720 laid down that no man, having served the years of his apprenticeship, should be received 'to his entrie' until he paid the necessary fees. This suggests that in Elgin masons did not join the lodge as entered apprentices until after their formal trade apprenticeships had been completed. So far as is known this was unique in the early Scottish lodges: in all other cases where evidence survives it was usual for the apprentice to enter the lodge a few years after his apprenticeship had begun.

Several years normally elapsed in Elgin between entry to the lodge and promotion to fellowship, and as the 1720 act laid down that a entered apprentice must have served at least four years as a journeyman before promotion to fellow craft it looks as though becoming an entered apprentice may have been almost simultaneous with becoming a journeyman at the end of apprenticeship. By the act the lodge also ruled that an apprenticeship should be for a minimum of five years (plus one year serving the same master for 'meat and fee'),[106] so the career of an Elgin mason would seem to be five years as a trade apprentice, after which he would become a journeyman and entered apprentice. Four or so years later he could become a fellow craft master in the lodge, and presumably (as there was no separate incorporation), this also made him a freeman master able to undertake work on his own account and employ others. Thus here the two parallel and interlocking hierarchies found in the mason's career in Edinburgh, where both incorporation and lodge were involved, has been simplified. Journeyman and entered apprentice have virtually been combined, as have fellow craft master freeman master (though of course many men entitled to take work for themselves as masters would continue in practice to work for others as journeymen/servants).

The 1720 act also sought to put strict limits on numbers of apprentices: no master was to have more than three apprentices 'all the days of his life'. This was presumably based on memories of the First Schaw Statutes of 1598, but in Elgin exceptions were made. A master's own sons or the sons of other freemen could be taken as apprentices in addition to the three, so the limitation only concerned apprentices from families not already involved in the trade.[107] Concern was shown also for ensuring that the mason trade remained distinct from others. In 1713 strict limitations were placed on masons working for men of a different 'science' without permission of the lodge.[108] In this the lodge was exercising jurisdiction outside as well as inside the burgh—work in quarries is specifically mentioned—but in other respects it seems to have distinguished between Elgin itself and the surrounding area. In 1709 Andrew Brodie paid one merk for having worked in the burgh for the past year (the money being given to a lodge member's wife who was in need). Evidently he was not a lodge member and was not normally entitled to work within the burgh itself.[109] As elsewhere, masters employing journeymen who were not members of the lodge are recorded paying booking money for them (from 1714), and men who were not fellow crafts were only permitted to undertake small jobs, worth under £10, on their own account.[110]

Sparse though the information given in the Kilmolymock minutes in the first years after 1704 is, the impression is of a quite large and well organised lodge, though meetings are only recorded once or twice a year. Accounts do not survive, but the lodge seems to have been run efficiently, as the fact that it had 300 merks out on loan in 1719 indicates. In the same year it began to invest its funds permanently, by buying property in the burgh.[111] One mystery about the lodge remains, however. How did the Elgin Lodge become called Kilmolymock? Until 1782 Kilmalemnock was a separate parish, then being united to Lhanbryd. The name has now disappeared, but its church was at Kirkhill, two miles east of Elgin. The lodge never met there in the years under review, but when in 1744 it applied for affiliation to Grand Lodge it described itself as the Lodge of Kilmolymock 'kept at Elgin'.[112] As in Perth, Elgin masons doubtless took the name of their lodge from a place outside the burgh to symbolise their independence from the burgh authorities: but not having a major abbey handy, they settled for the much humbler ecclesiastical site at Kilmolymock.

15 The Mason Box of the Lodge of Aberdeen
Three lodge officials were keyholders, and all had to be present
before it was opened
From Miller, *Lodge of Aberdeen*

9

EARLY SCOTTISH FREEMASONRY

By 1710 lodges of freemasons were scattered throughout Lowland Scotland, from the Borders to the fringes of the Highlands. All the larger towns and a number of smaller settlements had lodges, and in addition to the twenty-five or so known lodges there were probably others which have left no trace of their existence. Moreover, there were freemasons who belonged to no lodge, both operatives and non-operatives often being initiated outside the lodges, a practice some lodges accepted, others sought to suppress.

Even when allowance is made for a few lost lodges and for non-lodge freemasons, it is clear that the number of initiates in the country was still small, but a list of the earliest known references to lodges (appendix 1) shows that the rate at which lodges were emerging was accelerating: from the 1670s onwards several lodges appear in each decade and, though this may partly reflect accidents in the survival of evidence, most of these lodges were new ones, rather than old ones emerging from obscurity. Indeed it is possible that virtually no new lodges were created between the great burst of energy associated with William Schaw's reforms in the years around 1600, all the lodges first heard of between 1601 and 1670 (Glasgow, Dundee, Linlithgow, Scone) having originated in Schaw's time. Even if this is not the case, the impression remains that after Schaw's establishment of the lodge system relatively few new ones appeared until late in the century. Undoubtedly the increasing number of new lodges from the 1670s onwards owes much to increasing interest in freemasonry shown by gentry non-operatives, demonstrated by their irruption into older lodges (as at Kilwinning) as well as by their creation of new lodges like Dunblane, Kelso and Haughfoot. But this is not the whole story. The foundation of Canongate Kilwinning, Canongate and Leith, and Edinburgh Journeymen owe nothing directly to gentry influence. But though they arose largely from disputes among operative masons, it is possible that the increasing interest of men of high status in the movement led operatives to take a new pride and interest in freemasonry, reviving or reorganising old lodges as well as founding new ones.

As to why gentry interest increased late in the century, several explanations can be offered. The increasing numbers of references in non-masonic sources to the Mason Word indicates that knowledge of the existence of a movement with intriguing secrets was spreading—and obviously gentlemen had to know freemasonry existed before they could seek to join lodges. New social and intellectual interests could be satisfied by the movement. As interest increased in the emerging sciences and (above all through the work of Isaac Newton) it became widely accepted that the most powerful key in describing and understanding the universe was mathematics, a movement which claimed that the skills of the mason/architect/mathematician were central too it could hardly fail to be intriguing to outsiders. And in the existing organisation of masonic lodges men found a framework within which the growing passion for informal sociability could be satisfied. In lodges men could find—or at least seek— brotherhood and companionship, a forum for serious discussion of shared interests as well as sociable eating and drinking. In addition freemasonry offered what new clubs or societies could not: the satisfaction of belonging to an organisation which claimed ancient origins, arcane knowledge, and elaborate secret rituals.

The ritual side of the life of the lodge is of course the hardest to reconstruct because of the secrecy surrounding it. Even when, in the 1690s, written catechisms appear they outline rather than detail the rituals. Nor is it clear how those who underwent ritual initiation, and helped initiate others, regarded what they were doing. Did they treat it with high seriousness, or as great fun, silly horseplay? Doubtless the answer varied from lodge to lodge and from member to member. Outsiders often find it hard to conceive of grown men engaging in such antics, but rituals nearly always appear strange and even ridiculous to outsiders, and it could be argued that there was (and is) nothing that was inherently more ridiculous in masonic ritual than in many religious practices and civic ceremonies when seen from outside. Moreover initiations of various types were commonplace in organisations and occupational groups throughout society in the seventeenth century: masonic initiations might be unusually prolonged, but the concept of initiation would have been taken for granted. In all probability masonic initiations were taken seriously by the great majority of those involved—but this was not seen as incompatible with fooling about and having fun at the unfortunate initiate's expense (literally as well as metaphorically, as the initiate would give presents of gloves to lodge members and pay for food or drink). Initiations probably varied to some extent from lodge to lodge and from one candidate to another. Though it is only in Dumfries Lodge that the minutes indicate that gentlemen were let off lightly, it is hard to imagine anywhere that an earl was treated to the sort of ritual terrifying and humiliation that could be safely inflicted on a teenage apprentice stonemason.

Men of gentry status or above were very different from other members of a lodge. Having a broad social mix of members might demonstrate masonry's claim to unite men of all ranks, but it cannot have failed to lead to difficulties. Many gentry members of course only attended their lodge on the occasion of their initiation. They may have taken freemasonry seriously (after all Sir Robert Moray was obsessed with it, but is only known to have attended Edinburgh Lodge twice), but they saw nothing in the social and other activities of the lodge to attract them back to it on later occasions. Those gentry who did attend lodges regularly tended to seek to change their nature, recruiting more members who shared their social and educational background and were thus more likely share their interests. Obviously the emergence of distinct groups of members within the same lodge was likely to be divisive. And gentlemen members were unlikely to be satisfied with the kinds of food and drink that the artisan members could afford.

Such tensions are part of the reasons for the way in which gentlemen come to dominate some lodges, sometimes even founding them, for a period and then disappear. Equally important must have been changes in fashion at the local level, a sudden craze for freemasonry among local gentry dying out. This was to be a feature at a national level of British freemasonry even in its great century, the eighteenth, with periods of intense interest in freemasonry alternating with slumps in which lodges declined. But the fact that there was an element of fashion in the attraction of membership of masonic lodges need not imply that it was not taken seriously.

One sign of this is the fact that though from the middle of the seventeenth century there was clearly widespread interest among outsiders in the Mason Word, they found it hard to discover what the secrets of the word were until late in the century—and the lack of any mention of lodges except in masonic sources in Scotland in the seventeenth century suggests that the attempt to keep their existence secret was largely successful. This could not have been the case if gentlemen who only attended lodges once, and perhaps thereafter lost their interest in freemasonry, had felt free to discuss their initiation with outsiders. Most must have faithfully kept the oaths of secrecy they had taken during initiation.

From artisans to earls, men who were not stonemasons joined masonic lodges in seventeenth-century Scotland. Analysis of these men reveals few consistent and clear trends. The tendency for their numbers to increase towards the end of the century is obvious, though even this does not apply to every lodge. A scattering of members with mathematical interests reflects the claim of masons to be architect/mathematicians, but there were far more men with such interests who did not belong to lodges. Where groups of men with similar political views appears in lodges this usually seems to reflect the friendship of the individuals concerned rather than a political bias in the lodge. Doubtless the Lodge of Edinburgh was happy to welcome its group of officials and courtiers in the 1630s: friends in high places are always worth having. But that the lodge was not positively committed to the regime of Charles I was demonstrated by the lodge's initiation of rebel generals a few years later. Admitting the generals can be seen as indicating positive support for the rebel cause, but enthusiasm for the covenanters was so widespread at that time that this does not represent a distinctive bias in the lodge. Similarly, the appearance of men unhappy with, or actively opposed to, the Restoration regime and its religious policies in the Lodges of Edinburgh and Kilwinning in the 1660s and 1670s is probably of limited significance, though it does suggest that the lodges shared the widespread dissatisfaction of Scots with the regime. The closest approach to a politically committed lodge was Dunblane in the 1690s, but even in this case there is no evidence of any attempt to use the lodge to help the Jacobite cause.

William Schaw had intended his lodges to be local bodies coordinated and supervised at the national level by the general warden of the masons—and perhaps to some extent by the Sinclairs of Roslin as patrons of the craft. But Schaw's early death, the disappearance of the office of general warden, and the failure of the Sinclairs after the 1630s to make any attempt to assert their claims meant that in practice each lodge was left to develop on its own. Edinburgh Lodge had been declared the first lodge of Scotland, but showed no interest in developing this role. Kilwinning had been acknowledged as having authority over other lodges in the west, but seldom (if ever) sought to assert this power—though when looking for some superior authority to sanction the establishment of a new lodge in the 1670s Kilwinning Lodge was the most plausible body the Canongate masons could find.

If the lodges were indeed (as this book argues) essentially the creations of William Schaw, then it is not surprising that the removal of his guiding hand so soon after their foundation led individual lodges to develop in notably different ways in such matters as their relationship with the local incorporation (if any) and their attitudes to such matters as recruiting non-operatives and initiating members outside lodges. Indeed, what is perhaps surprising is not that variety existed, but that the lodges managed to remain so similar in essentials in the generations that followed. This is all the more the case in that the surviving records indicate that lodges generally ignored each other's existence: proud of their autonomy, they never consulted other lodges in difficult cases or about general policy. Though the Medieval mythology and organisation of the craft had owed much to the fact that many masons were mobile, often working far away from their homes, the Schaw lodges never attempted to cater for the needs of such men: instead, like the incorporations, they tended to be exclusive in their outlook, trying to prevent men who were not members working in their localities. Visitors from one lodge attending a meeting of another are unknown, though the treasurer of Kilwinning was entertained by the officials of Hamilton Lodge. Sometimes (as at Hamilton and Dunblane, for example) lodge minutes record the admission of men as members (rather than as visitors) who do not need to be initiated as they could prove that they had been initiated in another lodge, but this is unusual. Nonetheless, contacts between masons from different lodges must have been important in preserving a large measure of uniformity in ritual and secrets: indeed secret modes of recognition—words, answers to set questions, gestures, postures and embraces—would obviously be useless unless they were uniform. But such contacts almost always took place not in lodges but on building sites or elsewhere, where masons from different lodges may be imagined meeting together and performing rituals, and reciting the Old Charges for their own sake or in the course of initiations.

By 1710 freemasonry was well established in Scotland, though the composition and fortunes of individual lodges varied considerably. But long before this the activities of Scottish freemasons had begun to exert an influence south of the Border, in England. Most masonic historians have seen freemasonry as English in origin, and certainly the Old Charges, so important to early freemasonry, are English in origin. But when the English and the Scottish evidence for the development of seventeenth-century freemasonry are considered side by side, the evidence is far more copious north of the Border than south of it, though Scotland was much the smaller and poorer of the two nations. Looking at the surviving sources without the Anglocentric preconception that England must have been first, whatever the weight of the evidence, it appears that the freemasonry which was emerging in England by the end of the seventeenth century was overwhelmingly Scottish in character. The secrets of the Mason Word, the grades of entered apprentice and fellow craft or master, the initiation rituals, were all Scottish in origin. So to was the organisational framework of the movement, the system of permanent lodges with fixed memberships.

The first record of a masonic initiation in England is, appropriately, that of Scots by a Scottish lodge—the initiation of two Scottish generals at Newcastle in 1641 by the Lodge of Edinburgh. The first truly English initiation known was that of Elias Ashmole (a man with mathematical interests, significantly) by a lodge in Warrington in 1646. In the decades that follow there are a number of scattered references to freemasons, initiations and lodges. But the lodges, so far as can be seen, were very different from the Scottish lodges. They (or at least the great majority of them) were not permanent institutions, but occasions. Early English freemasons did not 'belong' to lodges, because there were no permanent lodges for them to be members of. A lodge in England was not an institution, but an occasion on which freemasons meet together, to carry out an initiation or for some other purpose, attendance depending on who the person organising the occasion decided to invite. Thus an early English 'lodge' was far more like the meetings sometimes held outside lodges in Scotland to carry out initiations than a Scottish lodge, even if the name is the same. Only at the very end of the century do more permanent lodges appear in England, copied from Scotland.

As to why the organisation of freemasonry in England is at first so nebulous compared to Scotland, the most likely answer is that whereas freemasonry began in Scotland with the foundation of lodges around 1600, in England it began with individual initiates, sometimes (as in London) deriving their ritual and secrets from English operative masons but increasingly under the influence of the thriving freemasonry of the Scots. Thus many of the essentials of modern freemasonry were alien imports from the north, rather than features adopted directly from the beliefs and practices of English working stonemasons. This meant that even when permanent lodges did emerge in England they were different in character from most of their Scottish counterparts. Whereas most Scottish lodges long retained close links with working stonemasons, who usually indeed still formed a majority of members, and made at least token gestures at trade regulation, the English lodges were founded by gentlemen enthusiasts who felt little or no need to seek legitimacy by developing links with 'real' stonemasons.

Some remnants of earlier English masonic organisation and terminology were retained, and indeed the very name of the movement, freemasonry, is English. Further, though so much about English freemasonry at the beginning of the eighteenth century is Scottish, the difference in membership of lodges between the two countries was of major importance for the future. Not constrained by operative traditions, functions, or members, the gentry in the

English lodges could innovate, basing their lore and practices on the Old Charges and on lodge organisation, degrees of initiate, secrets and rituals derived from Scotland, but altered according to their own needs and tastes. In this freedom for the gentry to 'do their own thing' in their new lodges probably lies much of the answer to the question of how it is that English freemasonry in the early eighteenth century, though based on Scottish freemasonry and continuing to owe much to it, almost immediately began to develop very rapidly in membership, in elaboration of ritual and in mythology. English freemasons did not feel confined by the Scottish system they had largely adopted, so could adapt and elaborate it in ways which made it more widely attractive, while ironically Scottish freemasonry was shackled by its strong traditions and the dominant and conservative operative presence in the lodges. By the end of the second decade of the eighteenth century the tide of influence which had flowed south to give England the essentials of freemasonry was being reversed: the influence of English innovations in freemasonry on Scottish lodges becomes discernible—which is the justification for ending this book in the second decade of the century.

If the seventeenth century was 'Scotland's century' in the development of modern freemasonry, the eighteenth was to be England's. The old Scottish lodges were faced with a new world, and had to decide in some respects whether to stick with traditional Scottish practices or to adopt English adaptations of them. But though English influence became strong, many of the Scottish lodges of freemasons to this day display evidence that in its origins freemasonry in Scotland differs from that in England. Many lodges still proudly bear the word 'operative' in their titles, and it is far more common for working men to be freemasons in Scotland than England.

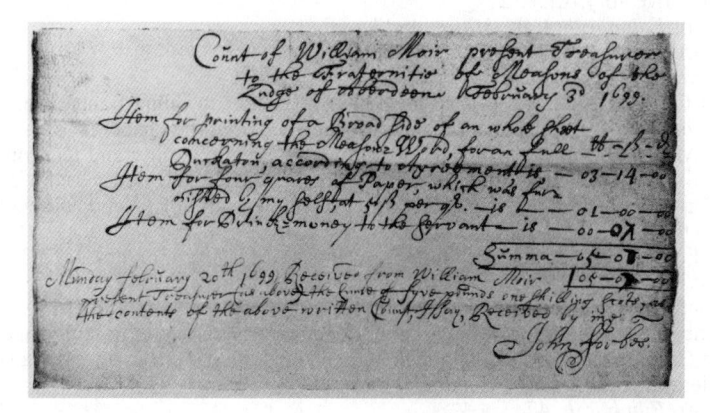

16   Lodge of Aberdeen: accounts
This account the 'Treasurer to the fraternitie of Measons of the Lodge of Aberdeen' records in 1699 a payment for the printing of 'a Broadside of an whole sheet concerning the Meason Word.' This is the first time a masonic lodge ever commissioned a printed work - one containing the secrets of the 'word.' No copies survive
From Miller, *Lodge of Aberdeen*

NOTES

CHAPTER 1 Masons and Freemasons, pp. 1-11

1. This chapter provides background for the studies of individual lodges by briefly summarising some of the main arguments of my *The origins of freemasonry. Scotland's century* (Cambridge, 1988), and the documentation which lies behind my arguments and assertions will be found detailed there.
2. I have followed the long-established practice of masonic historians of calling the two charters the 'St Clair' charters, though the Sinclair lairds of Roslin did not spell their name that way in this period.
3. F.A. Yates, *The art of memory* (London, 1966), 303-5.

CHAPTER 2   Edinburgh, pp. 12-51

1. See Inventory, 7.1, 15.1.
2. Mylne, *Master masons*, 61.
3. Carr, *Edinburgh*, 12.
4. See Inventory, 15.3-12.
5. Carr, *Edinburgh*; Carr, *Mason and burgh*.
6. Carr, *Edinburgh*, 8.
7. *Ibid.*, 8.
8. SRO, RD 1/502, ff. lr-4r. I owe this reference to John Bannatyne. Carr, *Edinburgh*, 69; states that the incorporation acquired the chapel in 1618.
9. J. McMillan, 'A study of the Edinburgh burgess community and its economic activities, 1600-1680' (University of Edinburgh Ph.D. thesis, 1984), 56-7.
10. Carr, *Mason and burgh*, 54; H. Carr, 'Apprenticeship in England and Scotland up to 1700', *AQC*, 69 (1956), 84.
11. Edinburgh Incorporation minutes (see Inventory, 15.6), i, reversed, 72-3.
12. Mylne, *Master masons*, 61, 108.
13. Carr, 'Apprentices', 57.
14. The stages and timing of the Edinburgh mason's career were first fully analysed in Carr *Mason and burgh*, though he explained the pattern in terms of a single hierarchy rather than two parallel ones.
15. Carr, *Edinburgh*, 47.
16. McMillan, Burgess community, 108.
17. *Ibid.*, 33, 37.
18. Edinburgh Incorporation minutes, i, 1-2, iv, 19.
19. *Ibid.*, ii, 60-5, iv, 88. An Alexander Robesone became an entered apprentice in the lodge in 1688, though his master was Robert Mylne, not William Fulton, Carr, *Edinburgh*, 208.
20. *Ibid.*, 196-7.

21. Lyon, *Edinburgh*, 19-20; Carr, *Mason and burgh*, 51-2; Carr, *Edinburgh*, 29; Edinburgh Incorporation minutes, i, 189. Carr wisely concluded that either the reference was garbled or the definition of the essay was a joke!
22. Edinburgh Incorporation minutes, i, 193.
23. *Ibid.*, ii, 100.
24. *Ibid.*, iii, 3 Nov. 1706.
25. Eg., *ibid.*, i, 14, 26, 180, and, reversed, 3.
26. *Ibid.*, i, 187.
27. *Ibid.*, ii, 193; H. Armet (ed.), *Extracts from the records of the burgh of Edinburgh. 1689 to 1701* (Edinburgh, 1962), 164-5.
28. NLS, Ms. Acc. 7332, box 2, bundle 1a; Colvin, *Architects*, 755.
29. SRO, RH.9/14/30. In a dispute in 1682 it was stated that the mason deacon of the incorporation in 1650 had protested against the making of the Portsburgh contract, Incorporation minutes, i, 104, 105-6, 109. For Portsburgh see RCAHMS, *Edinburgh*, lix-lx.
30. Edinburgh Incorporation minutes, i, 62, 100, 115, 130, 161, 184, 222, ii, 5, 31, 44, 56, 58, 115, etc.
31. W. Wood (ed.), *Extracts from the records of the burgh of Edinburgh. 1626 to 1641* (Edinburgh, 1936), 184.
32. J.R. Anderson (ed.), *The burgesses and guild brethren of Glasgow, 1573-1750* (SRS, 1925), 84.
33. *Edinburgh records, 1626-41*, 123-5.
34. R.K. Hannay and G.P.H. Watson, 'The building of the Parliament House', *Book of the Old Edinburgh Club*, xiii (1924), 30-1.
35. Colvin, *Architects*, 301; *Edinburgh records, 1626-41*, 210; C.B.B. Watson (ed.), *Roll of Edinburgh burgesses, 1406-1700* (SRS, 1926), 40; J.K. Hewison, *The covenanters* (2nd. edn., 2 vols., Glasgow, 1913), i, 485, 489. It is usually assumed that the William Aytoun who was master mason at Heriot's Hospital was the mason of that name rewarded by the council with a burgess-ship in 1640, as no others of the name are recorded being made burgesses. But (if a nineteenth century publication is to be trusted) in Aytoun's 1631 contract with Edinburgh council he is already referred to as a burgess of Edinburgh: either this is erroneous, or, perhaps, he had been promised burgess-ship but for some reason this did not materialise until 1640, *Inventory of original documents in the archives of Heriot's Hospital* (Edinburgh, 1857), 45.
36. J.D. Marwick (ed.), *Extracts from the records of the burgh of Edinburgh, 1573-89* (SBRS, 1882), 58.
37. *RPCS, 1673-6*, xxxii-xxxiii, 422-4.
38. M. Wood (ed.), *Extracts from the records of the burgh of Edinburgh. 1665 to 1680* (Edinburgh, 1950), 301-2, and *1689 to 1701* (Edinburgh, 1962), 20.
39. Edinburgh Incorporation minutes, ii, 94, 116; *Edinburgh records, 1689-1701*, 75-6.
40. Edinburgh Incorporation minutes, i, 22.
41. *Ibid.*, ii, 50.
42. Sir John Lauder of Fountainhall, *Historical notices of Scotish affairs* (2 vols., Bannatyne Club, 1848), i, 93, 96, 97; Carr, *Edinburgh*, 273.
43. *Ibid.*, 14.
44. *Ibid.*, 57-8.
45. *Ibid.*, 22.
46. *Ibid.*, 90-124.
47. *Ibid.*, 3-4.
48. *Ibid.*, 4
49. *Ibid.*, 42.

50. *Ibid.*, 42, 44, 46, 47.
51. *Ibid.*, 21.
52. W. Wood (ed.), *Extracts from the records of the burgh of Edinburgh.1655 to 1665* (Edinburgh, 1940), 391.
53. Carr, *Edinburgh*, 43.
54. *Ibid.*, 35.
55. *Ibid.*, 21, 49, 53. Yellowlees became Dingwall Pursuivant in 1603 and died in 1614, F.J. Grant (ed.), *Court of the Lord Lyon* (SRS, 1946), 33; SRO, CC.8/8/49, f.124r-v.
56. Carr, *Edinburgh*, 52, 54, 55, 58, 59.
57. *Ibid.*, 25, 61, 65.
58. Lyon, *Edinburgh*, 52-3; Carr, *Edinburgh*, 49-51.
59. *Ibid.*, 132.
60. *Ibid.*, 89-90.
61. Colvin, *Architects*, 567-70; Carr, *Edinburgh*, 97-8. For Mylne's epitaph see Mylne, *Master masons*, 159-60 and Stevenson, *Origins*, chapter 5.
62. Carr, *Edinburgh*, 99-114.
63. *Ibid.*, 107; Lyon, *Edinburgh*, 94; Mylne, *Master masons*, 141; SRO, CC.8/8/61, ff.19v-20r; Inventory, 30.5. Alexander Waterston became a fellow craft without being an entered apprentice in August 1635, and it has been suggested that he was one of this group of non-operatives, Carr, *Edinburgh*, 108. But there are a number of similar cases, and there was a mason burgess of Edinburgh of this name, so he was probably an operative.
64. Carr, *Edinburgh*, 114, 115, 116; Lyon, *Edinburgh*, 90.
65. M. Lee, *The road to revolution. Scotland under Charles 1, 1625-37* (Urbana and Chicago, 1985), 15, 30, 84-5, 101.
66. I. Grimble, *Chief of Mackay* (London, 1965), 3-9; G. Burnet, *The memoires of the lives and actions of James and Wiliam dukes of Hamilton* (London, 1677), 6-15.
67. Carr, *Edinburgh*, 111-13.
68. *Ibid.*, 118-20. For Moray see D. Stevenson, 'Masonry, symbolism and ethics in the life of Sir Robert Moray, FRS', *PSAS*, 114 (1984), 403-31, and Stevenson, *Origins*, chapter 7.
69. Carr, *Edinburgh*, 131-2
70. H. Paton (ed.), *Register of marriages for the parish of Edinburgh, 1595-1700* (SRS, 1905), 369; H. Paton (ed.), *Register of interments in the Greyfriars Burying-Ground, Edinburgh, 1658-1700* (SRS, 1902), 349; M. Wood (ed.), *Extracts from the records of the burgh of Edinburgh. 1642 to 1655* (Edinburgh, 1938), 322.
71. Carr, *Edinburgh*, 136-7.
72. *Ibid.*, 138-9.
73. *Ibid.*, 141; C.H. Firth (ed.), *Scotland and the Protectorate* (SHS, 1899), xlviii; *Edinburgh records, 1655-65*, 167; Canongate Incorporation minutes (Inventory, 9.2), i, 10 May 1660; HMC 29: 14th Report, Appendix ii, *Portland*, iii (1894), 252.
74. Carr, *Edinburgh*, 144; Watson, *Edinburgh burgesses*, 377; F.J. Grant (ed.), *Register of apprentices of the city of Edinburgh, 1583-1666* (SRS, 1906), 137; Paton, *Register of marriages*, 513. Neilson died in 1665, SRO, CC.8/8/72, ff.127r-128r.
75. Carr, *Edinburgh*, 160; *Scots peerage*, vi, 12-16; J. Patrick, 'The origins of the opposition to Lauderdale in the Scottish parliament of 1673', *Scottish Historical Review*, liii (1974), 19; *DNB*, xxviii, 231-5. Both Carr and Lyon, *Edinburgh*, 97, state that Hume was a lawyer, Lyon claiming that he was a member of

the faculty of Advocates. This is an error evidently arising from confusing him with his namesake, Sir Patrick Hume of Lumdsen, who was an advocate, F.J. Grant (ed.), *The faculty of advocates in Scotland* (SRS, 1944), 102.
76. Carr, *Edinburgh*, 152, 161; W.G. Scott-Moncrieff (ed.), *The Records of the proceedings of the justiciary court, Edinburgh, 1661-1678* (2 vols., SHS, 1905), i, 139.
77. Carr, *Edinburgh*, 161-2; A. Pringle, *Records of the Pringles or Hoppringills of the Scottish Border* (Edinburgh, 1933), 189-91; C.B. Gunn (ed.), *Records of the baron court of Stitchill* (SHS, 1905), 32n, 40n, 231; J.R. Jones, 'The Scottish constitutional opposition in 1679', *Scottish Historical Review*, xxxvii (1958), 38; J.M. Simpson, 'The advocates as Scottish trade union pioneers', G.W.S. Barrow (ed.), *The Scottish tradition* (Edinburgh, 1974), 170-4; Grant, *Faculty of advocates*, 174.
78. Carr, *Edinburgh*, 162; Patrick, 'Opposition to Lauderdale', 19, 21; R. Wodrow, *History of the sufferings of the church of Scotland* (4 vols., Glasgow, 1828-30), iii, 434; Jones, 'Scottish constitutional opposition', 38; Fountainhall, *Historical notices*, i, 409, 435; Simpson, 'Advocates', 171-4; Grant, *Faculty of advocates*, 97.
79. Carr, *Edinburgh*, 175; *Edinburgh records, 1655-65*, 93.
80. E.G.R. Taylor, *The mathematical practitioners of Tudor and Stuart England* (Cambridge,1954), 239; J. Corss, *Mercurius coelius* (Glasgow, 1662 and Edinburgh, 1663); J. Corss, *A new prognostication* (Edinburgh, 1675 and 1679); J. Corss, *Uranoscopia* (Edinburgh, 1662).
81. Watson, *Edinburgh burgesses*, 119.
82. Carr, *Edinburgh*, 220.
83. *Ibid.*, 230; Edinburgh Incorporation minutes, ii, 14 Aug. 1696, iv, reversed, accounts 1705-7.
84. Carr, *Edinburgh*, 236; Edinburgh Incorporation minutes, ii, 19 Mar. 1709.
85. Carr, *Edinburgh*, 240, 241,243.
86. Colvin, *Architects*, 530-1.
87. Edinburgh Incorporation minutes, ii, 30 Apr., 2 July, 3 Sept. 1709, iii, 20. For Clerk see J.M. Gray (ed.), *Memoirs of the life of Sir John Clerk of Penicuik* (SHS, 1892).
88. Carr, *Edinburgh*, 244.
89. *Ibid.*, 270-1; Lyon, *Edinburgh*, 161.
90. RCAHMS, *Edinburgh*, liii-lv; *Edinburgh records, 1626-41*, 328-34; M. Wood (ed.), *Book of records of the ancient privileges of the Canongate* (SRS, 1955), 3-4.
91. *Ibid.*, 25-6; APS, v, 562-3.
92. Eg., Canongate Incorporation minutes (see Inventory, 9.2-3), i, ff.21v, 81r, ii, see acts of crafts no. 63 and under 3 May 1679 and 3 May 1690.
93. *Ibid.*, i, ff.93r,113r, 114v, etc. See A.A.A. Murray, 'Freeman and cowan, with special reference to the records of Lodge Canongate Kilwinning', *AQC*, 21 (1908), 185-203 and Carr, *Mason and burgh*, 52.
94. Canongate Incorporation minutes, i, f.83r.
95. See *ibid.*, i, list of members and H. Armet (ed.), *Register of the burgesses of the burgh of the Canongate* (SRS, 1951).
96. Canongate Incorporation minutes, i, ff.88r, 89r, 91r, 101r, 103r, 108v, etc.; Murray, 'Freeman and cowan', 198-200.
97. West Register House, RD.13/427/1661.
98. Canongate Incorporation minutes, i, list of members and f.83r.
99. Carr, *Kilwinning*, 98-9.
100. GLS, Cartulary, i, 1-2; A. Mackenzie, *History of the Lodge Canongate Kilwinning* (Edinburgh, 1888), 9, 44.

101. Paton, *Edinburgh marriages*, 552; F.J. Grant (ed.), *Parish of Holyroodhouse or Canongate. Register of marriages, 1564-1800* (SRS, 1915), 575; Watson, *Edinburgh burgesses*, 114; Canongate Incorporation minutes, i, 9 May 1677. The John Wilson who was a mason burgess of Edinburgh was mason deacon in 1675-7, and is thus unlikely to have been the founder of Canongate Kilwinning of that name.
102. Eg., Carr, *Edinburgh*, 102.
103. *Ibid.*, 182-3.
104. *Ibid.*, 199; Armet, *Burgesses of the Canongate*, 44, 70. The master of one of the apprentices had died, leaving his widow as the apprentice's 'master'.
105. Aitchison's Haven minutes (see Inventory, 7.1-2), i, 27 Dec. 1684. This was presumably the Alexander Baxter who became a Canongate burgess and master of the incorporation in 1674, having become a fellow craft of Aitchison's Haven in 1665 and deacon of that lodge in 1670, Armet, *Burgesses of the Canongate*, 9; Canongate Incorporation minutes, i, list of members; Aitchison's Haven minutes, i, 27 Dec. 1665 and 27 Dec. 1670.
106. RCAHMS, *Edinburgh*, lv-lvi.
107. J.S. Marshall, 'A social and economic history of Leith in the eighteenth century, (University of Edinburgh Ph.D. thesis, 1969), 86-7, 92.
108. *Ibid.*, 98.
109. D. Robertson (ed.), *South Leith records* (Edinburgh, 1911), 107, 118.
110. Carr, *Edinburgh*, 47-8.
111. *Ibid.*, 205.
112. Canongate Incorporation minutes, ii, list of members; Armet, *Burgesses of the Canongate*, 54.
113. In the first edition of this book I incorrectly stated that none of the nine deserters could be traced in St Mary's Chapel Lodge. I owe the correction to Dr Lisa Kahler. Carr, *Edinburgh*, 209.
114. GLS, Cartulary, i, 35-6; C.M. Douglas, *A history of the Lodge Canongate and Leith, Leith and Canongate, No. 5* (Edinburgh, 1949), 32-4. In 1736 Mary's Chapel Lodge objected to the recognition of Canongate and Leith by Grand Lodge, still regarding it as a schismatic lodge, *ibid.*, 29-30.
115. C.R. Dobson, *Masters and journeymen: a pre-history of industrial coflict 1717-1800* (London, 1980), 47; Knoop, *Genesis*, 57-8.
116. See Carr, *Mason and burgh*, 28, 34-6.
117. Carr, *Edinburgh*, 163-6, 169.
118. *Ibid.*, 192-4.
119. *Ibid.*, 194-5.
120. *Ibid.*, 204-5.
121. *Ibid.*, 213.
122. *Ibid.*, 218-20.
123. *Ibid.*, 215-16.
124. W. Hunter, *Incidents in the history of the Lodge of Journeymen Masons Edinburgh No. 8* (Edinburgh, 1884), 235-6.
125. Carr, *Edinburgh*, 234-5. Carr says that it was agreed that journeymen should inspect the accounts as they contributed to lodge funds by paying 12 shillings yearly. But the journeymen who gained access to these accounts were members of the lodge, while those paying the 12 shillings were not.
126. Carr, *Edinburgh*, 235.
127. *Ibid.*, 247-8.
128. *Ibid.*, 249-51.
129. *Ibid.*, 251-2.

130. Edinburgh Incorporation minutes, iii, 41-2.
131. *Ibid.*, iii, 50.
132. Carr, *Edinburgh*, 252-4.
133. Edinburgh Incorporation minutes, iii, 55-6.
134. *Ibid.*, iii, 56, 63.
135. J.S. Seggie and D.L. Turnbull, *Annals of the Lodge of Journeymen Masons No. 8* (Edinburgh, 1930), 55-6; Edinburgh Incorporation Minutes, iii, 59.
136. Seggie, *Annals*, 56-60.
137. Carr, *Edinburgh*, 256-8.
138. Edinburgh Incorporation minutes, iii, 60.
139. Seggie, *Annals*, 61-8.
140. Carr, *Edinburgh*, 261.
141. Edinburgh Incorporation minutes, iii, reversed.
142. Carr, *Edinburgh*, 266-8, 353.
143. Edinburgh Incorporation minutes, iii, 76, 84, 103, iv, 16 Sept. 1721.
144. Edinburgh Journeymen minutes (see Inventory, 16.1).
145. See Inventory, 16.4.

CHAPTER 3 Lothians, pp. 52-62

1. Unless otherwise stated information in this section is taken from R.E. Wallace-James, 'The minute book of the Aitchison's Haven Lodge, 1598- 1764', *AQC*, 24 (1911), 30-46, and R.J. Meekren, 'The Aitchison's Haven minutes and early Scottish freemasonry', *AQC*, 53 (1940), 147-88.
2. Aitchison's Haven minutes (Inventory, 7.1-2), ii, reversed, 26 Dec. 1713.
3. Wallace James, 'Minute book', 36-7, 41; Aitchison's Haven minutes, i, 29 May 1689, ii, 27 Dec.1703.
4. SRO, E.70/70/8 and E.70/70/10.
5. Vernon, *History*, 16, 20.
6. The first known minute book of the Lodge of Dalkeith began in 1724 but is now missing. References in it are said to have shown that the lodge had existed many years earlier (National Register of Archives (Scotland), Survey No. 1956), so it is possible that Dalkeith had its own lodge by the end of the seventeenth century.
7. Aitchison's Haven minutes, i, 1.
8. Meekren, 'Minutes', 174-80.
9. Wallace-James, 'Minute book', 36-7.
10. See Inventory, 1.3.
11. J. Paterson, *History of the regality of Musselburgh* (Musselburgh, 1857), 57, refers to the Musselburgh masons having a society for the support of their poor, but this could possibly be a reference to Aitchison's Haven Lodge. Lyon, *Edinburgh*, 433 refers to the lodge regulating trade 'in conjunction with the Incorporation' but gives no indication of which incorporation he means: he may simply be assuming that there must have been one parallel to the lodge.
12. Wallace-James, 'Minute book', 36.
13. Aitchison's Haven minutes, i, 27 Dec. 1670.
14. *Ibid.*, i, 24 Feb., 27 Dec. 1671.
15. Meekren, 'Minutes', 173. It was Meekren's work, based on Aitchison's Haven minutes, that first demonstrated that entered apprentices and fellow crafts constituted two separate grades, each with its own secrets, thus destroying the long-held belief that there was only one grade in early Scottish freemasonry.
16. Wallace-James, 'Minute book', 35-6; Lyon, *Edinburgh*, 434; Aitchison's Haven minutes, i, 1667 etc, ii, 21, and, reversed, 27 Dec. 1702.

17. Wallace-James, 'Minute book', 33; Aitchison's Haven minutes, i, 20 Nov. 1599' 27 Jan. 1600.
18. Inventory, 1.3.
19. W.A. Laurie, *History of freemasonry and the Grand Lodge of Scotland* (2nd. edn. Edinburgh, 1859), 450.
20. Aitchison's Haven minutes, ii, 8.
21. Laurie, *History of freemasonry*, 450-1.
22. Aitchison's Haven minutes, ii, 27 Dec. 1722.
23. Wallace-James, 'Minute book', 41-2.
24. *Ibid.*, 41; Aitchison's Haven minutes, i, 27 Dec. 1682.
25. Wallace-James, 'Minute book', 33; *Scots peerage*, viii, 595; J. Fullerton (ed.), *History of the house of Seytoun* (Bannatyne Club, 1829), i, 196.
26. Wallace-James, 'Minute book', 33, 34; Aitchison's Haven minutes, i, 27 Dec. 1677, 27 Dec. 1693.
27. Lyon, *Edinburgh*, 193-4.
28. Wallace-James, 'Minute book', 41; Aitchison's Haven minutes, i, 27 Dec. 1670, ii, reversed, 27 Dec. 1688.
29. B.L.H. Horn, 'List of references to the Pre-Reformation altarages in the parish church of Haddington', *Transactions of the East Lothian Antiquarian and Field Naturalists Society*, x (1966), 71-2.
30. SRO, B.30/22/9 (see Inventory, 18.7).
31. SRO, B.30/22/2; SRO, B.30/18/4, Haddington Incorporation minutes, 1616-1751.
32. *Ibid.*, 27 Sept. 1674.
33. Laurie, *History of freemasonry*, 375-6.
34. Haddington Incorporation minutes, under dates cited.
35. Lyon, *Edinburgh*, 441.
36. Haddington Incorporation minutes, under dates cited.
37. Lyon, *Edinburgh*, 441-2.
38. Haddington Incorporation minutes, 14 Sept. 1696.
39. Lyon, *Edinburgh*, 441.
40. Carr, *Edinburgh*, 144.
41. Poole, *Gould's History*, iii, 247.

CHAPTER 4 The West, pp. 63-89

1. Lyon, *Edinburgh*, 435; Carr, *Kilwinning*, 20. In 1680, 1686 and 1693 the minutes refer to the lodge as the ancient lodge of Kilwinning, *ibid.*, 114, 118, 128.
2. Ayr Incorporation minutes (see Inventory, 24.6); G.S. Pryde (ed.), *Ayr burgh accounts, 1534-1624* (SHS, 1937), see index under Dowok and Liddell. The reference in *ibid.*, 203 to 'the masons ludge' in 1599-1600 is to a lodge in the sense of a shelter for masons to work in.
3. *Muniments of the royal burgh of Irvine* (2 vols., Ayrshire and Galloway Archaeological Association, 1890-1), ii, 64-9; A.F. McJannet, *Royal burgh of Irvine* (Glasgow, 1938), 346-7.
4. In 1779 the lodge changed the date of the annual meeting to 21 December, St Thomas' Day, claiming that this had been the 'ancient day of meeting', the 20 December meetings 'having by an error continued for many years past', Carr, *Kilwinning*, 271. This is not convincing: it is hardly likely that no one had noticed the error since 1599, the date of the Second Schaw Statutes which set the annual meeting on 20 December. It seems that the lodge had long forgotten the real significance of its meeting date, so rationalised it as an error

for 21 December: in 1735 a minute had made another attempt at explanation by erroneously calling 20 December St John's Day, *ibid.*, 201. One possible significance is that 20 December was the day of five early Christian martyrs, executed in the third century. St Ammon and four others were identified as Christians when they cast looks, 'streched out their hands and made gestures with their bodies' to encourage a man under trial to remain steadfast in his Christian faith: Eusebius, *The ecclesiastical history*, ed. K. Lake and J.E.L. Oulton (2 vols., London, 1926-32), ii, 109. The martyrdoms took place in Egypt, which of course held special significance for masons. Is it possible that Kilwinning masons had originally commemorated St Ammon and his colleagues as they sacrificed their lives through making signs and gestures to encourage a man to stand up for the truth, seeing parallels with the secret gestures and postures of their own Mason Word? This seems unlikely, given the obscurity of St Ammon and the lack of any other evidence connecting him with the mason craft; but the fact that Kilwinning Lodge has completely forgotten why 20 December was important suggests that the point was indeed obscure!

5. Eg., Carr, *Kilwinning*, 27, 35, 44.
6. *Ibid.*, 20-1, 79; SRO, CC.9/7/32, 24 Oct. 1661.
7. Carr, *Kilwinning*, 17-28.
8. *Ibid.*, 33.
9. *Ibid.*, 77-8.
10. *Ibid.*, 128.
11. *Ibid.*, 54.
12. J.R. Anderson (ed.), *Burgesses and guild brethren of Glasgow, 1573-1750* (SRS, 1925), 110; SRO, CC.9/7/35, 8 Feb. 1666; Carr, *Kilwinning*, 33-5, 44, etc.; *Archaeological and historical collections of the county of Renfrew* (2 vols., Paisley, 1885-90), ii, 192.
13. Carr, *Kilwinning*, 44, 68; MacGibbon, *Architecture*, iv, 30-1; W.M. Metcalfe, *A history of Paisley* (Paisley, 1909), 471-526.
14. *Inventory*, 4.10.
15. Carr, *Kilwinning*, 118-19.
16. *Ibid.*, 34, 35, 39, 42-3, 133.
17. *Ibid.*, 83-4, 94; Anderson, *Glasgow burgesses*, 75; J. Cruikshank, *Sketch of the Incorporation of Masons and the Lodge of Glasgow* (Glasgow, 1879), 70.
18. Carr, *Kilwinning*, 85, 94-5.
19. *Scots peerage*, ii, 482-4; J.R. Jones, 'The Scottish constitutional opposition in 1679', *Scottish Historical Review*, xxxvii (1958), 39.
20. Carr, *Kilwinning*, 83.
21. *Ibid.*, 54, 86, 98, 104: Carr shows indecision as to King's status. F.J. Grant (ed.), *The commissariot record of Glasgow. Register of testaments, 1547-1800* (SRS, 1901), 261.
22. Carr, *Kilwinning*, 86. Carlurg died within a few months of entering the lodge, T. Thomson (ed.), *Inquisitionum ad capellam regis retornatarum abbreviatio* (3 vols., 1811-16), i, Ayrshire, no. 706.
23. J. Sheddon-Dobie (ed.), 'Corshill Baron-Court Book', *Archaeological and Historical Collections relating to the Counties of Ayr and Wigton*, iv (1884), 93-4, 108, 122, 124, 125, 135.
24. Carr, *Kilwinning*, 88-9.
25. W. Fraser, *Memorials of the Montgomeries, earls of Eglinton* (2 vols., Edinburgh, 1859), i, 96.
26. Carr, *Kilwinning*, 104; Sheddon-Dobie, 'Corshill baron-court book', 107, 109, 132.

27. Carr, *Kilwinning*, 89.
28. *Ibid.*, 90; Sheddon-Dobie, 'Corshill baron-court book', 79.
29. *Scots peerage*, iii, 350-1.
30. Carr, *Kilwinning*, 91, 93.
31. *Ibid.*, 98.
32. *Ibid.*, 103-5.
33. Carr, *Edinburgh*, 182-3.
34. Carr, *Kilwinning*, 103, 104, 117, 118; Grant, *Commissariot record of Glasgow*, 545.
35. Carr, *Kilwinning*, 142.
36. *Muniments of the royal burgh of Irvine*, ii, 281, 282, 305.
37. *Complete baronetage*, ii, 385, iv, 285.
38. *Scots peerage*, iii, 452-3.
39. J.D. Marwick (ed.), *Extracts from the records of the burgh of Glasgow, 1573-1642* (SBRS, 1876), 203, 205-6; [T.A. Reid and R. Renwick], *The Incorporation of Wrights in Glasgow* (5th edn., Glasgow, 1928), 49-62.
40. H. Lumsden (ed.), *The records of the Trades House of Glasgow, 1605-1678* (Glasgow, 1910), 9, 27-8, 402-3.
41. Cruikshank, *Incorporation of Masons*, 99.
42. I.M. MacDonald, 'The Lodge of Glasgow St John No.3[bis]. An historical sketch', *GLSYB* (1959), 71.
43. Glasgow Incorporation minutes (see Inventory, 17.5-6), i, f 27r; Anderson, *Glasgow burgesses*, 50.
44. Glasgow Incorporation minutes, i, f.25r.
45. E.S. Lawrie, *The Lodge of Glasgow 'St John', No. 3[bis], with a note on the Incorporation of Masons in Glasgow* (Glasgow, 1927), 27.
46. Glasgow Incorporation minutes, under dates cited by Lawrie.
47. Cruikshank, *Incorporation of Glasgow*, 53; Glasgow Incorporation minutes, i, f.28r.
48. Lumsden, *Trades House*, 48. Some mason apprentices were booked at the Trades House, but most were booked or entered in the incorporation's minutes. In at least one case booking took place at both places. Robert Myllar's indenture was dated March 1618; he was booked with the incorporation in May 1619, and with the Trades House in November 1620, *ibid.*, 92; Glasgow Incorporation minutes, i, f.25v.
49. *Ibid.*, i, f.30v; Cruikshank, *Incorporation of Glasgow*, 54.
50. *Ibid.*, 70.
51. Lawrie, *Lodge of Glasgow*, 27; Glasgow Incorporation minutes, i, f.68v.
52. J.D. Marwick and R. Renwick (eds.), *Extracts from the records of the burgh of Glasgow, 1663-1690* (SBRS, 1905),259. It is possible that this was the Alexander Thom, mason burgess of Dumfries, who is recorded taking an apprentice there in 1675, SRO, RD.2/61, pp.749-51.
53. Glasgow Incorporation minutes, ii, under dates cited.
54. Marwick, *Glasgow records, 1663-90*, 345, 363, 375, 378, 506.
55. Inventory, 17.7.
56. Inventory, 17.2.
57. Lawrie, *Lodge of Glasgow*, 36, 61-2
58. *Ibid.*, 31.
59. Smith, *Dumfries*, 8; Dumfries Lodge minutes (see Inventory, 11.1), 20 May 1687. It could perhaps be thought that the minutes make a distinction between the 'honourable company' of masons and the lodge into which it was being converted. But the titles are synonymous—the term honourable company

meaning the masters of a lodge is found in the early catechisms of the Register House group.
60. Smith, *Dumfries*, xviii, 10; Dumfries Lodge minutes, 27 Dec. 1687, 27 Dec. 1718.
61. W. Dickie, 'Incorporated trades of Dumfries. With special reference to the weavers', *Transactions and Journal of Proceedings of the Dumfries and Galloway Natural History and Antiquarian Society*, xviii, pt.5, (1905-6), 412, 414.
62. C.M. Armet (ed.), *Kirkcudbright sheriff court deeds, 1676-1700* (2 vols., 1953), i, 223, ii, 558.
63. *Ibid.*, ii, 637, 845.
64. *Ibid.*, ii, 563, 573, 840.
65. SRO, RD.3/6, pp.565-8; SRO, RD.2/43, pp.752-3; H. Carr, 'Apprenticeship in England and Scotland', *AQC*, 69 (1956), 66; Strathclyde Regional Archives, RU.9/3/3/1; SRO, RD.2/10, p.397.
66. Marwick, *Glasgow records, 1573-1642*, 206.
67. Armet, *Kirkcudbright sheriff court deeds*, ii, 822-3.
68. Smith, *Dumfries*, 8, 10; Dumfries Lodge minutes, 27 Dec. 1704.
69. Smith, *Dumfries*, 8.
70. *Ibid.*, 9; Armet, *Kirkcudbright sheriff court deeds*, i, 388, 411, ii, 529, 613, 680; *Index to particular register of sasines for sheriffdom of Dumfries*, ii (1933), 221-2.
71. Dumfries Lodge minutes, under dates cited.
72. W. McDowall, *History of the burgh of Dumfries* (2nd. edn., Edinburgh, 1873), 422.
73. Dumfries Lodge minutes, 27 Dec. 1704; Armet, *Kirkcudbright sheriff court deeds*, i, 390, 399, 628, 843.
74. Smith, *Dumfries*, 14.
75. *Ibid.*, 14, 61; Dumfries Lodge Minutes, 27 Dec. 1712, 18 May 1713, 27 Dec. 1717.
76. Smith, *Dumfries*, 13.
77. *Ibid.*, 14.
78. *Ibid.*, 13-14, bowdlerises the episode by omitting from his transcript the fact that Fleming was drunk and swearing! Dumfries Lodge minutes, 8 Feb. 1711. Fleming had been admitted as an entered apprentice in 1704, he then being a journeyman, *ibid.*, 6 Sept. 1704.
79. Smith, *Dumfries*, 11, 12.
80. *Ibid.*, xviii; Dumfries Lodge minutes, 12 Nov. 1698, 27 Dec. 1705, 27 Dec. 1706.
81. Inventory, 4.6.
82. Smith, *Dumfries*, xviii; Dumfries Lodge minutes. 27 Dec. 1718.
83. Smith, *Dumfries*, 70; Inventory, 4.4.
84. Smith, *Dumfries*, 61; Dumfries Lodge minutes, 27 Dec. 1712.
85. GLS Cartulary, i, 45-6.
86. M.B. Johnston and C.M. Armet (eds.), *Kirkcudbright town council records, 1576-1604* (1939), 360; W. Mackenzie, *History of Galloway* (2 vols., Kirkcudbright, 1841), ii, app., pp.14-15.
87. Armet, *Kirkcudbright sheriff court deeds*, i, 214, ii, 645-6, 764.
88. Eg., B. E. Jones, *Freemasons' guide and compendium* (London, 1950), 127, and Poole, *Gould's History*, iii, 225.
89. Hamilton Lodge minutes (Inventory, 19.2), f.lr.
90. Hamilton Lodge papers and documents (Inventory, 19.1), bond.
91. Hamilton Lodge minutes, f.3r.
92. R.K. Marshall, *The days of Duchess Anne. Life in the household of the duchess of Hamilton, 1656-1716* (London, 1973),191-207.

93. C.A. Malcolm (ed.), *The minutes of the justices of the peace for Lanarkshire, 1702-1723* (SHS, 1931), 126.
94. Marshall, *Duchess Anne*, 65.
95. Hamilton Lodge minutes, f.5v; Malcolm, *Justices*, 29, 31, 53, 153, 164.
96. Hamilton Lodge minutes, ff.4v, 5v.
97. Marshall, *Duchess Anne*, 64, 74; Malcolm, *Justices*, 29, 31, 153, 175.
98. Hamilton Lodge minutes, f.6r.
99. Hamilton Lodge papers and documents, scroll minutes, 1 Feb. 1704, 27 Dec. 1705.
100. Malcolm, *Justices*, 31, 153, 164; Hamilton Lodge papers and documents, scroll minutes, 27 Dec. 1705.
101. *Ibid.*, list of members; Hamilton Lodge early papers (Inventory, 19.4), accounts 1712-13.
102. Hamilton Lodge papers and documents, scroll minutes, 2 Jan. 1710, 27 Dec. 1711; Malcolm, *Justices*, 102, 136, 152, 155, 156, 164, 165; *Scots peerage*, ii, 42; *Complete Baronetage*, iv, 415.
103. Hamilton Lodge early papers, minute, 6 June 1715, and accounts, 1714-15 (charge).
104. Hamilton Lodge minutes, f4r.
105. *Ibid.*, f.2v.
106. Hamilton Lodge papers and documents, accounts, 1696-8, in scroll minutes.
107. Hamilton Lodge minutes, f.6v; Hamilton Lodge papers and documents, 1701 statutes, and scroll minutes 16 Jan., 2 Apr. 1701.
108. Inventory, 19.3.
109. Hamilton Lodge papers and documents, scroll minutes, 5 Nov. 1702; Hamilton Lodge Minutes, f.5v.
110. Hamilton Lodge early papers, accounts, 1703-10.
111. *Ibid.*, accounts, 1712-13.
112. Hamilton Lodge papers and documents, scroll minutes, 1 May 1701, 28 Dec. 1702, 1 Feb. 1704, 27 Dec. 1710.
113. Hamilton Lodge early papers, accounts, 1703-10.
114. Carr, *Kilwinning*, 131, 143, 146.

CHAPTER 5   Fife and Tayside, pp. 90-7

1. Carr, *Edinburgh*, 43.
2. Lyon, *Edinburgh*, 66.
3. *Ibid.*, 68.
4. G.R.T. Wilson, *History of Lodge 'St Andrews'*, No. 25 (St Andrews, 1894), 2.
5. Lyon, *Edinburgh*, 68. Lyon records only John Burn as accepting the charter for Dunfermline, but the earlier (though not always reliable) transcript by Father Hay also records the name of Robert Alison among signatures which are now missing (see Inventory, 2.4, 2.5). Alison was among the masons and wrights who advised the burgh council of Dunfermline about repairs to the tolbooth in 1626, A. Shearer (ed.), *Extracts from the burgh records of Dunfermline in the 16th and 17th centuries* (Dunfermline, 1951), 154.
6. See Inventory, 14.1, 14.2.
7. Dunfermline Lodge minutes, (Inventory, 14.3).
8. Dunfermline Central Library, transcript of the Book of the Hammermen, c.1585-c.1689; E. Henderson, *Annals of Dunfermline* (Glasgow, 1879), 350.
9. *Ibid.*, 401; SRO, B.20/13/4, Dunfermline burgh council minutes, 1696-1726, 19 Jan 1719.

10. Dunfermline Lodge minutes, 27 Dec. 1698 and, e.g., 18 Jan. 1699, 18 Jan. 1704, 23 Jan. 1710.
11. *Ibid.*, 27 Dec.1701.
12. *Ibid.*, 27 Dec.1700.
13. *Ibid.*, 28 Dec. 1700.
14. *Ibid.*, 8 Jan. 1701; Henderson, *Annals*, 370.
15. H. Carr, 'Apprenticeship in England and Scotland up to 1700', *AQC*, 69 (1956), 66-8.
16. Dunfermline Lodge minuses, 27 Dec. 1711, 1712 and 1716, 18 Nov. 1714.
17. Henderson, *Annals*, 403-4.
18. Carr, *Edinburgh*, 43.
19. A. M. Smith, *The three united trades of Dundee. Masons, wrights and slaters* (Abertay Historical Society, 1987), 45-6, 79; *RPCS.*, 1629-30, xxvi-xxvii, 118, 127-8, 135-6, 227; J.D. Marwick (ed.), *Extracts from the records of the convention of the royal burghs of Scotland, 1615-1676* (Edinburgh, 1878),297-8.
20. A.J. Warden, *Burgh laws of Dundee, with the history, statutes, and proceedings of the guild of merchants and fraternities of craftsmen* (London, 1872), 584, 595.
21. Both the John Mylne of the petition and his father had been burgesses of Dundee, but they may be exceptions to the rule, being respected architects; or it could be that exclusion of masons from burgess-ship had been a result of the 1629 episode.
22. Dundee District Archive, Dundee register of deeds, 1760-4, pp.903-5. There are other copies of the act in Dundee Society papers (Inventory, 13.3). The act is dated 26 April 1659, but as it was acted on by the masons on 11 March it must have been agreed earlier.
23. Warden, *Burgh laws,* 578; Inventory, 4.8, 4.9.
24. *Ibid.*, 579-80; Dundee Society minutes (Inventory, 13.1), 11 Mar. 1659.
25. Dundee Society register (Inventory, 13.2), 11 Mar. 1659.
26. Dundee Society papers, act of 8 Feb. 1695.
27. Dundee Society register, *passim*.
28. Dundee Society papers, act of 17 Nov. 1677.
29. Dundee Society minutes, 27 Dec. 1669, 20 Nov. 1677.
30. *Ibid.*, 28 Dec. 1705, 27 Dec. 1706, 9 May, 27 Dec. 1707; Warden, *Burgh laws,* 581.

CHAPTER 6   Central, pp. 98-112

1. Mr of works accs., ii, 1, 12, 81, 136, 168, 299; R. Renwick (ed.), *Extracts from the records of the royal burgh of Stirling, 1519-1666* (Glasgow, 1887), 174; RCAHMS, Stirling, ii, 289; SRO, CC.21/5/5, 8 Feb. 1646.
2. Mr of works accs., ii, 164, 232; RCAHMS, *Stirling*, 289.
3. Mr of works accs., ii, 251, 370; CC.21/5/5, 20 Oct. 1644.
4. D.B. Morris, 'The Incorporation of Omnium Gatherum of Stirling', *Transactions of the Stirling Natural History and Archaeological Society*, (1931-2), 9-12; D.B. Morris, 'The Incorporation of Mechanics of Stirling', *ibid.*, (1930-1), 9-10; W. Harvey, 'Masonry in Stirling: The Ancient Ludge', *ibid.*, (1922-3), 29-31.
5. Central Regional Council Archives, Stirling, PD.7/12/9 (Inventory, 30.9), papers of 27 Nov. 1660 and c.1660.
6. PD.7/12/6 (Inventory, 30.6), f.lr-v.
7. PD.7/12/4 (Inventory, 3.3 and 30.4); Morris, 'Mechanics', 37-44.
8. PD.7/12/6, ff.2r-3r; PD.7/12/4, ff.28r, 34r.
9. PD.7/12/4, f.4r; Morris, 'Mechanics', 17.

10. PD.7/12/4, f.7r; Morris, 'Mechanics', 17. Parts of the entry have become illegible since Morris transcribed it.
11. PD.7/12/4, f.28r.
12. Harvey, 'Masonry', 35; W.J. Hughan, *The 'Ancient Stirling Lodge' manuscript of the Old Charges* (London, 1893), 3-4 (Inventory, 4.12 and 30.2).
13. Morris, 'Mechanics', 27.
14. PD.7/12/11 (Inventory, 30.11), paper of 7 Apr. 1674. It was intended that the litsters as well as the building crafts should be included in the new incorporation, *ibid.*, undated letter addressed to 'Your Grace'.
15. R. Renwick (ed.), *Extracts from the records of the royal burgh of Stirling, 1667-1752* (Glasgow, 1889), 16-17; Morris, 'Mechanics', 12-13.
16. *Ibid.*, 28-9.
17. *Stirling records, 1667-1752*, 117, 393.
18. Morris, 'Mechanics', 14-15, 30-6.
19. Eg., Harvey, 'Masonry', 43; W.J. Hughan, 'The "Ancient Stirling Ludge"', *AQC*, 6 (1893), 109; T.W.R. Johnston, 'Stirling Ancient No. 30. The lodge's history, taken from its records, 1741-1905', *Stirling Ancient 30. Book of the bazaar* (Stirling, 1905), 1.
20. GLS, Minute book, i, 58.
21. GLS, Cartulary, i, lists of members, 55.
22. Carr, *Edinburgh*, 43.
23. Inventory, 29.1.
24. Mylne, *Master masons*, 159. This family history valiantly upheld the story of the long line of Mylne master masons to the king, though the author had difficulty reconciling it with the evidence. The reference to John Mylne (died 1621) as holding the office in the 1580s, Lord J. Somerville, *Memorie of the Somervills* (2 vols., *Edinburgh*, 1815), i, 459-60, occurs in a work written in the late seventeenth century when the Mylne myth was well established, and is thus not reliable evidence. A 1589 contract called Mylne simply mason in Dundee, Mylne, *Master masons*, 66. See Colvin, *Architects* 567-70 for summaries of the careers of the three seventeenth-century John Mylnes.
25. J. Maidment (ed.), *The chronicle of Perth* (Maitland Club, 1831), 8.
26. T.H. Marshall, *History of Perth* (Perth, 1849), 420, 439-40; Mylne, *Master Masons*, 100.
27. The transcript in *ibid.*, 129, omits the name of one of the masters, James Roch.
28. Perth Incorporation minutes (Inventory, 29.6), 94.
29. Perth Incorporation minutes (Inventory, 29.5), 26 Dec. 1670, 1 Apr., 3 May 1671, 18 Oct. 1673.
30. *Ibid.*, 28 Sept. 1669, 11 Jan. 1687, 26 Dec. 1695.
31. Perth Incorporation minutes (Inventory, 29.4), f.11r, and (Inventory, 29.5), 4 Oct. 1671; *Index to the register of deeds, 1661* (1929), 87.
32. Perth Incorporation minutes (Inventory, 29.5), 3 Oct. 1683; Perth and Kinross District Archive, Sandeman Library, Perth, B.59/8/21, Perth register of deeds, 18, 120, 121, 122, 173, 224, 332.
33. B.59/8/25, 203.
34. *Ibid.*, 202.
35. *Ibid.*, 202-3.
36. *Ibid.*, 201-2.
37. *Ibid.*, 167-8.
38. The initial of the Brown who signed the 1658 agreement has been read as D in the published transcripts, but may well in fact be an H.
39. A.F. Hatten, "Early minute book of the Lodge of Dunblane', *AQC*, 67 (1954), 86.

40. *Ibid.*, 84, 87.
41. The transcript in Lyon, *Edinburgh*, 442 states that James Grahame was to be depute eldest fellow craft, but that in Hatten, 'Dunblane', 87 shows that a marginal note merely states that a Grahame (no Christian name being given) was to be depute. It seems most likely that John Grahame, the procurator fiscal, was meant, and that he was to act as depute to the clerk, James Turner.
42. *Complete peerage*, xii, 371; RPCS, 1689, 121-2, 194, 304.
43. A. Mackenzie, *History of the Camerons* (Inverness, 1884),199, 204-5, 231, 283.
44. *Ibid.*, 209.
45. A.B. Barty, *History of Dunblane* (Stirling, 1944), 159-60.
46. *Ibid.*, 155-6; W.B. Cook (ed.), *The Stirling antiquary* (3 vols., Stirling, 1893-1904), ii, 209-10; [J. Drummond], *Memoirs of Sir Ewen Cameron of Lochiel* (Abbotsford and Maitland Clubs, 1842), xl, 218, 269, 270, 281, 287-8.
47. SRO, RH.11/25/3, Register of deeds and protests of the regality of Dunblane, 1698-1747, pp.14, 50.
48. Barty, 'Dunblane, 112, 113, 114-15, 117; Hatten, 'Dunblane', 110.
49. *Ibid.*, 91.
50. *Ibid.*, 101.
51. *Ibid.*, 95.
52. *Ibid.*, 89.
53. *Ibid.*, 100.
54. *Ibid.*, 88, 90-1; Barty, *Dunblane*, 161.
55. *Ibid.*, 162-3.
56. Hatten, 'Dunblane', 90.
57. Barty, *Dunblane*, 161-2.
58. Hatten, 'Dunblane', 90, 96-7.
59. *Ibid.*, 96.
60. *Ibid.*, 107.
61. *Ibid.*, 107.

CHAPTER 7 The Borders, pp. 113-123

1. Vernon, *History*, 58-63; Inventory, 4.1, 27.1.
2. Vernon, *History*, 12.
3. *Ibid.*, 13-14; Inventory, 27.3.
4. M.H.B. Sanderson, *Scottish rural life in the sixteenth century* (Edinburgh, 1982) 99, 108, 125.
5. Vernon, History, 7; C.S. Romanes (ed.), *Selections from the records of the regality of Melrose* (3 vols., SHS, 1914-17), iii, 357n-363n.
6. RMS, *1593-1608*, no. 1756.
7. Romanes, *Melrose*, iii, 49-51.
8. Mr of works accs., i, 366; R. Renwick, *The burgh of Peebles. Gleanings from its records, 1604-52* (2nd. edn., Peebles, 1912), 159-61.
9. Vernon, *History*, 7-11.
10. Melrose Lodge minutes (Inventory, 27.2), 40, 41, 43, 46, 47, 50, 52, 58, 243. I am most grateful to the Lodge of Melrose for lending me a typed transcript of their first minute book.
11. Vernon, *History*, 16.
12. *Ibid.*, 16-17.
13. *Ibid.*, 18, 19.
14. *Ibid.*, 24.

15. *Ibid.*, 20.
16. *Ibid.*, 21; Melrose Lodge minutes, 17.
17. Vernon, *History*, 24.
18. Melrose Lodge minutes, 36.
19. *Ibid.*, 248.
20. Vernon, *History*, 24; Melrose Lodge minutes, 53, 249.
21. Romanes, *Melrose*, iii, 22-4, 28, 36.
22. SRO, CH.2/386/2, Melrose Kirk Session minutes, 1668-1702, 26 Oct. 1690, 21 Aug. 1692.
23. Vernon, *History*, 14, 15. Vernon mistranscribed 'Ffall' as 'Hall': see Melrose Lodge minutes, 245.
24. R.W.D. McGregor, *History of freemasonry in New Jersey. Commemorating the one hundred fiftieth anniversary of the Grand Lodge of... New Jersey, 1787-1937* (n.p., n.d.), 15; G.P. Insch, *Scottish colonial schemes, 1620-1686* (Glasgow, 1922), 276-7; W.A. Whitehead, *Contributions to the early history of Perth Amboy* (New York, 1856), 41, 47-8; W. Nelson (ed.), *Calendar of records in the secretary of state's office* (Documents Relating to the Colonial History of the State of New Jersey, 1st series, xxi, 1899), 106, 198, 211-12, 231, 272. McGregor, *History*, 16-17, claims that a second member of the Lodge of Melrose, the Quaker Andrew Robson or Robeson, emigrated to West Jersey in the 1680s, becoming surveyor general of the province and later settling in Pennsylvania and giving the name Roxborough to a township. But though this Robeson came from Roxburghshire he cannot be identified convincingly with the man of the same name who signed the Melrose Lodge agreement of 1675. The Quaker emigrant can be traced being persecuted for his religious beliefs in the 1660s (eg., *RPCS, 1661-4*, 266, 275, 281-2, 339, 596, 616, 626, *RPCS, 1665-9*, 135, 139, 428). But by 1677 he was settled in Ireland, and was described as having formerly been a merchant in London (Nelson, *Calendar*, 405). Thus he had probably left Scotland several years before 1675.
25. Vernon, *History*, 85, 87.
26. *Ibid.*, 85, 93.
27. *Ibid.*, 14, 15, 86. He is described as Deacon Faa in the Kelso minute, but what he was deacon of is uncertain. There is not known to have been an incorporation in Kelso containing masons, unless (as Vernon assumed) they belonged to the Incorporation of Hammermen.
28. *Ibid.*, 26n, 89n.
29. Carr, *Edinburgh*, 162; A. Pringle, *Records of the Pringles of the Scottish Border* (Edinburgh, 1933), 189-91, 311-12.
30. Vernon, *History*, 87-91.
31. *Ibid.*, 94-5.
32. *Ibid.*, 96.
33. H. Carr (ed.), 'The minute-book of the Lodge of Haughfoot, 1702-1763', pt. i *AQC*, 63 (1950), 256-7.
34. *Ibid.*, pt. 1, 258-63.
35. *Ibid.*, pt. 1, 258, 264-6, and pt. 2 *AQC*, 64 (1951), 9.
36. *Ibid.*, pt. 1, 269-71; Carr, *Edinburgh*, 162.
37. Carr, 'Haughfoot', pt. 1, 272, 274-6.
38. *Ibid.*, pt. 1, 272-3, 278-83.
39. *Ibid.*, pt. 1, 267-8, 284-5, 292-4, pt. 2, 9-11, 13; F.J. Grant (ed.), *The faculty of advocates of Scotland* (SRS, 1944), 152.
40. Carr, 'Haughfoot', pt. 2, 15, 17.
41. *Ibid.*, pt. 1, 267.

42. *Ibid.*, pt. 2, 38-40.
43. *Ibid.*, pt. 1, 301, pt. 2, 13.
44. *Ibid.*, pt. 2, 8, 16.
45. *Ibid.*, pt. 2, 14-15.

CHAPTER 8   The North, pp. 124-55

1. J. Stuart, *Extracts from the council register of the burgh of Aberdeen, 1398-1570* (Spalding Club, 1844), 39, 52, 68, 199; J. Stuart (ed.), *Extracts from the council register of the burgh of Aberdeen, 1570-1625* (Spalding Club, 1848), 267; Miller, *Aberdeen*, 9-11; A.M. Munro, 'Notes on the history of masonry in Aberdeen', *The Masonic Bazaar, Aberdeen. 8th, 9th and 10th October 1896* (Aberdeen, 1896), [3-4].
2. E. Bain, *Merchant and craft guilds. A history of the Aberdeen incorporated trades* (Aberdeen, 1887), 238-41; Stuart, *Council register of Aberdeen, 1398-1570*, 176.
3. Bain, *Guilds*, 236; Miller, *Aberdeen*, 15.
4. A.M. Munro (ed.), 'Register of burgesses of guild and trade of the burgh of Aberdeen, 1399-1631', *Miscellany of the New Spalding Club*, i (1890), 27, 52, 53, 55, 57.
5. Miller, *Aberdeen*, 13.
6. Stuart, *Council register of Aberdeen, 1398-1570*, 457. The burgh register of apprentices records the apprenticing of several sons of masons to other trades, but not apprentices being bound to the mason trade, A.M. Munro, 'Register of indentures of the burgh of Aberdeen', *Scottish Notes and Queries*, first series, x (1896-7), 163-5, 188-90, xi (1897-8), 11-12, 43-4, 60, 73-4, 118-19, 150-1, xii (1898-9), 6-7, 39-40, 54-5; second series, i (1899-1900), 78-9, 109-10, 163-5. But one indenture relating to the craft survives elsewhere in the burgh records: dated 1573, it is nearly a century older than any other known Scottish mason's indenture, 'Indenture of apprenticeship of Andrew Jamesone', *Scottish Notes and Queries*, i, no. 2 (July 1887), 24-5; H. Carr, 'Apprenticeship in England and Scotland up to 1700', *AQC*, 69 (1956), 65.
7. A.M. Munro (ed.), 'Aberdeen burgess register, 1631-1700', *Miscellany of the New Spalding Club*, ii (1908), 406.
8. Eg., *ibid.*, 89, 409.
9. Mylne, *Master masons*, 113.
10. L.B. Taylor (ed.), *Aberdeen shore work accounts, 1596-1670* (Aberdeen, 1972), 111, 122, 125; Stuart, *Council register of Aberdeen, 1570-1625*, 338-40; Munro, 'Burgesses, 1399-1631', 125, 135. I am grateful to Mr Duncan Macniven for bringing Watson's case to my attention.
11. SRO, PS.1/61, Register of the privy seal, f.47r; Miller, *Aberdeen*, 11-12; Stevenson, *Origins*, chapter 3.
12. See Inventory, 6.4-6.
13. Miller, *Aberdeen*, 18.
14. See Inventory, 6.1.
15. Miller, *Aberdeen*, opposite p.19.
16. *Ibid.*, 44. The printer, John Forbes, had taken the son of an Aberdeen mason as an apprentice in 1667, SRO, RD.2/35, pp.371-3. Thus it is possible that some link between the printer and the mason craft helped reassure the lodge that the secrecy of the catechism would not be jeopardised by printing it for members.

17. Poole, *Gould's History*, iii, 210-20.
18. W. Fraser, *The Elphinstone family book* (2 vols., Edinburgh, 1897), 91; SRO, CC.21/5/10, ff.79v-80v.
19. F.J. Grant (ed.), *The faculty of advocates in Scotland* (SRS, 1944), 4.
20. P.J. Anderson (ed.), *Fasti Academiae Mariscallanae Aberdonensis: Selections from the records of the Marischal College and University* (3 vols., New Spalding Club, 1889-98), ii, 53.
21. *Ibid.*, ii, 53,252.
22. 'It may be urged that the register was not written in 1670; but the objection will carry no weight, there being abundant internal evidence to confirm the antiquity of the document. Furthermore, the style of caligraphy and orthography and the declaration of the penman, all confirm the fact that the record was compiled in the year named, that it is a *bone fide* register of the members of the Lodge of Aberdeen for 1670', Poole, *Gould's History*, iii, 213-14. In fact, of course, the internal evidence proves conclusively the very opposite, and the claim that the precise year in which a document was written can be determined by its handwriting and spelling is obviously an absurdity.
24. J. Stuart (ed.), *List of pollable persons within the shire of Aberdeen. 1696* (2 vols., Aberdeen, 1844), ii, 276.
25. H. Scott (ed.), *Fasti Ecclesiae Scoticanae* (7 vols., Edinburgh, 1915-28), vi, 202; T. Mair (ed.), *Records of the parish of Ellon* (Edinburgh, 1876), 203-5.
26. Aberdeen District Archives, City Archives, Council register, lvii (1682-1704), 117-18.
27. Bain, *Guilds*, 117-18.
28. Munro, 'Burgesses, 1631-1700', 456.
29. P.J. Anderson (ed.), *Officers and graduates of University and King's College, Aberdeen* (New Spalding Club, 1893), 201; Scott, *Fasti*, iii, 128, vi, 197.
30. J.A. Parker (ed.), *Roll of the members and masters of the Lodge of Aberdeen* (2nd. edn., Aberdeen, 1929), 8-9.
31. See Miller, *Aberdeen*, facsimile opposite p. 20.
32. A.L. Miller, 'The connection of Dr James Anderson of the "Constitutions" with Aberdeen and Aberdeen University', *AQC*, 36 (1923), 91.
33. A.M. Munro, 'Notes on the history of masonry in Aberdeen', *The Masonic Bazaar, Aberdeen, 8th, 9th and 10th October 1896* (Aberdeen, 1896), [21]; Miller, *Aberdeen*, 24; Inventory, 6.3.
34. Inventory, 6.4; Miller, *Aberdeen*, 43.
35. *Ibid.*, 57-65.
36. Carr, 'Apprenticeship', 60, 61, 71.
37. Miller, *Aberdeen*, 66.
38. *Scots peerage*, iv, 35-6.
39. Munro, 'Burgesses, 1631-1700', 435, 444.
40. L.B. Taylor, *Aberdeen council letters* (6 vols., Oxford. 1942-61), vi, 181, 195, 209, 215, 257-60.
41. SRO, E.72/1/4, pp. 26-7.
42. *RPCS, 1688-9*, 119.
43. Aberdeen District Archives, Ms council letters, vol. 7, no. 95.
44. C.B.B.Watson (ed.), *Roll of Edinburgh burgesses, 1406-1700* (SRS, 1926), 173; H. Paton (ed.), *Register of interments in the Greyfriars Burying-Ground, Edinburgh, 1658-1700* (SRS, 1902), 207.
45. R.W.D. McGregor, *History of freemasonry in New Jersey. Commemorating the one hundred fiftieth anniversary of the Grand Lodge of... New Jersey, 1787-1937* (n.p., n.d.), 11-12; W.A. Whitehead, *East Jersey under the proprietary governments*

NOTES, CHAPTERS 8   179

(2nd. edn., Newark, New Jersey, 1875), 475; W.A. Whitehead, *Contributions to the early history of Perth Amboy* (New York, 1856), 27-8, 80-4.

46. For the Scots settlers in East Jersey in the 1680s see G.P. Insh, *Scottish colonial schemes, 1620-1686* (Glasgow, 1922), 145-85, and N.C. Landsman, *Scotland and its first American colony, 1683-1765* (Princeton, 1985).
47. *Ibid.*, 105.
48. J.E. Pomfret, *The New Jersey proprietors and their lands, 1664-1776* (Princeton,1964), 38.
49. Taylor, *Council letters*, v, p.xxi; vi, p.xviii. For early Scottish Quakers see G.B. Burnet, *The story of Quakerism in Scotland* (London, 1952) and J. Torrance, 'The early Quakers in Northeast Scotland', *Banffshire Field Club Transactions*, xiii (1936), 67-87. For their persecution in Aberdeen see Taylor, *Council letters, RPCS*, and J. Stuart (ed.), *Extracts from the council register of the burgh of Aberdeen, 1625-1747* (SBRS, 1872).
50. *Ibid.*, 292, 307.
51. See the article on Barclay in DNB.
52. J. Barclay, *Diary of Alexander Jaffray.... with memoirs of the rise, progress and persecution of the people called Quakers in the North of Scotland* (3rd. edn., Aberdeen, 1856), 290, 305; Taylor, *Council letters*, vi, p.xvi note; Anderson, *Records of the Marischal College*, ii, 230, 232; J.F.K. Johnstone and A.W. Robertson, *Bibliographia Aberdonensis* (2 vols, Third Spalding Club, 1829-30), 441, 447, 449, 450; G.M. Fraser, 'A rare tract on persecution in Scotland', *Journal of the Friends Historical Society*, vi (1909), 108.
53. Anderson, *Records of the Marischal College*, ii, 241; Bain, *Guilds*, 45; Poole, *Gould's History*, iii, 211.
54. Paterson's portrait is reproduced in Stevenson, *Origins*, Whyte's in the present book.
55. W.F. Miller, 'Gleanings from the records of the yearly meeting of Aberdeen, 1672-1786', *Journal of the Friends Historical Society*, viii (1911), 53; W. Nelson (ed), *Calendar of records in the secretary of state's office, 1664-1703* (Documents relating to the Colonial History of New Jersey, first series, xxi, 1899), 58, 98, 234, 245, 251; McGregor, *Freemasonry in New Jersey*, 13.
56. Taylor, *Council letters*, vi, p.xvi note; Munro, 'Burgesses, 1631-1700', 410, 451. The published burgess list erroneously converts the younger Mure from a hookmaker into a bookmaker!
57. Grant, *Advocates*, 4; J.A. Henderson (ed.), *History of the society of advocates in Aberdeen* (New Spalding Club, 1912), 80; P.J. Anderson (ed.), *Charters and other writs illustrating the History of the royal burgh of Aberdeen* (Aberdeen, 1890), 412; Anderson, *Records of the Marischal College*, iii, 232.
58. Whitehead, *East Jersey*, 467-8; Nelson, *Calendar*, 112, 121, 334; McGregor, *Freemasonry in New Jersey*, 13.
59. *Ibid.*, 13; Insh, *Scottish colonial schemes*, 263-7; Nelson, *Calendar*, 71, 74, 79, 103; A. and H. Tayler, *The house of Forbes* (Third Spalding Club, 1937), 352-3, 356, 357; Whitehead, *Perth Amboy*, 41; Barclay, *Alexander Jaffray*, 249; R.W.D. McGregor, 'Contributions to the early history of freemasonry in New Jersey', *The Master Mason*, i (Masonic Service Association of America, Washington: New Jersey edition only, 1925-7), Dec. 1925, 99-100. McGregor's articles were the first to establish the link between Aberdeen freemasons and New Jersey: unfortunately he did not cite his sources. He asserted that both the duke of York and James Drummond, earl of Perth (active in the colonisation project, Perth Amboy being named after him) were freemasons (ibid., 98). There is no evidence whatever for York being a mason, and that for Perth

is not convincing. The latter consists of a brass tobacco box bearing masonic symbols, the date 1670, and a Drummond coat of arms, which it is asserted belonged to the earl. But the elaborate masonic symbolism of the box belongs to a much later period, and the date 1670 remains a mystery. J. Yarker, 'Drummond—earls of Perth', *AQC,* 14 (1901), 138.

60. W.F. Skene, *Memorials of the family of Skene of Skene* (New Spalding Club1887), 78; Mair, *Ellon,* 180-1; Barclay, *Alexander Jaffray,* 267-8, 272-8, 305, 312; Johnstone and Robertson, *Bibliographia Aberdonensis,* ii, 447, 450.
61. McGregor, *Freemasonry in New Jersey,* 13-15.
62. P.W. Filby and M.K. Meyer (eds.), *Passenger and immigration Lists* (3 vols., Detroit, 1981), iii, 1957, under Skein; R. Proud, *The history of Pennsylvania* (2 vols., Philadelphia, 1797-8), i, 160.
63. J.E. Pomfret, *The province of West New Jersey, 1609-1702* (Princeton, 1956), 153, 160, 161-2, 166, 232; A. Leaming and J. Spicer, *The grants, concessions and original constitutions of the province of New Jersey* (reprint, Somerville, New Jersey, 1881), 456-8; Nelson, *Calendar,* 411, 412, 464; Macgregor, 'Contributions', *Master Mason,* i, Jan. 1926, 117-18. McGregor's references to the Aberdeen masons in New Jersey were copied in a number of American masonic publications, eg., G.D. Love, 'The first mason in America'. *New York Masonic Outlook,* Sept. 1926, 13, 28; A. Cerza, 'New Jersey', *Colonial freemasonry,* ed. L.C.W. Cook (Transactions of the Missouri Lodge of Research, vol. 30, 1973-4), 106. H.L. Haywood, *Supplement to Mackey's Encyclopedia of Freemasonry* (Chicago, 1946, being vol. iii of the Encyclopedia), 1151, wrongly states that Skene came to New Jersey in 1684, and implies that he came in the ship for which Harry Elphinstone was a booking agent. But he corrects this in his *Masonic essays* (Missouri Lodge of Research, 1963), 61.
64. McGregor, 'Contributions', *Master Mason,* i, Jan. 1926, 120.
65. See the list of the entered apprentices in Poole, *Gould's History,* iii, 212 and compare with Stuart, *Pollable persons* and the Old Aberdeen burgess list in A.M. Munro, *Records of Old Aberdeen* (2 vols., New Spalding Club, 1899-1909), i.
66. *Ibid.,* i, 241; Stuart, *Pollable persons,* ii, 575.
67. Aberdeen District Archives, Old Aberdeen council minutes, 1697-1719, 24 Dec. 1698; Munro, *Records of Old Aberdeen,* i, 173. Another of the apprentices, Kenneth Fraser, is sometimes referred to as being the king's master mason (eg., Poole, *Gould's History,* iii, 215). He never held this office, but it may be that he was master mason to King's College in Old Aberdeen and that this has led to confusion.
68. The details of members are taken from Parker, *Roll of Members,* 9-10. Parker lists William Donald, who joined the lodge in 1716, as a mason burgess, thus suggestng that the burgh had begun to admit masons as craft burgesses. In fact Donald was a maltman, Aberdeen District Archives, Register of burgesses, ii (1694-1760), 145.
69. Anderson, *Records of the Marischal College,* i, 146.
70. Poole, *Gould's History,* iii, 216, 217.
71. *Ibid.,* iii, 217-18.
72. *Ibid.,* iii, 215; *The constitution of the Aberdeen Mason Lodge* (Aberdeen, 1853), appendix, xvii.
73. B.E. Jones, *Freemasons' guide and compendium* (London, 1950), 387-92.
74. *Constitution of the Aberdeen Mason Lodge,* appendix, xvi.
75. J. Jamieson, 'The St John or Aberdeen Lodge, No. 34', *Aberdeenshire Masonic Reporter* (1879), 17, quoted Poole, *Gould's History,* iii. 215.

76. Munro, 'Notes on the history of masonry', [22]; Miller, *Aberdeen*, 14, and facsimile of accounts opposite p. 50.
77. Stuart, *Pollable persons*, ii, 617; Aberdeen District Archives, Register of deeds, 1689-1703, 27 June 1700.
78. Aberdeen District Archives, B.1/1/53, ff.9r-v, 25v-26r.
79. J. Gordon, *Abredoniae vtrivsque descriptio. A description of both touns of Aberdeen* (Spalding Club, 1842).
80. T. Friedman, *James Gibbs* (London, 1984), 3-6; B. Little, *The life and work of James Gibbs* (London, 1955), 5-19; Colvin, Architects, 337-9.
81. For the younger Anderson's family background see Miller, 'James Anderson', 89-103 and Miller, *Aberdeen*, 46-7.
82. L. Vibert, 'Introduction' to the facsimile edition of Anderson's 1723 and 1738 *Constitutions* published by the Quatuor Coronati Lodge (London, 1976).
83. A. Ross, *Freemasonry in Inverness: being an account of the ancient lodges of St John's Old Kilwinning, No. 6 of Scotland, and St Andrews Kilwinning, No. 31 of Scotland* (Inverness, 1877), 7-9; GLS Minutes, i, 34-5; GLS, Cartulary, i, 19-20.
84. H. Paton, *The Mackintosh muniments, 1442-1820* (Edinburgh, 1903), 142.
85. W. Mackay and G.S. Laing (eds.), *Records of Inverness*, ii (New Spalding Club, 1922), 278.
86. *Ibid.*, 262, 272-3.
87. *Ibid.*, 353, 355; W. Mackay (ed.), *The letter-book of Bailie John Steuart of Inverness, 1715-1752* (SHS, 1915), 112, 126, 128, 139, 141, 176.
88. Ross, *Freemasonry in Inverness*, 16, 55, 63-6.
89. W.J. Hughan, 'Specimens from a masonic quarry, No. 1, operative masonic lodges', *The Freemason*, i, no.1 (13 March 1869), 5. This transcript of the minute appears to be corrupt in places.
90. W. Cramond (ed.), *The annals of Banff* (2 vols., New Spalding Club, 1891-3), ii, 255.
91. *Ibid.*, i, 181.
92. *Ibid.*, ii, 73, 292.
93. Eg., *GLSYB* (1986), 128, Lodge No. 45.
94. Kilmolymock Lodge minutes (Inventory, 23.1), 5.
95. *Ibid.*, 8, 9.
96. W. Cramond (ed.), *The records of Elgin, 1234-1800* (2 vols., New Spalding Club, 1903-8), i, 362.
97. Kilmolymock Lodge minutes, 11.
98. *Ibid.*, 6, 7, 13.
99. Cramond, *Records of Elgin*, i, 379; E.D. Dunbar (ed.), *Documents relating to the province of Moray* (Edinburgh, 1895), 14.
100. Kilmolymock Lodge minutes, 6; Cramond, *Records of Elgin*, i, 377, ii, 312, 34, 325.
101. Kilmolymock Lodge minutes, 5, 9, 16.
102. Cramond, *Records of Elgin*, i, 346, ii, 397.
103. Kilmolymock Lodge minutes, 6, 7.
104. *Ibid.*, 7, 8.
105. *Ibid.*, 7.
106. *Ibid.*, 22-3.
107. *Ibid.*, 22; Carr, *Edinburgh*, 37.
108. Kilmolymock Lodge minutes, 11-12.
109. *Ibid.*, 9.
110. *Ibid.*, 10, 23.
111. *Ibid.*, 17-19, 21-2.
112. GLS, Cartulary, i. pp. 60-1

APPENDIX 1

LIST AND MAP OF EARLY (PRE-1710) MASONIC LODGES IN SCOTLAND

Lodges are listed on the left according to the dates of the earliest authentic references to them. On the right are listed the modern lodges (with their numbers on the roll of the Grand Lodge of Scotland) which can trace their origins to these early lodges: where there are doubts as to the continuity of the modern lodge with the early lodge this is indicated.

1 Aitchison's Haven, 9 January 1599[1]	(Extinct about 1866)
2 Edinburgh, 31 July 1599[1,2]	Lodge No. 1
3 St Andrews, 27 November 1599[1,2]	
4 = Kilwinning, 28 December 1599	Lodge No. 0
4 = Stirling, 28 December 1599[2]	Lodge No. 30
6 Haddington, 1599[1]	Lodge No. 57?
7 Dunfermline, 1600-1[1,2]	Lodge No. 26
8 Glasgow, 31 December 1613[2]	Lodge No. 3[bis]
9 Dundee, 1627-8[2]	
10 Linlithgow, 2 March 1654	Lodge No. 17?
11 Scone (Perth), 24 December 1658	Lodge No. 3
12 Aberdeen, 1670?	Lodge No. 1[3]
13 Melrose, 28 December 1674	Lodge No. 1[2]
14 Canongate Kilwinning, 20 December 1677	Lodge No. 2
15 Inverness, 27 December 1678	Lodge No. 6
16 Dumfries, 20 May 1687	Lodge No. 53
17 Canongate and Leith, Leith and Canongate 29 May 1688	Lodge No. 5
18 Kirkcudbright, c. 1691?	Lodge No. 41
19 Hamilton, 25 March 1695	Lodge No. 7
20 Dunblane, April 1695	Lodge No. 9
21 Kelso, 2 June 1701	Lodge No. 58
22 Haughfoot, 22 December 1702	(Extinct about 1763)
23 Banff, 1703	Lodge No. 52
24 Kilmolymock (Elgin), 27 December 1704	Lodge No. 45
25 Edinburgh Journeymen, 1707-12	Lodge No. 8

[1,2]Parties to the First (1600-1) and Second (1627-8) St Clair Charters.

APPENDIX 1

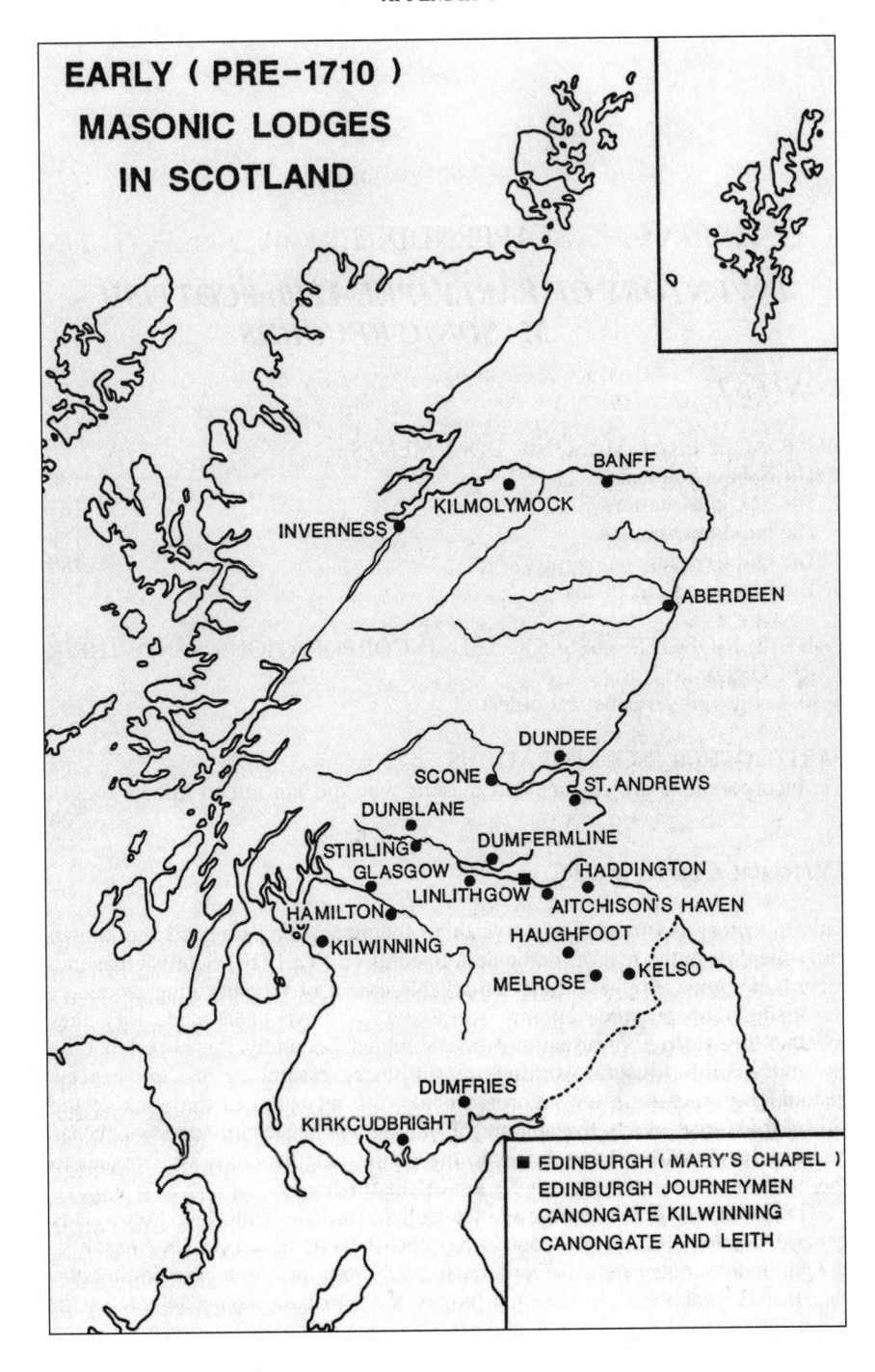

EARLY (PRE-1710) MASONIC LODGES IN SCOTLAND

- BANFF
- KILMOLYMOCK
- INVERNESS
- ABERDEEN
- DUNDEE
- SCONE
- ST. ANDREWS
- DUNBLANE
- DUMFERMLINE
- STIRLING
- GLASGOW
- LINLITHGOW
- HADDINGTON
- HAMILTON
- AITCHISON'S HAVEN
- KILWINNING
- HAUGHFOOT
- MELROSE
- KELSO
- DUMFRIES
- KIRKCUDBRIGHT

■ EDINBURGH (MARY'S CHAPEL)
EDINBURGH JOURNEYMEN
CANONGATE KILWINNING
CANONGATE AND LEITH

APPENDIX 2

INVENTORY OF EARLY (PRE-1710) SCOTTISH MASONIC RECORDS

CONTENTS

PART 1: GENERAL MASONIC DOCUMENTS
1. The Schaw Statutes   186
2. The St Clair Charters   187
3. The Falkland Statutes   188
4. The Old Charges   189
5. The Masonic Catechisms   191

PART 2: LODGES, ASSOCIATED INCORPORATIONS, AND THEIR RECORDS
6-30. Lodges (in alphabetical order)   192

PART 3: OTHER INCORPORATIONS
31. Incorporations which included masons who did not attend known lodges   204

INTRODUCTORY NOTE

This Inventory is intended to serve three functions. By listing all the known early (here as in the rest of the book defined as up to *c*.1710) Scottish masonic records it should emphasise the remarkable extent of the surviving evidence. Surprisingly no previous attempt seems ever to have been made to gather together the scattered information here assembled. Secondly, it is hoped that the Inventory will be a useful working tool for others researching masonic history, encouraging interest in the records. Finally, the inclusion in the book of the Inventory has cut down the amount of bibliographical information which has had to be included in the endnotes to the various chapters, cross-references to the inventory being provided in the notes where relevant.

    The scope of the Inventory is indicated by the Contents list. Part 1 lists general documents directly concerned with the emergence of freemasonry: the Falkland Statutes are a borderline case, but merit inclusion here through the fact that in practice only masonic lodges seem to have taken an interest in them. Part 2 lists lodge records, and also (where appropriate) the records of the

APPENDIX 2

incorporation or incorporations which significant numbers of the members of a lodge belonged to. In some instances burgh masons belonged to an incorporation but are not known to have had lodges before 1710: the records of these incorporations are listed in Part 3. Incorporations, of course, have no direct part in the emergence of freemasonry, but inclusion of their records in the list seems justified by the facts that they were often closely associated with lodges, and that in trying to understand the position of masons in the various burghs lodges and incorporations need to be studied side by side.

The arrangement of the Inventory means that some documents are listed twice under different headings: one appears three times, as the Dumfries No. 4 Ms. is a copy of the Old Charges (4.7) which includes a Catechism (5.7) and belongs to a lodge (11.5)! In all sections each entry relating to a document (or the first entry, if the document appears more than once) is followed by further information headed a, b and (in some cases) c:

a. Where transcripts or facsimiles of, or extracts from, documents have been published these are listed. In a few cases, like the Schaw Statutes, documents have been published many times, so only the best and most easily accessible versions are noted.

b. Ownership of the document. In most cases the owner has retained possession of documents, but where this is not the case a separate entry appears under c.

c. Location of the document, in cases in which it has been deposited by the owner in a library or archive for safe keeping.

It is sad that there are so few entries of this last type, for the inventory reveals that a substantial number of documents have been lost, mislaid or destroyed in the past century, though in some cases published transcripts or extracts survive. The present day lodges which can trace their history back into the seventeenth century are justifiably proud of their past, for they are the oldest lodges in the world. But it is surely misguided pride which makes most of them insist on retaining possession of unique records that they do not have the facilities to care for properly, however much they may revere them. Lodge officials change frequently, providing repeated opportunities for the records for which they are responsible to be lost sight of, and even if kept in a lodge safe they can be neglected and roughly treated as other items are put in or taken out. The Lodge of Scoon and Perth has deposited its prized 1658 agreement in the National Archives of Scotland; the Lodge of Dunfermline's early records are in Dunfermline Burgh Library; the Lodge of Dumfries has placed its records in the library of the Grand Lodge of Scotland. Would that other lodges would follow these enlightened examples! Sturdy independence and local pride are all very well, but insistence on retaining actual possession of valuables can be counter-productive, as the Inventory entries recording lost documents clearly demonstrate. Depositing records in a library or archive need not mean the loss either of ownership or of control of access to them.

As the first attempt at a complete list of early Scottish masonic records this Inventory is bound to contain omissions and inaccuracies. The more of the former there are the better, for omissions detected means that there are surviving pieces of evidence of which I am ignorant—but would be delighted to hear about. And these need not only be documents. Carved chests and a velvet purse are included in the inventory, and it may well be that other lodges have such intriguing items dating from the seventeenth century in their possession. If this Inventory encourages lodge officials to rummage in their safes and cupboards it will have served an additional function.

PART 1: GENERAL MASONIC DOCUMENTS

1. THE SCHAW STATUTES

Issued by William Schaw as master of works to the king and general warden of the masons.

THE FIRST SCHAW STATUTES

Edinburgh, 28 Dec.1598. Addressed to all master masons in Scotland.1.1— 1.3 are in the same hand, all three copies having evidently been made when the statutes were drawn up or soon afterwards. 1.1, 1.2 and 1.5 are signed by William Schaw. 1.3 was probably also originally signed by him but the part of the page that would have carried his signature has been cut off.

1. Eglinton. **1.1**
   Probably originally belonged to Kilwinning Lodge as it was found in the archives of the earls of Eglinton.
   a. W. Fraser, *Memorials of the Montgomeries, earls of Eglinton* (2 vols., Edinburgh, 1859), ii, 239-41 (transcript).
   b. Grand Lodge of Scotland.

2. Edinburgh. **1.2**
   Contained in Edinburgh Lodge's minute book, 1599-1686 (15.1).
   a. Lyon, *Edinburgh,* 9-11 (transcript, with partial facsimile opposite p.9); Carr, *Edinburgh,* 36-9 (transcript, with partial facsimile opposite p.37); GLSYB (1986), 86-8 (transcript).
   b. Lodge of Edinburgh (Mary's Chapel) No. 1.

3. Aitchison's Haven 1. **1.3**
   Contained in Aitchison's Haven Lodge minute book, 1599-1764 (7.1).
   b. Grand Lodge of Scotland.

4. Aitchison's Haven 2. **1.4**
   Early 18th century? Contained in Aitchison's Haven Lodge minute book,1769-1852 (7.2), pp.23-6. Evidently copied from 1.3 but misdated 28 Dec.1599.
   b. Grand Lodge of Scotland.

THE SECOND SCHAW STATUTES
Holyroodhouse, 28 Dec. 1599. Addressed to Kilwinning Lodge.

1. Eglinton. **1.5**
 Probably originally belonged to Kilwinning Lodge as it was found in the archives of the earls of Eglinton.
 a. Fraser, *Memorials,* ii, 241-4 (transcript); Lyon, *Edinburgh,* 12-14 (transcript, wih partial facsimile opposite p.12); Carr, *Kilwinning,* 4-6 (transcript); *GLSYB* (1986), 89-91 (transcript).
 b. Grand Lodge of Scotland.

2. THE ST CLAIR CHARTERS
Appointing the Sinclairs of Roslin patrons and protectors of the mason craft, and claiming that they held this position hereditarily. Masonic historians invariably refer to the documents as the 'St Clair' Charters, though at the time of issue the lairds of Roslin generally spelt their name 'Sinclair'.

1. First St Clair Charter. **2.1**
 1600-1 (dated by offices held by some of the signatories). Granted by the masons of Scotland, with the consent of William Schaw, to William Sinclair of Roslin. Signed by Schaw and representatives of lodges. Part of the sheet of paper (perhaps containing additional signatures) has been torn off.
 a. Lyon, *Edinburgh,* opposite p.65 (facsimile). See also under 2.5 below.
 b. Grand Lodge of Scotland.

2. Second St Clair Charter. **2.2**
 1627-8 (dated by offices held by some of the signatories). Granted by the masons and hammermen of Scotland to Sir William St Clair of Roslin. Signed by representatives of Lodges. Part of the sheet of paper (perhaps containing additional signatures) has been torn off.
 a. Lyon, *Edinburgh,* opposite p.68 (facsimile). See also under 2.5 below.
 b. Grand Lodge of Scotland.

3. Register House. **2.3**
 Early or mid 17th century copy of 2.1 and 2.2, with some differences in spellings and signatures.
 b. SRO, RH.9/17/14/1.

4. Hay 1. **2.4**
 End of 17th century. Copy by Richard Augustin Hay of both charters, evidently copied from 2.3 or a similar copy rather than directly from the originals, 2.1 and 2.2.
 b. NLS, Ms. Adv.32.6.2, Notebook of R.A. Hay, ff.49v-52r.

5. Hay 2. **2.5**
   c.1700. Copy by R.A. Hay of both charters, probably copied from 2.4 but with minor differences and the addition of 'Ed[inburgh]: 1630' before the signatures.
   - a. A. Lawrie, *History of Freemasonry* (Edinburgh, 1804), 297-304 (transcript); Lyon, *Edinburgh*, 65-8 (transcript copied from Lawrie). The transcripts in *GLSYB* (1986), 92-6 are evidently based on these earlier transcripts, with some corrections from 2.1 and 2.2.
   - b. NLS, Ms. Adv.34.1.9, Hay's Memoirs. Or a collection of several things relating to the historical account of the most famous families of Scotland, ii, 549-54.

3. THE FALKLAND STATUTES

26 Oct. 1636. Acts and statutes issued by Sir Anthony Alexander, master of works and general warden, at Falkland, addressed to the artificers and craftsmen of the building trades.

1. Aitchison's Haven 1. **3.1**
   1637. Contained in what later became the 1769-1852 minute book of Aitchison's Haven Lodge (7.2), pp.1-7, with minutes of 14 Jan. 1637 and 17 Mar. 1638 accepting the statutes.
   - a. W.A. Laurie, *History of Freemasonry* (2nd. edition, Edinburgh, 1859), 445-52 (transcript).
   - b. Grand Lodge of Scotland.

2. Aitchison's Haven 2. **3.2**
   Early 18th century. Contained in what later became the 1769-1852 minute book of Aitchison's Haven Lodge (7.2), pp.27-32. Transcript of 3.1.
   - b. Grand Lodge of Scotland.

3. Stirling. **3.3**
   1637. Contained in a fragmentary volume of records of the Society of Mechanics of Stirling (30.3), ff.1-3, with a minute of 5 Nov.1637 accepting the statutes, f.4r. Incomplete, with both beginning and end now missing and the rest of the text damaged.
   - a. D.B. Morris, 'The Incorporation of Mechanics of Stirling', *Transactions of the Stirling Natural History and Antiquarian Society* (1930-1), 37-44 (transcript, made when text was more complete).
   - b. Central Regional Council Archives, Stirling, in PD.7/12/4.

4. Haddo. **3.4**
   Mid 17th century? Copy of the latter half of the statutes, starting at the top of a page numbered '7'. Thus an incomplete copy rather than an intentionally shortened version of the statutes.
   - b. SRO, GD.33/65/7, Gordon of Haddo Papers.

5. Aberdeen. **3.5**
'1670'. Copy of the second half of the statutes, headed 'Laws and statutes for masons gathered out of their old writings', in the Aberdeen Lodge mark book (6.1). As 3.4 and 3.5 begin at the same point it is highly likely that the latter was copied from the former.
    a. Miller, *Aberdeen*, 41-3 (summary).
    b. Lodge of Aberdeen No. 1^3.

4. THE OLD CHARGES

Only versions of Scottish provenance are included in this listing. Each version of the Old Charges is identified by a code abbreviation, which consists of a letter (indicating the textual family to which it belongs) and a serial number. In the two larger families a second letter is used as well to indicate a particular branch. Brief descriptions of all the versions of the Old Charges known to that time may be found in Poole, *Gould's History*, i, 48-76. Additions to the list are noted in *AQC*, 90 (1977), 177-93 and 96 (1983), 98-110. A full list of versions up to 1985 is available in Wallace McLeod, *The Old Charges. With an appendix reconstituting the 'standard original' version* (Prestonian Lecture: Toronto, 1986) 51-6. I am grateful to Professor McLeod (who has introduced the coded abbreviations for the Old Charges) for his help in preparing this section of the Inventory.

1. Aberdeen Ms. **4.1**
'1670'. Contained in the mark book of Aberdeen Lodge (6.1). Grand Lodge family: D.i.11.
    a. Miller, *Aberdeen*, 66-74 (transcript).
    b. Lodge of Aberdeen No. 1^3.

2. Aitchison's Haven No. 1 Ms. **4.2**
19 May 1666. Contained in what later became the 1769-1852 minute book of Aitchison's Haven Lodge (7.2), pp.10-19. Written by the lodge secretary, John Auchinleck. The beginning (pp.10-11) is now missing. Tew family: T.2.
    b. Grand Lodge of Scotland.

3. Aitchison's Haven No. 2 Ms. **4.3**
Early 18th century. Contained in what became the 1769-1852 minute book of Aitchison's Haven Lodge. (7.2), pp.34-41. A transcript of 4.2. Tew family: T.10.
    a. Lyon, *Edinburgh*, 123-30 (transcript, with facsimile of first page opposite p.123).
    b. Grand Lodge of Scotland.

4. Dumfries No.1 Ms. **4.4**
Late 17th century. Three sheets of paper, probably written by the lodge secretary William M'George. Grand Lodge family: D.h.21.

a. Smith, *Dumfries*, 72-84 (transcript).
b. Lodge Dumfries Kilwinning No. 53.
c. Grand Lodge of Scotland.

5. Dumfries No. 2 Ms. **4.5**
   Late 17th century. Paper roll with beginning missing. Grand Lodge family: D.h.24.
   a. W.J. Hughan, 'The Dumfries Kilwinning Mss', *The Freemason*, xxix (Christmas No., 21 Dec. 1892), 8-9 (transcript).
   b. Lodge No. 53.
   c. Grand Lodge of Scotland.

6. Dumfries No. 3 Ms. **4.6**
   Late 17th century. Parchment roll. Grand Lodge family: D.g.25.
   a. Smith, *Dumfries*, 85-104 (transcript).
   b. Lodge No. 53.
   c. Grand Lodge of Scotland.

7. Dumfries No. 4 Ms. **4.7**
   Early 18th century. Paper booklet. Includes a catechism (5.7). Sundry group: H.1.
   a. Knoop, *Catechisms*, 52-68 (transcript); J. Lane, *AQC*, 6 (1893), 36-44 (transcript).
   b. Lodge No. 53.
   c. Grand Lodge of Scotland.

8. Dundee No. 1 Ms. **4.8**
   11 Mar. 1689. Fragment: the invocation or prayer from the opening of the Old Charges, copied into the minute book of the masons of Dundee (13.1) before the first entry.
   a. A.J. Warden, *Burgh laws of Dundee* (London, 1872), 579 (transcript).
   b. The Three United Trades of Masons, Wrights and Slaters, Dundee.
   c. Messrs. Gray, Robertson and Wilkie, 27 Bank St., Dundee.

9. Dundee No. 2 Ms. **4.9**
   Late 17th or early 18th centuries. Three sheets of paper glued together. Grand Lodge family: D.?.58.
   b. The Three United Trades of Masons, Wrights and Slaters, Dundee.
   c. Dundee District Archives, in Box GD/GRW/M3/1.

10. Kilwinning Ms. **4.10**
    Late 17th century. Grand Lodge family: D.a.8. (Missing, 1985).
    a. Lyon, *Edinburgh*, 116-23 (transcript).
    b. Lodge Mother Kilwinning, No. 0 (formerly).

11. Melrose No. 2 Ms. **4.11**
   1-4 Dec. 1674. Paper roll. Copied from a lost English original dated 1581 by 'A.M.', almost certainly Andrew Mein. Grand Lodge family: D. Sundry.12.
   a. Vernon, *History*, 58-63 (transcript).
   b. Lodge of Melrose St John No. 1².

12. Stirling Ms. **4.12**
   Late 17th century. Parchment. Includes texts of two unique certificates or testimonials to be signed by employers of masons expressing their satisfaction with their work.
   a. W.J. Hughan, *The 'Ancient Stirling Lodge' manuscript of the Old Charges, A.D. 1650 (circa)* (London, 1893), 5-9 (transcript).
   b. Lodge Ancient Stirling No. 30.

5. THE MASONIC CATECHISMS

Eight written catechisms exist, or are known to have existed, which predate the earliest surviving printed catechisms, published in London in 1723-6. Of the eight five are Scottish in provenance, two are Irish and one English. Of the three of non-Scottish provenance, one (5.3) clearly describes Scottish practices, being almost identical to 5.1 and 5.5. Internal evidence indicates that 5.6 also describes Scottish rituals (though perhaps adding some English innovations). 5.1, 5.3, 5.4 and 5.5 form a distinct group of very closely related texts.

1. Register House Ms. **5.1**
   1696.
   a. Knoop, *Catechisms*, 31-4 (transcript); J.M. Allan, *AQC*, 43 (1930), 154-5 (facsimile); *GLSYB* (1956), opposite p.100 (facsimile).
   b. SRO, RH.9/17/14/2.

2. Aberdeen. **5.2**
   Feb. 1699. Aberdeen Lodge paid 'for printing of a Broad Side of an whole sheet concerning the Measone Word'. This was almost certainly a catechism, but no copy survives.
   a. Miller, *Aberdeen*, 44 (transcript of reference, with facsimile opposite).

3. Chetwode Crawley Ms. **5.3**
   c.1700.
   a. Knoop, *Catechisms*, 35-8 (transcript).
   b. Grand Lodge of Ireland.

4. Haughfoot Fragment. **5.4**
   22 Dec.1702. The final 29 words of a catechism precede the first minute in the minute book of Haughfoot Lodge (20.1), the rest having evidently been torn out in the interests of secrecy.
   a. Knoop, *Catechisms*, 7 (transcript); Vernon, *History*, 282 (transcript);

H. Carr, *AQC*, 63 (1950), 258 and opposite 257 (transcript and facsimile).
b. Lodge St John No. 32, Selkirk.

5. Kevan Ms. **5.5**
c.1714-20. Found in Duns, Berwickshire, with list of lands and rents in the area on the back.
   a. Knoop, *Catechisms*, 41-4 (transcript); Carr, *Kilwinning*, 321-4 (transcript); G. Draffen, *AQC*, 67 (1954), opposite p.139 (facsimile); G. Draffen, *GLSYB* (1955), opposite p.118 (facsimile).
   b. Grand Lodge of Scotland.

6. Sloane Ms. **5.6**
Early 18th century.
   a. Knoop, *Catechisms*, 45-9 (transcript).
   b. British Library, Sloane Ms. 3329, ff.142r-143v.

7. Dumfries Ms. No. 4. **5.7**
Early 18th century. Included in a version of the Old Charges (4.7, 11.5). Possibly postdates the earliest printed catechisms.
   a. Knoop, *Catechisms*, 52-68 (transcript); J. Lane, *AQC*, 6 (1893), 36-44 (transcript).
   b. Lodge Dumfries Kilwinning No. 53.
   c. Grand Lodge of Scotland.

8. Trinity College, Dublin Ms. **5.8**
Feb. 1711.
   a. Knoop, *Catechisms*, 69-70.
   b. Library of Trinity College, Dublin.

9. Airlie MS. **5.9**
About 1700.
   a. Not published.
   b. SRO, GD.16/58/52, Airlie Muniments.

10. 1708. **5.10**
   a. Not published.
   b. Location withheld until a study of it is published by the scholar who discovered it.

   5.9 and **5.10** are recent discoveries which were not listed in the first edition of this book.

PART 2: LODGES, ASSOCIATED INCORPORATIONS, AND THEIR RECORDS

6. LODGE OF ABERDEEN

(As it has not been possible to examine the records of this lodge the following list of its early records is provisional).
   1. '1670', Mark Book. The date is incompatible with the names **6.1** of members listed. Contains 28 pages of the original, pasted into a new book in 1748. Pagination suggests the original had at least 147 pages. Contains:

APPENDIX 2

Decorated title page (Miller, *Aberdeen*, opposite p.19, facsimile).
Illustrations of masons' tools (Miller, *Aberdeen*, opposite p.42, facsimile).
'1670' list of lodge members and their mason marks (Poole, *Gould's History*, iii, 210-12, transcript; Miller, *Aberdeen*, opposite pp. 20, 22, 28, facsimiles of some pages).
Names of their successors in the mason craft.
'27 Dec. 1670', Laws and statutes of the lodge (Miller, *Aberdeen*, 57-65, transcript).
Mason Charter, or Old Charges (Miller, *Aberdeen*, 66-74, transcript; see 4.1).
Laws and statutes of masons 'gathered out of their old writings'. An incomplete text of the Falkland Statutes (see 3.5).
    a. Lodge of Aberdeen No. 1^3.
2. 1679-1720, a minute book covering this period is said to   **6.2**
have existed at one time.
    a. Miller, *Aberdeen*, 43 (mentioned).
3. 1680 or 1682, A printed copy of the '1670' laws and statutes   **6.3**
of the lodge is said to have existed at one time, but the evidence is weak.
    a. Miller, *Aberdeen*, 24 (mentioned).
4. 1690s, photocopies of some loose minutes. The whereabouts of   **6.4**
the originals is unknown, but they were in England when these copies were made.
    b. Lodge No. 1^3.
5. From late 17th century (?), miscellaneous papers, interleaved   **6.5**
in a bound volume.
    b. Lodge No. 1^3.
6. 1696-1779, minute book, recording admissions and elections   **6.6**
only.
    b. Lodge No. 1^3.
7. 1697, authority to the boxmaster to collect debts due to the   **6.7**
lodge. Contained in 6.5?
    a. Miller, *Aberdeen*, 44 (mentioned).
    b. Lodge No. 1^3.
8. 3 Feb. 1699, account of the treasurer with a printer   **6.8**
(see 5.2). Contained in 6.5?
    a. Miller, *Aberdeen*, 44 (transcript, with facsimile opposite).
    b. Lodge No. 1^3.
9. 1699-1700, boxmaster's account. Contained in 6.5?   **6.9**
    a. Miller, *Aberdeen*, opposite p.50 (facsimile).
    b. Lodge No. 1^3.
10. 1709, wooden chair 'James Mackie, 1709'. Mackie   **6.10**
joined the lodge in 1693 and was elected master for 1696-7.
    b. Lodge No. 1^3.
11. 1710, wooden chair 'Will Thomson elder   **6.11**
slater 1710'. Thomson joined the lodge in 1687, and the chair has carvings of the tools of his trade.
    b. Lodge No. 1^3
12. From 1719, cash books.
    b. Lodge No. 1^3.

Lodge No. 1[3] also possesses a charter chest with three locks, perhaps that mentioned in the '1670' statutes. The junior warden's chair is dated 1646. but it is not known how long it has been in the lodge's possession.

Incorporation of Coopers, Wrights and Masons of Aberdeen
5 Aug. 1527, seal of cause.
6 May 1541, new seal of cause. Each of the three crafts already had its own deacon, but it is not clear whether they were intended to come together as a single incorporation or were to form separate ones. But by *c.*1600 the wrights and coopers formed a single incorporation. (E. Bain, *Merchant and craft guilds. A history of the Aberdeen incorporated trades,* Aberdeen, 1887, 115, 238-41). Masons had no recognised incorporation or society in the 17th century.

7. LODGE OF AITCHISON'S HAVEN

1.9 Jan. 1598/9—1764, minute book, including a copy of the First Schaw Statutes (1.3). **7.1**
    a. R.E. Wallace-Jones, *AQC*, 24 (1911), 34-42 (extracts).
    b. Grand Lodge of Scotland.
2. 1769-1852, minute book, prefaced by a 1637 transcript of Falkland Statutes (pp. 1-7; see 3.1); the lodge's acceptance of the statutes (pp.7-9); a 1666 transcript of the Old Charges (pp.10-19, beginning missing; see 4.2); and 18th century transcripts of these documents (pp. 27-34, 34-41; see 3.2, 4.3) and of the First Schaw Statutes (pp. 23-6; see 1.4). Also includes (reversed) miscellaneous notes and minutes, 1662-1790. **7.2**
    b. Grand Lodge of Scotland.

Incorporation of Wrights of Musselburgh
It is not clear whether or not masons belonged to this body; all those whose trades are mentioned in the first minute book are wrights, but trades of most members are not specified.
1. 1668-1785, minute book. **7.3**
    b. SRO, B.52/8/1.

8. LODGE OF BANFF

1. 1703—?, minute book. (Destroyed by fire). **8.1**
    a. W.J. Hughan, 'Specimens from a masonic quarry, No. 1, operative masonic lodges', *The Freemason,* i, No. 1 (13 Mar. 1869), 5 (transcripts of minutes of 1708 and 1773).
    b. Lodge of St Andrew, Banff, No. 52 (formerly).

9. LODGE OF CANONGATE KILWINNING

No early records.
1. 13 Feb. 1735—10 June 1760, minute book. **9.1**
    a. Lodge Canongate Kilwinning No. 2.

Incorporation of Wrights and Coopers of the Canongate
Included masons.
1595, list of members begins.
6 Apr.1612, seal of cause (M. Wood, ed., *Book of records of the ancient privileges of the Canongate,* SRS, 1955, 25-6).
   1. 1630-90, minute book, including list of members 1585-1648. **9.2**
      b. Edinburgh City Archives.
   2. 1670-1750, minute book, including list of members 1585-1674. **9.3**
      b. Edinburgh City Archives.

10. LODGE CANONGATE AND LEITH, LEITH AND CANONGATE
No early records.
   1. From 1808, cash books. **10.1**
      b. Lodge Canongate and Leith, Leith and Canongate No. 5.
   2. From 1830, minute books. **10.2**
      b. Lodge No. 5.

Incorporation of Wrights and Coopers of the Canongate
See 9.2—9.3.

11. LODGE OF DUMFRIES
   1. 20 May 1687—Nov. 1788, minute book. **11.1**
      a. Smith, *Dumfries,* 8-32 (extracts).
      b. Lodge Dumfries Kilwinning No. 53.
      c. Grand Lodge of Scotland.
   2. Late 17th century, Old Charges, Dumfries No. 1 Ms. (see 4.4). **11.2**
   3. Late 17th Century, Old Charges, Dumfries No. 2 Ms. (see 4.5). **11.3**
   4. Late 17th century, Old Charges, Dumfries No. 3 Ms. (see 4.6). **11.4**
   5. Early 18th century, Old Charges, Dumfries No. 4 Ms. **11.5**
   (see 4.7). Includes a Catechism (5.7).

Incorporation of Wrights or Squaremen of Dumfries
Included masons.
   1. 1725-1781, minute book. **11.6**
      b. Ewart Library, Dumfries.

12. LODGE OF DUNBLANE
   1. 28 Jan. 1696—27 Dec. 1775, minute book, prefaced by **12.1**
   fragmentary accounts, Apr. 1696—1713.
      a. A.F. Hatten, *AQC,* 67 (1954), 85-109 (extracts).
      b. Lodge of Dunblane No. 9.

Incorporation of Masons of Dunblane
In c.1722-32 the lodge was sometimes referred to as one of the six craft incorporations of the burgh.

13. LODGE OF DUNDEE

1. 11 Mar. 1659—20 July 1960, 'Lockit book' (minute book) **13.1**
of the mason trade. The first minute refers to the organisation as a lodge, and it is preceded by an invocation from the Old Charges (4.8).
    a. A.J. Warden, *Burgh laws of Dundee* (London, 1872), 579-83 (a few extracts).
    b. The Three United Trades of Masons, Wrights and Slaters, Dundee.
    c. Messrs. Gray, Robertson and Wilkie, 27 Bank St., Dundee.

2. 11 Mar.1659—1779, 'Register of journeymen masons'. The **13.2**
first minute refers to the organisation as a lodge. In spite of the title there are more entries concerning apprentices and freemen than journeymen. Also miscellaneous minutes.
    b. The Three United Trades, Dundee.
    c. Dundee District Archive.

3. 27 Dec.1660—19th century, miscellaneous papers. Includes **13.3**
minutes from 1660, and a copy of the Old Charges (see 4.9, 13.4).
    b. The Three United Trades, Dundee.
    c. Dundee District Archive, Box GD/GRW/M3/1.

4. Mid—late 17th century, Old Charges, Dundee No. 2 Ms. **13.4**
(in 13.3; see 4.9).

Society or Incorporation of Masons of Dundee
    See 13.1—13.3. The society also acted as a lodge.

1. 6 March 1592, charter of James VI to the masons, **13.5**
wrights, slaters, etc. in Dundee giving them rights to elect a deacon etc. Registered in SRO, PS.1/63, ff.208r. There is no sign of any attempt to implement the charter.
    a. A.M. Smith, *The three united trades of Dundee* (Abertay Historical Society, 1987), 79 (transcript).
    b. The vestry, St Andrews Church, Dundee.

14. LODGE OF DUNFERMLINE

1. 27 Dec. 1673, obligation to attend lodge meetings on **14.1**
St John's day, signed by over 50 members (some signing after 1673). Parchment.
    b. Lodge of St John, Dunfermline No. 26.
    c. Dunfermline Central Library.

2. 27 Dec. 1688, obligation to attend lodge meetings on St John's day, **14.2**
signed by nearly 200 members (many signing after 1688). Parchment.
    b. Lodge No. 26.
    c. Dunfermline Central Library.

APPENDIX 2

   3. 27 Dec. 1698—28 Dec.1728, minute book. **14.3**
      b. Lodge No. 26.
      c. Dunfermline Central Library.

Incorporation of Masons of Dunfermline
19 Jan. 1719, seal of cause renewed, as the original gift was nearly illegible through its antiquity (SRO, B.20/13/4, Dunfermline burgh council minutes, 1696-1726).

15. LODGE OF EDINBURGH (MARY'S CHAPEL)
   1. 31 July 1599—25 Dec.1686, minute book, prefaced by **15.1**
   First Schaw Statutes (1.2).
      a. Carr, *Edinburgh*, 35-202 (transcript).
      b. Lodge of Edinburgh (Mary's Chapel) No. 1.
   2. 27 Dec.1687—25 Dec. 1751, minute book. **15.2**
      a. Carr, *Edinburgh*, 203-47 (transcript to 1738).
      b. Lodge No. 1.

Incorporation of Masons and Wrights of Edinburgh (Mary's Chapel)
15 Oct. 1475, seal of cause (Lyon, *Edinburgh*, 247-9, transcript).
   1. 1594-1834, miscellaneous papers. 4 boxes, including papers **15.3**
   1594-1706 (box 1, bundles 1-4) and 1647-1707 (box 2, bundles 1-7).
      b. NLS, Accession 7332.
   2. 1601—19th century, miscellaneous papers. 1 box. **15.4**
      b. NLS, Accession 8617.
   3. 1666-1866, miscellaneous papers. 1 box. **15.5**
      b. NLS, Accession 7344.
   4. 1669-1755, minute books. 7 volumes, including: **15.6**
   i. Minutes 1669-86, with accounts 1670-85.
   ii. Minutes 1686-96, with accounts 1685-95.
   iii. Minutes 1696-1709, with financial notes etc. 1697-1705.
   iv. Minutes 1709-20, with accounts 1697-1749.
      b. Edinburgh City Archives.
   5. Late 17th—19th centuries, miscellaneous papers. 2 boxes. **15.7**
      b. NLS, Accession 7056.
   6. Late 17th—19th centuries, miscellaneous papers. 1 box. **15.8**
      b. NLS, Accession 7257.
   7. Late 17th—19th centuries, miscellaneous papers.1 folder. **15.9**
      b. NLS, Accession 7260.
   8. Late 17th—19th centuries, miscellaneous papers. 1 box. **15.10**
      b. NLS, Accession 8351.
   9. 1724-1832, miscellaneous papers. 1 folder. **15.11**
      b. NLS, Accession 7494.
   10. 1724-1949, minute books and miscellaneous papers. **15.12**
   54 volumes, boxes and folders, including minute books 1755-1842.
      b. Incorporation of Mary's Chapel.
      c. NLS, Deposit 302.

16. EDINBURGH LODGE OF JOURNEYMEN MASONS

1. 1707-1820, record or minute book. The earliest records of **16.1**
the lodge were evidently kept on loose papers, some of which were copied into this book c.1740. Includes:
Constitution (statement as to how the lodge was founded).
1707, 1710, acts.
18 Nov. 1708, list of members and their contributions.
1709-1802, lists of members and payments.
1 Nov .1709—30 Oct.1767, abstracts of laws and acts.
  - a. W. Hunter, *Incidents in the history of the Lodge of Journeymen Masons* (Edinburgh, 1884), 235-6 (transcript of 1708 membership list).
  - b. Lodge of Journeymen Masons No. 8.

2. 8 Jan.1715, decrees arbitral (containing deed of **16.2**
submission, 29 Nov. 1714), extracted from the burgh register of deeds.
  - a. J.S. Seggie and D.L. Turnbull, *Annals of the Lodge of Journeymen Masons* (Edinburgh, 1930), 55-60 (transcript).
  - b. Lodge No. 8.

3. 13 July 1715, Letters of Horning against the **16.3**
Incorporation of Mary's Chapel.
  - a. Seggie and Turnbull, *Annals,* 61-8 (transcript).
  - b. Lodge No. 8.

4. 1715, bag or purse of red satin, with blue labels. **16.4**
The labels (sewn on later) bear the words 'A gift from the Lords of Council and Session 1715' in gold letters. The Lords are said to have presented the purse to the lodge after the case which led to the decreet arbitral.
  - b. Lodge No. 8.

Incorporation of Masons and Wrights of Edinburgh (Mary's Chapel)
See 15.3- 15.12.

17. LODGE OF GLASGOW

1. '5 Oct. 1051' (or '1057'), supposed charter of Malcolm III **17.1**
founding the lodge and/or the incorporation. An obvious forgery (18th century?), though largely illegible. There are doubts as to whether the 'translations' published correspond to the text.
  - a. J. Cleland, *Annals of Glasgow* (2 vols., Glasgow, 1816), ii, 484-6, and E.S. Lawrie, *The Lodge of Glasgow* (Glasgow, 1927), 75-4 (transcripts of supposed translation).
  - b. Strathclyde Regional Archives, T-TH.12/6.

2. 1686, carved wooden box inscribed 'God Save the King and **17.2**
St John's Lodge 1686'. Probably presented to the lodge by Alexander Thom (see 17.7) but subsequently in the possession of the incorporation and used as its deacon's box.
  - a. Lawrie, Lodge of Glasgow, 62 (mentioned).
  - b. Lodge of Glasgow St John No. 3bis (?—unconfirmed).

Incorporation of Masons of Glasgow
1551, seal of cause (with coopers and wrights).
1569, coopers separate.
1600, wrights separate, leaving the incorporation to the masons (J.D. Marwick, ed., *Extracts from the records of the burgh of Glasgow, 1573-1642*, SBRS, 1876, 205-6).
- 1. Oct.1551, seal of cause. **17.3**
    - a. J. Cruikshank, *Sketch of the Incorporation of Masons and the Lodge of Glasgow* (Glasgow, 1879), 3-6 (transcript).
    - b. Strathclyde Regional Archives, T-TH.12&7.
- 2. 1582-1667, miscellaneous papers (concerning property). **17.4**
    - b. T-TH.12/8-12.
- 3. 1600-1681, minute book. **17.5**
    - b. T-TH.12/1/1(1).
- 4. 1681-1772, minute book. **17.6**
    - b. T-TH.12/1/2.
- 5. 1684, carved wooden box inscribed 'God save the King and **17.7** the Masons Craft 1684'. Given to the incorporation by Alexander Thom, 2 June 1684 (see 17.6, under date), but later in possession of the lodge.
    - a. Lawrie, *Lodge of Glasgow*, frontispiece and 60-2 (photographs and description).
    - b. Lodge of Glasgow St John, No. 32.
    - c. People's Palace Museum, Glasgow.
- 6. 1690-1737, account book. **17.8**
    - b. T-TH.12/4/1.

18. LODGE OF HADDINGTON

- 1. 1599, minute, otherwise illegible, stated to have recorded **18.1** a meeting in Gullane Church. (Lost).
    - a. W.A. Laurie, *History of Freemasonry* (2nd. edn., Edinburgh, 1859), 375-6 (summary).
    - b. Lodge St John Kilwinning No. 57, Haddington (formerly).
- 2. 2 Feb.1682, bond granted to the lodge. (Missing, 1985). **18.2**
    - a. Lyon, *Edinburgh*, 441 (summary).
    - b. Lodge No. 57 (formerly).
- 3. 29 May 1697, contract or agreement between the lodge and **18.3** John Crumbie. (Missing, 1985).
    - a. Lyon, *Edinburgh*, 441-2 (transcript).
    - b. Lodge No. 57 (formerly).
- 4. From 1713, minute books. (Up to 1761 missing, 1985). **18.4**
    - b. Lodge No. 57.

Incorporation of Wrights and Masons of Haddington
25 Sept. 1647, seal of cause renewed, as its predecessor had been lost (SRO, B.30/22/9).

1. 1616-1751, minute book. **18.5**
　　b. SRO, B.30/18/4.
2. 1671-1751, account book. **18.6**
　　b. SRO, B.30/18/6.
3. 1533-1915, miscellaneous papers, mainly relating to the incorporation. **18.7**
　　b. SRO, B.30/22.

19. LODGE OF HAMILTON

1.25 Mar. 1695—19th century, 'Papers and documents'. **19.1**
1 folder. Includes:
25 Mar. 1695, bond.
27 Dec. 1697—1730, scroll (draft) minutes.
1700-3, accounts of the boxmaster.
4 Apr.1701, statutes of the lodge signed by members.
1703 or 1709 (endorsed 1703, but the date at the head of the list has been altered and there are additions after 1709), list of members.
1704-9, lists of quarterly payments by members.
　　b. Lodge Hamilton Kilwinning No. 7.
2.27 Dec. 1695—4 Jan. 170[1], 28 Dec. 1796—19 June 1816, minute book. **19.2**
　　b. Lodge No. 7.
3. 1701, Bible (London, 1698) and Psalms (Edinburgh, 1698) presented to the Lodge by David Crawford in 1701. **19.3**
　　b. Lodge No. 7.
4. 1703-1779, 'Early papers'. 1 folder. Includes accounts of payments by the boxmaster, 1703-10. **19.4**
　　b. Lodge No. 7.

20. LODGE OF HAUGHFOOT

1. 22 Dec. 1702—27 Dec. 1763, minute book, prefaced by a fragment of a Catechism (5.4). **20.1**
　　a. Vernon, *History,* 282-98 (Extracts); H. Carr, *AQC*, 63 (1950), 255-303, and 64 (1951), 5-60 (transcripts).
　　b. Lodge St John No. 32, Selkirk.

21. LODGE OF INVERNESS

1.27 Dec. 1678—27 Dec. 1736, summary of entries in a minute book (now lost) relating to the election of office holders, contained in a petition to Grand Lodge, 1737. **21.1**
　　a. A. Ross, *Freemasonry in Inverness* (Inverness,1877), 7-9 (transcript).
2. From 1737, minute books.
　　b. Lodge Old Inverness Kilwinning St John's No. 6.

22. LODGE OF KELSO

1. 27 Dec.1701—27 Dec. 1706, 31 Dec. 1716— **22.1**
5 Feb. 1753, minute book.
    a. Vernon, *History,* 85-110 (extracts).
    b. Lodge of Kelso No. 58.
2. 27 Dec.1710, bond or ticket acknowledging a debt to the **22.2**
lodge.
    a. Vernon, *History,* 94-5 (transcript).
    b. Lodge No. 58.

Incorporation of Hammermen of Kelso
Possibly included masons.
1658, mentioned (Vernon, *History,* 86n).

23. LODGE OF KILMOLYMOCK (ELGIN)

1. 27 Dec.1704—14 Feb. 1786, minute book. **23.1**
    b. Lodge of Kilmolymock No. 45.

24. LODGE OF KILWINNING

1. 28 Dec. 1598, First Schaw Statutes: copy probably **24.1**
originally belonging to the lodge (1.1).
2. 28 Dec.1599, Second Schaw Statutes: copy probably **24.2**
originally belonging to the lodge (1.5).
3. 20 Dec.1642—Dec. 1758, minute book. **24.3**
    a. Carr, *Kilwinning,* 17-250 (transcript 1642-51, mainly 'in modern language and spelling'; thereafter extracts and abstracts).
    b. Lodge Mother Kilwinning No. 0.
4. 20 Dec.1643, 20 May 1644, 20 Dec.1693, 20 Sept. 1735, **24.4**
loose minutes. (Lost).
    a. Lyon, *Edinburgh,* 29-30 (partial transcripts 1643-4); Lyon, *Freemason's Magazine and Masonic Mirror,* new series, ix July—Dec. 1863), 433, 233 (partial transcripts, 1693, 1735); Carr, *Kilwinning,* 27-8, 128, 201 (partial transcripts taken from Lyon).
    b. Lodge No. 0 (formerly).

5. Late 17th century, Old Charges, Kilwinning Ms. (4.10). **24.5**
(Missing, 1985).
    b. Lodge No. 0 (formerly).

Incorporation of Squaremen or Masons and Wrights of Ayr **24.6**
1. Apr. 1582—10 Oct. 1724, minute book, prefaced by
statutes and oaths, 1556, 1567 and 1569.
    b. Carnegie Library, Ayr (Kyle and Carrick District Library), B.6/24/1.

Incorporation of Squaremen or Wrights of Irvine
May have included masons from foundation; certainly did so later.
3 July 1646, seal of cause to wrights and other incorporations.
   1. 3 July 1646, seal of cause to the Seven Incorporated   **24.7**
   Trades.
       a. *Muniments of the royal burgh of Irvine* (2 vols., Ayrshire and Galloway Archaeological Association, 1890-1), ii, 64-9.

25. LODGE OF KIRKCUDBRIGHT
No early records.
   1. Jan.1735—Dec. 1785, minute book.   **25.1**
       b. Lodge St Cuthbert Kilwinning, Kirkcudbright No. 41.

Incorporation of Wrights of Kirkcudbright
Existed by the late 17th century, and probably included masons.

26. LODGE OF LINLITHGOW
No early records.

27. LODGE OF MELROSE
   1. 1-4 Dec. 1674, Old Charges, Melrose No. 2 Ms. (4.11)   **27.1**
   2. 28 Dec. 1674—28 Dec. 1792, minute book (mainly   **27.2**
   financial).
       a. Vernon, *History*, 12-37 (extracts); Lodge No. 1^2 possesses a typed transcript.
       b. Lodge of Melrose St John No. 1^2.
   3. 29 Jan. 1675, mutual agreement of members of the lodge.   **27.3**
       a. Vernon, *History*, 13-14 (transcript).
       b. Lodge No. 1.
   4. 1680, petition of masons and portioners of Newstead to the   **27.4**
   Earl of Haddington. Endorsed as a petition of 1683, but the earl's agreement to the petition is dated 14 Feb. 1680.
       a. Vernon, History, 16-17 (transcript).
       b. Lodge No. 1^2.

28. LODGE OF ST ANDREWS
No early records.

29. LODGE OF SCONE (PERTH)
   1. 24 Dec. 1658, contract or mutual agreement, signed by 40   **29.1**
   members of the lodge (some signing many years after 1658). Parchment.
       a. Mylne, *Master masons,* 128-30 (transcript); D.C. Smith, *History of the Ancient Masonic Lodge of Scoon and Perth* (Perth, 1898),

45-7 (transcript, with facsimile opposite p. 44). Both transcripts are unreliable where some of the signatures are concerned.
    b. Lodge of Scoon and Perth No. 3.
    c. SRO, GD.1/613/1.
  2. 1725-77, minute book. **29.2**
    a. Lodge No. 3.

Incorporation of Wrights of Perth
Included masons.
1519, earliest records.
  1. 1519, 1526-1621, minute and account book **29.3**
    b. NLS, Ms.19288.
  2. 1659-70, minutes and accounts, included in **29.4**
a private account book kept by a Perth wright.
    b. NLS, Ms.19289.
  3. 26 Oct.1664—16 Sept 1698, court or minute book. **29.5**
    a. Perth Museum and Art Gallery.
  4. 5 Oct. 1698—1 Oct.1734, court or minute book. **29.6**
    a. Perth Museum and Art Gallery.
  5. 1616-1727, miscellaneous papers. 2 bundles. **29.7**
    a. Perth Museum and Art Gallery.

30. LODGE OF STIRLING
  1. '5 Nov.1147', supposed charter of David I founding the **30.1**
lodge. An obvious forgery, known only through what purports to be an English translation of it inserted in the lodge's minute book (30.3) in accordance with an order dated 15 Apr. 1777.
    a. W.J. Hughan, *AQC*, 6 (1893), 112 (transcript of 'translation').
    b. Lodge Ancient Stirling No. 30, minute book 1741-1822, 432-3.
  2. Late 17th century, Old Charges, Stirling Ms. (4.12). **30.2**
  3. 28 Dec. 1741—10 Aug. 1822, minute book. **30.3**
    b. Lodge No. 30.

Society or Company of Mechanics of Stirling
Emerged in the early 17th century from the Omnigatherum. At least in the late 1630s it seems to have acted as a lodge.
  1. 1636-c.1725, fragments of a volume, containing the **30.4**
Falkland Statutes (3.3), a few minutes of 1637-90, and lists of payments of annualrents, early 18th century.
    b. Central Regional Council Archives, Stirling, PD.7/12/4.
  2. 15 May 1637, precept by Sir Anthony Alexander. **30.5**
    b. PD.7/12/5.
  3. 1637-9, minutes of the court of artificers and of the **30.6**
lodge and company of Stirling, and a receipt of 1656.
    b. PD.7/12/6.

4. 1637-91, papers relating to the mechanics. **30.7**
    b. PD.7/12/7.
5. 1650-97, accounts and receipts. **30.8**
    b. PD.7/12/8.
6. 1660-3, papers relating to a seat in the kirk. **30.9**
    b. PD.7/12/9.
7. 1663-74, lists of journeymen mechanics. **30.10**
    b. PD.7/12/10.
8. 1674, papers relating to the attempt to gain **30.11**
a charter of incorporation.
    b. PD.7/12/11.
9. 1676-1712, account book (fragmentary). **30.12**
    b. PD.7/12/12.
10. 1697-1767, accounts. **30.13**
    b. PD.7/12/13.
11. 1701-78, accounts and receipts. **30.14**
    b. PD.7/12/14.
12. 1703-4, agreements between mechanics and two dyers. **30.15**
    b. PD.7/12/15.

PART 3: OTHER INCORPORATIONS

31. INCORPORATIONS INCLUDING MASONS WHO DID NOT ATTEND KNOWN LODGES

BURNTISLAND: INCORPORATION OF HAMMERMEN
Dominated by smiths and wrights, but possibly included masons.
1. 1648-1741, minute book. **31.1**
    b. St Andrews University Library, B.9/13/2.

CRAIL: INCORPORATION OF SQUAREMEN
Probably included masons.
1. 1668-1743, court book. **31.2**
    b. St Andrews University Library, B.10/11/9.

JEDBURGH: INCORPORATION OF WRIGHTS, MASONS AND COOPERS
1. [19 Mar.] 1560—25 Feb. 1696, minute book. **31.3**
    b. Queen Mary's House, Jedburgh.

LANARK: INCORPORATION OF MASONS AND WRIGHTS
26 Feb. 1674, seal of cause renewed, as previous seal had become illegible (R. Renwick ed., *Extracts from the records of the royal burgh of Lanark, 1150-1722*, Glasgow, 1893, 195-8).

PEEBLES: WRIGHTS AND MASONS

15 Dec. 1684, reference indicates that the masons and wrights had some sort of organisation admitting or 'brothering' apprentices and journeymen (W. Chambers, ed., *Charters and documents relating to the burgh of Peebles..., 1165-1710*, SBRS, 1872, 115-16.

29 Apr. 1713, agreement that the masons, wright, glaziers and smiths should be incorporated (ibid., 185-7).

RUTHERGLEN: INCORPORATION OF MASONS AND WRIGHTS

1. 5 Nov. 1636, seal of cause. **31.4**
   b. Strathclyde Regional Archives, RU.9/3/1.
2. 1659-1710, collectors' or treasurers' accounts. **31.5**
   b. RU.9/3/2/1-17.

SANQUHAR: INCORPORATION OF SQUAREMEN

Included masons.
Existed by 1714, but in 1714-39 was merged with the hammermen as a single incorporation (*Dumfries and Galloway Notes and Queries*, part 1, 1910, 44.)

SELKIRK: INCORPORATION OF HAMMERMEN

Included smiths, masons, wrights and coopers.

1. 1681, seal of cause (T.C. Brown, *History of Selkirkshire* **31.6**
   or chronicles of Ettrick Forest, Edinburgh, 1886, ii, 214).

APPENDIX 3

WILLIAM GEDDES'S ENCOMIASTICK EPIGRAM, 1690

The following verse, unearthed in 1999, adds to the evidence of the interest being taken by non-masons in Scotland in the myths and organisation of the mason craft that were giving birth to freemasonry. The legend of the two antediluvian pillars in which human knowledge was preserved is repeated, the importance of symbolism to masons stressed, reference made to the secrets relating to identification that masons had, and it is emphasised how it is masons who provide the settings for the grandeur and pomp of great courts. A rather more unusual touch is the claim that God himself was a stonemason, for with mallet and chisel He engraved the Ten Commandments on stone for Moses.

Though the poem is printed, only a single copy is known to survive, in the National library of Scotland (APS. 4. 83. 24). The broadside is headed, with what seems inappropriate formality, by a decorative woodcut featuring the Scottish royal coat of arms, a type of ornament commonly used to head official acts and proclamations. The sides and foot are decorated, even more oddly, with woodcuts showing silhouettes of coasts as seen from the sea, presumably taken from some 'ruttier' or 'rutter'- guides containing instructions to sailors which featured such silhouettes to help them identify the landfalls they made. Thus in decorating the broadside poem the printer has randomly used some woodcuts he happened to have in stock. The figures giving the date of the publication, 1690, are placed round the text, and the place may be assumed to be Edinburgh.

The poem shows that Geddes was interested by masonry, but there is no evidence that he was an initiate. His family came from Moray, and he graduated as a master of arts at King's College, Aberdeen, in 1650. In the same year he was appointed schoolmaster at Keith, and in 1652 he was tutor to Hugh Rose of Kilravock. In 1659 he became minister of Wick, moving to the parish of Urquhart in 1677, but he resigned in 1682 rather than take the Test Act Oath, which many believed threatened protestantism. However, after the Revolution of 1688-9 he was re-admitted to the ministry, at Wick in 1692, and he died two years later. In terms of church government, he served under presbyterian government from 1659 to 1661, episcopalian from 1661 to 1682, and presbyterian again in 1692 to 1694. Which system he preferred is unknown.

Geddes was a man of considerable literary energy, preparing a Memoriale Historicum, covering Biblical times, 'the Universal Histories of the Four

Monarchs,' and Scottish, English, French and Turkish history, as well as works on arithmetic, geography and Hebrew. In March 1683 the privy council of Scotland recommend these valuable works to the public, and granted Geddes copyright of them for nineteen years *(RPCS, 1682-4, 93)*. Such official favour to a man who had lost his job the previous year for opposition to a central plank of government policy suggests that Geddes had friends in high places. However, even with the council's support, the books never appeared.

Thus his only works to be printed were his verse on the mason craft and *The saint's recreation. Third part. Upon the estate of grace* (Edinburgh, 1683), which set hymns and spiritual songs to the tunes of popular ballads. Of parts one and two nothing is known, and the text of the third part is preceded by an apology for the author's delay in producing the texts over which the privy council had given him copyright. Many generous persons had advanced the price of the books, he admitted, and they might wonder why they have not received them long ago. He had used all diligence possible but his 'pious and worthy designe' had 'been obstructed several wayes, which are not altogether pertinent to be divulged,' perhaps a hint at political complications *(Fasti) Ecctesiae Scoticanae*, ed. H. Scott, 10 vols., 1915-81, vi, 409, vii, 141; *DNB*).

An *ENCOMIASTICK EPIGRAM*
Upon the most ANTIENT and HONOURABLE TRADE

OF

MASONS.

By Mr. *WILLIAM GEDDES*, Late Minister at *Urquhart*.

	Among *Mechanicks*, MASONS I extoll
	And with the best I doubt not to Enroll.
*Antiquity and	Before the *Flood** Antiquity they Claime,
Noble Precedents	The MASON then must have an antient Name.
	When Godly* *Enoch* by his *Divine Art*,
*Joesphus de	He did foretell how that the World should smart
1 Antiq. Jud.	By Fire and Water, he two Pillars made,
Jude Epist.	The one with *Brick*, and one with *Stone* was laid:
	He wrote thereon all *Sciences* and *Arts*,
	Some knowledge to Diffuse in all Men's hearts.
	If Water came, the *Stone* might it endure;
	The *Brick* the Fire; so all continued sure.
*Exod. 32.	The* Moral-Law, in writ none could it have,
	Till *GOD* Himself in *Stone* he must it Grave.
Honourable and	For *Hewing Stone*, none can put you to shame,
mysterious Badge	The *Corner Stone*, to *JESUS* is a Name:
	For this I think the MASON must be Blest,

6

*A Metaphore taken from a part of the Coat of Arms	From antient times he hath a *Divine* Crest. A *Character* whereby they know each other, And yet so *Secret,* none knows but a Brother. All Temples, Turrets,* Pallaces of Kings, All Castles, Steeples, and such other things:
Noble and Stately Works.	Strong Holds and Houses, which do long endure, Do owe all what they have to Masons Cure. All Courts great Grandeur, and Magnifick State, What Pomp they have, from MASONS they do get;
Laws and Order.	The strictest Laws they have for *Common-well,* The *greatest Charity* when BRETHREN fail.
The Sum of all.	Symbols *Divine,* * *Pomp, Dwelling, Law* and *Love*; Few are the *Men who do such Tradsmen* prove.

APPENDIX 4

ALLAN RAMSAY, TO DR JOHN THEOPHILUS DESAGULIERS

Desaguliers was one of the outstanding figures in the emergence of freemasonry in England, being elected Grand Master in 1719 and serving as Deputy Grand Master in 1722-4 and 1726. His scientific interests led to his publishing *The motion of water and other fluids. Being a treatise on hrydrostaticks, written in French by Mariotts, translated into English. Together with a treatise of the same author, giving practical rules for fountains or jets d'eau* (London, 1718), and he was much involved in designing the water supply for the great house at Canons in Middlesex of the duke of Chandos, who employed him as his chaplain.

At the end of July 1721 John Campbell, the provost of Edinburgh, dined at Canons (C.H.C. & M.I. Baker, *The life and circumstances of James Brydges, first duke of Chandos*, Oxford, 1949, 194), his presence probably being due, in part at least, to his seeking expert advice for a planned new water supply for Edinburgh. Desaguliers was present at the dinner, and Campbell evidently arranged for him to visit Edinburgh the following month as an advisor to the burgh council on the water supply.

Once in Edinburgh Desaguliers came into contact with Scottish freemasons and asked for a meeting with them. The Grand Lodge of England's masonic activities were at this time concerned only with a few London lodges, and Desaguliers was no doubt glad of the opportunity to discover at first hand something of the activities of Scottish lodges. On 24 August 1721 he was admitted to the Lodge of Edinburgh (Mary's Chapel), and the following day he was present when the lodge admitted the provost of Edinburgh and other leading burgh officials. Several more local dignitaries joined on 28 August (Carr, *Minutes*, 269-71. See page 35 above). It seems certain that it was Desaguliers who inspired this admission to the lodge of the burgh hierarchy.

Apart from the well-known entries in the Mary's Chapel minutes almost nothing is known of Desaguliers' visit to Edinburgh apart from his work for the council, but Alan Ramsay's lines printed below indicate that his social contacts included literary figures. Ramsay was a sociable, clubable man, and had been a prominent member of the Easy Club. His lines indicate that he had enjoyed Desaguliers' company enough to mark their meeting in the Scots verse he was seeking to revive in an age of anglicisation. It is notable that the poem is dated 25 August, a day on which Desaguliers must have been busy arranging the admission of the provost and his colleagues to Mary's Chapel, but no reference is made to his masonic interests.

The text of poem said to have been found in a copy of Ramsay's *Poems* (Edinburgh, 1721), presumably the copy of the book he had given Desaguliers. Subsequently Desaguliers retained enough contact with the Scots poet to become a subscriber to his *Poems* of 1728 (A. Ramsay, *Works*, STS, 6 vols., 1951-74, ii, 16, iv, 259, vi, 191. The permission of the Scottish Text Society to print this text is gratefully acknowledged).

TO DR JOHN THEOPHILUS DESAGUEIERS ON

PRESENTING HIM WITH MY BOOK.

Is then, the famous Desagulier's son
To learn the dialect of our Calidon? *Caledonia (Scotland)*
Wiel, Doctor, since you think it worth your while
Sometimes on my laigh landart shrine to smile, *Lowland*
Accept the haleware, and, when ye gae hame, *whole work*
Stand by your poet, and haud up his fame. *hold*
Gin ill-haird buckys girn and shae their spite, *When surly bigots snarl; show*
Your good word will gang far, and put them hyt. *go, get them enraged*
'Tis sport to see a critick fuf and fling, *lose their tempers and caper about*
And, like a dron-bee, daftly tine his sting; *lose*
But the industrious whid frae flower to flower *flat*
Suck frae the sweet, and trip out o'er the sour. *turn away from*
While Arthur's Seat shall my Parnassus be,
And frae its twaesome tap my nag can flee *double peak*
Around this nether-warld, its be my care
To gather images handwal'd and rare, *hand picked*
And gin I be sae kanny aft to please *when; so skillful as often*
The best - my mind will be at muckle ease, *great*
Then, with a willing heart and fancy keen,
Its be my study still to strike at spleen

O worthy wight, whase genius great refines, *man*
And puts in practice Euclid's unko lines, *extraordinary*
Be ever blyth, and keeps a saul in heel, *retain courage to the end*
Sae beneficial to the common weal.
Aug. 25th, 1721.   Allan Ramsay

INDEX

The names of initiated freemasons are followed by an abbreviation of the name of their lodges in brackets, which should be self-explanatory: see the list of lodges in Appendix 1 on p.182. These abbreviations are also used in subject entries in the index to refer to lodges. Other abbreviations used are: F = Freemason (used to identify freemasons initiated outside lodges or in unknown lodges); and OC = Old Charges.

Entries in **bold** in the form of two figures separated by a full stop (eg., '**1.2**') refer to the reference numbers to the right of the entries in Appendix 2, pp. 186-205.

Aberdeen, 124-5; Futtie (Footdee), 147; Futtiesmyre, 147-8; King's College, 130, 206; Marischal College, 127-8, 140, 143, 146-7, 149; Old Aberdeen, 145; St Nicholas' Church, 124; site lodge in, 2, 124; tolbooth, 125

Aberdeen, Incorporation of Hammermen of, 130, 146

Aberdeen, Incorporation of Coopers, Wrights and Masons of, 124

Aberdeen, Incorporation of Tailors of, 146

Aberdeen, Incorporation of Wrights and Coopers of, 124, 130, 146

Aberdeen, Lodge of, 63, 104, 124-50, 178-80, 182; catechism, 127, **5.2**; Mark Book, 126-31, 133-7, 140-1, 144, 149, 178, **3.5, 4.1, 6.1**; records, **6.1-12**

Aberdeen, Society of Barber-Surgeons of, 130

Aberdeen Ms. (OC), 126, 136, **4.1, 6.1**

Aberdeenshire, 125

Able family (AH), 53

Adamson, Henry, 103-4

Agnew, Alexander, glazier (Dumf.), 81

Airlie, Ms, **5.9**

Airth, Stirlingshire, 92

Aitchison's Haven, East Lothian, 52

Aitchison's Haven, Lodge of, 4-5, 12,18, 35, 39, 52-62, 67, 69, 76, 80, 99, 113, 166-7, 182; records, **1.3-4, 3.1-2, 4.2-3, 7.1-2**

Aitchison's Haven Mss. Nos. 1-2 (OC), 58, 93, **4.2-3**

ale houses, inns, taverns, 47, 50, 66, 88, 111

Alerdis, *see* Allardyce, Alexander

Alexander, Sir Anthony (Edin.), 26-7, 57, 99, 188

Alexander, Henry, 2nd earl of Stirling (Edin.), 27, 57, 99

Alexander, Sir William, 1st earl of Stirling, 27

Alexander, William, Lord (Edin.), 26-7

Alexander of Peffermiln, Mr George, advocate (Aber.), 142-3

Alexander of Peffermiln, Mr John, advocate, 142-3

Alison, Robert (Dunf.), 172

Alison, Robert, clerk (Edin.), 33

Alison family (Kilw.), 67

Allardyce (Alerdis) of that Ilk, Alexander (Edin.), 27

Alloa, Clackmannanshire, 93

Alvah, Mill of, Banffshire, 151

America, first freemasons in, *see* New Jersey

Anderson, James, glazier (Aber.), 126, 128, 130-1, 149-50

INDEX

Anderson, Dr James, 111, 149-50
Anderson, John (AH), 61
Anderson, Michael (Kilm.), 153
Anderson, Patrick, wright (Edin.), 33
Anderson, Robert, wright (Dumf.), 79, 82
apprenticeship, apprentices, 13-14 *and passim*
aprons, 134-5
Archibald, David, tailor (Sco.), 106
architecture, Renaissance concept of, 7-8, 10, 28
Argyll, earl of, *see* Campbell, Archibald,
Ashmole, Elias, antiquarian, 160
Auchingown, Renfrewshire, 68
Auchinleck, John, clerk (AH), 58
Ayr, 64, 67, 92
Ayr, Incorporation of Squaremen (Masons and Wrights) of, 64-5, 74-5; records, **24.6**
Ayrshire, 39, 64, 66, 72-3, 78
Aytoun family (AH), 18, 53
Aytoun, George, clerk (AH), 57-8
Aytoun, John (AH), 53
Aytoun, William (AH), 18, 54, 57, 163

Baillie of Ashiesteill, Alexander (Hau.), 122-3
Baillie of Woodside, John, clerk (Ham.), 84
Balgonie, Milton of, Fife, 92
Banff, 151
Banff, Lodge of, 151-2; records, **8.1**
Banffshire, 125
banquets, dinners, eating and drinking; Aber., 133, 135, 146; Dumf., 81; Dunb., 111; Edin., 20-2; Ham., 87-8; Hau., 123; Mel., 115
Barbour of Aldowry, James (Inv.), 150
Barclay of Urie, Robert, 139-40
Barr, Alexander (CL), 41
Barton, Hugh, wright (Dumf.) 79
Baverley, John, cordiner (Aber.), 145
Baxter, Alexander (AH), 39, 56
Baxter, William (Dunb.), 108
Beck, Robert, writer (Dumf.), 81
Bellenden family, 36
Bellenden of Broughton, William, 36
Beltrees, Renfrewshire, 68
Bennet, James (Ban.), 151
Bennet, Lieutenant (Kel.), 118
Bennet of Grubet, William (Kel.), 118

Betson of Killerie, Robert (Dunf.), 91
Bible, 87
Boaz, 142
Borland, Mathew, "lover (Sco.), 106
Borlands, Thomas, in Kingstables, 19
Borthwick, John (Hau.), 122
Borthwick of Falahill younger, William (Hau.), 122
Boswell of Auchinleck, John, 24-5
Bothwell, Lanarkshire, 85
Bothwell Bridge, Battle of, 72
boxes, 50; AH, 59; Aber.,131,133,135; Glas., 76-8; Kel., 118; Kilm., 153
Boyle, Mr James, secretary (Ham.), 85
Brenche, Patrick, mason, 36
Brodie, Andrew, 154
Brodie, Francis (Kilm.), 153
Brodie, William (Edin., EJ), 47-50
Broughton, barony of, 36
Brown, Dr (Kel.), 118
Brown, Henry, notary (Sco.?), 106-7, 174
Brown, John (Edin.),24
Brown, William, 115
Brownhill, James, wright (Edin.), 47-8
Bruce, Alexander, 2nd earl of Kincardine, 91-2
Bruce, Alexander, 3rd earl of Kincardine (Dunf.), 91-2
Bruce, Jean, 127
Bryson, James (Ham.), 86
Buchanan, John, mason, 100-1
Bunzie, Andrew, weaver ((Mel.), 114
Bunzie family (Mel.), 113-14, 116
burghs, convention of the royal, 94
Burlington, 143
Burn, John (Dunf), 172
Burnet, Alexander, archbishop of Glasgow, 76
Burnet of Lethenty, Robert, 142-3
Burnet, Daniel, 142
Burntisland, Fife, 92
Burntisland, Incorporation of Hammermen of, 31.3

Caddell, William, innkeeper, 111
Caddell of Fossochie, William (Dunb.), 108-9, 111
Cairncross, George (Hau.), 122
Cairncross, William (F, Hau.), 121-2
Calderwood, Thomas (AH), 56

Caldwell, John (Kilw.), 68
Caldwell, John, younger (Kilw.), 68
Caldwell, Mathew, mason, 68
Caldwell, Robert, mason, 68
Caldwell family (Kilw.), 67-8
Cameron, Alexander (Dunb.), 107-9
Cameron of Lochiel, Ewen, 108
Cameron of Lochiel younger, John (Dunb.), 107-9
Camick, Mr George, innkeeper (Dumf.), 81
Campbell, Archibald, 9th earl of Argyll, 31, 108
Campbell, Patrick (Had.), 61
Canongate, 17, 21, 35-6, 39-41, 85
Canongate and Leith, Leith and Canongate, Lodge of, 40-2, 44, 52, 88, 156, 166, 182; records, **10.1-2**
Canongate, Incorporation of Wrights and Coopers of, 30, 36-9, 166; records, **9.2-3**
Canongate-Kilwinning, Lodge of, 37-41, 72, 156, 159, 166, 182; records, **9.1**
Carmichael of Balmeadow, James (Dunf.), 91
Carmichael of Bamblea, James (Dunf.), 91
Carr, Harry, historian, 24, 70
Carrick, Ayrshire, 64, 67
Carruth, John, (Kilw.), 68
Carruth, Robert (Kilw.), 68
Cassillis, earl of, *see* Kennedy, John
catechisms, masonic, 4, 105, 119, 123, 127, 171, 177, **5.1-8**
Catholicism, Catholics, 5, 10, 139, 147
Chapman, Lawrence, wright (Sco.), 106
Charles I, King, 27, 94, 103-4, 158
Charles II, King, 31, 138
charters to lodges, forged, **17.1, 30.1**
Chetwode Crawley Ms. (catechism), 5.3
chocolate-houses, 10
Church of Scotland, 2, 9-10, 116; *see also* presbyterianism
Clerk, Sir John, of Penicuik (Edin.), 33-4
clubs, 10, 157
Cochrane, David, maltman (Sco.), 106
Cochrane, William (CK) 38
Cochrane, Sir William, 1st Lord, 71-3
Cockburn, John (Mel.), 116, 145
coffee-houses, 10, 50
Colleonard, Banffshire, 152
Copland of Udoch, Patrick, 125

Coplands of Udoch, 125-6
Corsehill, barony of, 70-1
Corss, James (Edin.), 32
covenanters, 28
Cowane, John, 98
cowans, 22, 79; AH, 57; CK, 36-7; Edin., 22; Glas., 75; Had., 61; Ham., 86; Kilw., 69; Mel., 116; Sco., 105; Stir., 99
Cowie, John, merchant (Aber.), 140, 142
Craich, Thomas (Sco.), 104
Craig, William (Hau.), 122
Craigdallie, Thomas, litster (Sco.), 106
Crail, Incorporation of Squaremen of, **31.2**
Crawford, David (Ham.), 85, 87
Crawford family (Kilw.), 67
Crombie, William (Kilm.), 153
Cromwell, Oliver, 30
Crumbie, John (AH), 61-2
Cubie, Mr Robert (AH), 59
Cullen of Sachs, William (Ham.), 85, 88
Cunison, John, clerk (Ham), 85
Cunningham, Alexander (Stir.), 99
Cunningham, Ayrshire, 64, 66-7
Cunningham of Carlurg, Joseph (Kilw.), 70
Cunningham of Corsehill, Sir Alexander (Kilw.), 70-1, 73
Cunningham of Robertland, Sir David (Kilw.), 72-3
Cunninghams of Robertland, 72

Dalkeith, Midlothian, 52-3, 56, 115
Dalkeith, Lodge of, 167
David I, King, 204
Dawson, Archibald (AH) 61-2
deacons, *see* lodge officials
Deans, John, writer (Aber.), 146
Dee, River, 132
degrees, masonic, 4, 14, 152-3, 161, 167
Deism, 140
Denmark, 5
Desaguliers, John Theophilus (Edin.), 35, 93-4, 209-10
Dick, James (Inv.), 151
Dobie, Mr William (Sco.), 106-7
Don of Smailholm, Andrew (Kel.), 118
Donald, William, maltman (Aber.), 180
Donaldson, Alexander, officer (Sco.), 106
Donaldson, John (Hau.), 122

Douglas, Charles Hamilton, 2nd earl of Selkirk, 85
Douglas, William, mason, 61
Drummond, Cornet (Kel.), 118
Drummond, James, 4th earl of Perth, 179-80
Drummond, John, 1st earl of Melfort, 108
Drummond, William, 1st Lord Strathallan, 107-10
Drummond of Balhaldie, Alexander (Dunb.), 107-9
Duffus, Kirkton of, Morayshire, 153
Dumbarton, 66, 79; castle, 98
Dumfries, 53, 81, 170
Dumfries, Incorporation of Squaremen (Wrights) of, 78, **11.6**
Dumfries, Lodge of, 69, 78-83, 92, 157, 170-1, 182; records, **11.1-5**
Dumfries Nos. 1-4 Mss. (OC), 82, **4.4-7**
Dumfries No. 3 Ms. (OC), 82, **4.6**
Dumfries No. 4 Ms. (OC and catechism), **4.7, 5.7**
Dunblane, 107
Dunblane, Incorporation of Hammermen of, 110
Dunblane, Incorporation of Masons of, 109-10
Dunblane, Lodge of, 107-12, 123, 151, 156, 159, 175, 182; records, **12.1**
Dunblane, regality of, 109
Duncan, Alexander, 147
Duncan, John, merchant (Edin.), 33
Dundas, Mr James, merchant (Dund.), 97
Dundee, 23, 92, 173; site lodge in, 2
Dundee, Lodge of, 94-7, 156, 182; records, **13.1-4**
Dundee, Lord, *see* Grahame, John
Dundee, Society or Incorporation of Masons of, 95-7, 99; records, **4.8-9, 13.5**
Dundee Mss. Nos. 1-2 (OC), 95, **4.8-9**
Dunfermline, 172; tolbooth, 172
Dunfermline, earls of, *see* Seton, Alexander, Charles, *and* James
Dunfermline, Incorporation of Masons of, 92-3
Dunfermline, Lodge of, 5, 56, 69, 90-4, 105, 113, 172, 182; records, **14.1-3**
Dunkirk, 30
Duok (Dowok), Hew, wright, 65
Duthie, John (Dunb.), 108, 110

Duthie, Robert (Dunb.), 108, 110

East Jersey, *see under* New Jersey
Edinburgh, 56, 68, 79, 92, 122, 130; castle, 98, 114; Easy Club, 209; Greyfriars' Church, 33; Heriot's Hospital, 18, 54, 57, 163; incorporations, 12; Mary's Chapel, 12-13; Niddry's Wynd, 12, 19; Parliament House, 18; site lodge in, 98; tolbooth, 48; university, 18
Edinburgh (Mary's Chapel), Incorporation of Masons and Wrights, 12-50 *passim*, 57, 60; records. **15.3-12**
Edinburgh (Mary's Chapel), Lodge of 4-5, 8, 12-50 passim, 53, 56-7, 59-60, 62-3, 67-8, 72, 74, 80, 88, 90, 92-3, 118, 158, 160, 166, 182, 209; records, **1.2, 15.1-2**
Edinburgh Journeymen, Lodge of, 20, 42-51, 88, 156, 182,; records, **16.1-4**
Eglinton, earls of, **1.1, 1.5**; *see also* Montgomery, Alexander.
Egypt, 1, 6-8, 32, 169
Elgin, 153-5; tolbooth, 153
Elgin, Lodge of, *see* Kilmolymock, Lodge of
Ellon, Aberdeenshire, 143
Elphinstone, William, wright (Edin.), 33
Elphinstone of Airth, Charles, 127
Elphinstone of Airth, Richard, 127
Elphinstone of Calderhall, Sir Thomas, 127, 138
Elphinstone of Melgum, Harry, tutor of Airth (Aber.), 127, 138, 143, 180
England, 1, 3-4, 9-11; early freemasonry in, 11, 149-50, 159-61
Enlightenment, the. 9-11
Enoch, 207
Entered apprentices, 4, 14 *and passim;* refusal of promotion by, 43-5, 59, 93
Erroll, earls of, *see* Hay, Gilbert *and* John
essays, 16-17, 36, 61, 66-7, 76, 146, 163
Euclid, 1
Evelick, laird of (Dunf.), 91

Faa (Fall), George (Kel., Mel.), 116-18, 176
Falkland Statutes, 27, 57-8, 99, 126, **3.1-5**

INDEX

fellow crafts, 4, 14 *and passim*
Fergushill, Robert, clerk (Kilw.), 71-2
feuars, 68, 114
Fife, 90, 92
Findlater, earl of, *see* Ogilvie, James
Finlayson, Christopher, merchant (Dunb.), 110
Fisherrow, 52, 57
Fleming, John, mason (Dumf.), 81, 171
Fleming, John, wright, 83
footballs, 105
Forbes, Alexander, 2nd Lord Pitsligo (Aber.), 138, 143
Forbes, Alexander, slater (Aber.), 130
Forbes, John, merchant (Aber.), 143, 145
Forbes, John, printer, 177
Forbes of Boyndlie, Alexander, 143
Forbes of Tulloch, William (Aber.), 146
Forres. 17
Forsyth, Alexander, glazier (Ban.), 151-2
Forsyth, Alexander, younger, glazier (Ban.), 151-2
Forsyth, James, glazier (Kilm.), 153
Foveran, Aberdeenshire, 143
France, 5
Fraser, Kenneth (Aber.), 180
Fraser, Mr William, minister of Slains (Aber.), 128-9
freemasons; use of term, 28, 75, 113; *see also* non-operative freemasons
Frier, James (Hau.), 123
Frier, Thomas (Hau.), 123
Frog, Alexander, tidesman (Dumf.), 81
Fulton, John (Edin.), 39
Fulton, William (Edin.), 14, 162
Fulton family (Kilw.), 67
Fyvie, Aberdeenshire, 128-30

Galashiels (Gala), Selkirkshire, 120, 122-3
Galt, Alexander (Kilw.) 70
Geddes, William, 206-8
George, Mr Alexander, advocate (Aber,) 127
Gib, Thomas (CK), 38
Gibb (Gibbs), James architect, 147, 149
Gibb, Peter (Patrick), merchant, 147
Gibson, Archibald, clerk, 24
Gilfillan, John, cordiner (Stir.), 101

Girdleness, Kincardineshire, 133, 136, 147
Glasgow, 18, 32, 64, 68-9, 74, 79; Trades' House, 75, 170
Glasgow, archbishop of, *see* Burnet, Alexander,
Glasgow, Incorporation of Masons, 69, 74-7, 170; records, **17.3-6**
Glasgow, Incorporation of Masons and Wrights, 74
Glasgow, Incorporation of Masons, Wrights and Coopers of, 74
Glasgow, Lodge of, 5, 74-8, 156, 182; records **17.1-2**
gloves, 55, 71, 86-7, 95, 104-5, 113, 134-5, 157
Golden Lion, 143
Gordon, George, mathematician (Aber.), 146
Gordon, Robert, cardmaker (Aber.), 142
grades, *see* degrees
Grahame, James, lorimer (Dunb.), 108, 175
Grahame, John 1st Vis. Dundee, 108
Grahame, John, younger (Dunb.), 108-9
Grand Lodge of England, 94, 149-50
Grand Lodge of Scotland, 37, 41, 62, 82-3, 101, 150-2, 155, 166
Gray of Crichie younger, John (Aber.), 128, 138
Gray, George (F. Hau.), 122
guilds, 1-2, 8-10, 12, 17, 19, 21 ,30, 33, 35, 42, 64, 84, 94-5, 99, 109, 124, 154
Gullane Church, East Lothian, 60

Haddington, 60-1; Nungate, 61
Haddington, earl of, *see* Hamilton, Charles
Haddington, Incorporation of Wrights and Masons of, 60-2
Haddington, Lodge of, 5, 60-2, 182; records, **18.1-7**
Halket, Capt., 93
Halket of Pitfirrane, Sir Peter, 93-4
Hamilton, 84-6
Hamilton, Alexander, general of the artillery (Edin.), 28-9

Hamilton, Anne, duchess of, 84-5
Hamilton, Mr Archibald (Ham.), 85, 88
Hamilton, Charles, 5th earl of Haddington, 115, **27.4**
Hamilton, James, 3rd marquis of, 27
Hamilton, John, mason, 16
Hamilton, John (F, Ham.), 88
Hamilton, Lodge of, 83-9, 105, 111-13, 123, 159, 182; records, **19.1-4**
Hamilton, regality of, 85
Hamilton of Barncleuch, John (Ham.), 85
Hamilton of Dalyell, James (Ham.), 85, 88
Hamilton of Rosehall, Sir James (Ham.), 85, 88
Hamilton Palace, 84
Harper of Cambusnethan, Sir John, 31-2
Hasilton, Alexander, slater (Sco.), 106
Haughfoot, Lodge of, 31, 69, 119-23, 156, 182; records **20.1**
Haughfoot Fragment (catechism), 120, **5.4**
Hay, Gilbert, 11th earl of Erroll (Aber?), 128-30, 138
Hay, John, 12th earl of Erroll (Aber?), 128-30, 138, 143
Hay, John, 2nd earl of Tweeddale, 31-2
Hay, Father Richard Augustin, **2.4-5**
Henderson of Fordell (Dunf.), 91
Henry and Francis, 138
Hermes Trismegistus, 6-8
Hermeticism, 6, 10
Hinschaw, James (Ham.), 84
Holland, *see* Netherlands
Holyrood, abbey of, 35
Holyroodhouse, 24, 63
Hoppringle, *see* Pringle
Houlet, John (Mel.), 115
Hume of Lumsden, Sir Patrick, advocate, 165
Hume of Polwarth, Sir Patrick, 1st earl of Marchmont (Edin.), 31, 164-5

Inchinnan, Renfrewshire, 66
incorporations, *see under names of individual incorporations*
indentures of apprenticeship, 13-14, 55, 79, 170, 177
identification rituals, 2-4, 20, 159
initiation rituals, 2-5, 8, 20, 156-61; AH, 53, 58-9; Aber., 136, 139, 145.,
Dumf., 82, Dunb., 109, 111; Dund., 95; Dunf., 93; Edin., 14, 20-3, 26, 28, 49; EJ, 47; Glas., 76; Ham., 87-8; Haul., 122; Kilm., 153; Kilw., 66, 69-70, 72; Mel., 115-16; Sco., 103; outside lodges, 39, 53, 59, 69, 72, 79-80, 92, 115, 121, 122, 159, 160
inns, *see* ale houses
intenders; Aber., 136; AH, 53-4, 58; Ham., 88; Kilw., 66-7
Inveresk, Midlothian, 52-3, 58; church, 53
Inverkeithing, Fife, 92
Inverness, 151
Inverness, Lodge of, 150-1, 182; records, **21.1-2**
invisibility, 103
Irvine, Ayrshire, 64-5
Irvine, Incorporation of Squaremen (Wrights) of, 65; records, **24.7**
Irvine, Mr Alexander (Aber.), 130

Jachin, 142
Jack, John, 62
Jacobites, 108
Jaffray of Kingswells, Alexander (Aber.), 146
James VI and I, King, 3, 94, 103, 125
James VLT and II, King (former duke of York), 31, 80, 108, 138-9, 179
Jamesone, Andrew, 177
Jedburgh, Incorporation of Wrights, Masons and Coopers of, **31.3**
Jenking, *see* Jonkin
Jerusalem, temple of, *see* Solomon's Temple,
Jesus, 207
Johnston, James (Dumf.), 79, 81
Johnston, John (AH), 39
Johnston, John, mason (F), 36, 38
Jonkin (Jenking), Hercules (Edin.), 30
journeymen, grievances of, 35, 38, 41-51

Keith, 206
Keith, William, 5th Earl Marischal, 27
Kelburn Castle, 68
Kelso, 116
Kelso, Incorporation of Hammermen of, 176
Kelso, Lodge of, 116-17, 120-1, 123, 156, 176, 182; records, **22.1-2**

INDEX

Kennedy, John and Mrs, innkeepers, 88
Kennedy, John, 7th earl of Cassillis (Kilw.), 69-71, 73
Kennedy, Mr John, schoolmaster (Kilm.), 153
Ker, Robert, 1st earl of Roxburgh, 36
Ker of Breakenhills, John (Kilw.), 72
Kerr of Banf Milns, Gilbert (Kel.), 118
Kerr of Chirtrees (Kel.), 118
Kerr of Greenheid younger, Andrew (Kel.), 118
Kevan Ms. (catechism), **5.5**
Kilbarchan, Renfrewshire, 66-7, 70
Killiecrankie, Battle of, 108
Kilmolymock, Morayshire, 155
Kilmolymock, (Elgin) Lodge of, 152-5, 182; records, **23.1**
Kilwinning, 64
Kilwinning, Lodge of, 24, 63-74, 78, 80, 86, 88-9, 92-3, 102-3, 111, 113-14, 138, 150-1, 156, 158-9, 182; and CK, 37-9, 72; and Schaw Statutes, 5, 25, **1.1, 1.5**; records, **24.1-6**
Kilwinning Ms. (Old Charges), 69, **4.10**
Kincardine, earls of, *see* Bruce, Alexander,
Kincardineshire, 17, 125, 133
King, James (Kilw.), 70, 73
King, John (Ham.), 84
King, Thomas (Edin.), 43
Kinross, 79, 92-3
Kirkcudbright, 83
Kirkcudbright, Incorporation of Wrights of, 83
Kirkcudbright, Lodge of, 82-3, 182; records, **25.1**
Kirkcudbrightshire, 79
Kyd of Craigie, Patrick (Dund.), 97
Kyle, Ayrshire, 64, 67

Lanark, Incorporation of Masons and Wrights of, 204
Lanarkshire, 32, 79, 85, 114; Nether Ward of, 64, 88-9
Largo, Fife, 92
Lauderdale, earl of, *see* Maitland, John,
Laurie, William, historian, 60
Leith, 17, 21, 30, 39-41; North, 36-7, 39-40; South, 36, 39-41

Leith, Incorporation of Hammermen of, 40
Leith, Incorporation of the Wrights of, 40
Leyden University, 31
Liddel, Mr George, mathematician (Aber.), 127-8, 146
Liddell, George, glazier, 65
Liddell, Hugh (Edin.), 44
Linlithgow Palace, 62, 98
Linlithgow, Lodge of, 30, 62, 156, 182
Livingstone, Lieu. John (Dumf.) 80
Lochwinnoch, Renfrewshire, 68
lodge finances: expenditure (banquets, benefits, food and drink, etc.); AH, 55-7; Aber., 131, 133-5, 146; Dunb., 111; Edin., 20-2, 44-6, 48-9; EJ, 45-7, 49-51; Glas., 76-7; Ham., 87-9; Hau., 123; Kel., 117; Mel., 115
lodge finances: income (dues, fees, fines, gifts, etc.); AH, 56-7, 59-60; Aber., 126-7, 133-6, 146; Ban., 151; Dunb., 109-11; Dund., 95-6; Dunf., 92-3; Edin., 44-9; EJ, 45-7, 49-51; Had., 61; Ham., 84, 86-9; Hau., 123; Kel., 117-18; Kilm., 153-4; Kilw., 66-7, 70-1, 73; Mel., 113, 116; Sco., 104, 106
lodge laws, statutes, agreements, contracts, obligations; signed by members, (Dunf.) 91-2, (Ham.) 86-7, (Mel.) 113, 115, (Sco.) 102-6; unsigned, (Aber.) 126, 131-6, (AH) 59, (Dumf) 78-80, (Dund.) 95-6, (Kel.) 117, (Kilw.), 65-6
lodge management committees (and other groups monopolising power in lodges); Dunf., 93; Edin., 45-7; Ham., 86, 89; Kilm, 152-3
lodge meetings: places; AH, 52-3, 55; Aber., 133, 136, 148-9; Dumf, 79; Dunb., 111; Dunf., 93; Edin., 13; EJ, 47; Had., 60-1; Ham., 88; Hau., 120, 123; Kilm., 155; Kilw., 66; Mel., 113-14; Sco., 105
lodge meetings: timing and frequency; AH, 52, 55-6, 59; Aber., 135; Dumf., 81-2; Dunb., 109; Dund., 96; Edin., 20-2; Glas., 78; Ham., 87-8; Hau., 120-1; Inv., 150; Kilm., 154; Kilw., 65, 69

lodge officials (deacons, wardens, masters, etc.); AH, 56-7; Aber.,133, 147; Dumf., 78-9; Dunb., 107-10; Dund., 96-7; Dunf., 92-3; Edin., 13, 22-4, 45, 50; Glas., 74, 76; Had., 62; Ham., 86; Hau., 121-2; Inv., 150-3; Kel., 117; Kilm., 152; Kilw., 66, 69-73; Mel.,115; Sco., 102-5; Stir., 99-100

lodge regulation of the mason trade; AH, 53-60; Aber., 131, 136; Dumf., 81; Dunb., 109-12; Dund., 95-6; Dunf., 93; Edin., 19-22, 25, 60; Had., 61; Ham., 86-7, 112; Kel., 117; Kilm., 153-4; Kilw., 68-9, 73-4; Mel., 116; Sco., 105; Stir., 99-100

lodges; as benefit societies, 56, (AH) 56-7, (Aber.) 131, 133-5, (Edin.) 20-1, 44, 46, (EJ) 45-7, 49-50, (Hau.) 123, (Kel.) 117, (Kilm.) 154; of freemasons, 2-11,156-61, *see also under names of individual lodges and subject entries*; examination of members in masonic lore, (AH) 58, 76, (Dunf.) 81-2, (Glas.) 76, (Kel.) 119, (Kilw.) 66 (Mel.) 115-16; occasional, 160; site, 2-3, 124

Logie Buchan, Aberdeenshire, 130
London, 146, 160
Loudoun, James, manufacturer (Ham.), 85, 88
Lourie, Robert (Hau.), 120-1
Lushington, Thomas, merchant (Aber.) 146
Lyall, John (Dunf.), 93
Lyon, David M., historian, 16, 24

McAlexander, Robert, dragoon (Dumf.), 80
McBean, John (Inv.), 150
McClellan, Sir Samuel, merchant (Edin.), 33
MacDugall of Stodrig, Thomas (Kel.), 118
M'George of Inglistoun, clerk (Dumf.), 80, 82, 189
McGill, Mr Alexander, architect (Edin.), 33
Mack, James (Ham.), 86
Mackay, Sir Donald, Lord Reay, 27
Mackintosh, Lachlan, 150

Mackintosh of Elrig, William (Inv.), 150
Macleod, laird of, 150
Maitland, John, 2nd earl and 1st duke of Lauderdale, 31-2, 71
Malcolm II, King, 198
Manuscript Constitutions, *see* Old Charges
Marshall, Mr William, clerk (Edin.), 33
mason craft; mobility, 1-2, 159; career structure, 13-15, 95-6, 154
mason marks, 24-5, 28, 31, 87, 91, 96, 126
Mason Word, 4, 11, 22, 37, 48-9, 58-61, 64, 69, 75, 80, 82, 84, 88, 97, 103-4, 107, 120-1, 123, 126, 130-1, 134, 142, 156, 158, 160, 169, **5.2**
masonic catechisms, *see* catechisms, masonic
masonic records, 184-205
master masons, 14-15, *and passim*; presiding in lodges, *see* lodge officials
master masons, king's, 25; *see also* Mylne family
masters of works, king's, 3, 5, 26-7, 57, 159
mathematics, 1, 3, 7-8, 10, 32, 127, 146, 157, 160
Maxwell, Dr William (Edin.) 25, 28
Maxwell of Tinwald, Francis (Dumf.), 81-2
Mean, Mr Nicol (Mel.), 114
Mein, Alexander, in Maxwellheugh (Mel., Kel.), 115, 117-18
Mein, Alexander, mason (c.1635), 114
Mein, Andrew (Mel.), 115
Mein, Andrew (Mel.), 113, 191
Mein, Andrew mason (c.1615), 114
Mein, Mr Andrew (Mel.), 114
Mein, David (Mel.), 115
Mein, James (Mel.), 114
Mein, James younger (Mel.), 114
Mein, James 'Byres', (Mel.), 116
Mein, James 'Townheid' (Mel.), 116
Mein, John, maltman (Mel.), 114
Mein, John, osler (Mel.), 114-15
Mein, John 'Wynd', clerk (Mel.), 115
Mein, Richard (Mel.), 115
Mein, Robert (Richard), mason (1613), 114
Mein, Robert, mason (c.1635), 114
Mein family (AH, Mel.), 53,113-14,116

Melfort, earl of, *see* Drummond, John,
Melrose, 114
Melrose, Lodge of, 53, 63, 67-8, 113-18, 123, 145, 176, 182; records, **27.1-4**
Melrose Mss. Nos. 1-2 (OC), 113, 115, **4.11**
memory, art of, 6-7, 58, 103
Middle Ages, 1-4, 6, 9, 42, 159
Midlothian, 119
Mill, Alexander (Ban.), 151
Miller, Wiliam (Ham.) 85
Miller of Watersaugh, John (Ham.), 85
Millhaven, East Lothian, 52, 55
Milnathort, Kinross-shire, 93
Milne, John, wright (Sco.), 106
Mitchelson of Middletoun, John, advocate (Hau.), 122
Montgomery, Alexander, 8th earl of Eglinton (Kilw.), 71-3, 138
Montgomery, James, wright (Kilw.), 73
Montgomery, William (Aber.), 145
Moray, Mr William (Edin.), 31
Moray, Sir Robert (Edin.), 28, 31, 91, 140, 157
Moreis, James (Dunf.), 93
Morison, John, younger, cooper, 100
Morrison's Haven, East Lothian, 52
mortcloths, 56-7, 110-11, 116
Moses, 206
Mostede, George, clerk, 24
Moultray of Rescobie, James (Dunf.), 91
Mowbray, Robert, wright (Edin.), 33
Mudie of Ardbickie younger, James (Dunf.), 91
Mure (Moore), Alexander, hookmaker (Aber?), 142
Mure (Moore), Alexander, younger, hookmaker (Aber?), 142, 179
Murray, David (Aber.), 145
Murray, David (Hau.), 120-1
Muschett, Thomas (Dunb.), 108
Muschett, William (Dunb.), 110
Musselburgh, 52, 56-9, 167; church, 53
Musselburgh, Incorporation of Wrights of, **7.3**
Myllar, Robert, mason, 170
Mylne, John (d.1621), 102-4, 173-4
Mylne, John (d.1657), (Sco?), 102-4, 125, 173
Mylne, John (d.1667), (Edin.), 25-6, 28, 94, 98, 10³

Mylne, Robert, mason, (Edin.), 17, 43, 162
Mylne, Thomas, mason, 102
Mylne family, 25, 102-3, 174

Naismith, Arthur, clerk (Ham.), 84-5
Naismith, James, wright (Ham), 84
Naismith, John, surgeon (Ham.), 84
Napier of Merchison, John, 32
National Covenant, 18
Neilson, James (Lin., Edin.), 30, 33, 62
Neilson, William, merchant (Edin.), 33
Netherlands (Holland), 32, 147
New Jersey, 128, 138, 142-3, 179-80; East, 116, 138, 139, 142-3; West, 139, 143, 145, 176
New Perth, *see* Perth Amboy
New York, 116
Newall, John, clerk (Dumf.), 81
Newall, Robert, wright (Dumf.), 79
Newark, New Jersey, 116
Newbattle, 33, 55-6; abbey, 52
Newcastle upon Tyne, 28, 160
Newstead, Roxburghshire, 113-16
Newton, Isaac, 157
Newtyle, Aberdeenshire, 143
Nicolson, Alexander (Inv.), 150-1
Nicolson, John (F, Ham.), 88
Nicolson, Robert (Inv.), 151
Nigg, Kincardineshire 132
Nisbet, Mr Alexander, surgeon (Edin.), 33
non-operative freemasons, 8-9, 24-5, 156-61; AH, 58-9; Aber., 127-30, 136, 138-46; Ban., 152; Dumf., 80-1; Dunb., 107-12; Dund., 97; Dunf., 91-3; Edin., 25-35, 164-5; Glas., 78; Had., 62; Ham., 84-6, 88; Hau., 119-23; Inv., 150-1; Kel., 117-19; Kilm., 153; Kilw., 66, 69-73; Mel., 114; Sco., 106-7; Stir., 101
Norie, Andrew (Sco.), 104
Norie, Andrew, younger (Sco.), 105
North Leith, *see under* Leith
North Queensferry, 92

Ogilvie, George (Kilm.), 153
Ogilvie, James, 3rd earl of Findlater (Aber.), 138
Old Aberdeen, 145

INDEX

Old Charges (Ms. Constitutions), 1-2, 4, 6-7, 58, 149, 159, 161, 189, **4.1-12**; *see also under names of individual versions*
omnigatherums (omnigadrums), 39, 98-100
Orr, James (Kilw.), 68

Paisley, Renfrewshire, 66, 68, 75, 79
Paterson, Alexander, armourer (Aber.), 130, 140, 179
Paton, Andrew (F, Ham.), 88
Patten, Andrew (AH), 54
Pattoun, Mr David (Dunb.), 111
Peachfield, New Jersey, 143
Pearson, James, 108
Pearson of Kippenross, John (Dunb.), 107-8, 111
Pedden family (AH), 53
Peebles, 114
Peebles, Incorporation of Masons and Wrights of, 204
Pennsylvania, 138, 143, 176
pentacle, 28, 31
Perth, 23, 92, 155; bridge at, 103-4
Perth, earl of, *see* Drummond, James
Perth, Incorporation of Masons and Wrights of, 105-6; records, **29.3-7**
Perth, Lodge of, *see* Scone, Lodge of
Perth Amboy (New Perth), 116, 143, 179
Petticrief, James (AH), 57
Petticrief family (AH), 53
Philp, Agnes, 115
pillars of the Temple, 132, 142, 207
Pitsligo, Lord, *see* Forbes, Alexander
Plewlands, Morayshire, 153
Portsburgh, Edinburgh, 17, 19, 36, 163
Prentice, Robert (CK), 38
presbyterians, 31-2, 71, 80-1, 116, 149, 206
Preston of Valleyfield, Sir William (Dunf.), 91
Prestonpans, East Lothian, 52, 56-7
Pringle, James (Hau.), 120
Pringle, James, brother of Pringle of that Ilk (Hau.), 120-1
Pringle, John, wright (Hau.), 120-1
Pringle of Clifton, Robert (Kel.), 118
Pringle of Graycrook, Mr Walter, advocate (Edin.), 31, 118, 121

Pringle of Stitchel, Sir Robert (Kel.), 31, 118, 121
Pringle (Hoppringle) of that Ilk (of Torsonce), John, 120-2
Pringle of Torwoodlie, James (Hau.), 122
Protestants, 2, 5; *see also* Church of Scotland *and* presbyterians

Quakers, 138-40, 142-3, 176
Quarrywood, Morayshire, 153

Rait of Mideple, George (Aber.), 128, 138
Ramsay, Allan, 209-10
Ramsay, David (Edin.), 27
Rankin, George (CL), 41
Reay, Lord, *see* Mackay, Sir Donald
Reformation, 2, 10, 35
Register House Ms. (catechism), **5.1**
Renaissance, 3, 5-8, 11
Renfrew, 66-7
Renfrewshire, 64, 66, 68, 73, 78
Renton, Robert, 111
Restoration (1660), 30, 158
Revolution (1688), 108, 116, 130, 206
Rhynd, James (Stir.), 98
Richard, James, messenger (Dunf.), 93
Risk, Renfrewshire, 68
Ritchie, John, 18
rituals, 2-11 *passim*, 23, 42, 49, 73, 78, 80-2, 87, 105, 112, 115, 119, 132, 139-40, 142, 157, 161; *see also* initiation rituals *and* identificaton rituals
Robertson, James, cowan, 79
Robertson, John, clerk (Ham.), 85
Robertson, Thomas (St A), 90
Robesone, Alexander (Edin.), 14, 162
Robson (Robeson), Robert (Mel.), 176
Roch, James (Sco.), 104
Roch, Thomas (Sco), 106, 107
Roland (Ronald), John (Aber.), 125, 147
Rome, Scots College in, 147
Rose, Hugh, of Kilravock, 206
Rosicrucianism, 103
Roslin, Midlothian, 25
Ross, Andrew (Inv.), 150-1
Ross, Donald (Inv.), 150
Ross, James (Kilm.), 153
Ross, James, clerk (Kilw.), 65
Ross, John (Kilm.), 153
Roxborough, Pennsylvania, 176
Roxburgh, earl of, *see* Ker, Robert,
Roxburghshire, 121

Rutherglen, 79
Rutherglen, Incorporation of Masons and Wrights of, **31.4-5**
Rye House Plot, 31

St Ammon, 169
St Andrews, 92; 1600 meeting in, 23-4, 56, 90, 94, 101
St Andrews, Lodge of, 5, 23, 56, 90-1, 182
St Andrew's Day, 55
St Clair Charters, 5, 62, 64, 162; First, 5, 24, 56, 61, 74, 90-1, 98, **2.1-5**; Second, 5, 25, 61, 64-5, 75-6, 91, 94, **2.2-5**
St Clair of Roslin, *see* Sinclair of Roslin,
St John's Day (27 December), 65; AH, 52, 59; Aber., 135-6; Ban., 151; Dumf., 80-1; Dunb., 109; Dund., 96; Dunf., 91; Edin., 20,; Glas., 78; Ham., 87-8; Hau., 120-1; Inv., 150; Kel., 117, 119; Mel., 113, 115
St Machar, Aberdeenshire, 145
St Thomas' Day, 168
St Wynnyn's Day, 65
Sandilands, William (AH), 59
Sanquhar, Incorporation of Squaremen of, **31.6**
Schaw, William, 3-25 *passim*, 35,37, 56, 58, 63-4, 74, 90, 94, 98, 100, 102-3,138, 156, 158-9, 186-7; death of, 5, 20, 25, 159
Schaw Statutes, 3-5, 66; First, 22-3, 43, 53-4, 57, 60-1, 63, 88, 154, **1.1-4**; Second, 5, 23-5, 63-5, 78, 88, 98, 168, **1.5**
sciences, modern, 156-7
Scone, abbey of, 102, 105
Scone (Perth), Lodge of, 26, 101-7, 113, 153, 182; records, **29.1-2**
Scott, Andrew (Inv.), 151
Scott, Capt. John, surgeon (Hau.), 122
Scott, Thomas (Hau.), 120
Scott, Walter (Hau.), 122
Scott, Walter, merchant (Kel.), 118
Scott of Gala, Sir James (Hau.), 120-2
Scott of Gala younger, Hugh (Hau.), 122
Scott of Thirlestane, William, advocate (Kel.), 118
Second Sight, 103
secret societies, 5-6

Selkirk, 123
Selkirk, earl of, *see* Douglas, Charles Hamilton,
Selkirk, Incorporation of Hammermen of, **31.6**
Selkrig, James (Dumf.), 79
Service, John (Stir.), 98-100
session, court of, 48-9
Seton, Alexander (AH), 58-9
Seton, Alexander, 1st earl of Dunfermline, 138
Seton, Alexander, 3rd earl of Dunfermline (Aber?), 128-9,138
Seton, Charles, 2nd earl of Dunfermline (Aber?), 128-9, 138
Seton, George, 4th earl of Winton, 58
Seton, Mr George, minister of Fyvie (Aber.), 128
Seton, Ensign George (Aber.), 146
Seton, James, 4th earl of Dunfermline (Aber?), 128-9, 138
Sheriffmuir, Battle of, 108
Sinclair, Edward, dragoon (Dumf.), 80
Sinclair of Roslin, William, 5, 187
Sinclair of Roslin, Sir William (d.1650), 5, 25, 65, 187
Sinclair of Roslin, 5, 159, 162, 187
Skene, John, merchant (Aber.), 128, 143-4, 180
Skene of Newtyle, Alexander, merchant, 143
Slains, Aberdeenshire, 128
Slater, David (Gla.), 75
Sloane Ms. (catechism), **5.6**
Smellie, William (Edin.), 47-9
Smith, Hew, cooper, 66
Smith, Mr James (Edin.), 17, 33, 43, 84-5
Smith, John (Kilw.), 71
Smith, Thomas, miller (Ham.), 85
Smith, William, clerk (AH), 58-9
Snodgrass, Malcolm, mason, 75
Solomon's Temple, 1, 7, 102; pillars of, 132, 142
Somerville, James (Dunf.), 93
South Leith, *see under* Leith,
squares, 93
stars, 28-9
Steill, John, wright (Ham.), 84
Steill, John younger (Ham.), 84
Stenton, East Lothian, 61
Stevenson, Thomas (Kilw.), 89

Stewart, David (Kilw.), 70-1
Stewart, John, elder (Glas.), 75
Stewart, John, younger (Glas.), 75
Stewart of Blackhall, Sir Archibald, 70
Stewart of Hesselsyd, Archibald (Edin.), 27
Stewarton, Ayrshire, 70-1
Stirling, 98; castle, 98, 101; Cowane's Hospital, 98
Stirling, earls of, *see* Alexander, Sir William *and* Henry,
Stirling, Lodge of, 5, 98-101, 182; records, **30.1-3**
Stirling, Omnigatherum of, 98-100
Stirling, Society of Mechanics of, 99-101; records, **3.3, 20.4-15**
Stirling Ms. (OC), 100, **4.12**
Stirling of Kippendavie, Charles (Dunb.), 111
Stirlingshire, 92
Stockbridge, 121
stoic philosophy, 28
Stow, Midlothian, 119, 122-3
Strachan, Capt. John, 80
Strachan, Robert (Sco.), 105
Strachan of Thornton, Sir Archibald (Edin.), 26-7
Strathallan, Lord, *see* Drummond, William,
Stuart, Prince Charles Edward, 'the Young Pretender', 108
Stuart, James, 'the Old Pretender', 108
sundials, 18, 98
Sutherland, William, land waiter (Dumf.), 81
Sweetheart, Kirkcudbrightshire, 80

Tait, Mr Andrew (Mel.), 114
Tarbet, James, merchant (Kilw.), 73
Tay, River, 103-4
Temple, James (F), 37
Tessin, Hans Ewald (Edin.), 30
Thom, Alexander, mason (Glas.?), 76-7, 170
Thomson, Andrew, clerk, (Hau.), 120-2
Thomson, James (Edin.), 30
Thomson, John (Stir.), 98
Thomson, John, younger, mason, 93
Tod, James (Dumf.), 79
Tolerated Communities, 101
toleration, religious, 9

Torsonce, Midlothian, 120
Tosoch, Andrew, slater (Sco.), 106
Trinity College Ms. (catechism), **5.8**
Tulliallan, Fife, 92
Turke, John, painter, 69
Turke, Walter (Kilw.), 69
Turner, James, writer (Dunb.), 108, 175
Tweeddale, earl of, *see* Hay, John,
Twynholm, Kirkcudbrightshire, 79
tylers, 147

Urquhart, 206

Vitruvius Pollio, Marcus, 7, 28

Wallace, Lawrence, merchant (Kilw.), 71, 73
Wallace of Shewalton, 71
wardens; general, 3, 5, 24, 40-1, 158-9; of lodges, *see* lodge officials; regional, 126
Wardrop, John, wright (Edin.), 33
Warrington, 160
Waterston, Alexander (Edin.), 164
Watson, James (Edin.), 47-8, 50
Watson, John (Sco.), 105
Watson, Thomas, mason, 125
West, Andrew (Dund.), 96
West, John (Dund.), 96
West Jersey, *see under* New Jersey
West Kilbride, Ayrshire, 130
Whyte, James, merchant (Sco.), 106
Whyte, John, merchant (Sco.), 106
Whyte, Patrick, hookmaker (Aber.), 129, 132, 142, 146
Wick, 206
Wilson, Henry, mason, 16
Wilson, John (CK), 38
Wilson, John (Edin.), 166
Wilson, John, weaver (Sco.), 106
Wilson, Thomas (St A), 90
Winchester, James, merchant (Kilm.), 153
Winram, Robert (Edin., EJ), 47-9
Winton, earl of, *see* Seton, George
Witherspoone, James (AH), 57

Yates, Frances, (historian), 7
Yellowlees, John, clerk, 24
Yester House, 33
York, duke of, *see* James VII,
Young, Alexander, surgeon (Hau.), 122
Young, John (Hau.), 122
Young, William, clerk (AH), 58
Younger, John, writer (Dumf.), 81
Younger, John, writer (Hau.), 122